THE ABOSLUTE FAILURE

of

CHRISTIANITY, JUDAISM, ISLAM, HINDUISM AND BUDDHISM

THE ABOSLUTE FAILURE

of

CHRISTIANITY, JUDAISM, ISLAM, HINDUISM AND BUDDHISM

Including Critical Commentaries on
The Gospel of Matthew, Genesis,
Exodus, the Mitzvot And The Quran

DALE ANTHONY PIVARUNAS

CITI OF BOOKS

CITIOFBOOKS, INC.
3736 Eubank NE Suite A1
Albuquerque, NM 87111-3579
www.citiofbooks.com
Hotline: 1 (877) 389-2759
Fax: 1 (505) 930-7244

Ordering Information:
Quantity sales. Special discounts are available on quantity purchases by corporations, associations, and others. For details, contact the publisher at the address above.

Printed in the United States of America.

| ISBN-13: | Softcover | 979-8-89391-064-3 |
| | eBook | 979-8-89391-065-0 |

Library of Congress Control Number: 2024908125

TABLE OF CONTENTS

INTRODUCTION

There are five major religious organizations in the world, major in either adherents and or influence: Hinduism, Judaism, Buddhism, Christianity, and Islam. Hinduism is approximately 8000 years old, Judaism 3800 years old, Buddhism 2500 years old, Christianity 2000 years old and Islam 1400 years old. Adherents of these religions represent about 80% of the world's population and adding another 6% for those people who adhere to a non-major religion, it is seen that over 85% of the world's population adhere to some religion.

What is a religion? A religion is a set of beliefs about life, the origin of the universe, life after death, good and evil, moral behavior, the meaning of life, ceremonies, rituals, prayers, etc.

There are hundreds of thousands of organizations that have evolved around religions. Whether they are called congregations, temples, synagogues, churches, mosques, etc., they are organizations.

These organizations mandate allegiance from their members usually with the threat of eternal damnation. These organizations have hierarchical structures; some simple and some such as the Catholic Church very complex. Most of these organizations also claim that their religious organization is the source of all truth, and that the other organizations are false.

The vast majority of people have not developed their understanding of God and theology on their own, but rather have accepted the theology from the religious organization they are affiliated with. This is because most people have been raised from birth in their current religious organization.

People's understanding of God, the Nature of God, sin, justice, the afterlife, etc. are based on the teachings of their religious organization. And each of these religious organizations mandate what their adherents are to believe under threat of eternal damnation. And virtually every major religion bases its theology on the oral and written teachings of real, mythical, and legendary individuals.

Thirty years ago, I began to realize the world's religious organizations were an absolute failure, and this applied especially to Christianity, specifically Pauline Christianity. There is significantly more evil in the world today than at the time of the birth of Jesus Christ, God, Who had become human to teach humankind how to live. The teachings of Jesus should have lessened the amount and severity of evil over the last 2000 years, but they did not. Was it the teachings of Jesus Christ that failed humanity for the last 2000 years or was it the distorted Christianity developed and promoted by Paul and Augustine that failed humanity and continues to fail humanity?

I was on my way to dinner on January 17, 1991, when the US began an aerial and naval assault on Iraq which lasted five weeks. I was so shocked and numb that I could not eat. How could I eat when the US was raining bombs and missiles on another country which had not attacked us? The US had created a coalition of thirty-six countries including itself. The so-called coalition flew over 100,000 sorties and dropped 89,000 tons of bombs and for the first time used dirty bombs – bombs that contained depleted uranium. Later I found out that up to 50,000 Iraqis were killed, 75,000 wounded and 80,000 captured.

For the first time, news media coverage of this conflict showed some of the horrors of war for people to view on television. Of course, the horrors viewed by the Iraqi soldiers and civilians were far worse than what was depicted on television.

This was not a defensive war but a military attack by the United States. Iraq did not attack the United States, the United States attached Iraq. When I reflected that at the time of this military assault on Iraq, seventy-five percent of the US population considered itself Christian, I was shocked that no leaders among the various Christian organizations had protested these actions by the United States. Jesus taught non-violence and love of neighbor. The Christian leaders in the United States and the thirty-five countries that were part of the coalition were hypocritically silent. They preached Christianity but they did not practice Christianity. Or was there a difference between the Christianity prevalent today and the Christianity of Jesus?

While the total percent of adherents of Judaism, Islam, Hinduism, and Buddhism at the time was five percent of the US population, the leaders of these organizations were also shamefully silent.

When I further reflected on the FIFTY wars that the United States has engaged in, what leaders of Christian organizations took any position on the immorality of these wars and the fact that war is un-Christian based on the teachings of Jesus Christ. And not just the leaders, but also the members and those who participated in these wars. And this applied to the leaders and members of Judaism, Islam, Hinduism, and Buddhism.

And to think that approximately seventy-five percent of the participants in the military assault on Iraq in 1991 were Christians, and they felt no guilt in killing people and wounding people and destroying critical life-sustaining infrastructure. I wondered how these Christians and the leaders of the various Christian organizations could reconcile their actions with the teachings of Jesus Christ: Blessed are the peacemakers, for they will be called children of God. You have heard that it was said, 'You shall love your neighbor and hate your enemy.' But I say to you, love your enemies, bless those who curse you, do good to those who hate you, and pray for those who spitefully use you and persecute you, that you may be children of your Father in heaven; for He makes His sun rise on the evil and on the good, and sends rain on the just and on the unjust. For if you love those who love you, what reward have you. Do not be overcome by evil but overcome evil with good.

Because evil is the absence of good, it is not destroyed but must be overcome, offset, or filled in with good. How can politicians, military leaders and soldiers who claim to be Christians engage in offensive wars when such events or activities are totally inconsistent with the teachings of Jesus.

War is one of the greatest evils known to humanity. Yet, religious leadership, that is, the leaders of the various religious organizations (Catholics, non-Catholic Christians, Orthodox Christians, Jews, Muslims, Hindus, Buddhists, etc.) have condoned and supported war for thousands of years. Every major religious organization has failed to prevent and minimize war and violence against the lower class by the upper class for the entire length of their existence: Judaism – 3000 years, Christianity – 2000 years, Islam – 1400 years, Hinduism – 5000 years, Buddhism – 2500 years. And there are many cases in history where the leaders of religious organizations have actually promoted war.

All the major religious organizations, Catholics, non-Catholic Christians, Orthodox Christians, Jews, Muslims, Hindus, Buddhists, etc.; in theory exist to provide moral leadership, moral direction, and moral guidance to their members and to society in general. Their common position is that all deliberate human actions are either good (moral) or bad (immoral). The primary purpose of the executives, directors, and managers of these religious organizations (pope, cardinals, patriarchs, bishops, priests, ministers, rabbis, sheiks, imams, gurus, etc.) is to instruct members and society in general concerning moral matters. Unfortunately, virtually every major religious organization has abandoned their responsibility of moral leadership and has focused almost exclusively on culture, rituals, prayers, and beliefs and not on actions – working against the evils which impact society and the majority of people.

In the past 2000 years' history of global civilization, social evils have been ignored by the leadership of the major religious organizations. Wars, slavery, abuse of women; discrimination against women, minorities, the handicapped, and those without property; abuse and mistreatment of children (including child labor), poverty, homelessness, torture, extreme forms of imprisonment, experiments on humans (psychological, drugs, vaccines, etc.), nuclear attacks by the United States (Hiroshima and Nagasaki), assassinations, false imprisonments, genocide, population control/reduction, state terrorism, covert military actions, evictions, human trafficking, organ trafficking, sanctions against whole countries resulting in hundreds of thousands of deaths, suicides, drug addictions and numerous other evils have not decreased and in fact have increased in terms of the number of people impacted.

The world seems to be getting worse and worse from a good/evil point of view especially because of technology which allows evil people to cause harm to great numbers of people. I do not mean to imply that technology is evil, but rather that it can be used to do extensive evil. Nuclear technology can be used for both good and evil purposes. Communication technology especially social media can be used for good purposes, but it can also be used for evil purposes such as mass propaganda, silencing the truth, smearing the reputation of an individual, restricting access to information, and invading a person's privacy. Chemical technology also can be used for both good and evil purposes. GMO's, Roundup, and the patenting of plant genes which allows a corporation to sue and/or take over farms that have even inadvertently used the corporation's patented gene are just some examples of chemical technology being used for evil purposes. Medical technology can be used for good and for evil. Pharmaceutical companies such as Perdue marketing and selling OxyContin and corporations that sell vaccines that are not really needed by the general population but do so for the sake of profits are just two examples of medical technology being used for evil purposes.

We are in the midst of the greatest crisis in all history. The Global Ruling Elite, those extremely wealthy individuals who control most heads of state, most news organizations, most social media organizations, and the heads of most of the largest corporations, have formed a plan and are executing that plan to both reduce and control the world's population.

Every current major political and social policy should be viewed within the context of the Ruling Elite's plan to both reduce and control the world's population.

The individuals comprising the Global Ruling Elite feel that they are superior to virtually all other people and because of their superiority, they can and will decide who should live and who does not need to live, what every person should do, where each person should live, what each person should think and say, how each person should live and how long each person should live.

They are doing this at this time in history because they feel that technology will allow them to use automation and not humans to serve them. Robots, drones, autonomous vehicles, policing robots, military robots, sensors, cameras, and satellite networks will blindly, efficiently, and effectively allow the Ruling Elite to rule the entire world – every human being other than those comprising the Ruling Elite.

How foolish are two groups of people: those who support the puppets of the Ruling Elite, and those who are blindly accepting without questioning and without resisting the theft of their freedoms and rights. Do these people really think that if they give up their freedom, their rights, and their property – they will be happy?

The reality of this should be extremely frightening for people, yet most people are either too blind, too naïve, or too stupid to realize what is going on. And this is because the leaders of the major religious organizations, Christianity, Judaism, Islam, Hinduism, and Buddhism, say nothing about what is going on. Either these leaders are stupid, or they are puppets of the Global Ruling Elite.

The Ruling Elite are absolutely amoral because they consider themselves above everything, even morality. They are the greatest threat to humankind, far greater than any pandemic, war, climate change, or natural disaster. The Ruling Elite are evil. They are atheists who have contempt for God and the natural laws of God and are actively engaged in undermining all religions and directing the allegiance of all people from God to themselves, for they consider themselves to be gods.

And the Ruling Elite have started a war against the entire world, and people need to understand that this is a war, the greatest war between good and evil of all time.

And now we are in the middle of the so-called "great reset" which has as its purpose the absolute control of virtually every country and every person by the super-rich elite of the world, who feel that they are superior to everyone else, and they will decide what is right for everyone. 'You will own nothing and be happy'. The ruling elite will own everything, and the masses will be happy because the exalted ruling elite will tell them what they need to do – happiness comes from obeying the ruling elite of the world? Absurd!

And this great reset is being supported and promoted by technology, the communications industry, and the medical industry, because the leaders of the major communication and medical corporations are part of the super-rich elite. This effort on the part of the super-elite of the world is the greatest evil to affect the world since the beginning of time. And what do the leaders of the organized religions have to say about the great reset – nothing. The leaders of the Catholic Church, the Orthodox Church, the Christian churches, the synagogues, the mosques, and the temples are complicit in the "great reset" because they do nothing! And they themselves are evil since they do not do what is right and oppose this great evil. Not to oppose error is to approve it. Not to defend truth is to suppress it. To neglect to confront and resist evil men, when we can do so, is no less a sin than to encourage them.

We must resist the Great Reset. The Great Reset being promoted by the World Economic Forum and the heads of most states on behalf of the Global Ruling Elite is evil and must be resisted. The absolutely, absurd oxymoron of this program 'you will own nothing and be happy' must be condemned – it is false and against the Natural Law of God. Property is one of the basic rights of an individual, and property ownership is necessary for a person to live a complete and human life.

The right to own property is a human and inalienable right. This right is critical and essential to the preservation of life, the support of liberty and the pursuit of happiness. Among the most essential things that a person must own is a home, and this implies that every person should own a home. Homeownership is intimately bound to being human. Homeownership brings freedom, independence, security, and stability to the homeowner. A person's right and ability to build or buy a home and live in it must be protected. Home ownership is not only good for the individual and the family; it is good for the economy. The economy expands as homeownership increases and contracts as home ownership decreases. The Ruling Elite want to own all property and force all people to rent from them. "You will own nothing and be happy" is a claim by the World Economic Forum. But if the people own nothing, who will own everything – the Ruling Elite.

Besides a home, people have the right to buy and must own their own furniture, appliances, means of transportation, means of communication, etc. in order to live a human life. The Ruling Elite want to own everything: furniture, appliances, vehicles, etc. and have people rent from them. And they want to own and control all the means of production and distribution.

The Ruling Elites of the late 1800s and early 1900s attempted this with their factory or company towns. The company owned the workers homes, their furniture, and their appliances. Workers were paid in the company's money, could only buy food from the company store, could only go to the company doctor, could only send their children to the company school. The workers were serfs or slaves. And this is the goal of the Ruling Elite, but they want to do this on a global scale and extend the model of the company town to virtually everyone.

Ten percent of the world's population live in extreme poverty living on less than $1.90 a day. Over fifty percent of the world's population live in poverty living on less than $2.50 a day. There are 600,000 homeless people in the United States and over 100 million people globally who have no home, while the number of people globally with inadequate housing is over 1.6 billion - 1.6 billion!

And yet, twenty-two men (white men) have as much wealth as the lowest fifty percent of the world's population - almost 4 billion people. Does this please God, Yahweh, Allah, Buddha, or whatever name religious organizations give to the Creator and Sustainer or the world? And why have the leadership of the Catholics, non-Catholic Christians, Orthodox, Jews, Muslims, Hindus, Buddhists, etc. failed since their inception to reduce and minimize poverty which results in suffering and in many cases extreme suffering? Poverty leads to suicides, physical health issues, mental health issues, crime, prostitution, homelessness, and the breakup of families, and it is quite obvious that the leaders of the Catholics, non-Catholic Christians, Orthodox Christians, Jews, Muslims, Hindus, Buddhists, etc. don't care in spite of their claims to be the representatives of Jesus, God, Yahweh, Allah, Buddha, or whatever name religious organizations give to the Creator and Sustainer or the world?

I do not and cannot believe that God does not care about the poor. The leaders of the organized religions do not want to upset the super-wealthy rulers of the world because it might impact their comfortable lifestyle and their perceived reputation for being highly moral and virtuous individuals who represent God on earth and speak for God. These leaders are whitened sepulchers, who outwardly appear to be holy but actually are morally corrupt, not necessarily by actions but rather by the lack of action.

If the purpose and the reason for existence of the major religious organizations is to promote good and avoid evil, they have all drastically failed.

Why haven't the various organized religions (Catholic, Orthodox, Christian, Muslim, Jewish, Hindu, Buddhist, etc.) publicly taken a moral stand on the militarization of the police, the increase of nuclear weapons, enhanced interrogation, drone murders, snipers, Iraq, Afghanistan, Sudan, regime change in Libya, Ukraine and Egypt, the devastating sanctions on Iran, Venezuela, Cuba, Syria and North Korea; telling their followers to cease and desist from such practices?

HYPOCRISY OF RELIGIOUS LEADERS

Virtually every religious organization teaches and promotes a belief in Heaven. Unfortunately, they all hold that membership in their organization is a requirement to gain Heaven and that is a major point of diversity and disharmony among them and a source of confusion to the majority of people. Catholics hold, in general, that you have to be Catholic to go to Heaven. Protestants hold that you have to believe in Jesus Christ to go to Heaven. Judaism holds that you have to be Jewish to go to Heaven. Muslims, Hindus, and Buddhists (and every other organized religion) hold pretty much the same. What makes things worse is that not only is membership in a particular organized religion a requirement for Heaven, but also the practice of rituals and rules unique to the various religious organizations. You cannot eat pork, you have to say these prayers, you have to attend these ceremonies, you have to be baptized; these and countless other practices and mechanics are specified by organized religions. Membership and rituals seem to be all that is required for a person to go to Heaven.

The leadership of the organized religions have always pandered to the rich and those in power. It is obviously easier for the leadership of organized religions to allow people to pursue a life of wealth, prosperity, comfort, and luxury with the false hope that they can go to Heaven because of Church membership and the practice of rituals and ceremonies, than it is to promote the living of a good life in the sense of the Sermon on the Mount and the teachings of Jesus in the passage on the Sheep and the Goats. Some organized religions have even gone so far as to equate the "good life" (good life in the sense of a prosperous life involving riches and property) with a sign that God has blessed a person – prosperity Christianity.

This "good life" is, in fact, inconsistent with leading a good life and the direct opposite of being good. A person pursuing the 'good life" (prosperous life) directs and subordinates everything to themselves. They seek to maximize wealth which involves exploiting others. Since the global economy (wealth and property) is finite, the more one person takes decreases what is available to all others. This does not imply that all people should own an equal amount of property, but rather that there needs to be a moral and legal limit (both upper and lower) on the amount of property that a person owns. The rich feel justified in stealing from the poor and the middle class because of the various capitalist amoral philosophies that have been developed, and no one from the so-called conscience of society (leaders of religious organizations) says anything.

It seems as though all organized religions have lost the understanding of what is truly important in life and what is absolutely necessary to go to Heaven, and that is living a good life, a good life meaning loving your neighbor (all neighbors) as you love yourself. Living a good life transcends all of the practices, beliefs, and rituals of all organized religions. It's really so simple, yet seemingly beyond the grasp of the leadership of organized religions: a person needs to live a good life.

The real reason why Pauline Christianity (not the Christianity of Jesus), Judaism, Islam, Hinduism, and Buddhism have failed as religions is that they are all false religions and man-made religions. They were all founded by men, not God, and are based on myths, legends, and distorted understandings of God and His nature. And their leaders arrogantly and falsify claim that they speak in the name of God. And most religions exist to maintain and support their clergies and the comfortable lifestyles of their clergy.

The members of these religions need to step back and question the motives of their clergy and whether the rituals, practices, sacraments, and beliefs are really leading to a good life and a better world for all people.

In the words and actions of Jesus living a good life involves three things. First, good is to be done and promoted, and evil is to be avoided. Second, treat others in words and actions as you would have them treat you in words and actions which is also expressed in Christianity as 'love your neighbor as yourself'. Third, respect the absolute dignity and equality of each and every human being.

Christianity teaches that human beings, all human beings, are made in the image and likeness of God. Jesus taught this principle through both his words and his actions. The absolute dignity of the human being applies to all human beings not just the rich, the powerful, the educated, men, older people, the healthy, the educated, the members of specific religions, specific nationalities, specific races or the beautiful. The absolute dignity of the human being applies to the rich and the poor, the powerful and the powerless, the educated and the uneducated, women and men, the old and the young, the healthy and the sick, the members of all religions, the members of all nationalities, all races and the beautiful and the ugly. The absolute dignity of each and every human being is the basis for the rights of each and every human being and the Christian imperative that every person is treated with dignity and respect in their social lives, their economic lives, their political lives, and their private lives. This is what is needed to live a good life and get to Heaven.

Religious leadership will pay lip-service to the above principles, yet in practice they ignore them.

Most people have heard of the phrase 'evil exists because good people do nothing to overcome it'. This is incorrect. In fact, evil exists because there are too few good people to overcome it. Goodness of its very nature moves or acts to offset evil which is the lack of or absence of goodness. In fact, there are not enough good people in the world to overcome the evil in the world. And this is the fault of the leadership of the various religious organizations.

Evil is often associated with an individual who steals, or drinks to excess, or who takes drugs, or assaults others or murders. While this is true, the greatest evils are war, genocide, human trafficking, slavery, human exploitation, and denial of human rights; all of which have existed for thousands of years even to this very day. If there were enough good people, there would be virtually no war, no genocide, no human trafficking, no slavery, no denial of human rights, and far less murders, assaults, and thefts.

Natural Law is the principle that certain rights and values apply to human beings by their very nature as human beings and that certain ethical behaviors are incumbent on all human beings.

Respect for other's life, liberty, person, dignity, and property because they are human beings is the basis of Natural Law. Natural Law defines how a person should treat other persons both on an individual basis as well as within a society of persons. Natural Law only applies to human persons and not to artificial persons such as the oxymoron that originated in the United States that refers to a corporation as a person. Natural Law is the law that is derived through the intellectual activity of a rational human being.

This book is not about religion but rather about organizations which purport to promote religion though it can be difficult to distinguish between the two since these organizations have had and continue to have the greatest influence on the principles and practices of each religion. Hinduism, Judaism, Buddhism, Christianity, and Islam are the dominant religions which have developed and are controlled by organizations consisting of ruling elites who claim to be the enlightened ones inspired and selected by God to lead and direct the adherents of the religion as the representatives of God or Yahweh or Buddha or Allah.

'THIS IS THE WORD OF GOD' – THE GREATEST MARKETING TOOL AND SCAM EVER DEVISED

At their inceptions, the various religious organizations devised a tactic to get their followers to blindly accept their teachings and that was to claim that certain original teachings were the word of God. Followers were to accept these teachings without question since to do so was to question God. In spite of many inconsistencies in the writings themselves as well as between these writings and science, history, and common sense; followers were to accept these teachings as though they came from God. And this applies to Christianity, Judaism, Islam, Hinduism, and Buddhism as well as many small religious organizations.

The Hebrew Bible, which is also called the Tanakh, and which Christians call the Old Testament was written over a period of approximately 500 years from 600 BCE to 100 CE. It is a compilation of many different documents from many different sources, edited and blended together to provide the theme that the Jews were God's Chosen people, above all other people and who had a mission to somehow dominate the world. As the Hebrew Bible was taking its final form, its promoters positioned it as the work of God or the word of God explaining that the writers and editors were directly inspired by God. The intended implication of this was that a person could not and should not question anything in the Hebrew Bible because to do so would be to question God. People were to accept everything in the Bible as the absolute truth, coming directly from God.

This was perhaps the most successful marketing tool in all human history up to this day. From the Jews to the Christians (who borrowed and used this same idea for their writings which they call the New Testament), followers blindly accepted the Hebrew Bible (the Old Testament) and the Christian Bible (the New Testament) as the absolute truth without question because they were told it was the word of God, that is written by God. Muslims also copied this marketing tool with respect to the writings of Mohammed. The followers of Islam are to accept the writings of Mohammed without question and accept these writings as the word of Allah or God. The same can be said though in a lesser extent for Hinduism and Buddhism.

A critical study of the Hebrew Bible shows that there is little to no historical or scientific accuracy to these writings. It is highly doubtful whether Adam, Eve, and Noah ever existed and most likely that Abraham and Moses either did not exist or the actual individuals were not at all what is written of them. The pious writings of the Hebrew Bible are just that, the writings of pious individuals. The stories of the major individuals who wrote the Hebrew Bible are either myths or legends; myths having no historical basis and legends based a few historical facts greatly exaggerated by the author(s).

The Scriptures of the major religious organizations, the Old Testament, the New Testament, the Quran, the Veda, and The Tripitaka, while purporting to be the written word of God almost dictated by God are in fact mostly fabrications by these religious groups to show that God established and endorses their organization. And yet, these religious groups support and justify actions such as war using their books when these actions are in fact against the Natural Law which people using their God-given conscience understand to be wrong.

How can anyone except for a person who has a distorted understanding of the nature of God think that God condones and even commands people to wage war to kill men, women, and children or allows slavery, or inequality? How can anyone think that God wants you to kill some else?

CHRISTIANITY, THE GOSPELS, PAUL AND THE EARLY CHRISTIANITY ORGANIZATION – THE CATHOLIC CHURCH

Christianity has approximately 2.6 billion followers and Catholicism is the largest branch of Christianity with 1.3 billion followers. Christians account for 32 percent of the world population of 8 billion people.

It takes little reflection to realize that there is almost no influence of the basic principles of Christianity on business and economics. Businesses and economies throughout the world are actually pagan. Unfortunately, the vast majority of Christians have closed their minds to the inconsistencies between their faith and the philosophies and practices of the business world which falsely claim that business is outside the realm of morals as expressed in the statement 'it is neither right nor wrong, it is just business'.

The Christian morality of Jesus is based on the commandment 'love your neighbor as yourself'. This is certainly not applied to the unemployed, the underemployed, those making minimum wage, those living in poverty, those who are having or have had their homes repossessed, those who are slaves to payday loans or title loans, those who have been cheated through rent-to-own, lease-option or lease-purchase contracts and countless others suffering financially.

Unfortunately, this has to do primarily with Pauline Christianity. Pauline Christianity actually allows for the inconsistencies between the Christianity of Jesus and the philosophies and practices of the business world which falsely claim that business is outside the realm of morals. This is because Pauline Christianity places most of its focus on faith (belief in Jesus and belief in the tenets of Pauline Christianity), protestations of that faith, and rituals. Pauline Christianity allows its followers to have two lives, one public in their business, economics, and political world, and another life in their private world. And Pauline Christianity allows these two lives to be independent and inconsistent.

The Christianity of Jesus promotes justice, fairness, balance, cooperation, and mutual respect within business, economics and politics and is based on three principles: good is to be done and promoted and evil is to be avoided; love your neighbor as yourself and the absolute dignity and equality of each and every human being.

Christianity teaches that human beings, all human beings, are made in the image and likeness of God. Jesus taught this principle through both his words and his actions. The absolute dignity of the human being applies to all human beings not just the rich, the powerful, the educated, men, older people, the healthy, the educated, the members of specific religions, specific nationalities, specific races or the beautiful. The absolute dignity of the human being applies to the rich and the poor, the powerful and the powerless, the educated and the uneducated, women and men, the old and the young, the healthy and the sick, the members of all religions, the members of all nationalities, all races and the beautiful and the ugly. The absolute dignity of each and every human being is the basis for the rights of each and every human being and the Christian imperative that every person is treated with dignity and respect in their social lives, their economic lives, their political lives, and their private lives.

Unfortunately, Pauline Christianity does not accept the equality of each and every human being. For it places those with wealth and power

(power within government, politics, economics, and organizations) above others.

Christian Economics is based on Natural Law and the teachings of Jesus Christ and is the application of these principles in the practice of economics in a person's public and private lives. Unfortunately, most Pauline Christians separate Economics and Christianity taking the position that the two are mutually exclusive. This is wrong, absurd, and contrary to the mission and teachings of Jesus Christ.

Again, the Christianity of Jesus promotes justice, fairness, balance, cooperation, and mutual respect within business, economics and politics and is based on three principles: good is to be done and promoted and evil is to be avoided; love your neighbor as yourself and the absolute dignity of each and every human being.

Can these principles be applied to the economy regarding prices, jobs, business practices, the minimum wage, wages in general, the outsourcing of jobs, pensions in private industry, home foreclosures, home repossessions, how employers treat their employees, how managers treat their subordinates, etc.? Are prices, jobs, business practices, the minimum wage, wages in general, the outsourcing of jobs, pensions in private industry, home foreclosures, home repossessions, employer-employee relationships, and manager-subordinate relationships based on the principles 'that good is to be done and promoted, and evil is to be avoided', 'love your neighbor as yourself', the absolute dignity and equality of each and every human being and the imperative of treating every person with dignity and respect? Certainly not!

It takes little reflection to realize that there is almost no influence of these basic principles of Christian Economics, economics based on the teachings of Jesus, within virtually every economy in the world. The economies of the world for all practical purposes are pagan, and are based, managed, and directed by economic theories which disconnect morality and economic behavior and activities. And this is wrong, absolutely wrong.

Every human action within business, between businesses, involving a contract, involving a transaction, the relations between employers and employees, the relations between managers and subordinates, the relations between businesses and customers; these are all subject to morality, that is, they are either right or wrong from an ethical point of view as well as from a Christian point of view. Current economic theories actually support the disparity between the rich and the working class and promote the economic dominance of the wealthy class.

The philosophy expressed in the statement "it is neither right nor wrong, it is just business" is not only false but it is evil. And it has been used intentionally to disconnect business to morality so that business can be totally unconstrained to do whatever it wants.

But how does God want people to act within their economic lives: their jobs, their businesses, their business transactions, how they treat employees, how they pay employees, how they treat business subordinates, how they deal with tenants, how they set prices, how they deal with other businesses, how they market their products and services, how they advertise, the quality of their products and services, etc.?

It is extremely unfortunate that the vast majority of Christians have totally disconnected their economic lives from their religious lives and their religious beliefs. Most Christians exclaim their belief, loyalty, and love of God within church but totally deny Him within their economic lives acting as though God does not exist. Most Christians are pagans in their economic lives because of Pauline Christianity, and this is totally inconsistent with the Christianity of Jesus.

How is the Christian mandate to love your neighbor as yourself to be applied in business, economics, and politics?

And when the Son of man shall come in His majesty, and all the angels with Him, then shall He sit upon the seat of His majesty. And all nations shall be gathered together before Him, and He shall separate them one from another, as the shepherd separates the sheep from the goats. And He shall set the sheep on His right hand, but the goats on His left. Then shall the King say to them that shall be on His right hand: Come, you blessed of My Father, possess the kingdom prepared for you from the foundation of the world. For I was hungry, and you gave me to eat; I was thirsty, and you gave me to drink; I was a stranger, and you took me in; naked, and you clothed Me: sick, and you took care of Me; I was in prison, and you came to Me. Then the just will ask Him, saying: Lord, when did we see You hungry and fed You; thirsty, and gave You a drink? And when did we see You a stranger, and took You in; or naked and clothed You? Or when did we see You sick or in prison, and assisted You? And the king will answer them saying: Amen I say to you, as long as you did it to one of these My least brethren, you did it to Me.

Then He shall say to those on His left: Depart from Me, you cursed, into the everlasting fire which was prepared for the devil and his angels. For I was hungry, and you did not feed Me; I was thirsty, and you did not give me a drink. I was a stranger, and you did not take Me not in; naked and you did not clothe Me; sick and in prison, and you did not care for Me. Then they will ask Him, saying: Lord, when did we see You hungry, or thirsty, or a stranger, or naked, or sick, or in prison, and did not minister to You? Then He shall answer them, saying: Amen I say to you, as long as you did not do so to one of these least, neither did you do it to Me.

Christians have heard this passage from the bible many times. And yet, so few Christians understand its true meaning and even less apply this passage to their economic, business, and political lives. Who are the hungry, the thirsty, the naked, the strangers, the sick, and the imprisoned in modern society? Obviously, it is the homeless, the unemployed, those living in poverty, those who are underemployed, those who have had their homes repossessed, those who are physically, mentally, and emotionally sick; and all those imprisoned physically, financially, and emotionally. Jesus identifies with these people and Christians are to see Jesus in these people.

Do Christians see Jesus in the homeless, the unemployed, those living in poverty, those who are underemployed, those earning minimum wage, those who have had their homes repossessed, those who are physically, mentally, and emotionally sick; and all those imprisoned physically, financially, and emotionally? The vast majority do not.

What is worse is that many people who call themselves Christian actually deride these people. Christians claim to praise God in Church on Sunday but then they ignore and mistreat Him every day when they ignore and mistreat the homeless, the unemployed, those living in poverty, those who are underemployed, those who have had their homes repossessed, those who are physically, mentally, and emotionally sick; and all those imprisoned physically, financially, and emotionally. The following is a more contemporary expression of Matthew chapter 25.

At the end of the world when God judges everyone, He will separate the good from the bad based on the commandment to 'love your neighbor as yourself'. He will say to the good, 'Come you blessed and inherit the kingdom prepared for you from the beginning of time. For I was poor, and you helped Me out of poverty. I was unemployed and you helped Me to find a job, or you gave Me a job, or you created a job for Me. I did not have health insurance and you helped Me to obtain insurance. I was not making a living wage and you worked to have My employer pay a living wage. I was homeless and you helped me find a place to live. My house was in foreclosure, and you helped prevent it from being repossessed. I was old and you helped Me with a socially based income and health insurance. I was uneducated and you helped to educate Me. I was in prison, and you helped change the system from retribution based to restorative based. I was discriminated against, and you helped stop the discrimination.' And the righteous will ask Him, 'Lord, when did we see You in poverty or unemployed or without insurance or making less than a living wage or homeless? When did we see Your home in foreclosure or You uneducated or old and without an income or health insurance? When did we see you in prison or being discriminated against?' And God will answer, 'Whatever you did for any of my brothers or sisters, you did for me.' Then he will say to the others, 'Depart from me. For I was poor, and you ignored Me. I was unemployed and you did nothing but say that it was My fault. I did not have health insurance and you resisted any means to provide Me with public health insurance. I was not making a living wage and you said that My employer should determine how much I was worth and that there should not be a minimum wage let alone a living wage. I was homeless and you crossed the street so that you would not have to walk by Me. My house was in foreclosure, and you did nothing. My house was re-possessed, and you helped with My eviction. I was old and you worked to take away my government mandated pension and health insurance that I paid for. I was uneducated and you said that only those that can afford an education should be educated. I was in prison, and you threw away the key. I was discriminated against, and you did nothing to stop the discrimination.' And the unrighteous will ask Him, 'Lord, when did we act this way to you?' And God will answer, 'What you did or did not do to your fellow human beings, you did to Me.'

Thirty-one percent of people in the world identify themselves as Christians, so it would be logical to see a significant influence of Christianity within the various economies and political systems. And yet, that is certainly not the case. With such a high percentage of Christians, there is obviously a very high percentage of so-called Christians within banking, the defense and weapons industry, the pharmaceutical industry, the chemical industry, the diversified manufacturing industry and within government (all levels and all branches).

And yet the Christians in these industries and within government make no effort to apply Christian principles within their jobs. How could a Christian working within the banking industry support the foreclosure of over fifteen million homes and the repossession of over five million homes? How could a Christian person working for the banking industry personally apply and enforce policies that took people's homes away knowing that this affected women, children, and senior citizens? How could a Christian sheriff or Christian police officer forcefully evict a family from their home removing their belongings and placing the family's belongings on the street while the family watched? How could a Christian help the corporation that they work for to outsource jobs to another country knowing that it results in the loss of employment for hundreds or thousands of employees and their families just to increase profits? How can a Christian work for a company that manufactures military weapons that helps promote military conflicts so that the company can sell its products and services? How can a Christian work for an employer who either directly or indirectly operates factories that employ young girls and even children paying them extremely low wages and making them work excessively long hours? How can a Christian employer pay adults with families at the minimum wage rate or less than the minimum wage? How can a Christian manager force employees to work without a break for ten or twelve hours at time? How can a Christian manager lay off workers a day before a holiday so that the workers are not paid for the holiday? How can a Christian work for a company that intentionally reduces the hours of its employees so that it does not have to provide health insurance? How can a Christian work for a pay day loan company or a title loan company which has interest rates between 300 and 750 percent or higher? How can a Christian work for a company that pays male workers much higher than it pays female workers for the exact same work? How can a Christian work for a hospital or medical center which charges a person without insurance more than a person who has insurance because the insurance company gets a discount? (The person does not have insurance because they cannot afford insurance). How can a Christian work for a company that discriminates against older applicants? How can a Christian in government ignore the millions of people who are unemployed, the millions of people who are under-employed, the millions of people who have to work two jobs, the millions of people who live from paycheck to paycheck, and the millions of people living in poverty?

The current economic and political crises throughout the world are the direct result of Christians not practicing their faith in their daily lives and this includes their business lives, their economic lives, and their political lives. Unfortunately, the vast majority of Christians have closed their minds to the inconsistencies between their faith and the philosophies and practices of the business world which falsely claim that business is outside the realm of faith and morals as expressed in the statement 'it is neither right nor wrong, it is just business'. Good is to be done and promoted, and evil is to be avoided in all things including business and politics. The commandment to love your neighbor as yourself does not stop when it comes to business and politics; it applies to every facet of a Christian's life. If the failure of Christians to practice their faith in their economic lives is the cause of the current economic and political crises, then the solution is the application of Christian Economics to the economy and political system by Christians practicing the Christianity of Jesus.

<u>JESUS, HIS LIFE</u>

Most scholars estimate that Jesus was born between 6 and 4 BC, that Jesus' public life began around AD 27–29 and lasted up to three years, and that He died between AD 30 and 36.

Jesus came from the town of Nazareth in Galilee. This northern territory of Palestine was also his most important area of activity. Apart from the larger towns of Sepphoris and Tiberias, Galilee was a country area, and agriculture was the main occupation. The Lake of Gennesaret was famous for its fishing. In the time of Jesus, Galilee was surrounded by a number Greek cities. There was also in Galilee a group of ten Greek towns, the Decapolis.

During the time of Jesus, 500,000 – 600,000 people lived in Palestine only half of which were Jews. The vast majority of Jews did not live in Palestine. It is estimated that the total number of Jews living at the time of Jesus both within Palestine and outside of Palestine was about 3.1 million. That means that the number of Jews living in Palestine was only about 10 percent of the global Jewish population.

Jerusalem was a city of some 50,000, but during major feasts, could swell to 100,000.

There also was some exchange of populations: some Jews lived in Gentile cities, such as Scythopolis, and some Gentiles lived in some Jewish cities and towns, and this included Greeks and Romans. The fact that the inscription that Pilate had placed on the cross of Jesus was written in Aramaic, Greek and Latin support the cosmopolitan nature of Jerusalem. This fact also shows that there were educated Greeks and Romans who lived in Jerusalem since only the educated could read.

Extreme poverty was present, but never reached a socially dangerous level. At the other end of the economic spectrum, few Palestinian Jews had great fortunes except for the royalty and the Jewish aristocrats with large estates, and this included the merchants who supplied the Temple and the Sadducees, the party of high priests.

THE GOSPELS

The original manuscript of the Gospel of Mark was written between supposedly AD 66–70, the original manuscripts of the Gospels of Matthew and Luke supposedly around AD 85–90, and the original manuscript of the Gospel of John supposedly AD 90–110. It should be pointed out, that these writings came from anonymous authors, and it was only well over a hundred years later that the Christian organization at the time claimed the authorship of these works were from some individuals named Mark, Matthew, Luke, and John probably to promote the idea that these works were by individuals with some direct relationship to Jesus. For a multitude of reasons based on research, the Gospels were not written by any individuals who had any direct relationship to Jesus. The simple fact that the Gospels were written in Greek with sophisticated prose, and that the pseudo-claimed authors (Mark, Matthew, Luke and John) were uneducated individuals who spoke Aramaic shows the improbability of the authors being the Mark, Matthew, Luke or John alluded to in the Gospels themselves, though it is likely that these individuals were written into the Gospels intentionally to link the authorship of the Gospels to individuals in the Gospels as a marketing tool. However, to this day most Christians erroneously believe that Gospels were written by such individuals and that these individuals had a direct relationship to Jesus and even witnessed the events described in the Gospels.

There is very, very little historical information about Jesus. The Gospel writers who wrote the four gospels, who never met Jesus, who received their information from second and third-party sources and who were intent on their interpretation of Jesus' message provide almost nothing about the historical Jesus other than a few (very few) select incidents. And this was intentional since the Gospel writers were more intent on their commentaries on Jesus and transmitting their message to the reader.

The First Jewish Revolt against Rome lasted from 66 AD to 73AD and included the destruction of Jerusalem and the temple. This revolt was a disaster for Palestine and Judaism. Up to half of the Jewish population died, and the organizational structure of Judaism, the high priest, and the Sanhedrin, ceased to exist. When Jerusalem and the temple were destroyed in 70AD, there was a leadership and organizational crisis. With no temple, no high priest and no Sanhedrin, Judaism struggled to find direction. And it was during this crisis in Judaism that the Gospels were written. There is no doubt that the initial Gospel writers wanted to influence the direction of Judaism within this leadership and organizational crisis by promoting the acceptance of Jesus as the Messiah of Judaism and the integration of Judaism and Pauline Christianity.

The early Christians can be divided into two groups: the ordinary, lower-class people who lived in small towns and villages who were directly taught by Jesus and Mary, His mother; and the middle class and perhaps even upper-class Jews who did not live in Palestine and in fact did not ever live in Palestine. Virtually, all of the Jewish Christians of this second group were Hellenistic Jews or Roman Jews.

Before becoming Christians, the members of this second group were relatively devout Jews living outside of Palestine. In accepting Jesus, they did not give up their Judaism, but rather merged their Judaistic beliefs, rituals, and practices with Christian beliefs and with the newly developing rituals and practices of Christianity. While they are referred to as Jewish Christians, it is more appropriate to call them Judaistic Christians. The vast majority of these Judaistic Christians had friends, family and business associates who were still practicing Jews who did not accept Christianity.

The Gospels contain both fact and fiction. The analysis which follows later in the section entitled 'The Gospel of Matthew'. is an attempt to show to the reader what is most probably fiction and also to prove that the Gospels are not the word of God, that is written by God nor even inspired by God but rather just the words of men.

The Gospel writers did not intend on producing fact-based, eyewitness-based biographies of Jesus. Rather, their intention was to convince the Jews that Jesus was their Messiah, that they should believe the teachings of Jesus (as explained through the Pauline school) and that they should be converted to Pauline Christianity.

The Gospels writers were also interested in trying to show that Jesus intended to establish an organization which we call the Church with its hierarchical and male-dominated structure. And the Gospel writers wrote to influence the different Jewish factions especially the Pharisees and Essenes.

Some of the Gospels writers may have been Pharisees and Essenes themselves like Paul who was a Pharisee. Another important point is that the early Pauline Christians after the destruction of the Temple in 70 AD and the collapse of the governmental structure of Judaism (no High Priest and Sanhedrin) wanted Judaism to continue and saw their hybrid of Christianity and Judaism to be the solution. In addition, they saw the new Christian Church structure as the new structure for both Judaism (which they hoped to be converted to their hybrid Judaistic Christianity or Christian Judaism) and Christianity. And they hoped through their writings to accomplish this.

It would be better to consider the Gospels as commentaries on Jesus. They should absolutely not be considered biographies. The literary process used by the Gospel writers involved taking statements made by Jesus and actually modifying the words of Jesus to fit their commentary. Unfortunately, readers for the last 2000 years have read the Gospels thinking that what appears to be the words of Jesus are actually the words of Jesus, that is, actually spoken by Jesus and captured with exact accuracy. But this is not at all true. The Gospel writers added, deleted, and changed the words of Jesus to fit their purpose.

While this literary technique appears to be shocking, it is the same literary technique used by the writers of the Jewish Bible (what Christians call the Old Testament), the Quran (the Islamic scriptures), the Veda (the Hindu scriptures), and the Tripitaka (the Buddhist scriptures).

Further, it should be recalled that the Gospels were authored by many individuals over a long period of time like the narratives from the Jewish Bible regarding Adam and Eve, Noah, Abraham, Moses, David, etc. Things were added, changed, and removed from previous versions of the texts. Earlier versions of the Gospels focused on trying to convince the Jews to accept Jesus as the Messiah and convert to Pauline Christianity, while later versions of the Gospels focused on trying to show that Jesus intended to establish a Church similar to the structure of the Church when these versions were written.

Returning to the fact that the Gospel writers did not intend to write a fact-based, eyewitness-based account of what Jesus said and did, it should also be noted that they intended to provide their own views on Christianity. So almost everything in the Gospels was written as an interpretation (spin doctors in a certain sense) by the Gospel writers. This was a rather arrogant approach. It implies that the Gospel writers thought that they were smarter than their readers or their intended readers. They knew better. The Gospel writers are like the movie Matilda, where Matilda's father says, "Listen, you little wiseacre: I'm smart, you're dumb; I'm big, you're little; I'm right, you're wrong, and there's nothing you can do about it."

Who did the Gospel writers write for, that is, who was their intended audience? Since they wrote the Gospels in Greek, it was certainly not the Jews in Palestine who spoke Aramaic nor the lower-class Jews living outside of Palestine who did not speak Greek. It should be obvious that the four Gospel writers wrote specifically for the middle and upper-class Jews who lived outside of Palestine and who were involved in trade and finance with non-Jews throughout the Middle East and the entire Roman Empire. In addition, the gospels were written by men for men, and this is inconsistent with the nature of God and the mission of Jesus Who came to teach and minister to all: men and women, rich and poor, young and old, healthy and sick, educated and uneducated.

The Gospel writers did not intend on writing a factual account of Jesus, His teachings, or His actions. If they did, they would have interviewed those close to Jesus and especially Mary, His mother, who had the most and the best information and insights into the life, teachings, and personality of Jesus. Nor does it appear that the Gospels writers travelled to Palestine to visit the sites where Jesus lived and interview individuals who had contact with Jesus or Mary.

No, the Gospel writers wanted their readers to accept their view of Jesus and to do that they felt it necessary to reconcile Jesus with the teachings of Judaism as expressed in the Jewish Bible, what Christians call the Old Testament.

In Matthew 4:24 it was stated 'And the report of him went forth into all Syria'. This is a most interesting statement. It indicates that news about Jesus spread from inside Palestine to other countries and most probably to Jews living outside Palestine.

However, it cannot be ruled out that the news of Jesus spread outside Palestine to non-Jews as well since there were non-Jews in Palestine who heard and saw Jesus. Obviously, news spread from person to person since there were no newspapers or other media. The people who viewed the miracles performed by Jesus and listened to His teachings were eager to tell others of what they saw and heard. And this statement (Matthew 4:24) tells the extent of the spread of news regarding Jesus.

But if news of Jesus spread outside of Palestine, then it would seem logical that Paul and those individuals who wrote the Gospels would have heard of this news about Jesus. And if they did, why didn't they travel to Palestine to see Jesus in person and listen to what He said and to see the miracles that He was performing? Paul especially seems to have totally avoided researching Jesus through those who had contact with Him during His Life.

The Gospel writers used a writing style that blended facts with a fictional narrative as a means of persuading their readers to accept their proposals – that Jesus was the Messiah of the Jewish Bible and that Jesus' life, and actions were foretold by Jewish so-called prophets. The Gospel writers went to great lengths to link quotes from Jewish prophets (especially Isaiah) with events in the life of Jesus even when there is no historical basis for doing so. And the Gospel writers and those who edited the Gospels continuously until their final form was established during the time of Emperor Constantine actually fabricated events in the life of Jesus to link Jesus to the prophecies of the so-called prophets of the Old Testament.

The Incarnation of God as a human in Jesus had nothing to do with the Jews, their mostly fabricated Bible, their notion of a messiah who would be sent by God to save them from their enemies and make them the supreme nation with control over all other nations, their ridiculous laws and rituals, and their institutions. The reason why God took on human nature had nothing to do with the Jews and Judaism. God does not nor ever has had favorites, for God loves all people (all people and individuals) equally. The Jewish religious tenet that God has a special relationship with the Jewish people and established a special covenant with them is contrary to the nature of God.

In fact, all religions have erroneous teachings about God, Yahweh, Allah, etc. because of incorrect understandings about the nature of God. It was not until Thomas Aquinas who further developed Aristotle's ideas about God that we had and have a much more complete and correct understanding of God and the nature of God.

PAUL, THE FOUNDER OF PAULINE CHRISTIANITY

aul lived from 5 AD to 67 AD and half of his life was contemporaneous with the life of Jesus, including his adult life. Paul was in Jerusalem for the stoning of Stephen in 34 CE, and it would be safe to assume that he visited Jerusalem during the public life of Jesus. It would also be safe to assume that Paul knew about Jesus. Yet, there is no report of Paul having seen, heard, or speaking to Jesus while Jesus was alive even though Paul could have since he lived at the same time and travelled to Jerusalem probably at times such as the Passover when Jesus was there.

The theology developed by Paul of Tarsus which was adopted by the early organization which claimed to be the Christian Church, and which was later enhanced by the leaders of the Christian Church claimed and taught that God became a human for the sole purpose of offering a death sacrifice to appease God and to atone for Original Sin (coined by Augustine) and the personal sins of all humans throughout all time. Paul surpassed all previous Jewish writers including those who created the creation myth, the Noah myth, the Abraham myth or legend, and the Moses myth or legend.

This claim or teaching of Paul that God took on human nature for the sole purpose of offering a death sacrifice to appease God and to atone for sin is the core and central tenet of Pauline Christianity. But is this true?

Paul developed his ideas of Christianity based on his own personal paradigm. This paradigm was based on Jewish teachings, some Greek philosophers, Paul's upbringing, his relationships with the upper classes of the Jews outside Palestine, the non-Jewish upper classes of Syria particularly Damascus and Antioch, and possibly even the upper classes of Roman.

Paul's ideas on Christianity were not based on listening to Jesus speak, nor interviews with the disciples of Jesus, nor interviews with Mary, the mother of Jesus, who alone had the greatest insights on the personality, mission, and teachings of Jesus.

While Paul was not a disciple of Jesus, nor an apostle of Jesus, he made himself out to be an apostle in order to convince his readers and his followers that what he was teaching was somehow connected directly to Jesus.

In the Acts of the Apostles it is written, "Meanwhile, the witnesses laid their coats at the feet of a young man named Saul…Saul approved the stoning of Stephen…At that time the church in Jerusalem suffered terribly. All of the Lord's followers, except the apostles, were scattered everywhere in Judea and Samaria. Saul made a lot of trouble for the church. He went from house to house, arresting men and women and putting them in jail."

It would seem that Paul (Saul) was present at the council of the Sanhedrin which condemned Stephen since he was present at the stoning which took place immediately afterwards.

It is also likely that Paul actually participated in the stoning of Stephen. The statement 'the witnesses laid their coats at the feet of a young man named Saul" is probably a fabrication. First of all, Paul was not a young man at this time. Second, he himself was a witness who approved the stoning. Third, there was no reason for the participants to take off their coats, lay them down on the ground, and have someone watch their coats. Were they afraid that someone was going to steal them?

Certainly not! The writers of the Acts of the Apostles would obviously try to downplay Paul's involvement in the stoning because they were followers of his.

The statement "He went from house to house, arresting men and women and putting them in jail" is also very interesting. Paul was obviously very close to the high priests and elders and obviously knew about Jesus and Christianity, and he seems to have had an intense hatred for Christianity.

These passages raise some important questions about Paul, his knowledge of Jesus and His teachings, and possibly his involvement with the death of Jesus.

It is certainly likely that Paul knew of Jesus, the activities of Jesus especially His miracles, and the teachings of Jesus since they both lived as adults at the same time,

While there is no evidence or testimony that Paul ever saw Jesus or heard Him speak, it is certainly possible. And it is certainly possible that Paul was in Jerusalem at the time of the Crucifixion and may have witnessed the trial and death of Jesus.

What was Paul doing from the time of Stephen's death to his conversion? Was he still going about from house to house in Jerusalem arresting Christians?

While the conversion of Paul is written as miraculous, it was not necessarily so. It could have been that Paul came to the realization that Christianity was of God based on his witnessing of the trial and stoning of Stephen and Stephen's testimony. It could have also been based on the possibility of Paul having witnessed the trial and crucifixion of Jesus. It is estimated that Paul's conversion was between one and four years after the stoning of Stephen and four to seven years after the death of Jesus.

Paul was on his way to Damascus when he supposedly had a vision that changed his life according to his words in Galatians 1:16. More specifically, Paul states that he saw Jesus 1 Corinthians 9:1, though the Acts of the Apostles claims that near Damascus he saw a blinding bright light. No proof that any of this actually occurred. Paul probably made up the story of his vision as well as his claim that he was an apostle in order to promote his ideas.

Following this so-called revelation, which supposedly led Paul to believe that God had chosen Jesus to be the promised Messiah, he went into the Arabian Peninsula, and then to Damascus, Galatians 1:17 " I did not go up to Jerusalem to see those who were apostles before I was, but I went into Arabia. Later I returned to Damascus". And three years later he went to Jerusalem to become acquainted with the Apostles there.

So, right after his conversion, why didn't Paul return to Jerusalem to ask forgiveness of the people that he had arrested and learn from the disciples about Jesus and His teachings?

In Acts of the Apostles chapter 9 it is written "Meanwhile, Saul was still breathing out murderous threats against the Lord's disciples. He went to the high priest and asked him for letters to the synagogues in Damascus, so that if he found any there who belonged to the Way, whether men or women, he might take them as prisoners to Jerusalem… Saul spent several days with the disciples in Damascus. At once he began to preach in the synagogues that Jesus is the Son of God…After many days had gone by, there was a conspiracy among the Jews to kill him, but Saul learned of their plan. Day and night they kept close watch on the city gates in order to kill him. But his followers took him by night and lowered him in a basket through an opening in the wall."

Facts or fiction? How could Paul "take prisoners to Jerusalem" from Damascus? What kind of legal jurisdiction would he have to arrest people in another country and take them as prisoners to Jerusalem?

Also, in Damascus "at once he began to preach in the synagogues that Jesus is the Son of God", but a few days earlier he had such hatred of

Jesus that he was on his way to arrest followers of Jesus in Damascus. It is not likely that he would or did so. He would have been contrite and sorrowful over what he had done to Jesus and His followers for the past number of years in Jerusalem. And what did Paul really know about Jesus immediately after his so-called conversion?

After escaping from Damascus, Paul spent three years in the Arabian desert. And after this time in the Arabian desert, he returned to Damascus where he was supposedly persecuted before heading to Jerusalem to meet with the Apostles for the first time after which he supposedly began his ministry which lasted thirty years.

After the meeting in Jerusalem with some of the apostles, Paul began his missionary journeys. During the next approximately twenty years, he established churches in Asia Minor and Europe. All of these churches were based on this new version of Christianity, Pauline Christianity, not the Christianity of Jesus. But what was Paul doing in the Arabian desert?

Paul was obviously a very devout and dedicated Jew who knew Jewish theology, Jewish law, and Jewish Scriptures. Judaism was how Paul viewed the world.

Jesus would have been conundrum for Paul. Acceptance of Jesus would have not been an immediate or quick process, but rather a long process involving a paradigm shift. The three years that Paul spent in the Arabian desert probably involved an intense process of trying to reconcile Jesus with Paul's Judaism. This process resulted in the development of Pauline Christianity, the theology and beliefs created by Paul, which he successfully preached, and which became the core theology and beliefs of the Christian Church, the organization which claimed that it represented Jesus on earth. And Pauline Christianity influenced most of the books of the New Testament.

Paul retained the following tenets of Judaism in his new theology involving Jesus:

- the sin of Adam

- everyone is a sinner

- necessity to be clean

- necessity to be spotless

- washing to become clean

- transferring the sins to the thing being sacrificed

- sacrifice to atone for sin by destroying the thing upon which the sins have been transferred

- God can get angry, is vindicative, and punishes those who disobey Him

- there is only one God who is infinite and eternal

Paul added in his new theology:

- sin is an infinite offense because sin it is an offense against an infinite being - God

- sin being an infinite offense against God can only be atoned for by an infinite sacrifice

- an infinite sacrifice involves the sacrifice of an infinite being

- but if sacrifice involves the destruction of the thing being sacrificed, how can an infinite being, God, be destroyed?

- Jesus was both God and human, so the sacrifice of Jesus on the cross was a sacrifice of both a human and God

- Jesus, as God, made an infinite sacrifice of Himself as an atonement for the sins of all people past, present, and future

- the sins of all people were transferred to Jesus

- all people are guilty of sin through the sin of Adam

- only those people who believe in Jesus can really be cleansed of their sins

These are rather absurd statements that the followers of Paul (almost all Christians) accept without question.

First of all, how can so-called Original Sin be imputed against babies and children who have not reached the age of reason?

How can a finite person commit an infinite offense?

While it is said in John 3:16, 'For God so loved the world, that he gave his only begotten Son, that whosoever believeth in him should not perish, but have everlasting life.', what about people who never had the opportunity to know and believe in Jesus, are they damned, and will not reach everlasting life no matter how good they were? Is it not possible to believe in God or Allah, or Yahweh or whatever name one has of God, live a good life loving God and neighbor, and attain to eternal life?

In Matthew 18:21-22 'Then Peter came up and said to him, "Lord, how often will my brother sin against me, and I forgive him? As many as seven times?" Jesus said to him, "I do not say to you seven times, but seventy times seven.' Does this not apply to the Infinite God, Who will forgive infinitely?

Is a sacrifice necessary for forgiveness?

It should be clear that the theology of Paul (Pauline Christianity) was developed by him during this time period of three years without interviewing Mary, any disciples of Jesus, anyone who actually heard Jesus, or anyone who was cured by Jesus. This indicates great arrogance on the part of Paul. He knew better than those who lived with, spoke with, and listened to Jesus.

In addition, the motivation of Paul for creating his version of Christianity may not have been virtuous. Paul was first intent on rising through the Jewish hierarchy as a Pharisee. Was this because he truly thought that Judaism was pleasing to God or because he was ambitious and wanted to feel important and have people look upon him as important. Perhaps, having been frustrated in his attempts to rise to a very high level in the Jewish leadership hierarchy, he seems to have moved to a belief in Jesus Christ. Was this because he truly believed in Jesus, or because he saw this as an opportunity to achieve his objectives in life of being looked upon as important? In founding Pauline Christianity, Paul achieved and surpassed his goal of being considered important so much so that his Church considers him a saint.

Paul came to the conclusion that Jesus lived in heaven, that Jesus was the Messiah and God's Son, and that He would soon return, all of which influenced the writers of the Gospels. The teaching of Paul that

Jesus would return soon influenced his followers, but obviously this teaching was wrong.

The Christianity of Paul is based on the next life. Very useful for people who want to do what they want during this life with the expectation that they can still enjoy Heaven in the next life even though they do not follow the Law of Jesus. The Law of Jesus and the Christianity of Jesus is based on this life. Jesus is Love. To love Jesus is to love your neighbors in this life.

Sin, sacrifice and atonement for sin is central in the Hebrew Bible – the Christian Old Testament. It was first narrated in the Cain and Abel myth. In the Book of Genesis, Cain and Abel, the first two sons of Adam and Eve, make sacrifices to God. Why? Obviously, the authors of this myth wanted to establish the existence and use of sacrifices from what they considered the beginning of time. Cain was a farmer and Abel was a shepherd. They made sacrifices to God, produce and a sheep. But supposedly God favored the sacrifice of the animal over the sacrifice of the produce. Was this intended to imply that God favored animal sacrifices? And do the authors of the Hebrew Bible intend to imply that God even favors human sacrifices more than animal sacrifices with the myth of Abraham and his son Isaac?

Judaism looked upon God or Yahweh as a Supreme King with extensive rules for humans, Who liked to punish those who disobeyed, Who got angry, Who was vindicative, Who treated humans unequally, Who preferred males over females, Who regretted having created humans and Who had no problem killing humans and animals because they did not obey (the so-called Flood).

The theological paradigm of Paul retained this notion of God. Paul held because of his Judaistic views, that humans had infinitely offended God through the sins of Adam and Eve (an extreme twist of logic to state that all humans share in the supposed sins of Adam and Eve) as well as the personal sins of humans.

Note that Paul, his followers, and the Christian organization hold that sin is an infinite offense because it is an offense against an infinite being, God.

This seems to be somewhat inconsistent with the statement of Jesus that we must forgive those who offend us seventy times seven times. It would seem that this would apply to God as well. And while it is not clear in the Gospels, it should be noted that forgiveness of another should occur before and without even being asked. God like a parent does not hold grudges and loves humans unconditionally.

According to Paul, because sin is supposedly an infinite offense, it required an infinite act of atonement – the sacrifice of the life of Jesus the Son of God Who was one with God and therefore infinite Himself. And this is the theology of Paul and the theology of the Christian churches today which are based on Pauline Christianity – the Christianity developed by Paul and his followers.

The theology of Paul which became the theology of the Christian organizations or churches is inconsistent with the nature of God and the teachings of Jesus Christ Who was God. And this basic tenet of Pauline Christianity has undermined the pursuit of good based on the teachings of Jesus and has led to innumerable evils since the time of Paul and the early Christian organization.

For Paul and Pauline Christianity, people need to have faith and believe in this central tenet of Pauline Christianity that God in the person of Jesus offered an infinite sacrifice to atone for the infinite sins of humans for all time. Unfortunately, since the time of the early Christian Church many people have been ostracized, tortured, and even put to death for not believing this. Who can reconcile this with the true nature of God (not the nature of God as described in the Old Testament) and the teachings of Jesus Who was God?

Paul's theme that Jesus became human for the sole reason of dying for the sins of humankind, provides a rather convenient opportunity for people to avoid having to live a good life: doing good in all things (business, politics, and economics), loving your neighbor as yourself (all humans are your neighbors), and respecting the absolute dignity and equality of each and every human being. Instead, people can now say that Jesus saved them, and that they are saved implicitly implying that they do not have to do anything except to believe because Jesus has done everything. And this is the summary of Pauline Christianity.

DOES GOD WANT SACRIFICE?

Does God want sacrifices or is this notion just a human construct that fits a human paradigmQ?

Sacrifice was a major component of Jewish theology and was based on the anthropomorphic theme of Judaism. Anthropomorphism is the ascribing of human qualities to God because of a defective understanding of who and what God is, that is, the nature of God.

Besides Judaism, most religions up to the time of Jesus were anthropomorphic. It must be emphasized that this notion was absolutely incorrect and inconsistent with the true notion of God. The nature of God was partially discovered (or understood) by Aristotle (300 years before the birth of Jesus) and more fully discovered and elaborated by Thomas Aquinas in the 1200's.

Judaism ascribed human characteristics to God, among these they ascribed human defects such as pride and arrogance. The Jews looked upon God as a king and considered the relationship between God and humans to be the same as that between earthly kings and subjects. So, because earthly kings demanded retribution against un-loyal and disrespectful subjects, so the Jews assumed that God wanted the same.

41

However, they quickly replaced animals with humans in their incorrect notion that God's anger (God does not get angry) would be appeased by this sacrifice.

God does not and has never wanted sacrifices. Sacrifices are an absurd invention of humans. God does not get angry and is not offended by human mistakes. Consider the words of Jesus (God) on the cross Who said, "forgive them for they know not what they do". Because God is Love, something that the Jews did not understand, He only wants the best for humans and does not want to destroy them or even animals through the incorrect idea of sacrifice.

THE CHRISTIANITY OF JESUS?

Why God took on human nature?

One of the main reasons why God became human was to provide the correct view of the relationship between God and humans and to correct the incorrect view that the Jews and virtually all other nations had of this relationship. The Jews looked upon God with fear because they thought that God was this king who required absolute obedience and if you did not obey God or respect God, you would be punished perhaps even with eternal suffering. Though the notion of eternal suffering was borrowed from the Greeks by the Jewish writers and the early Christian writers, it fit into Jewish and Pauline Christian theology.

The Jews did not believe in equality. They certainly held that men were superior to women; the priestly class, the king and the royal family were superior to everyone else, the Jews were superior to Samaritans, the healthy were superior to the unhealthy, and that the Jews were superior to non-Jews (Gentiles). And the Jewish writers and the early Christian writers applied this to God. According to them, God prefers men, people in authority, and the learned. This is absolutely inconsistent with the nature of God and the teachings and actions of Jesus.

God took on human nature to provide the correct description of Who God was and to tell people how they should live their lives. The world believed in multiple gods and gods with human characteristics and deficiencies. Even the Jewish writers attributed human characteristics and deficiencies to God. The Jews believed that God was mean, could get angry, could be vindicative, played favorites, punished people by illness and death, tricked people, etc.

Jesus and the nature of God hold that all people are equal. Human beings, all human beings, are made in the image and likeness of God. Jesus taught this principle through both his words and his actions. The absolute dignity and equality of the human being applies to all human beings not just the rich, the powerful, the educated, men, older people, the healthy, the members of specific religions, specific nationalities, specific races or the beautiful. The absolute dignity and equality of the human being applies to the rich and the poor, the powerful and the powerless, the educated and the uneducated, women and men, the old and the young, the healthy and the sick, the members of all religions, the members of all nationalities, all races and the beautiful and the ugly. The absolute dignity and equality of each and every human being is the basis for the rights of each and every human being and the Christian imperative (based on the Christianity of Jesus and not the Christianity of Paul) that every person is to be treated with dignity and respect in their social lives, their business lives, their economic lives, their political lives, and their private lives.

He stood up to read, and the scroll of the prophet Isaiah was handed to him. Unrolling it, he found the place where it is written: 'The Spirit of the Lord is on me, because he has anointed me to proclaim good news to the poor. He has sent me to proclaim freedom for the prisoners and recovery of sight for the blind, to set the oppressed free, to proclaim the year of the Lord's favor.' Then he rolled up the scroll, gave it back to the attendant and sat down. The eyes of everyone in the synagogue were fastened on him. He began by saying to them, 'Today this scripture is fulfilled in your hearing.'" (Luke 4:17-20).

The Jews (and this certainly applied to the writers of the Gospels and the other books of what is called the New Testament) viewed God in the same way that they viewed earthly kings, people who demanded absolute respect and obedience. And anyone who disobeyed the king or disrespected the king could and would be severely punished and perhaps even put to death.

The Jews and biblical writers also held the view that God was always testing people to see if they were faithful (respectful and obedient) to God. Consider the test in the so-called Garden of Eden for Adam and Eve or the test of Abraham when according to the narrative God wanted Abraham to sacrifice Isaac.

Jesus taught that this view of the relationship was wrong. The relationship between God and humans is similar to that of a parent and children, except in a way that humans will never fully understand. For how are humans to understand Infinite Love? When Jesus taught this to the common people, they understood it, but it was not understood or perhaps ignored by the upper class, the ruling class and the writers of the New Testament including the Gospel writers and Paul himself. It is also possible that the writers did not have a very good understanding of the love of a parent for his or her children, having been raised in families where the father was like a king in their home since that was part of the established culture of Judaism.

While it is likely that Jesus used the word parent instead of father to describe the correct relationship between God and humans, the writers would have replaced parent with father since parent did not fit their paradigm. They held that men were superior to women and that fathers were superior to mothers.

Most people get the impression that Jesus was always speaking to men only, and this is absolutely incorrect. Jesus spent most of His time in small villages, living among the common people (and the poor) speaking with them and teaching them. These people had a much different view of the relationship between a parent and their children. In fact, in most cases it is the relationship between a mother and her children that best begins to describe the relationship between God and humans at least as much as we can understand that relationship.

Because the region where Jesus was mixed, that is, Jews, Samaritans, Greeks, Syrians, and Romans lived there; Jesus interacted with these other groups. And because of this, it is most likely that Jesus spoke Aramaic, Hebrew, Latin, and Greek.

Jesus as God would not have considered these other people as different or lower than Jews. He would have considered them as equals, all children of God. In addition, even though the society in which Jesus lived was male dominated, he would not have treated women as inferiors.

Nor would Jesus have distinguished social classes: rich, poor, slaves, etc.; for all are equal in the eyes of God. Jesus had friends and associates (work, discussion groups, etc.) who were Jews, Samaritans, Greeks, Syrians, Romans, both men and women, rich and poor, free and indentured, employed and unemployed, healthy and sick. Jesus' mission to humankind did not start when he was thirty, but as soon as he was of the 'age of reason' (from a human point of view) and was able to interact with others.

During Jesus' so-called non-public life (his life not captured in the Gospels), he attended weddings, parties (birth, anniversary, etc.), festivals and other types of celebrations. Obviously, when Jesus was younger, he attended with his parents. As he became older (boys were considered adults by the age of 13 or 14), Jesus attended these celebrations alone.

Since Jesus had made friends with non-Jewish people especially through this work as a laborer, He probably was invited to the weddings and parties of non-Jews. When Jesus attended weddings, parties, festivals, and other types of celebrations, He obviously interacted with the people at these gatherings. In speaking with people, He would have discretely spoke about things related to His mission of teaching people (all people) how to live a good life, the equality of all people (Jews, Romans, Greeks, etc., men, women, old, young, rich, poor, educated, uneducated, healthy, and sick), and to love your neighbor as yourself. Either the Gospel writers did not know of these things, or they intentionally chose to ignore them since these actions of Jesus did not fit into their paradigm or their objectives in writing the gospels.

Jesus did not intend to start an organization like the one that developed a hundred years after His death, and which developed into a hierarchically structured corporation with aspirations of ruling the world and which allowed slavery, supported wars, and continuously grew in wealth up to today.

The notion that Jesus wanted to establish a Church and immediately began with His Public Life to do so as narrated in the Gospels was certainly a fabrication of the Pauline organization which was trying to give itself legitimacy just like the myth or legend of Abraham was used to try to give legitimacy to Judaism.

It is also most likely that Mary accompanied Jesus in virtually all of his travels and co-taught with him. Who understood the teachings of Jesus from the perspective of a human better than Mary?

So, when Jesus travelled from village to village, teaching the people, Mary was also there teaching the people about the true Word of God (since Jesus was the Word of God).

Though He was born a Jew, Jesus did not follow Jewish philosophy and the belief that Jews were better than non-Jews or Gentiles. This belief led people to avoid contact with Gentiles. Jesus was God and all people regardless of race, origin, ethnicity, gender, social class, health, or mental ability are equal and equally precious to God. God loves all people equally in the same way that a parent loves their children equally. This natural virtue of loving one's children equally comes from God. Obviously, there are parents who do not love all of their children equally or even do not love their children at all, but that is an aberration and a psychological and/or philosophical defect in the parent.

The writers of the New Testament and the leaders of the early Christian organization especially Paul and Augustine completely mis-understood the message of Jesus regarding the relationship between God and humans. Paul, his school of followers, Augustine and the other individuals who were most influential in developing the theology of the Christian organization either did not have any idea of unconditional love or if they did, they denied its existence as well as even the possibility that it could apply to God. So, instead they applied their incorrect notion that God's love for humans was conditional.

UNCONDITIONAL VERSUS CONDITIONAL LOVE

When parents accept, love, and show affection to their children, even when they make mistakes or fall short of expectations, this is unconditional love. In other words, it is a form of love with no strings attached. Therefore, parents love their children for who they are, no matter what. Parents like God love their children equally. They do not give preference to the beautiful child or the smart child or the athletic child or the healthy child or the obedient child or the male child over the plain or even ugly child or the unintelligent child or the clumsy child or the sick child or the disobedient child or the female child.

Unconditional love, simply put, is love without strings attached. It's love you offer freely. You don't base it on what someone does for you in return. You simply love them and want nothing more than their happiness. This is the love that God has for every human being, though we will never completely understand God's love for us because God is Love and in fact is Infinite Love.

God does not need and does not want anything from humans. God does not want sacrifices or prayers or rituals or magnificent churches or statues. God is Love, God is Goodness itself, God is the absolute parent to all humans. What does God want? Does God want people to worship Her/Him? Does God want people to pray to Her/Him seven times a day? Does God want sacrifice? Does God want people to kill animals in sacrifice? Does God want people to kill other humans in sacrifice? Does God want people to kill other people because they don't believe some religious teaching? God wants humans to love each other without condition.

What does God want from humans? Above all, God wants humans to get along, not to fight, to help each other, to take care of each other – all others.

And when the Son of man shall come in His majesty, and all the angels with Him, then shall He sit upon the seat of His majesty. And all nations shall be gathered together before Him…Then shall He say… Come, you blessed of My Father, possess the kingdom prepared for you from the foundation of the world. For I was hungry, and you gave me to eat; I was thirsty, and you gave me to drink; I was a stranger, and you took me in; naked, and you clothed Me: sick, and you took care of Me; I was in prison, and you came to Me. Then the just will ask Him, saying: Lord, when did we see You hungry and fed You; thirsty, and gave You a drink? And when did we see You a stranger, and took You in; or naked and clothed You? Or when did we see You sick or in prison, and assisted You? And He will answer them saying: Amen I say to you, as long as you did it to one of these My least brethren, you did it to Me.

This is the Christianity of Jesus Who was God and not the altered Christianity of Paul.

This notion of the unconditional love of God for humans and the requirement that humans love each other with the same unconditional love imitating God existed among the early Christian followers within the poor and lower classes of people living in Palestine immediately after the death of Jesus. Yet, this notion did not enter into the Gospels or other writings of the New Testament. Why? Was it because the New Testament writers did not know about this because they did not interview actual individuals who lived with and listened to Jesus and Mary? Or was it because the unconditional love of God for humans as taught by Jesus and required of His followers did not fit into their Jewish paradigm?

DEVELOPMENT OF THE GOSPELS AND OF THE EARLY CHRISTIAN CHURCH

The vast majority of people think that one person decided to write a commentary on Jesus (a Gospel) and set about to do so, writing the actual document himself. And this was done four times, once for each Gospel.

However, this is not how the Gospels were written. The writers (usually more than one person) were identified by a Pauline Christian group by the leaders of the group, given the task of writing the commentary, provided with a high-level outline of what to write, provided the objectives of the commentary, specified the intended audience, and provided the financial means of support for the task. Also, because of the difficulty in writing and publishing: writers needed time to write, more than one person had to make copies, and the distribution of these copies required traveling, significant financial support was required in writing the Gospels and other books of the New Testament. And significant financial support could only come from wealthy individuals. And wealthy individuals would not allow anything to be written that would challenge or undermine their status and position economically and politically.

As the Gospel was being written, it was subjected to review by the group leaders and selected individuals of the group. During this review process, changes were made to satisfy the directives of the group leadership and wealthy patrons. Once completed, the leaders of the group visited other Pauline Christian groups to get their inputs into the document.

This review and editing process took place many, many times over many, many years before the final document was completed and endorsed by the hierarchy of the Pauline Christian Church.

The Gospel writers, editors, and sponsors did not intend to write a fact-based biography of Jesus, citing His travels, words, and actions. Rather, they were intent on writing a narrative based on their own views and objectives.

Obviously, most people would rather read a biography of Jesus, including His words and actions, and not someone else's interpretation. Unfortunately, the Gospel writers were 'spin doctors' who intentionally provided a biased interpretation of the life, teachings, words, and actions of Jesus in order to promote Pauline Christianity and the Pauline Christian Church.

It should be clear that these Pauline Christian groups were either founded by Paul himself, his companions, or his followers.

Paul himself established many communities which became churches. His approach in setting up these churches consisted of a few steps. In coming to the town, he would go to the local Jewish Synagogue preaching there in order to gain some followers by using his knowledge of the Hebrew Scriptures and his own developed ideas on the life of Jesus, Who He was, and His mission.

With an initial core group of followers, they would meet in peoples' homes. Paul then employed a strategy of selecting influential and typically wealthy individuals within the group to take on leadership roles.

Because Paul used wealthy and influential individuals as leaders of the new community/church, he was able to meet other wealthy and influential town members. He often used these same individuals to introduce him to similar wealthy and influential individuals in other towns and cities, and in some cases, Paul used these people to start communities in these other towns and cities without him. Paul used both wealthy men and wealthy women to both lead the new Pauline communities/churches and to start new Pauline communities/churches on their own.

Unfortunately, this strategy of establishing churches with leaders who were wealthy and influential within both the business and political communities had a negative impact on the practice of the Christianity of Jesus. In helping one's neighbor, a person will not have any excess wealth. Wealthy people are like the rich person in the Gospel of Matthew 19:20 The young man said to Him, all these things have I observed, what do I lack? Jesus said unto him, if you would be perfect, go, sell what you do not need, and give to the poor... But when the young man heard this, he went away sorrowful for he was one that had great possessions.

These rich people who were the leaders of the early Pauline Christian Church did not want to give up their wealth, but they did want to be saved, that is get to Heaven after they died. Paul knew this and made sure that he did not teach or say anything that would be disapproved of by these wealthy individuals because these individuals were his financial support. It is certainly much easier to sell the idea that a person does not have to really change their lives but only believe (or profess some beliefs) and practice some rituals.

Maintaining the approval and therefore the financial support of his wealthy friends was the primary reason why Paul supported slavery in spite of its obvious inconsistency with the Christianity of Jesus. And not only Paul but virtually the entire Pauline Christian Church up to the last century supported slavery. Why? Because the Church leaders did not want to lose the financial support of their wealthy members. And the wealth of most people over the last 2000 years was based on slavery and the exploitation of the lower class in society by the wealthy upper class.

Pauline Christianity has always supported uncontrolled capitalism, the absolute rights of the capitalist and the absolute denial of the rights of the worker. Why? Because the leaders of Pauline Christianity (the Catholic Church, the Orthodox Church, and the thousands of Protestant Churches) do not want to offend their wealthy supporters.

But, how did early Christianity go from poor, uneducated, fishermen and farmers with no organizational experience because they spent the majority of their time trying to support their families to a highly structured, very hierarchical organization led by very educated individuals with wealth and political power and influence? Why did Rome become the center of Christianity even before Constantine? Was Christianity highjacked by the ruling elite soon after the death of Jesus?

It certainly appears that Christianity (Pauline Christianity) was controlled by an elite group of individuals up to the time of Constantine, it was further organized and controlled by this elite group with the collaboration of Constantine and has been controlled by this elite group up to the present day. While the individuals of this elite group have changed over the last 2000 years, the leadership of the Pauline Christian Church organization has always been composed of wealthy and political ambitious people.

The original strategy of Paul of using wealthy and influential individuals when setting up communities/churches seems to have continued in the Pauline Christian Church even to this day. Most of the early bishops were wealthy and politically influential even within Rome by the time of Constantine.

Unfortunately, the history of the Pauline Christian Church is replete with examples of corrupt popes and bishops, wars started by the Church and the establishment of the so-called Holy Roman Empire, an attempt to create a political and spiritual empire over the world. This feat was the goal of Judaism where the Jewish leadership (High Priest and Sanhedrin) wanted to create a political and spiritual empire that would rule over both Jews and Gentiles.

It is amazing to realize how much evil has been ignored by the leadership of the Pauline Christian Church since its establishment because it did not want to offend the Ruling Elite. Here is one example that is somewhat recent.

King Leopold II was the king of the Belgians from 1865 to 1909 and, through will and effort, the absentee owner and autocratic ruler of the

Congo Free State (the present-day Democratic Republic of Congo) from 1885 to 1908.

At the Berlin Conference of 1884–1885, the colonial nations of Europe authorized his claim and committed the Congo Free State to him. Leopold controlled the Congo using mercenaries for his personal gain. He extracted a fortune from the territory, initially through ivory but later through natural rubber, all through forced labor from the native population.

Leopold's rule over the so-called Congo Free State was characterized by atrocities and brutality, including torture, murder, and the amputation of the hands of men, women, and children when the quota of rubber was not met all of which have been classified as crimes against humanity.

And yet, Leopold II was a Catholic in good standing with the Catholic Church and was given a Catholic funeral. Not one member of the hierarchy denounced him or attempted to exert political pressure on him to change. Outrageous!

And which Catholic leader or which leader of any religious group denounced World War I, World War II, the Korean War, the Vietnam War, the two Iraq Wars? None!

And which Catholic leader or which leader of any religious group denounced the bombing of civilian areas in Dresden, Germany or in Berlin, Germany or the firebombing of Tokyo or the destruction or Hiroshima and Nagasaki by nuclear bombs or the carpet bombing of five cities in North Korea? None!

There were multiple Christian groups that formed after the death of Jesus, but it was the group that was initially led by Paul and based on his teachings that succeeded. The Pauline Christian church was organized to appeal to Hellenistic Jews, Gentiles, the Aristocracy, the Greeks, and Romans, but above all the wealthy and politically influential.

Pauline Christianity spread because many Jews were merchants who travelled throughout the Mediterranean region, throughout the entire Roman empire and even throughout the areas conquered by Alexander the Great. These early Christians were Judaistic Christians and were actually more aligned to Judaism than to Christianity.

This early Christian Churches quickly lost or diluted the message of Jesus when they began to focus on the existence and importance of themselves as a new organization within society. Their leaders wanted to be recognized as leaders within society and because of this they entered into the political arena. This was the main reason why the so-called leadership of the early Christian Church established itself in Rome, the center of the Roman Empire.

The leaders of the early Pauline Christian Church, bishops, wanted to join the ruling classes and be part of it. This extended to both the areas of economics and politics. Theological disputes were more about different bishops vying for greater political power than what was best for the people and what was consistent with the true teachings of Jesus – His teachings by word, actions, and examples.

The Christian Churches of today look very favorably upon Roman Emperor Constantine and some even consider him a saint. However, Constantine was not a good person. Constantine was possibly the most murderous of all the Roman emperors of antiquity. He even murdered his eldest son and his second wife, Fausta. How can anyone reconcile Constantine's supposed Christian new faith with appalling murders, including those of his own family.

The story of the "sign-in-the-sky" where Constantine and his army saw a light in the sky with the Greek words "In this sign you shall conquer" and later that night he had a dream where Christ confirmed the message were stories fabricated by Eusebius. God would never direct a leader to enter a war for the purpose of conquering another country which involved the killing of men, women, and children and the enslavement of those remaining alive in the conquered country.

Constantine was very clever and a skilled politician. He also understood the political aspirations of the bishops including the Bishop of Rome. Constantine needed soldiers and he saw an opportunity to enlist Christians to be his soldiers by working with the Bishop of Rome. Constantine had a significant impact on the Church and the Church adopted many aspects of Roman culture.

Constantine completely altered the relationship between the Church and the imperial government beginning a process that eventually made

Christianity the official religion of the Roman Empire. Many converts were made including those who converted with the hope of advancing their career. This had serious negative impacts on the Church since many of these individuals took on influential positions within the Church.

Constantine elevated people to the position of bishop, obviously individuals who fit his requirements, supported him, and who would be controlled by him. He also personally oversaw councils of bishops indicating the influence and control that he had over the Church.

While there had been multiple competing Christian groups, Constantine was instrumental in elevating the Pauline Christian Church as the one and only official Christian Church as well as destroying documents that had views of Christianity (the teachings of Jesus) that differed from the tenets of Pauline Christianity.

Before Constantine, the New Testament was scattered scripts and there were competing documents. He was instrumental in defining the canon of the New Testament through Eusebius over whom Constantine had great influence.

While the leadership of the early Church had taken on political aspirations within the non-spiritual world, this aspiration was fulfilled starting with the Church's collaboration with Constantine and continued for 1200 years. These aspirations came in part from the Pauline Church's idea of replicating the goal of Judaism to become a religious empire that would rule the world as part of their destiny.

Jesus had no intention of starting either a religious empire (or organization) or a global state empire. As Jesus said to Pilate, "My kingdom is not of this world".

THE PUBLIC LIFE OF JESUS

The life of Jesus is usually divided into two periods: His private life from birth to perhaps around twenty-five to twenty-seven years of age and His public life, the time after His private life until His death.

It is certainly difficult to divide the life of Jesus into a private period and a public period. The reason why this has been done is because we have virtually no information about His life before the period described in the Gospels and this was either because they did not have any information about the life of Jesus before His so-called public life, or the life of Jesus during His so-called private life did not fit into their paradigm or was not well suited for their theme. Also, because the Gospel writers did not interview individuals such as Mary, the mother of Jesus, relatives, and friends, they did not obtain any information on the life of Jesus before His public life.

We can assume that Jesus interacted with the people in Nazareth while growing up and it is interesting to contemplate these interactions. Since Jesus was God with the mission of teaching people about the true nature of God, the correct relationship between God and humans and how people should live; Jesus would certainly have begun to teach by word and example to the people in Nazareth.

And we cannot discount how Mary, His mother, interacted with the people of Nazareth. As His mother, Mary knew about Jesus and what His mission was, and she would have assisted Him in His mission.

Once Jesus reached an age (perhaps around thirteen or fourteen) where He was expected to help support His family, He obviously would have accompanied Joseph to work sites and worked and interacted with the other workers and the people managing the projects.

The image given that Jesus was a carpenter that seemed to do all of His work out of their home in Nazareth is incorrect and misleading. Joseph and Jesus were carpenters, construction workers and laborers who travelled to where building construction was being done. While the Jews had construction projects, most of the major construction work involved the Greeks, Romans, and other non-Jews.

This period of approximately twelve to fifteen years when Jesus was working and interacting with Greeks, Romans and other non-Jews is most interesting. Obviously, Jesus learned to speak Greek and Latin in order to interact with the people on these projects. Somewhat proof of this is the conversation between Pilate and Jesus. Pilate probably spoke Latin and Jesus responded in Latin.

As noted above, since Jesus was God with the mission of teaching people about the true nature of God, the correct relationship between God and humans and how people should live; Jesus would certainly have begun to teach by word and example to the people He came in contact with on these work projects. And given that these projects where probably at such a distance from Nazareth that it was not feasible or even possible to travel home every day, we can assume that Joseph, Jesus, and perhaps even Mary lived in the areas where these construction projects were going on.

When Jesus transitioned from working fulltime to teaching fulltime, He initially spent most of his time with the common people in their villages. He did not spend time with the Hellenistic Jews who did not live in Palestine, and this included Paul and those individuals who wrote the Gospels.

There were significantly more Hellenistic Jews (living outside of Palestine) than Jews living in Palestine. Could Jesus have visited and spent time with the Jews living outside of Palestine? Of course, He could have, but He did not. Could Jesus have visited Paul (Saul of Tarsus) and spent time with him teaching him and making him one of His Apostles? Of course, He could have, but He did not. Could Jesus have spent time with those people who would later become the Gospel writers or Gospel re-writers? Of course, He could have, but Jesus did not!

Nor did Jesus spend time with the leaders of Judaism during His time; the High Priest, the members of the Sanhedrin, the Pharisees, the Sadducees, the Essenes, and the scribes except perhaps for a brief meeting when He was twelve years old, and on a few occasions when some Pharisees came to see Him. Note, He did not go to see them.

And why did Jesus spend most of his time with the common people in their villages and not the powerful and influential Jews in Jerusalem and outside of Palestine including Saul of Tarsus and those people who would become writers of the gospels? Obviously, Jesus knew that these people would not be open to His teachings, but the poor common people who comprised the working class would be. In fact, Jesus knew that these later individuals (the powerful and influential Jews in Jerusalem and outside of Palestine including Saul of Tarsus and those people who would become writers of the gospels) would not understand His message. This is very important point. If Jesus did not teach Paul and the writers of the gospels, did they really understand His mission, message, and teachings?

And how was it that the poor and working-class people understood the message of Jesus? They were basically uneducated, knew very little about the Jewish Scriptures except what they were told in the synagogues.

Is it possible that Jesus taught a message different from the message written by Paul and the Gospel writers and that only a few glimpses of this message are found in the so-called New Testament?

It is also very interesting to understand that when Jesus spent time with the people in their villages, He spent time with the women of the villages something that would not have been possible in dealing with the power elite of the Jewish organizations since they were male dominated and excluded women.

Jesus would travel from town to town and village to village without belongings or money. Did Mary Jesus' mother accompany Him on His mission? Most probably. Jesus would not have abandoned His mother in Nazareth to support herself and do all of the chores around their home. Besides, since the mission of Jesus was also directed to women, Mary's presence at the side of Jesus teaching with Him and ministering with Him would have been most effective for women.

CHRISTIAN, JEWISH, MUSLIM, HINDU AND BUDDHIST SCRIPTURES – FACTS OR FABRICATIONS OR BOTH

The Jewish scriptures (Christians call them the Old Testament) are called the Tanakh, after the first letters of its three parts or sections. T: Torah, is called the teaching of Moses and comprised the first five books. N: Nevi'im, are the books of the prophets. And Kh: Ketuvim, are for the writings including the psalms and wisdom literature.

Moses allegedly lived somewhere in the period between the 14th and 13th Century BCE, though there is absolutely no historical evidence that such a person ever existed and if there was some legendary person referred to as Moses, that person did not do what is attributed to him. The Tanakh was developed over between twelve to fourteen hundred years and for the greater part of this period, it was verbally passed from generation to generation. It was not fixed as a complete document until the second century CE or even later.

Later in this book, a more detailed analysis of the Torah will show the likelihood that it consists primarily of fiction and not facts.

Christian scriptures are called the New Testament by Christians and were developed over a period of over three hundred and fifty years.

The Christian Scriptures primarily the Gospels require a critical analysis, and the analysis will be done later in this book.

The Hindu scriptures are called the Veda and are divided into four sections: the Rig Veda, the Yajur Veda, the Sama Veda, and the Atharva Veda. The Veda was supposedly developed between the 16th and 13th centuries BCE and were passed on from generation to generation until it was written in the 6th century BCE, though only the oral version is considered authoritative, given the emphasis on the exact pronunciation of the sounds.

The Quran is the scripture of Islam and is believed by Muslims to be God's final revelation to humankind. The Quran was supposedly revealed to Muhammad by the Angel Gabriel over a period of 22 years, beginning in 610 CE and ending in 632 CE.

The Tripiṭaka are the scriptures of Buddhism and is composed of three main categories of texts: the Sutra Piṭaka, the Vinaya Piṭaka, and the Abhidhamma Piṭaka. The Tripitaka is considered to be a record of the words of the Buddha who allegedly lived between the 6th and 4th centuries BCE. It was written and fixed sometime between the 1st century BCE and the 1st century CE.

The following are just some examples from Christian scriptures and Jewish scriptures which contain questionable statements, that is, they are either inconsistent or contrary to the nature of God and show where the writer took great liberty adding his own views on the event.

Was John the Baptist the cousin of Jesus? If he was, it would seem that they would have had a very close relationship. And if so, wouldn't John know Jesus and perhaps know Who He was and what His mission was? Or was this narrative an attempt to promote the ritual (and later the sacrament) of Baptism as well as the idea that people had to be washed clean from their sins? Washing was a big thing in Judaism. Washing your hands, washing one's feet, women having to bathe after their menstrual cycle, washing, purification after childbirth, lepers having to wash, etc. It would seem that this narrative fit well into the goal of trying to convince the Jews to accept Jesus as their Messiah and to integrate Judaism and Pauline Christianity. But what is fact and what is fiction?

When Jesus started His public ministry, He did not immediately search out and select Apostles. In fact, it was probable that His Apostles were those who followed Him. The notion that Jesus chose twelve Apostles fit into the Jewish narrative (or legend) of the twelve tribes of Israel which in turn was based on the narrative (or legend) that these tribes were formed by the descendants of Jacob (another legend) the grandson of Abraham (another legend). Fact or fiction?

Matthew 21:18 Now in the morning as He returned to the city, He hungered. And seeing a fig tree by the wayside, He came to it, and found nothing thereon, but leaves only. And He said to it, let there be no fruit from you henceforward forever. And immediately the fig tree withered away. And when the disciples saw it, they marveled, saying, how did the fig tree immediately wither away? And Jesus answered and said to them, verily I say to you, if you have faith, and doubt not, you will not only do what has been done to this fig tree, but even if you shall say to this mountain, be taken up and cast into the sea, it will be done. And in all things, whatever you ask in prayer, believing, you will receive.

The passage regarding the fig tree is inconsistent with Jesus and His divine nature.

How could Jesus, Who was God Himself, express a human imperfection? This passage implies that Jesus became angry with the fig tree because He was supposedly hungry. In another passage it is stated that Jesus fasted for forty days and nights, so Jesus could control His hunger. Jesus would have known that it was not the season for figs to bear fruit, since He designed and sustains the Universe. It is actually absurd to think that Jesus would have even gone to the fig tree out of season looking for fruit. And the narrated anger of Jesus is childish and indicative of a person who cannot control his feelings. And then to imply that Jesus was so angry at a fig tree for being a fig tree that He cursed it and destroyed its life. The sentiments and actions of Jesus described in this passage are totally inconsistent with His Divine Nature.

This passage is not only untrue, but absolute fiction. Whoever wrote this passage was a theological idiot.

Similar passages which are even more absurd than the passage on the fig tree involve the figure of Abraham. The story of Abraham is in the Book of Genesis. Genesis itself is replete with contradictions, inconsistencies, and absurdities which I will comment on later in the book. However, I want to show the absurdity of the conversation between God and Abraham regarding Sodom. This passage implies that Abraham is more just than God.

The LORD appeared to Abraham by the oaks of Mamre, as he sat at the entrance of his tent in the heat of the day. He looked up and saw three men standing near him. When he saw them, he ran from the tent entrance to meet them, and bowed down to the ground. He said, "My Lord if I find favor with you, do not pass by your servant. Let a little water be brought, and wash your feet, and rest yourselves under the tree.

Let me bring a little bread, that you may refresh yourselves, and after that you may pass on - since you have come to your servant." So, they said, "Do as you have said." Abraham hastened into the tent to Sarah, and said, "Make ready quickly three measures of choice flour, knead it, and make cakes. " Abraham ran to the herd, and took a calf, tender and good, and gave it to the servant (the more appropriate word would be slave, Abraham had slaves – how could a person who owned slaves be considered a good and just person in the eyes of God?), who hastened to prepare it. Then he took curds and milk and the calf that he had prepared and set it before them; and he stood by them under the tree while they ate. They said to him, "Where is your wife, Sarah?" And he said, "There, in the tent." Then one said, "I will surely return to you in due season, and your wife Sarah shall have a son." And Sarah was listening at the tent entrance behind him. Now Abraham and Sarah were old, advanced in age; it had ceased to be with Sarah after the manner of women. So, Sarah laughed to herself, saying, "After I have grown old, and my husband is old, shall I have pleasure?"

The Lord said to Abraham, "Why did Sarah laugh, and say, 'Shall I indeed bear a child, now that I am old?' Is anything too wonderful for the Lord? At the set time I will return to you, in due season, and Sarah shall have a son." But Sarah denied, saying, "I did not laugh"; for she was afraid. He said, "Oh yes, you did laugh." Then the men set out from there, and they looked toward Sodom; and Abraham went with them to set them on their way.

The Lord said, "Shall I hide from Abraham what I am about to do, seeing that Abraham shall become a great and mighty nation, and all the nations of the earth shall be blessed in him? No, for I have chosen him, that he may charge his children and his household after him to keep the way of the Lord by doing righteousness and justice; so that the Lord may bring about for Abraham what he has promised him."

Then the Lord said, "How great is the outcry against Sodom and Gomorrah and how very grave their sin! I must go down and see whether they have done altogether according to the outcry that has come to me; and if not, I will know." So, the men turned from there, and went toward Sodom, while Abraham remained standing before the Lord.

Then Abraham came near and said, "Will you indeed sweep away the righteous with the wicked? Suppose there are fifty righteous within the city; will you then sweep away the place and not forgive it for the fifty righteous who are in it? Far be it from you to do such a thing, to slay the righteous with the wicked, so that the righteous fare as the wicked! Far be that from you! Shall not the Judge of all the earth do what is just?" And the Lord said, "If I find at Sodom fifty righteous in the city, I will forgive the whole place for their sake." Abraham answered, "Let me take it upon myself to speak to the Lord, I who am but dust and ashes. Suppose five of the fifty righteous are lacking? Will you destroy the whole city for lack of five?" And he said, "I will not destroy it if I find forty-five there." Again, he spoke to him, "Suppose forty are found there." He answered, "For the sake of forty I will not do it." Then he said, "Oh do not let the Lord be angry if I speak. Suppose thirty are found there." He answered, "I will not do it, if I find thirty there." He said, "Let me take it upon myself to speak to the Lord. Suppose twenty are found there." He answered, "For the sake of twenty I will not destroy it." Then he said, "Oh do not let the Lord be angry if I speak just once more. Suppose ten are found there." He answered, "For the sake of ten I will not destroy it." And the Lord went his way, when he had finished speaking to Abraham; and Abraham returned to his place.

This passage of the Old Testament attempts to show God as an angry person intent on revenge and punishment Who does not have compassion for people and Who will punish all the peoples of Sodom and Gomorrah, including women, children, and infants. It also implies that God does not know what is really going on in these two cities, 'Then the Lord said, "How great is the outcry against Sodom and Gomorrah and how very grave their sin! I must go down and see whether they have done altogether according to the outcry that has come to Me; and if not, I will know.' And Abraham is depicted as more compassionate than God when he tries to get God to stop the destruction of these two cities.

This passage really shows that the writer(s) did not comprehend the true nature of God and that they were trying to establish Abraham as a very virtuous person (in spite of the fact that he had slaves and mistresses among other significant personal defects). Obviously, this passage is a complete fabrication that has absolutely no basis in reality. And this passage has been passed off to Jews and Christians for 3000 years as the Word of God, something either written by God or dictated by God to the writer(s) with the objective of tricking or coercing people into believing it because it is the Word of God.

A scam is defined as a dishonest scheme or a fraud. This passage like virtually every other supposed narrative of the Old Testament is a scam.

In the Gospel writings regarding Jesus before Pilate, how was the detailed information captured? In John's gospel, it was said that the Jews did not enter the judgement hall of Pilate allegedly because they did not want to be defiled in which case, they could not eat the Passover meal. Certainly, absurd reasoning – the Jewish leaders would be defiled, not for trying to kill an innocent person, Jesus, but defiled because they would come into the presence of a non-Jewish Roman official.

So, Pilate had to go out of this hall to talk to the Jewish leaders. When he could not resolve their concerns, Pilate went back inside and called for Jesus to come to him. So, we now have Pilate and Jesus and no

Jews, and probably some of Pilate's attendants in the room where there are conversations between Pilate and Jesus. Who then would have captured and recorded to either written word or memory the exact words of the conversations between Pilate and Jesus and how was this communicated to the writers of the Gospels? This is especially a wonder regarding the conversation between Pilate and his wife; 'When he was set down on the judgment seat, his wife sent unto him, saying, have nothing to do with that just man: for I have suffered many things this day in a dream because of him.' Only attendants to Pilate and his wife may have heard this conversation (emphasis on 'may have heard' since there is no way to determine whether this is true or a fabrication to enhance the narrative of Jesus before Pilate), and again how was this communicated to the writers of the Gospels?

Another observation in the Gospel passages involves the inscription Pilate had placed on the cross of Jesus, 'Jesus the Nazarene, the King of the Jews'. It was written in Hebrew, Greek, and Latin. Obviously, there must have been a considerable number of people in Jerusalem who spoke only Greek or Latin and not Hebrew, and also why was there not an inscription in Aramaic?

The story of Judas may have been totally fabricated in order to draw more connections between the Old Testament so-called prophecies and Jesus; 'Then was fulfilled that which was spoken by Jeremy the prophet, saying, and they took the thirty pieces of silver, the price of him that was valued, whom they of the children of Israel did value... And gave them for the potter's field, as the Lord appointed me.'

These passages are just some of many, many passages in both the so-called New Testament and the so-called Old Testament that should lead an objectively minded person to conclude that both books contain fact and fiction. And it follows that if the Bible contains both facts and fictions, the objectively minded person should draw the conclusion that the teachings of the Christian Church and Judaism that the Bible was the word and work of God, written by God through the writers is false. It should be doubted that the Bible was even inspired by God, but rather was the work of men (yes, men since it appears that women were not allowed to be involved in the writings.)

THE CHRISTIANITY OF JESUS VERSUS PAULINE CHRISTIANITY

Pauline Christianity is based on faith alone, prayers, and the practice of rituals with very little focus on morality. In Catholic Churches which are Pauline Christian churches there is almost no regular teachings on morality (good versus bad actions) during Masses on Sundays and their holydays. Instead, virtually all instructions given on Sundays and holydays involves passages of the Old Testament and the epistles of Paul. In spite of the seriousness of present-day evils, there is no instruction or direction by the Catholic Church regarding these everyday evils which many Catholics are complicit in.

When has anyone heard during a Sunday sermon any talk about human trafficking, prostitution, the military acts of aggression by the United States, the apartheid actions of the Israeli government against the Palestinians, war crimes, the fact that the United States is the biggest arms dealer in the world, the fact that the United States spends over 810 billion dollars a year on its military while there are 40 million people living in poverty, the fact that the minimum wage in the US has not been raised since 2009, the greatest resurgence of Eugenics in the US since the early 1900's, the intentional price gouging involving energy, food, rents, the extreme interest rates for payday loans averaging 391 percent, that the credit card interest rates average between 20 and 25 percent, the outsourcing of jobs to lower wage countries, the existence of sweat shops, the opioid crisis being intentionally started and managed by large pharmaceutical corporations, the absolute drive for power, and the ubiquitous practice of placing profits over people?

Are these actions right or wrong? They are certainly wrong, but the Catholic Church, the pope, the cardinals, bishops, and priests say nothing. All of the above actions are contrary to the teachings of Jesus, so why is the Catholic Church silent? If it because of the practice instituted by Paul not to offend the wealthy and the politically influential and powerful? Most likely!

This is one of the reasons Pauline Christianity is significantly different than the Christianity of Jesus.

What could life and society be today if the Christianity of Jesus prevailed over the Christianity of Paul?

There is far more to the actions and teachings of Jesus than what is contained in the writings of the early writers after the time of Christ.

One of the reasons for this is the destruction of documents and the elimination of individuals that occurred before, during, and after the reign of Emperor Constantine, who in collaboration with the leadership of the Pauline Christian organization eliminated any Christian teachings that were contrary to the policies, practices, and teachings of the Pauline Christian Church as well as those individuals who promoted such teachings.

Slaves existed in Palestine during the time of Jesus. Large landowners owned slaves. Wealthy householders owned slaves. Herod owned many slaves. The chief priests owned slaves. And slavery was very prevalent throughout the Roman Empire. In fact, the wealth of most rich people at the time of Paul and the early Christian Church was due to slavery. So, Paul and the early Christian Church leaders allowed and even supported slavery, lest it upset their wealthy patrons

The Gospel writers would have ignored any of Jesus' statements against slavery since it was a very controversial topic that impacted many influential Jews.

The Gospel writers would have ignored any of Jesus' statements about women's equality since it was a very controversial topic that impacted many influential Jews.

The Gospel writers would have ignored any of Jesus' statements against prostitution since it was a very controversial topic that impacted many influential Jews.

Jesus was non-violent and preached non-violence, why did the Pauline Christian Church promote violence, war, and participation in war especially from the time of Constantine and Augustine who actually developed a theory on a just war.

You have heard that it was said, 'An eye for an eye, and a tooth for a tooth.' But I say to you, do not resist an evil person; but whoever slaps you on your right cheek, turn the other to him also. If anyone wants to sue you and take your shirt, let him have your coat also. Whoever forces you to go one mile, go with him two. Give to him who asks of you, and do not turn away from him who wants to borrow from you. You have heard that it was said, 'You shall love your neighbor and hate your enemy.' But I say to you, love your enemies and pray for those who persecute you.

Bless those who persecute you; bless and do not curse. Rejoice with those who rejoice, and weep with those who weep. Be of the same mind toward one another. Do not set your mind on high things but associate with the humble. Do not be wise in your own opinion.

Repay no one evil for evil. Have regard for good things in the sight of all men. If it is possible, as much as depends on you, live peaceably with all men. Beloved, do not avenge yourselves, but rather give place to wrath

The Law of Moses was to be replaced with the Law of Jesus: love one another, all people are equal, no war, no violence, no slavery, treat others as you want to be treated, one's wife is your equal; politics, business and economics based on love of neighbor, and all people are equal in the eyes of God, God is the parent of all people regardless of race, religion, economic level, gender, age, physical condition, physical appearance, social status; helping the poor, helping the disabled, giving comfort to those depressed, sheltering the homeless, feeding the hungry, clothing those who need clothes, teaching the unlearned – this was the Christianity of Jesus.

Pauls' Christianity was designed to be appealing to the wealthy, slave-owners, and those who controlled wives. Paul's idea of Christianity did not focus on the Law of Jesus but rather the Law of Self. Paul focused on the individual and how to save herself or himself. Jesus' kingdom was on earth, Paul's was in Heaven. Jesus spoke of the Kingdom of God thirty-two times. Paul spoke of the Kingdom of Heaven. What is the Kingdom of God? Jesus spoke of this Kingdom; Not he who says Lord, Lord will enter the Kingdom of God, but he/she that does the will of God. Since God is Love, Truth, Wisdom, and Peace; the Kingdom of God is the kingdom of Love, Truth, Wisdom and Peace. The followers of Jesus must seek the kingdom of Love, Truth, Wisdom, and Peace on earth.

PROSPERITY CHRISTIANITY

Prosperity Christianity is the philosophy, belief and practice that holds that prosperity or wealth is a sign that one is blessed by God, that seeking wealth is the same as seeking God's blessing, and that maximizing wealth is the same as maximizing God's blessing. Implicit in these beliefs is the position that a person who is not wealthy is not blessed by God.

There are many very wealthy individuals (millionaires, multi-millionaires, and billionaires) who accept and promote Prosperity Christianity in theory and in practice though not explicitly referring to the phrase Prosperity Christianity. And many of these individuals have leadership positions within corporations and within the various levels and branches of government. They boast of being practicing Christians as well as pursing ever-increasing wealth.

In past times, Christianity consisted in giving to the poor, feeding the hungry, clothing the naked, giving shelter to the homeless, caring for the sick and imprisoned, etc. and these actions were considered the means of seeking God's blessing. These actions were directed away from oneself and towards others and this practice is also called altruism. However, with Prosperity Christianity the direction of action is toward oneself. Prosperity Christianity of its nature is individualistic (directed towards oneself) and its main objective is the acquisition and control of wealth.

Because of this, Prosperity Christianity of its nature is selfish. A certain amount of selfishness is natural and good. However, when selfishness impacts others, denying others their natural rights and depriving others of what is due to them; then selfishness is wrong. Prosperity Christianity is an oxymoron and yet many, many people accept the idea as correct and even biblical.

But is the pursuit of wealth really synonymous with the practice of Christian principles? And if the pursuit of wealth is a Christian principle, then why has this notion only been discussed and promoted only within the last sixty years?

The principles of Christianity are those principles expressed and exemplified by the words and actions of Jesus Christ and can be summed up in three principles: good is to be done and promoted and evil is to be avoided; love your neighbor as yourself and the absolute dignity and equality of each and every human being. Prosperity Christianity is not Christian and is actually contrary to Christian principles, that is, those principles expressed and exemplified by the words and actions of Jesus Christ. Prosperity Christianity only benefits the rich and makes the poor submissive to the rich since the rich are allegedly God's blessed.

Unfortunately, most Christians are not critical thinkers but rather blind followers. They have been and are led by so-called Christian leaders who have aligned themselves with the economically elite. Many Christian leaders have espoused the false principles of Prosperity Christianity. The vast majority of Christians do not comprehend the inconsistencies of current business and economic practices with truly Christian principles and blindly follow their leaders who have been blinded by their own personal pride and greed.

How is the Christian mandate to love your neighbor as yourself to be applied in business, economics, and politics? How does God want people to act within their jobs, their businesses, their business transactions, how they treat employees, how they pay employees, how they treat business subordinates, how they deal with tenants, how they set prices, how they deal with other businesses, what they sell, how they market their products and services, how they advertise, what is the quality and safety of their products and services, etc.

Christianity is more than praying, attending church services, proclamations of faith, singing hymns, receiving sacraments, and performing religious practices. Christianity is a way of life and extends to every facet of a person's everyday life including their business, economic, and political lives.

The ten richest men in the world more than doubled their wealth from $700 billion to $1.5 trillion during the first two years of the recent pandemic, while the wealth of 99 percent of humanity fell and 160 million more people fell into poverty. Greed is at the base of the current economic disparity in the world. Greed that has no concern or compassion for others, literally billions of others some of whom live in extreme poverty. This is a moral crisis directly caused by the actions of certain people, and yet Pauline Christianity does nothing except for the pope to make some vague statement every now and then, while at the same time rubbing elbows with the rich and powerful and supporting the work of the Council of Inclusive Capitalism (oxymoron).

While there is not an infinite amount of money and material things, the human that desires these things as the object of his or her ultimate happiness will continually seek more and more money and wealth. So consuming and enslaving is this drive, that this person will do anything and everything to achieve this perceived objective: the acquisition of absolutely all wealth. Unfortunately, money and wealth will never bring happiness to a person. Human happiness consists in the attainment of union with Infinite Goodness, Infinite Truth, Infinite Order, Infinite Wisdom, and Infinite Beauty; that is to say God, Who alone can satisfy a human's desire for happiness and Who alone will complete that person.

Greed is the driving force behind Prosperity Christianity. The economic crisis which has impacted hundreds of millions of people has been and is caused by some very rich people who are intent on becoming even richer and more powerful. These people have neither sympathy nor empathy for their fellow human beings. These super-rich people are in fact the cause of the financial, emotional, and physical sufferings of these people, and they don't care.

Rather, these super-rich have contempt for those suffering from this economic crisis and actually blame them rather than themselves for their economic misery. And this is Prosperity Christianity, which is not the Christianity of Jesus.

THE LOVE OF GOD TAUGHT BY JESUS

Jesus taught that the relationship between God and humans is that of a Parent and child. God as a parent loves all people equally and desires the good of all people.

God is like a baby who does not see male or female, black, white, or brown, old or young, ugly or beautiful, healthy or sick, rich or poor, German, Italian, American, Jew, Chinese or Indian – all are the same for God.

Then why do religions have prejudices. Why does Judaism think that Jews are God's chosen people and better than non-Jews or gentiles? Why has and does virtually every major religion consider that men are superior to women (women should submit to men) in the eyes of God? Why has and does virtually every major religion consider that some people; kings, queens, government leaders, and those in authority are superior to everyone else? Why does Paul tell his followers to obey all authority not only government authorities, but also slave-owners, husbands, and himself?

Paul establishes the basis for blind obedience to so-called authority and equates the authority of government, leaders, and himself with the authority of God Himself.

'Let everyone be subject to the governing authorities, for there is no authority except that which God has established. The authorities that exist have been established by God. Consequently, whoever rebels against the authority is rebelling against what God has instituted, and those who do so will bring judgment on themselves. For rulers hold no terror for those who do right, but for those who do wrong. Do you want to be free from fear of the one in authority? Then do what is right and you will be commended. For the one in authority is God's servant for your good. But if you do wrong, be afraid, for rulers do not bear the sword for no reason. They are God's servants, agents of wrath to bring punishment on the wrongdoer. Therefore, it is necessary to submit to the authorities, not only because of possible punishment but also as a matter of conscience (words or teachings from Paul in letter to the Romans)

Obviously, Paul was trying to gain favor with those in authority including the rich, slave-owners, men, those with servants and the leaders of organized religions and factions of organized religions. And this is one of the main objectives of Pauline Christianity. The above passage from Paul's letter to the Romans is inconsistent with the teachings of Jesus. What was the basis for Paul making this claim? Certainly not his extensive conversations with Jesus – because he had none. Certainly not his extensive conversations with those who knew Jesus personally and spent considerable time with Jesus, listening to Him, talking to Him and ask Him questions – because he had no such conversations. The basis for Paul making this claim is Paul himself.

Paul lived from the year 5 AD to 64 or 67 AD. Jesus was born in the year 4 BC and died in between 30 and 33 AD. The years when Jesus taught and preached publicly were the last three or four years of His life, from 29 AD to 33 AD. Paul would have been 24 to 27 years old during this time. Given that Paul was supposedly a devout Jew and Pharisee, it would seem reasonable to assume that he followed happenings in Palestine even though he did not live in Palestine. It is also reasonable to assume that he travelled to Jerusalem every year.

In fact, the Jewish Bible instructs Jews to travel to Jerusalem three times a year, one of which is Passover. It is very hard to believe that Paul did not hear or meet Jesus while Jesus was living. It is also very hard to believe that Paul never had the opportunity of speaking with the family, friends, and close associates of Jesus, unless he intentionally chose not to, and if so – WHY?

Obviously, the one person who could provide the greatest insights into Jesus – Who He was, Why He became a human, what were His teachings, what did humans need to do to please God – was Jesus' mother, Mary. Why didn't Paul speak to Mary. He certainly could have. Paul was supposedly converted to Christianity a few years after the death of Jesus. It is said that Mary lived eleven years after the death of Jesus. Perhaps Paul did speak with Mary and perhaps he did not like what she said because it did not fit his own personal view of Jesus which became the basis of his theology and the basis of Pauline Christianity.

Who would know more about Jesus than His mother, Mary? She spent the most time with Him, she had the most personal relationship with him, she obviously had extensive conversations with Him. Why wouldn't Paul, the Gospel writers, and especially Luke who wrote the Acts of the Apostles and who was a companion of Paul have interviewed Mary.

When I reflect on the relationship between Mary and Jesus, I realize that she had the most unique relationship with Him far exceeding that of any other being including angels. Mary and Jesus had mother and son conversations which were at the same time conversations between a human being and God. As His mother, Mary asked Jesus questions and God answered. These conversations occurred daily for His entire life. It is a shame that no one was able to record for all generations what these conversations were about since the truths revealed in these conversations would have clarified the true purpose in God becoming a human, Who or What God was or is, what happens after death, what is Heaven like, does Hell exist, will the world come to an end or will it go on into infinity, etc.

Obviously, Mary was in awe and wonder from the time of the announcement by the angel that she would conceive a son by the power of God and that this child would be the Son of God. She must have tried to understand what this meant every day during her pregnancy.

She was bearing the Son of God, but who or what was the Son of God? Was the baby in her womb really God or just some prophet? If her baby was God, then He was also human? And if so, her son would be both God and man at the same time – an amazing consideration.

And the question certainly arose in Mary's mind, why was God becoming a human? Mary had to think about all of this and reflect on these things and try to understand this as much as she could every day during her pregnancy waiting for His birth and the opportunity to talk to this God-Human and ask all of her questions.

Mary would have had discussions with her husband, Joseph, about these things, and he in turn must have reflected on these things daily himself.

The birth of Jesus must have been absolutely astonishing event for Mary. She had given birth to a son Who she conceived without a man. She was told that she had conceived by the power of God, so God was the father of her son. As she looked at her son who she had waited for, reflecting on these things for nine months, was it obvious that He was also God? Mary knew that God was infinite, eternal, omnipotent, and all-present; and yet, this child that she just gave birth to was God! She obviously had these thoughts, and she was eager for the opportunity to talk to her son and ask Him questions that would help her in some little way to understand.

How soon Jesus began to talk is not known, but He certainly could have talked immediately after His birth. Mary would have been eager to talk to Jesus as well as observe the things that Jesus would do that would reflect His Divine Nature.

I would assume that Jesus had conversations with his relatives, Lazarus, Mary Magdalene, and other close friends where these individuals were able to ask Jesus questions and receive answers about Jesus, His mission, why God became a human, etc. Yet, all of these answers were lost probably because of the bias of the writers of the early Christians or because of the bias of those who copied and edited these writings.

The original manuscripts of the New Testament books are not known to have survived. The oldest document containing writings of the Old and New Testaments is the Codex Vaticanus from the 4th Century (300 – 325 CE). It and the Codex Sinaiticus (330- 360 CE) were part of a project ordered by Constantine to produce 50 copies of the Bible. This raises the question of how many copies of the Bible existed before 360 CE.

The original manuscripts of the New Testament are believed to have been lost or destroyed. Copies were made of copies which were made of copies without access to the original documents.

Are we to assume that in this process of copying documents there was no poetic license, artistic freedom, literary license, artistic license, narrative license, or writer's embellishment?

For God so loved the world, that He gave His only begotten Son, that whosoever believed in Him should not perish but have everlasting life (John 3:16). Implicit in this statement are a number of ideas or proposals. The reason why I use the word proposal is that these are proposals by Paul and his followers regarding the purpose of Jesus: why He became human, why He lived and why He died. Paul and his followers marketed these proposed ideas without any proof. Paul never met Jesus even though he lived at the same time as Jesus. Nor did Paul interview any of those who were related to Jesus (His mother, Mary, and His relatives) nor any of His close friends (Mary Magdalen, Lazarus) nor any of the people who spent time with Jesus and talked with Him personally and not in a public forum. How could Paul or rather how dare Paul claim to know more about Jesus than His family, friends, and close associates. Paul's Christianity is all about Paul and not about Jesus.

First of all, God showed His love for humankind by becoming a human. By this act God wanted to and wants to show people that He considers Himself an equal with us not someone superior to us. And if Jesus Who is God treats us as equals, then we need to treat others as equals. If Jesus did not act as a superior to us, then how can some of us act like they are superior to all others: leaders, government officials, judges, husbands, etc. After Jesus had washed the feet of His disciples, He instructed them saying If I then your Lord and Teacher, have washed your feet, you also ought to wash one another's feet. For I have given you an example, that you should do as I have done to you.

You have heard that it was said, 'An eye for an eye and a tooth for a tooth.' But I tell you not to resist an evil person. But whoever slaps you on your right cheek, turn the other to him also. If anyone wants to sue you and take away your tunic, let him have your cloak also. And whoever compels you to go one mile, go with him two. Give to him who asks you, and from him who wants to borrow from you do not turn away.

Bless those who persecute you; bless and do not curse. Rejoice with those who rejoice, and weep with those who weep. Be of the same mind toward one another. Do not set your mind on high things but associate with the humble. Do not be wise in your own opinion.

Repay no one evil for evil. Have regard for good things in the sight of all men. If it is possible, as much as depends on you, live peaceably with all men. Beloved, do not avenge yourselves. Therefore, if your enemy is hungry, feed him. If he is thirsty, give him a drink. Do not be overcome by evil but overcome evil with good.

In reading the gospels regarding of the Last Supper, a person should question the truthfulness of the narrative. The typical celebration of the Passover was a family event, attended by wives, children, and extended family. Would Jesus have intentionally excluded the families of the Apostles? Are we to accept that the wives and children were to have stayed home and either not celebrated Passover or celebrated it without the father of the family?

An objective person should also question the narratives in the gospels regarding the Apostles seemingly leaving their families. Would Jesus really want these men to leave their wives and children and require their wives to support and defend themselves and their children without their husbands/fathers? Life was difficult for working people during the time of Jesus. But it had to be especially difficult for families without a father.

If the husband/father died, then the father would be respected since he died from no fault of his own. But if the father abandoned his wife and children, people would have contempt for such a man.

This would certainly have impacted the Apostles' trustworthiness when preaching or teaching people. Since they would have had a reputation for abandoning their families, people would have questioned their moral authority as well as their message.

I would certainly have very serious doubts about a person and what they had to say about God and how to live a good life, if they had abandoned their families. While I will return to this topic later, for me this also applies to Augustine of Hippo who abandoned his wife and son. How can a man who abandons his wife and son be considered a saint and a doctor of the Pauline Christian Church?

Did the Apostles stop supporting their families when they became apostles, or did they continue to support their families while following Jesus part-time? I really think that the Apostles continued to support their families while following Jesus at the same time. This can be supported by the fact that the most early Christian priests were married, and this continued in the Eastern Christian Churches even to this day where priests are married and have families.

It was Augustine who was most instrumental in undermining the idea of married priests and teaching that celibate clergy are superior to married people. Augustine who abandoned his wife and son to pursue a celibate life had serious personal problems which influenced his thinking, which in turn influenced his writings and teachings.

And because Augustine was such an influence in the Roman Church (he was actually a bully who intimidated people who disagreed with him and had books burned and people who he considered heretics (actually people who disagreed with him) tortured and imprisoned by government authorities (first Christian inquisitions)). Augustine was instrumental in influencing Christian views on marriage up until this day and what the cause of so many problems for the last 1700 years.

THE LAST SUPPER AND PAULINE CHRISTIANITY

Jesus nor the Apostles would have excluded the wives and children of the Apostles from the Last Supper and in fact, it is most likely that Mary the mother of Jesus was also present at the Last Supper. It would make no sense otherwise. Mary was obviously in Jerusalem during the time of the Last Supper, since she was present the next day at the crucifixion of Jesus. Would Jesus have left His Mother by herself for this last Passover celebration? Certainly not!

The gospel writers intended to justify the existence and position of the Church organization and developed the gospel narratives with this objective and intentionally left out information that did not support their views and objectives. Because the early Church organization which was developed by Paul and his school was based on the Christianity of Paul and not the Christianity of Jesus, it was necessary for the gospel writers and the Pauline Christian School to try to establish some authenticity for the priesthood of the Church of Paul.

Paul wanted to create a new religious organization patterned after the religious organization of Judaism which had a hierarchy with priests.

Paul's organization would have priests and very quickly a hierarchy of priests: deacons, priests, bishops, and a chief priest who would later be called the pope.

Judaism was created and developed by individuals like Paul and the gospel writers who established Judaism based on alleged but really legendary figures like Abraham, Moses, and Melchizedek.

Paul and the gospel writers wanted to show that their organization consisting of priests and a priestly hierarchy was created by Jesus. Remember that the gospel writers were not eyewitnesses to the events of Jesus' life and seemingly refused to use interviews and quote eyewitnesses.

Like the Jewish writers who developed Judaism, Paul and the gospel writers used the gospels to supposedly prove that Jesus founded their Church and at the same time used their Church to claim that the gospels and the other writings of the so-called New Testament were the word of God, not just inspired by God but written by God. The Old Testament writers and the New Testament writers did this in order to actually coerce people into accepting both their writings and their institutions.

Of course, these arguments are logically incorrect. You cannot claim that the Church was instituted by Jesus using the gospels claiming that the gospels were written by God based on the authority of the Church. Their claim for the authority of the Church is based on the authority of the gospels and the authority of the gospels is based on the authority of the Church. While this is certainly illogical, yet why don't people see this?

Most people are aware of the teachings and position of the Church of Paul which developed into the Christian Church of today that Jesus instituted the priesthood at the Last Supper. This is why in the gospel narratives it was necessary to exclude all other persons except the Apostles from the Last Supper. Not that the presence of other individuals such as the wives and children of the Apostles and Mary the mother of Jesus would have prevented Jesus from ordaining His Apostles as priests, but the presence of only the Apostles made the narrative so much more compelling and supportive of the Pauline Christian Church's teachings on their priesthood.

The gospel narratives of the Last Supper which intentionally excluded people other than the Apostles shows the chauvinistic view of Paul and the gospel school regarding the superiority of men over women and their position that God in the person of Jesus regarded men as superior to women and the Apostles as superior to other men.

But is God chauvinistic? Was Jesus chauvinistic? Does God consider men superior to women? Did Jesus consider men superior to woman? Does God consider some men as superior to other men? Did Jesus consider some men as superior to other men? Does God hold that celibate people are superior to married people? (The view was promoted by Augustine because he considered that sex even within marriage other than specifically for bearing children was basically sinful and sex resulting in the conception of children the means for transmitting original sin.) Absolutely not!

The presence of woman at the Last Supper would have been a conundrum for Paul and the gospel writers as it is for present day Christian leaders especially within the Catholic Church. The Catholic Church holds that women cannot become priests primarily because Jesus supposedly chose only men to be His apostles and He only ordained men as priests at the Last Supper.

As mentioned before, Paul and the gospel school wanted to establish an institution (the Church) which would be very similar to the Jewish institution. Paul and the gospel school could not have accepted women at the Last Supper since this might imply that Jesus did ordain some women as priests, something that they could not accept within their new institution since they felt that they as men were superior to women.

What if Jesus did not have Apostles, what if these individuals like Peter, James, John, etc., were merely fervent followers who after the death, resurrection and ascension of Jesus took lead roles in the early Christian communities.

At Pentecost, the Holy Spirit descended on the disciples of Jesus, men, and women. In Luke Chapter 24, the risen Jesus appeared to His disciples, both men and women.

During the public life of Jesus, He visited small towns. Mary accompanied Jesus, and they stayed with the townspeople, working with them, eating with them, celebrating with them, teaching them, and then going to another town. Were the followers of Jesus chosen by Him or did they by their own decision chose to be followers of Him. And did the followers of Jesus as families, follow Him, husbands and wives, husbands, wives, and children?

The early Christian communities, that is, those groups of people who began to follow the teachings of Jesus were:

• 	the people in the small towns and villages where He stayed – they began to follow Him before His death; poor, uneducated, honest, hard-working families who were apolitical

• 	the groups formed by the individuals the gospels identify as apostles, though there were more of them than 12 – the number 12 was meant to link the institution of Paul to the 12 tribes of Israel.

Christian organizations lost the message of Jesus when they began to focus on the existence and importance of them as organizations within society. Their leaders wanted to be recognized as leaders within society and because of this they entered into the political arena. And because tends to corrupt, many leaders of the Pauline Christian Church became corrupt.

Power tends to corrupt

Power tends to corrupt at every level: what does that mean? A person in a position of authority over others is tempted to think that he/she is better than those over whom this authority is exercised. The teacher is tempted to think, "I am better than my students." The policeman is tempted to think, "I am better than these citizens." The boss is tempted to think, "I am better than those people that report to me." The judge is tempted to think, "I am better than those I am to judge." The mayor, the governor, the congressman, the president are all tempted to think, "I am better than all those over whom I have authority."

These thoughts come because of the prestige surrounding such positions. And if these thoughts are not over-come with the truth that the person in authority is meant to serve others and in this sense is subordinate to the needs of all those to be served, then the person with authority (teacher, policeman, boss, judge, mayor, governor, congressman, president) will first begin to think that they are better than others and then begin to act as though they are better than others. Unfortunately, most people with authority succumb to this temptation and consider themselves superior to those over whom they have authority. This is true historically and is still true today.

As the person in authority begins to think that they are better than their subordinates, they also begin to reverse the relationship between themselves and their subordinates. That is, they begin to think that their subordinates should serve them rather than they serve their subordinates. This, unfortunately, happens most often and leads to unjust effects. In fact, in the vast majority of cases, the superior believes that his/her subordinates are meant to serve them instead of he/she serving the subordinates.

CRITICAL ANALYSIS OF PAULINE SCRIPTURES

The Gospel of Matthew Commentary

(The Bible passages from Matthew, Genesis and Exodus are based on The World English Bible (WEB) which is a Public Domain (no copyright) Modern English translation of the Holy Bible, based on the American Standard Version of the Holy Bible first published in 1901, the Biblia Hebraica Stutgartensa Old Testament, and the Greek Majority Text New Testament.)

The so-called Gospel of Matthew (so-called because the author or authors are unknown, the use of Matthew in the title was not used until the second or third century, and there is almost no chance that the supposed Apostle wrote the first copy of this book) starts with an attempt to show the genealogy of Jesus from Abraham through David.

Working backwards in the text with the statement 'Jacob begat Joseph the husband of Mary, of whom was born Jesus, who is called Christ'.

A rational, objective person would have to question how the writer(s) of this Gospel would know who the father of Joseph was or his grandfather or his great-grandfather, etc. Since there were about three million Jews living at the time of Jesus and there were no computers, and no process for recording genealogy from generation to generation over supposedly 1200 yours – from Abraham to Jesus, it is almost certain that this text was either extreme hyperbole or extreme poetic license.

In addition, the tracing of Jewish descent in Judaism was defined through the maternal line or mother and not the father. Besides, Joseph was not the father of Jesus.

The intent of the writer(s) was to show that Jesus descended from both Abraham and David, because this was necessary for Jesus to be the Messiah according to the Gospel writers in order to convince the Jews that Jesus was the Messiah. However, the very existence of Abraham and David is doubtful, and there is absolutely no reason why God taking on human nature even had to be linked to the Jews in any way whatsoever.

One of many examples of fabrications made by the Evangelists to persuade their Jewish contemporaries to accept Jesus is the Bethlehem narrative found in two of the four gospels. The Messiah was supposedly prophesized to be born in Bethlehem by Micah 700 years earlier. Also, David was supposedly born in Bethlehem.

The writers of the Gospels of Luke and Matthew (or their editors after them) created the Bethlehem narrative and went for far as to create a Roman census as the reason why Mary gave birth to Jesus in Bethlehem. They also fabricated the killing of the infants in Bethlehem and the flight of Joseph, Mary, and Jesus to Egypt to complete what we would call today a 'wild story'.

There is absolutely no historical evidence that Rome decreed any type of census and the annals of Roman history regarding the period coinciding with the birth of Jesus are accurate and dependable.

The Gospel writers were more intent on linking Jesus to the Jewish Bible and its so-called prophecies, than finding out the true circumstances of the birth of Jesus. There is certainly no reason why Jesus could not have been born in Nazareth. Why didn't Luke and Matthew or the original writers of these Gospels interview people from Nazareth and Bethlehem? They certainly could have, but they did not? Why?

The writers of the Gospel Matthew would have had to interview people and search out records over the 1200 years from Abraham to Jesus (of course highly, highly unlikely), and they would have done extensive research into the circumstances of the birth of Jesus (and His early life), but they did not.

Every circumstance of these Gospel narratives (the census, the birth in Bethlehem in a manger, the Magi, the flight into Egypt) are all intended to link Jesus to the Jewish Bible and its so-called prophecies, and not to describe the actual circumstances of Jesus' birth. So, the nativity narratives of Luke and Matthew are doubtful, improbable, and most likely fiction.

In Matthew 4:1 Then was Jesus led up of the Spirit into the wilderness to be tempted of the devil. And when He had fasted forty days and forty nights, He afterward hungered. And the tempter came and said unto Him, If You are the Son of God, command that these stones become bread. But He answered and said, it is written, man shall not live by bread alone, but by every word that proceeds out of the mouth of God.

Then the devil taketh Him into the holy city; and He set him on the pinnacle of the temple, and said to Him, If You are the Son of God, cast Yourself down: for it is written, He shall give His angels charge concerning You, and on their hands, they will bear You up, lest You dash Your foot against a stone. Jesus said unto him, Again, it is written, you will not make trial of the Lord you God.

Again, the devil took Him unto an exceeding high mountain, and showed Him all the kingdoms of the world, and the glory of them; and He said to Him, all these things will I give you, if You will fall down and worship me. Then said Jesus to him, get away from Me, Satan: for it is written, you shall worship the Lord your God, and Him only shall you serve. Then the devil left Him; and behold, angels came and ministered unto Him.'

Is this passage fact or fiction? First of all, the passage implies that Jesus was alone during the entire sequence of events with the devil. If no one else was present, how were these events recorded? Did Jesus tell someone about these events?

The number of days that Jesus supposedly fasted, forty, was used many times in the Jewish Bible. The flood lasted forty days, Moses spent 40 years in Egypt, Moses fasted for forty days, etc. Obviously, the writer(s) of Matthew used the same duration of time since most Jews were familiar with this and would have accepted this without question.

Jesus was inspired by the Holy Spirit to go into the wilderness in order to be tempted by the devil. This makes no sense at all. It was stated in the passage that the devil knew that Jesus was the Son of God. And, if the devil knew this, He would know that Jesus could not fall into sin, so it would make no sense to tempt Him.

How could the devil transport Jesus to the top of the temple and the top of a mountain? How could the top of the mountain allow one to see every kingdom in the world? And how could it be said that the devil could give all of the kingdoms of the world to Jesus?

While Jesus may have fasted, this narrative might have been created in order to appeal to the Essenes, one the three main Jewish groups, who considered fasting to be performed by holy individuals.

Is this story about Jesus being tempted by the devil fact or fiction? Obviously, fiction!

The Apostles of Jesus

Matthew 4:18 And walking by the sea of Galilee, He saw two brothers, Simon who is called Peter, and Andrew his brother, casting a net into the sea; for they were fishermen. And He said to them, Come and follow me, and I will make you fishers of men. And they left their nets and followed Him.

And going further on He saw two other brothers, James the son of Zebedee, and John his brother, in the boat with Zebedee their father, mending their nets; and He called them. And they immediately left the boat and their father and followed him.

This passage implies that Jesus was intent on establishing an organization consisting of twelve men (the so-called Apostles) even before beginning to teach the People and choosing specific men. This is problematic for many reasons.

It is most likely that the individuals in this passage were married and had children. How could a virtuous, responsible person leave his wife and children forcing them to take care of themselves based on an invitation from a stranger who they never talked to before and who they knew nothing about. And would Jesus want His followers to abandon their spouses and children?

This passage also implies that Jesus travelled around Palestine by Himself. Jesus would not have abandoned His mother, Mary, during His public life. How would she support Herself? Mary was actually the first Apostle of Jesus chosen by Jesus and she accompanied Jesus as His mother and apostle.

We also get the impression that Jesus was always teaching only men. That is incorrect. Jesus' mission was to both men and women. Since Jesus would not have abandoned His mother, since His mission was to both men and women and since Mary was the first Apostle of Jesus, she would have accompanied Him on all of His travels focusing on teaching women the message of Jesus.

Since the mission of Jesus was to both men and women, and since those individuals who were fervent, dedicated followers of Him were His Apostles, it certainly follows that there were women Apostles either alone or with their spouses.

Also, since the mission of Jesus was to all people and since Jesus travelled though areas which contained both Jews and non-Jews (Matthew 4:25 And there followed him great multitudes from Galilee and Decapolis and Jerusalem and Judaea and from beyond the Jordan – the majority of people in Decapolis were Gentiles), it certainly follows that there were probably non-Jewish followers of Jesus who were His Apostles.

A more likely description of the beginning of the mission and modus operandi of Jesus follows.

In beginning of His so-called public life, Jesus, and Mary His mother (again Jesus would not have abandoned His mother) left their home and walked to a town close to their home. They may or may not have known anyone in this town. But meeting people in the town (many activities were done outside the house), Jesus and Mary with their friendly, warm, loving, and captivating demeanors would begin conversations with people leading people to realize that Jesus and Mary were rabbis or teachers and teachers who taught a different message than the Scribes, the Pharisees, the Sadducees, the Essenes, and the other so-called Jewish rabbis at that time.

Very quickly, the people whom Jesus and Mary first met in the town would introduce Jesus and Mary to others in the town. And Jesus and Mary would begin to teach the people, and in some cases heal the sick. The people of the town would invite Jesus and Mary to stay in their town, sleeping in their homes, sharing meals, working, and socializing together. Though guests, Jesus and Mary would have shared in the daily chores; cooking, taking care of children, tending to the animals, cleaning, etc. This would have been most endearing to the people and in sharp contrast to the arrogant, condescending attitude and behavior of the Jewish religious leaders, the Scribes, the Pharisees, the Sadducees, the members of the Sanhedrin, and the High Priest.

What was more amazing to the people in the town was how Jesus and Mary taught and showed by their example that all people were equal in the eyes of God and that everyone should be shown the same respect and love: men and women, old and young, beautiful and ugly, sick and healthy, smart and not smart, Jew and non-Jew.

As Jesus and Mary would leave this town to travel to another town, they left Christians – the first followers of Jesus and His teachings.

It is also likely that some people (single men, single women, and married couples and their children) travelled with Jesus and Mary from town to town, teaching and exemplifying the Christianity of Jesus. It is most likely that some of these followers became Apostles of Jesus, included both men and women, were more than twelve, some were non-Jews, and some of which were identified in the Gospels.

Unfortunately, because the writers of the Gospels were more Jewish than Christian and were followers of Paul and his school, they restricted the Apostles of Jesus to fit their paradigm and objectives for writing, one principle which was that men were superior to women (taught in Judaism and by Paul) another principle of Judaism was that Jews were superior to non-Jews and that because of this they ignored the female and non-Jewish Apostles.

Matthew 5:7 Sermon on the Mount

And seeing the multitudes, He went up into the mountain: and when He had sat down, his disciples came unto him and He opened his mouth and taught them, saying,

Blessed are the poor in spirit: for theirs is the kingdom of Heaven.

Blessed are they that mourn: for they shall be comforted.

Blessed are the meek: for they shall inherit the earth.

Blessed are they that hunger and thirst after righteousness: for they shall be filled.

Blessed are the merciful: for they shall obtain mercy.

Blessed are the pure in Heart: for they shall see God.

Blessed are the peacemakers: for they shall be called sons of God.

Blessed are they that have been persecuted for righteousness' sake: for theirs is the kingdom of Heaven. Blessed are you when men reproach you, and persecute you, and say all manner of evil against you falsely, for My sake. Rejoice, and be exceedingly glad: for great is your reward in Heaven.

You are the salt of the earth. But if the salt has lost its savor, how will it be salted? It is therefore good for nothing, but to be cast out and trodden under foot of men. You are the light of the world. A city set on a hill cannot be hidden. Neither do men light a lamp, and put it under a bushel basket, but rather on a stand so that it shines over all that are in the house. Even so let your light shine before men, that they may see your good works, and glorify your Father Who is in Heaven.

Do not think that I came to destroy the law or the prophets: I came not to destroy, but to fulfill. For verily I say to you, until Heaven and earth pass away, one jot or one tittle shall not pass away from the law, until all things are accomplished. Whoever therefore breaks one of these least commandments, and teaches men to do the same, will be called least in the kingdom of Heaven. But whoever does and teaches them, will be called great in the kingdom of Heaven. For I say to you, that unless your righteousness exceeds the righteousness of the scribes and Pharisees, you will not enter into the kingdom of Heaven.

While the beginning of the teachings in the Sermon on the Mount are consistent with the teachings of Jesus, this section on the law and the prophets seems to have been inserted by the Gospel writers to bring Jesus back to what they thought He should be, a good and faithful Jew.

You have Heard that it was said to them of old, do not kill and whoever kills shall be in danger of the judgment. But I say to you, that every person who is angry with his neighbor will be in danger of the judgment. And whoever says to his neighbor, raca, will be in danger of the council; and whoever says, you fool, will be in danger of the Hell of fire. If therefore you are offering your gift at the altar, and you remember that you and your neighbor are at odds with each other, leave there your gift before the altar, and go and be reconciled to your neighbor, and then come and offer your gift. Agree with your adversary quickly, while you are with him in the way; less your adversary deliver you to the judge, and the judge deliver you to the officer, and you are cast into prison. Verily, I say to you, you will by no means be released until you have paid the last farthing.

This passage is probably correct, that is, what Jesus taught (not on the Mount but somewhere at some time) but edited to put a Jewish spin based on the Gospel writer(s) paradigm and objectives in writing the Gospel. Raca and fool are the same thing, so the Gospel writer duplicated the idea that Jesus was trying to convey probably unintentionally.

Secondly, what is first cited as a disagreement between a person and their neighbor, expands into a contractual disagreement involving money or property. While Jesus would have spoken about not having disagreements with your neighbor, He would not have talked about civil law issues. This is most probably something that the Gospel writer or writers did to embellish on what Jesus was teaching.

Again, the Gospels were not written as biographies of Jesus describing His actions, words, and teachings, but rather a document to persuade Jews to accept Jesus as the Messiah and convert to Pauline Christianity.

You have Heard that it was said, you shall not commit adultery. But I say to you, that every one that looks on a woman to lust after Her has committed adultery with Her in his Heart. And if your right eye causes you to stumble, pluck it out, and cast it from you. For it is better for you that one of your members should perish, and not your whole body be cast into Hell.

And if your right hand causes you to stumble, cut it off, and cast it from you. For it is better for you that one of your members should perish, and not your whole body go into Hell. It was said also, whoever divorces his wife, let him give Her a writing of divorcement. But I say to you, that every man that divorces his wife, except for the cause of fornication, makes Her an adulteress, and whoever marries Her when after she is divorced commits adultery.

The Gospel writers wrote many years after the death of Jesus. And since the Gospels were edited (things changed, things added, things removed) many times from the first writing until their final forms hundreds of years later, those writers editing the Gospels inserted their personal views into the Gospels. And they were obviously influenced by different ideas being proposed during their lives. Some of these ideas had to do with sex, the notion that almost all sex was sinful (except for the specific purpose of producing children), and celibacy was to be preferred over marriage. It is against this background that the above passage from Matthew needs to be reviewed and understood.

It should also be noted that the Gospel writers relied on second-hand information and hearsay regarding Jesus, His words, and actions. And because of this, if the second-hand or hearsay account fit into the writer's paradigm and objective, it probably would have been included in the Gospel without substantiating the information.

The above passage implies that Jesus suggested that a person pluck out their eye or cut off their hand, Jesus would not have said that. It also implies that Jesus allowed divorce for a wife's infidelity, Jesus would not have said that.

How was all of this information from the so-called Sermon on the Mount captured? The only way to record such information was by writing it down. It would have been virtually impossible for a person or persons to capture all of the teachings of Jesus at the so-called Sermon on the Mount by writing as Jesus was speaking. In addition, writing was done on parchment or papyrus or scratched on potsherds or wax tablets and trying to write on these media while Jesus was speaking is virtually impossible.

This does not mean that Jesus did not say the things in the passage called the Sermon on the Mount (at least some of the things if not most), but most probably He uttered these words at different times in different places and not all at once as implied in this passage. Why couldn't the writer(s) of the Gospel have provided these teachings of Jesus as being taught at different times in smaller amounts as probably happened? Jesus being the Ultimate Teacher would not have taught so many things in one session since He knew that people could not possibly remember so much.

It certainly appears that the circumstance of the Sermon on the Mount was fiction, but most of the teachings (not all) are probably authentic.

Matthew 8:5 And when He entered into Capernaum, there came to him a centurion, beseeching Him, and saying, Lord, my servant lies in the house sick of the palsy, grievously tormented. And He said to him, I will come and heal him. But the centurion answered and said, Lord, I am not worthy that you should come under my roof, but only say the word, and my servant will be healed. For I also am a man under authority, having under myself soldiers, and I say to this one, go, and he goes; and to another, come, and he comes; and to my servant, do this, and he does it. And when Jesus heard it, He marveled, and said to those that followed, Verily I say to you, I have not found so great faith Israel. And I say to you, that many shall come from the east and the west, and shall sit down with Abraham, and Isaac, and Jacob, in the kingdom of heaven, but the sons of the kingdom will be cast forth into the outer darkness and there will be the weeping and the gnashing of teeth. And Jesus said to the centurion, go your way, as you have believed, so be it done for you. And the servant was healed in that hour.

Is this narrative fact or fiction or a combination of both fact and fiction? First of all, it is interesting to note that the Gospel writers noted that Jesus was in Capernaum. Generally, they fail to locate Jesus in any town or city. Capernaum was a somewhat large (fifteen hundred people) town and the location of one-third of the thirty-three recorded miracles that Jesus performed. This is one of only two miracles that He did in the presence of and for Gentiles.

The Gospel writers used the word servant and not the word slave probably intentionally even though the person the Centurion is entreating Jesus for is a slave. But the question must be asked, would Jesus not say something about slavery since this was obviously a sin, an extremely serious sin? Is it because Pauline Christianity does not consider slavery a sin and a moral and social evil?

In Ephesians 6:5 Paul states, "Slaves, be obedient to your human masters with fear and trembling, in sincerity of heart, as to Christ" which is Paul instructing slaves to obey their master. Similar statements regarding obedient slaves can be found in Colossians 3:22, Timothy 6:1, and Titus 2:9.

Jesus would not have condoned slavery. God, and Jesus as God, considers that all people are His children and are equal and that no person is beneath another or should be subject to another in a subservient way. Judaism condoned slavery and wealthy Jews during the time of Jesus owned slaves.

The Gospel writers would have ignored any teachings of Jesus regarding slavery so as not to offend their fellow Jews who were slave owners. But how arrogant of Paul and the Gospel writers to pick and choose from the teachings of Jesus in order to fit their paradigm and their form of Christianity.

Slavery with all of its related evils continued within the Christian world (and the non-Christian world) for more than 1900 years after the so-called New Testament was written because of the arrogance of Paul and his followers who thought that they knew more than God and were holier than God. Pauline Christianity not only condoned slavery but it supported slavery at times and even engaged in slavery.

Absolutely outrageous! And the Christian Church considers Paul a saint and apostle, disgraceful!

When Paul writes in Ephesians 6:5, "Slaves, be obedient to your human masters with fear and trembling, in sincerity of heart, as to Christ", he is not writing to slaves who could not read. He was writing to slave owners and telling them that Pauline Christianity is not a threat to their business and to their slave-ownership. Pauline Christianity allows people to be slave-owners and supposed Christians at the same time.

This attitude of the Pauline Christian Church supporting and not denouncing the evil practices of the wealthy ruling elite has continued to this day to the detriment of millions of people over the last 2000 years who have been immorally exploited by the wealthy ruling elite. Shame on Paul and his Church.

Matthew 8:17 That it might be fulfilled which was spoken through Isaiah the prophet, saying: Himself took our infirmities, and bare our diseases. Another example of the Gospel writers trying to link the actions of Jesus to passages in the Jewish Bible whether or not they were actually related.

Matthew 8:20 And Jesus saith unto him, the foxes have holes, and the birds of the Heaven have nests; but the Son of man does not have a place to lay his Head. This is a rather strange statement given that Jesus relied on the generosity of people for His food and lodging during His public life. Did Jesus really say this?

Matthew 8:21 And another of the disciples said to Him, Lord, allow me first to go and bury my father. But Jesus said to him, follow me, and leave the dead to bury their own dead. Another very strange statement. Did Jesus really say this? What was the demeanor and personality of Jesus really like? Was He a mean, intolerant, selfish person? Or was He a gentle, respectful, approachable, generous, humanitarian, magnanimous, self-denying, self-giving, and self-sacrificing person? The answer should be obvious. Why then do the Gospel writes try to depict Jesus as almost mean, intolerant, and selfish? Was it because that is how they thought that He should be?

It appears that the Gospel writers had an image of Jesus as a tough, no-nonsense person who could get angry (cursing the fig tree), use mean words, become impatient, and be condescending to others especially women including His mother (wedding celebration in Cana – 'Woman, what have I to do with you?').

Perhaps, this was the image of a real man according to the Gospel writers. But this is incorrect. Jesus was a gentle person, Who did not look down on anyone especially His mother. The alleged response of Jesus to His mother 'Woman, what have I to do with you?' is absurd and obviously a fabrication in the Gospel of John. Calling His mother, woman, is rather demeaning and something Jesus would not have done. Secondly, telling his mother, what have I do with you, is condescending and something that Jesus would not have said.

Matthew 8:28 And when He was come to the other side into the country of the Gadarenes, there met him two possessed with demons, coming forth out of the tombs, exceedingly fierce, so that no man could pass by that way. And behold, they cried out, saying, what have we to do with You, the Son of God? Have You come Here to torment us before the time? Now there was far off from them a Herd of many swine feeding. And the demons pleaded with Him, saying, If You cast us out, send us away into the Herd of swine. And He said to them, Go. And they came out, and went into the swine: and behold, the whole Herd rushed down the steep into the sea and perished in the waters. And they that fed them fled, and went away into the city, and told everything, and what happened to them that were possessed with demons. And the city came out to meet Jesus: and when they saw Him, they wanted Him to depart from their borders.

This passage may contain facts but definitely it contains fiction. First of all, this area was a non-Jewish area historically and as indicated by the statement they raised pigs, pigs being considered unclean by the Jews and to be avoided. Do demons really possess people? Would Jesus cause pigs to be killed or is this something that fit the Jewish narrative since the Jews hated pigs. Would the people of the town really be angry with Jesus for having supposedly freed the two men from their demons? This makes no sense. Instead, the people would have welcomed Jesus after this and not rejected Him. But this would not fit the Jewish paradigm of looking down on and not associating with Gentiles.

Matthew 9:35 And Jesus went about all the cities and the villages, teaching in their synagogues, and preaching the gospel of the kingdom, and healing all manner of disease and all manner of sickness. But when He saw the multitudes, He was moved with compassion for them, because they were distressed and scattered, as sheep not having a shepherd. Then He said to his disciples, the harvest indeed is plenteous, but the laborers are few. Pray you therefore the Lord of the harvest, that He send forth laborers into his harvest.

And He called unto him his twelve disciples, and gave them authority over unclean spirits, to cast them out, and to heal all manner of disease and all manner of sickness. Now the names of the twelve apostles are these: the first, Simon, who is called Peter, and Andrew his brother; James the son of Zebedee, and John his brother, Philip, and Bartholomew, Thomas, and Matthew the publican, James the son of Alphaeus, and Thaddaeus, Simon the Cananaean, and Judas Iscariot, who would also betray Him.

These twelve Jesus sent forth, and charged them, saying, go not into any way of the Gentiles, and enter not into any city of the Samaritans. But go rather to the lost sheep of the house of Israel. And as you go, preach, saying, the kingdom of Heaven is at hand. Heal the sick, raise the dead, cleanse the lepers, cast out demons: freely you received, freely give. Take no gold, nor silver, nor brass in your purses, no wallet for your journey, neither two coats, nor shoes, nor staff; for the laborer is worthy of his food. And into whatever city or village you enter, search out who in it is worthy; and there abide until you leave. And as you enter into the house, salute it. And if the house be worthy, let your peace come upon it: but if it be not worthy, let your peace return to you. And whosoever shall not receive you, nor hear your words, as you go forth out of that house or that city, shake off the dust of your feet. Truly, I say unto you, it will be more tolerable for the land of Sodom and Gomorrah in the day of judgment, than for that city.

Behold, I send you as sheep in the midst of wolves: therefore, be as wise as serpents, and harmless as doves. But beware of men: for they will deliver you up to councils, and in their synagogues, they will scourge you; you will be brought before governors and kings for my sake, for a testimony to them and to the Gentiles. But when they deliver you up, be not anxious how or what you shall speak: for it will be given you in that hour what you will say. For it is not you that speak, but the Spirit of your Father that speaks in you. And brother will deliver up brother to death, and the father his child: and children will rise up against parents and cause them to be put to death. And you shall be hated by all men for My name's sake. But he that endures to the end will be saved. But when they persecute you in this city, flee into the next:

for verily I say unto you, you shall not have gone through the cities of Israel, until the Son of man comes.

A disciple is not above his teacher, nor a servant above his lord. It is enough for the disciple that he be as his teacher, and the servant as his lord. If they have called the master of the house Beelzebub, how much more those of his household! Fear them not therefore: for there is nothing covered, that shall not be revealed; and hid, that will not be known. What I tell you in the darkness, speak in the light; and what you hear in the ear, proclaim upon the housetops. And be not afraid of them that kill the body but are not able to kill the soul. But rather fear him who is able to destroy both soul and body in Hell. Are not two sparrows sold for a penny? And not one of them will fall on the ground without your Father. Even the very hairs of your head are all numbered. Fear not therefore for you are of more value than many sparrows. Every person who will confess Me before men, I will also confess him before my Father who is in Heaven. But whoever denies Me before men, I also deny him before my Father who is in Heaven.

Do not think that I came to send peace on the earth: I came not to send peace, but a sword. For I came to set a man at variance against his father, and the daughter against Her mother, and the daughter-in-law against Her mother-in-law. And a man's enemies will be from his own household. He that loves his father or mother more than Me is not worthy of Me; and he that loves his son or daughter more than Me is not worthy of Me. And he that does not take his cross and follow after Me, is not worthy of me. He that finds his life will lose it, and he that loses his life for my sake will find it.

He that receives you receives Me, and he that receives Me receives Him that sent Me. He that receives a prophet in the name of a prophet will receive a prophet's reward, and he that receives a righteous man in the name of a righteous man will receive a righteous man's reward. And whoever will give a drink cold water only to one of these little ones, in the name of a disciple, truly I say to you he shall in no wise lose his reward.

This above passage, Matthew 9:35 – Matthew 10:42, is almost certainly fiction and was added to the Gospel for the specific purpose of trying to show that Jesus intended to establish an organization similar to the

Pauline Christian organization which came to exist with its hierarchical, male-dominated, rather intolerant, arrogant, and condescending structure. This was similar to the structure of Judaism with the High Priest, Sanhedrin, Sadducees, Pharisees, Scribes and Rabbis and the main centralized Temple and localized synagogues.

Did Jesus choose the so-called twelve Apostles or where there many individuals and couples who followed Him that should be called His Apostles and among these were women and non-Jews.

'These twelve Jesus sent forth, and charged them, saying, go not into any way of the Gentiles, and enter not into any city of the Samaritans.' This statement is inconsistent with the nature and mission of Jesus. God considers all people as His children. He has no favorites. The fabricated idea that God favors the Jewish people because of a supposed promise to Abraham is just that, a fabrication – there is no truth to it whatsoever. God loves all people equally and does not discriminate and does not have preferences. The Gospel writers obviously wanted to show the Jews who would read the Gospel that Jesus was just like them, biased and bigoted. Unfortunately, the writers did not understand the true nature of God and were more Jewish than Christian according to the Christianity of Jesus and not the Christianity of Paul.

As noted in earlier comments on the Gospel of Matthew, the writers wanted to depict Jesus as a 'tough guy' which is both false and misleading.

Matthew 11:1 And it came to pass when Jesus had finished commanding his twelve disciples, He departed from there to teach and preach in their cities (whose cities?). Now when John heard in the prison the works of the Christ, he sent by his disciples and said to him, are you He that is to come, or do we look for another? And Jesus answered and said to them, go and tell John the things which you hear and see, the blind receive their sight, the lame walk, the lepers are cleansed, the deaf hear, the dead are raised up, and the poor have good tidings preached to them. And blessed is he, whoever will find no occasion of stumbling in me.

How does this passage make any sense given Matthew 3:13-17 (within the same Gospel and verses before 11:1)?

Matthew 3:13-17 Then Jesus came from Galilee to the Jordan to be baptized by John. But John tried to deter Him, saying, "I need to be baptized by You, and do You come to me?" Jesus replied, "Let it be so now; it is proper for us to do this to fulfill all righteousness." Then John consented. As soon as Jesus was baptized, He went up out of the water. At that moment heaven was opened, and He saw the Spirit of God descending like a dove and alighting on him. And a voice from heaven said, "This is my Son, whom I love; with Him I am well pleased."

Obviously, Matthew 11:1 is absolute fiction and a literary blunder because of its inconsistency with Matthew 3:13-17.

Matthew 11:7 And as these went their way, Jesus began to say to the multitudes concerning John, what did you go out into the wilderness to see, a reed shaken with the wind? But what did you go out to see, a man clothed in soft raiment? They that wear soft raiment are in king's houses. But what did you go out to see, a prophet? Yes, I say to you, and much more than a prophet. This is he, of whom it is written, behold, I send My messenger before your face, who will prepare your way before you. Verily I say to you, among those that are born of women there has not arisen a greater person than John the Baptist, yet he that is but little in the kingdom of Heaven is greater than he. And from the days of John the Baptist until now the kingdom of Heaven suffers violence, and men of violence take it by force. For all the prophets and the law prophesied until John. And if you are willing to receive it, this is Elijah, that is to come. He that has ears to hear, let him hear. But to what should I liken this generation? It is like to children sitting in the marketplaces, who call unto their friends and say, we piped unto you, and you did not dance, we wailed, and you did not mourn. For John came neither eating nor drinking, and they say, he hath a demon. The Son of man came eating and drinking, and they say, behold, a gluttonous man and a drunk, a friend of publicans and sinners! And wisdom is justified by her works.

These verses are also a fabrication by the writers of the Gospel of Mathew in which they want to link Jesus to so-called prophets of the Jewish Bible. Also, the writers fail to cite the greatness of Mary, the mother of Jesus, who is greater than John the Baptist and this is because of their bias towards women.

Matthew 11:20 Then He began to rebuke the cities where most of His mighty works were done, because they did not repent. Woe to you, Chorazin, woe to thee, Bethsaida! If the mighty works had been done in Tyre and Sidon which were done in you, they would have repented long ago in sackcloth and ashes. But I say to you, it shall be more tolerable for Tyre and Sidon in the day of judgment than for you. And you, Capernaum, will you be exalted unto Heaven? No, you will go down unto Hell. For if the mighty works had been done in Sodom which were done in you, it would have remained until this day. But I say to you that it shall be more tolerable for the land of Sodom in the day of judgment, than for you.

Total fiction fabricated by the Gospel writers. Jesus would not condemn whole cities nor are whole cities to be judged at the end of time. Tyre and Sidon were prosperous Roman port cities. Early in Jesus' ministry, people from Sidon and Tyre heard about the things He did and came to see Him (Mark 3:8) and be healed by Him (Luke 6:17). Were these individuals Jews or Gentiles? And what were the writers of Matthew trying to imply by this passage? Lastly, again Jesus is depicted as a harsh, unforgiving person who He was not.

Matthew 12:46 While He was speaking to the multitudes, behold, His mother and His brothers stood outside, asking to speak to him. And a person said to Him, your mother and your brothers are outside and want to speak to You. But He answered and said to him that told Him, who is My mother and who are My brothers? And He stretched His hand towards His disciples, and said, behold, my mother and my brothers! For whoever does the will of My Father Who is in Heaven, he is my brother, and sister, and mother.

Jesus was speaking to the multitudes inside – 'His mother and His brothers stood outside'? There were no large indoor stadiums during the time of Jesus, so the statement that 'His mother and His brothers stood outside' makes no sense. Why wouldn't Mary and the brothers of Jesus already be within the group of Jesus' disciples to whom He was speaking? The Gospel writers seem to intentionally separate them to make the point supposedly made by Jesus. But did this really happen and did Jesus really say these things? Very doubtful!

Matthew 13:1 On that day went Jesus out of the house and sat by the seaside. Where was this at? What city or village? All of this would be more credible if the Gospel writers cited exactly where this took place geographically. While there were about 250 villages in Galilee during the time of Jesus, very few are cited in the Gospels – why? It would seem likely that Jesus and Mary could have and would have visited virtually every one of them in the span of over three years in Jesus' public life and it is possible that Jesus did start his ministry earlier than cited.

Matthew 13:2 And there were gathered before Him such a great multitude, that He entered into a boat, and sat; and the multitude stood on the beach. And He spoke to them many things in parables, … And the disciples came, and said to Him, why do you speak to them in parables? And He answered and said to them, to you it is given to know the mysteries of the kingdom of Heaven, but to them it is not given.

This makes no sense and cannot be true, that is, this is fiction, a fabrication made by the Gospel writers. In the midst of Jesus' teaching from the boat to the people on the beach, the disciples come to Him, how in another boat? Jesus would not intentionally try to deceive people. Jesus would not give preference to His so-called disciples, because all people are equal in the eyes of God. 'And He answered and said to them, to you it is given to know the mysteries of the kingdom of Heaven, but to them it is not given.' Absurd!

Matthew 13:12 For whoever has, to him shall be given, and he shall have abundance. But whoever has not, from him will be taken away even that which he has. Therefore, I speak to them in parables; because seeing they do not see, and hearing they do not hear, neither do they understand. And to them is fulfilled the prophecy of Isaiah, which says, by hearing you will hear, and will not understand. And seeing you will see, but in no wise perceive. For this people's heart is waxed gross, and their ears are dull of hearing, and their eyes are closed. Unless they should perceive with their eye, and hear with their ears, and understand with their heart, and repent, and I will heal them.

Is Jesus supposedly still speaking only to his disciples and not the multitude of people on the beach? Did Jesus really speak in parables in order to hide His teaching from people? I do not think so. More fiction!

The Gospel writers are more intent on trying to fulfill the so-called prophecies of Isaiah (their favorite prophet) than explaining what Jesus said and did. This is not only fiction it is outrageous. If people do not understand, what is the sense of speaking in parables that make it harder if not impossible to understand. Jesus wanted people to understand how they needed to live and not what they needed to believe. The above passage Matthew 13:12 clearly fits Pauline Christianity and not the Christianity of Jesus.

Matthew 13:34 All these things spoke Jesus in parables to the multitudes, and without a parable He spoke nothing to them that it might be fulfilled which was spoken through the prophet, saying, I will open my mouth in parables, I will utter things hidden from the foundation of the world.

The Gospel writers again are more intent on fulfilling the so-called prophecies of the so-called prophets than providing an accurate account of what Jesus said and did. This was because they were trying to persuade their Jewish readers and they wanted to link Jesus to the Jewish Bible prophets.

This notion that Jesus would only speak to the people in parables (though He supposedly spoke plainly to His Apostles) is incorrect. A teacher will try different methods to convey an idea to her or his students. Jesus certainly would not play such a game as cited by the Gospel writers.

Matthew 13:54 And coming into His own country, He taught them in their synagogue, and they were astonished, and said, where does this man get this wisdom and the ability to do such amazing works? Is not this the carpenter's son, is not his mother called Mary and His brothers James, and Joseph, and Simon, and Judas and his sisters, are they not all with us? How then is this man able to do these things? And they were offended by Him. But Jesus said to them, a prophet is not without honor, except in his own country, and in his own house. And He did not do many mighty works there because of their unbelief.

First of all, why wouldn't the Gospel writers state that Jesus came to Nazareth? Nazareth was a relatively small town of about 300 people. Assuming that this was Nazareth, are we to believe that this was the first time that Jesus returned home? This passage implies that Jesus both taught and performed miracles. It is extremely hard to believe that all the people of Nazareth were offended by what Jesus said and did. And are we also to believe that Jesus' relatives were also offended by him 'a prophet is not without honor except...in his own house' including Mary, His mother? All of this makes no sense, and we have to conclude that this is another fabrication by the Gospel writers and there is little to no truth in what is written.

Matthew 14:1 At that season Herod the tetrarch heard the reports concerning Jesus, and said to his servants, this is John the Baptist; he is risen from the dead, and therefore do these powers work in him.

How did the Gospel writers get this information regarding the personal conversation between Herod the tetrarch and his servants?

Matthew 14:3 For Herod had John arrested, and bound, and put in prison for the sake of Herodias, his brother Philip's wife. For John had said to him, it is not lawful for you to have her. And he wanted to put him to death, but he feared the people, because they counted him a prophet. But when Herod's birthday came, the daughter of Herodias danced in the midst, and pleased Herod. Herod promised with an oath to give her whatever she would ask. And she, being put told by her mother, said, give me here on a platter the head of John the Baptist. The king was grieved; but because of his oaths, and of them that were at dinner with him, he commanded it to be done. And had John beheaded in prison, and his head was brought on a platter, and given to the daughter of Herodias and she brought it to Her mother. And his disciples came, and took up the corpse, and buried him; and they went and told Jesus.

Matthew 14:13 Now when Jesus heard the news about John, the Baptist, He withdrew from where He was in a boat, to a desert place apart.

In Matthew 13:2 Jesus was in a boat and there was a multitude of people on the beach listening to Him. And in Matthew 13:54 Jesus came to His own country, taught in the synagogue, and healed people. And now in Matthew 14:13, Jesus was in a boat. Is this again in a boat or is He in the same boat as in Matthew 13:2, and Matthew 13:54 is misplaced. This is somewhat confusing, and it appears that the Gospel writers make no attempt to provide any accuracy. Of course, their intention was not to provide an accurate account of Jesus' travels and actions, but rather to tell their story.

And when the multitudes heard where He was, they followed Him on foot from the cities.

How did the people hear about where Jesus was? Perhaps, the disciples followed Him, but then they would have had to travel to the towns and cities to tell the people where Jesus was. But why? Did Jesus specifically tell his disciples to go the towns and cities? And given that the number of people from the towns and cities that came to see Jesus in the desert was well over fifteen thousand people (five thousand men, perhaps more than five thousand women, and at least five thousand children), they would have had to come from seventy-five or more towns and cities (assuming an average population of two hundred people per town and virtually all the people in the town went to see Jesus – rather unlikely). And the process of the disciples, travelling to seventy-five or more towns after leaving Jesus in the desert, and the people travelling to the desert to see Jesus would indicate a large duration of time.

Matthew 14:14 And He came forth and saw the great multitude.

Came forth from where? It would seem to imply that Jesus was in some sort of building, and He came out and saw this multitude of people (over fifteen thousand) who travelled from over seventy-five cities and towns and who all arrived at almost the same time.

He had compassion on them and healed their sick. And when evening came, the disciples came to Him, saying, this place is desert, and the time is late, send the people away, so that they may go into the villages, and buy themselves food.

But wouldn't most of the villages be empty because the people came to see Jesus in the desert? And won't the disciples realize this?

But Jesus said to them, they do not need to go away, you feed them. And they said to him, we have only five loaves, and two fishes. And He said, bring them to me. And He commanded the multitudes to sit down on the grass.

Grass? Is there grass in a desert?

And He took the five loaves, and the two fishes, and looking up to Heaven, He blessed, and broke and gave the loaves to the disciples, and the disciples to the multitudes. And they all ate, and were filled, and they took up that which remained over of the broken pieces, twelve baskets full. And they that did eat were about five thousand men, besides women and children.

Matthew 14:22 And straightway He constrained the disciples to enter into the boat, and to go before Him to the other side, until He would send the multitudes away.

I thought they were in a desert. While the miracle of Jesus feeding fifteen thousand people (or a lot of people) by multiplying the bread loaves and the fish could very well be true, the poetic license employed by the Gospels writers undermines the credibility of the account.

Mathew 14:23 And after He had sent the multitudes away, He went up into the mountain apart to pray and when evening came, He was there alone. But the boat was now in the midst of the sea, distressed by the waves; for the wind was contrary. And in the fourth watch of the night, He came to them, walking upon the sea. And when the disciples saw him walking on the sea, they were troubled, saying, it is a ghost, and they cried out for fear. But immediately Jesus spoke to them, saying be of good cheer, it is me do not be afraid.

And Peter answered Him and said, Lord, if it be You, allow me to come to you upon the waters. And He said, come. And Peter went down from the boat and walked upon the water to come to Jesus. But when he saw the wind, he was afraid, and beginning to sink, he cried out, saying, Lord, save me. And immediately Jesus stretched forth His hand, and took hold of him, and said, O you of little faith, why did you doubt? And when they entered the boat, the wind ceased. And they that were in the boat worshipped him, saying, truly You are the Son of God.

This is unnecessarily confusing. Jesus supposedly sent the disciples to cross the lake (do we assume the Sea of Galilee which was a lake eight miles wide and thirteen miles long) at late afternoon after which Jesus sent off the people who came out from the cities and towns to see Him. He then went up into a mountain to pray until it got dark. Since the Gospel writers did not say anything about the time of the year, we can assume that darkness came between six and eight o'clock.

The fourth watch is from three in the morning to six in the morning. If Jesus came to the disciples in the boat at three in the morning, the disciples would have been travelling in the boat from four or five in the afternoon the day before until three in the morning. That represents a time span of at least ten hours. In ten hours, the disciples could have travelled the length of the lake four times. All of this does not imply that Jesus did not walk on water out to the boat where the disciples were and calm the storm, but rather why did the Gospel writers again use poetic license?

And one additional point, Peter again and again acts like a doofus. Was he really a doofus, or did the Gospel writers intentionally portray him that was for some reason?

Matthew 15:21 And Jesus withdrew into the parts of Tyre and Sidon.

Tyre and Sidon were predominantly non-Jewish cities.

Matthew 15:22 And behold, a Canaanite woman came out from those borders, and cried, saying, have mercy on me, O Lord, son of David; my daughter is grievously vexed with a demon. But He did not answer her not a word. And his disciples came and besought him, saying, send her away; for she cries after us. But He answered and said, I was sent only to the lost sheep of the house of Israel. But she came and worshipped him, saying, Lord, help me. And He answered and said, it is not right to take the children's bread and cast it to the dogs. But she said, yes, Lord, but even the dogs eat of the crumbs which fall from their masters' table. Then Jesus answered and said to her, woman, great is your faith, be it done for you as you have asked. And her daughter was healed from that hour.

This passage is either complete fiction or it contains significant fabricated elements. Jesus was not sent to the Jews only, but to all people. Jesus would not have referred to non-Jewish people as dogs or cited the superiority of the Jews over non-Jewish people. The fabrications here are obviously to suit the Gospel writers intended Jewish readers. If perhaps, the Gospel writers actually believed as Jews that they were superior to non-Jews, they certainly did not understand the nature of God.

Jesus and the nature of God hold that all people are equal. Human beings, all human beings, are made in the image and likeness of God. Jesus taught this principle through both his words and his actions. The absolute dignity of the human being applies to all human beings not just the rich, the powerful, the educated, men, older people, the healthy, the members of specific religions, specific nationalities, specific races or the beautiful. The absolute dignity of the human being applies to the rich and the poor, the powerful and the powerless, the educated and the uneducated, women and men, the old and the young, the healthy and the sick, the members of all religions, the members of all nationalities, all races and the beautiful and the ugly.

The absolute dignity of each and every human being is the basis for the rights of each and every human being and the Christian imperative (based on the Christianity of Jesus and not the Christianity of Paul) that every person is to be treated with dignity and respect in their social lives, their business lives, their economic lives, their political lives, and their private lives.

It appears the Gospel writers did not understand the true mission of Jesus. The mission of Jesus was to provide the correct description of Who God was and to tell people how they should live their lives. The world believed in multiple gods and gods with human characteristics and deficiencies. Even the Jewish writers attributed human characteristics and deficiencies to God. The Jews believed that God was mean, could get angry, could be vindictive, played favorites, punished people by illness and death, tricked people, etc. This was absolutely false.

The relationship between God and humans is similar to that of a parent and children, except in a way that humans will never fully understand. For how are humans to understand Infinite Love? When Jesus taught this to the common people, they understood it, but it was not understood or perhaps ignored by the upper class, the ruling class and the writers of the New Testament including the Gospel writers and Paul himself. It is also possible that the writers did not have a very good understanding of the love of a parent for his or her children, having been raised in families where the father was like a king in their home since that was part of the established culture of Judaism.

Matthew 15:32 And Jesus called to him his disciples, and said, I have compassion on the multitude, because they continue with me now three days and have nothing to eat: and I would not send them away fasting, less they faint on the way. And the disciples said to Him, where can get so many loaves in a desert place as to feed such a great multitude? And Jesus said to them, how many loaves do you have? And they said, seven, and a few small fishes. And He commanded the multitude to sit down on the ground, and He took the seven loaves and the fishes, and He gave thanks and broke them, and gave to the disciples, and the disciples to the multitudes. And they all ate and were filled. And they took up that which remained, seven baskets full. And they that were fed were four thousand men, besides women and children. And He sent away the multitudes, and entered into the boat, and came into the borders of Magadan.

Isn't Matthew 15:32 and Matthew 14:14 the same? They probably are narratives of the same event and represent a literary error.

Matthew 16:21 From that time began Jesus to tell His disciples, that He must go unto Jerusalem, and suffer many things of the elders and chief priests and scribes, and be killed, and the third day be raised up.

This is a statement without any proof whatsoever. That is, what are the exact statements of Jesus, when and where does He make them, and to whom did He make them? And did Jesus really make these statements or where they fabricated by the gospel writer(s) to fit the teachings of Paul regarding Jesus and His mission?

Matthew 16:22 And Peter took Him, and began to rebuke Him, saying, be it far from You, Lord: this will never happen to You. But He turned, and said to Peter, get behind me, Satan: you are a stumbling-block to Me, for you do not mind the things of God, but the things of men.

Then said Jesus to his disciples, if any man would come after me, let him deny himself, and take up his cross, and follow me. For whoever would save his life shall lose it, and whoever shall lose his life for My sake shall find it. For what does it profit a man, if he gains the whole world, and loses his life? Or what will a man give in exchange for his life? For the Son of man will come in the glory of His Father with His angels, and then will render to every man according to his deeds.

Verily I say unto you, there are some of them that stand here, who will not die until they see the Son of man coming in his kingdom.

This passage appears to be the teachings of Paul, the Gospel writers, and the early Pauline Christian Church placed in the mouth of Jesus. This means that Jesus did not say these things but rather the Gospel writers wanted their intended audience to believe that Jesus said these things in order to be converted to Pauline Christianity. If Jesus had said: "there are some of them that stand here, who will not die until they see the Son of man coming in his kingdom" He would have been absolutely wrong which is inconsistent with the nature of God.

Matthew 17:1 And after six days Jesus took with Him Peter, and James, and John his brother, and brought them up into a high mountain, and He was transfigured before them. And his face shone as the sun, and His garments became white as the light. And behold, there appeared unto them Moses and Elijah talking with him.

And Peter answered, and said unto Jesus, Lord, it is good for us to be here. If You want, I will make here three tabernacles, one for You, one for Moses, and one for Elijah. While he was still speaking, behold, a bright cloud overshadowed them: and behold, a voice out of the cloud, saying, this is My beloved Son, in whom I am well pleased; hear Him. And when the disciples heard it, they fell on their faces, and were extremely afraid. And Jesus came and touched them and said, arise, and do not be afraid. And lifting up their eyes, they saw no one except Jesus.

And as they were coming down from the mountain, Jesus commanded them, saying, do not tell the vision to anyone, until the Son of man be risen from the dead. And His disciples asked him, saying, why then say the scribes that Elijah must first come? And He answered and said, Elijah indeed will come and will restore all things. But I say to you, that Elijah has come already, and they knew him not, but did to him whatever they would. Even so will the Son of man also suffer from them. Then understood the disciples that He spoke to them of John the Baptist.

Because the Gospel writers were good and faithful Jews, they believed the stories from their Bible that Elijah and Moses existed, were heroic figures, performed miracles, and did that while Moses died Elijah was assumed into Heaven. However, there is no historical evidence that these two individuals ever existed and there are only legends about them. So, while these events could have occurred, did they? Or was this just a fabrication by the Gospel writers again to link Jesus to the Jewish Bible figures in order to persuade their readers to accept Jesus as the person foretold as the Messiah.

How would Peter, James and John know that the two figures that were talking to Jesus were Elijah and Moses?

Similar to Matthew 3:17 (And a voice from heaven said, "This is my Son, whom I love; with him I am well pleased". Perhaps, this happened and perhaps not. It is certainly possible that Jesus transfigured without the figures of Elijah and Moses.

What does it mean that Elijah will restore all things? Certainly, seems like a fabrication by the Gospel writers.

If these events were true, it would seem that they would have greatly influenced the minds and hearts of Peter, James, and John especially God speaking and claiming that Jesus was the Son of God. And if so, then one would expect them to have acted differently during the arrest, trial, and crucifixion of Jesus.

Matthew 17:22 And while they abode in Galilee, Jesus said to them, The Son of man shall be delivered up into the hands of men, and they will kill him, and on the third day He will be raised up. And they were exceeding sorry.

Strange statements inserted here without any context, that is, were they just talking, and Jesus blurted this out. It would appear the those who heard the above statement of Jesus did not believe that Jesus would be raised up based on their actions after the death of Jesus. If they believed the statement, they would have expected Jesus to be raised up on the third day after His death.

Matthew 18:7 Woe to the world because of occasions of sinning! For it must needs be that the occasions come, but woe to that man through whom the occasion comes! And if your hand or your foot causes you to stumble, cut it off, and cast it from you. It is better for you to enter into life maimed or halt, rather than having two hands or two feet to be cast into the eternal fire. And if your eye causes you to sin, pluck it out, and cast it from you: for it is better for you to enter into life with one eye, rather than having two eyes to be cast into the Hell of fire. See that you despise not one of these little ones, for I say to you, that in Heaven their angels do always behold the face of My Father who is in Heaven.

For the Son of man came to save that which was lost. Don't you understand that if any man has a hundred sheep, and one of them goes astray, he will leave the ninety-nine, and seek that one that is lost? And if finds it, verily I say to you, he will rejoice more over it than over the ninety-nine which did not go astray. Even so it is not the will of your Father who is in Heaven, that one of these little ones should perish.

And if your brother sin against you, go and show him his fault between you and him alone. If he hears you, you have gained your brother. But if he does not hear you, take with you one or two more, that at the mouth of two witnesses or three every word may be established. And if he refuses to hear them, tell it to the church: and if he refuses to hear the church also, let him be to you as the Gentile and the publican. Verily I say to you, what things you will bind on earth will be bound in Heaven; and what things you will loose on earth will be loosed in Heaven. Again, I say to you, that if two of you agree on earth as touching anything that they ask, it will be done for them by My Father Who is in Heaven. For where two or three are gathered together in My name, there am I in the midst of them.

This passage is very similar to Matthew 5:21. Would Jesus repeat the same teachings, it is certainly possible. But it is also possible that the Gospel writers mixed up the teachings of Jesus from different sources. Also, it seems like the theme of this passage changes between warning about occasions of sin and children "See that you despise not one of these little ones, for I say to you, that in Heaven their angels do always behold the face of My Father who is in Heaven". Unfortunately, rather confusing! And what is the circumstance? Is Jesus speaking to a crowd of people, or to his disciples, or just to a few disciples?

Also, what about forgiving someone seven times seventy times. How does that teaching fit in with "And if he refuses to hear them, tell it to the church". Jesus certainly would not have used the word church, perhaps elders but not church. Also, this seems like another attempt by the Gospel writers to show that Jesus intended to establish a Church, in this case with a judicial structure.

Jesus would not have used the words, "let him be to you as the Gentile and the publican". This was a derogatory and demeaning statement indicating the superiority of the Jews. How would this reconcile with "love your neighbor as yourself" where neighbor implies all people and not just Jews.

Again, the Gospel writers as faithful Jews writing for and to other Jews would have supported the Jewish animosity that Jews had for Gentiles and publicans, but this was not the teaching of Jesus. Hence, this insertion is fabrication.

Matthew 18:21 Then Peter came and said to him, Lord, how often shall my brother sin against me, and I forgive him, up to seven times? Jesus said to him, I say to you, not up to seven times, but, up to seventy times seven. Therefore, the kingdom of Heaven is like a certain king, who would make a reckoning with his servants.

And when he had begun to reckon, one was brought to him, that owed him ten thousand talents. But in as much as he could not to pay, his lord commanded him to be sold, and his wife, and children, and all that he had, and payment to be made.

This person was obviously a slave based on the following statement where the king was going to sell the man, his wife, and children and all that he had. For only slaves could be sold.

This is a rather strange statement supposedly made by Jesus, if He did make it. The principle regarding forgiveness could certainly have been illustrated by another more relevant story especially given the listeners were probably not slaves and never had been slaves. And it certainly is questionable that Jesus would make these statements without drawing attention to the immorality of the idea that a person (in this case the king) would or even could sell a man, his wife, his children, and all that he had because of a monetary debt.

Matthew 18:26 The servant (or slave) therefore fell down and worshipped him, saying, Lord, have patience with me, and I will pay thee all. And the lord of that servant, being moved with compassion, released him, and forgave him the debt. But that servant went out, and found one of his fellow-servants, who owed him a hundred shillings, and he laid hold on him, and took him by the throat, saying, pay what you owe. So, his fellow-servant fell down and besought him, saying, have patience with me, and I will pay you. And He would not, but went and cast him into prison, until he should pay that which was due. So, when his fellow-servants saw what was done, they were exceeding sorry, and came and told their lord all that was done.

Then his lord called him, and said, you wicked servant, I forgave you your debt, because you besought me, shouldn't you also have had mercy on your fellow-servant, even as I had mercy on you? And his lord was angry, and delivered him to the tormentors, until he should pay all that was due. So, shall also my Heavenly Father do to you, if you do not forgive your brother from your heart.

Another passage without any circumstances, that is, where, who, and when. Also, is Jesus referring to what the Christian Church calls Purgatory and not Hell, the former lasting for a period of time, the later lasting forever? Again, the Gospel writers were intent on putting their words in the mouth of Jesus.

Lastly, how can this be reconciled with the teaching of Jesus to forgive another person seventy times seven times? Does God want us to forgive others, while He does not? Certainly not!

Matthew 19:3 And there came unto Him Pharisees, trying him, and saying, is it lawful for a man to put away his wife for every cause? And He answered and said, have you not read, that He who made them from the beginning made them male and female, and said, for this cause a man will leave his father and mother, and cleave to his wife, and the two will become as one flesh? So that they are no longer two, but one flesh. What therefore God has joined together, let not man put asunder.

This teaching is interesting with respect to a man and woman married within what is called common law marriage, one in which the couple lives together for a period of time but without ever going through a formal ceremony or getting a marriage license. Jesus seems to endorse the notion of common law marriage even though the Pauline Christian Church established marriage as a sacrament and only considers a couple married if they were married in the Church.

This is most interesting when applied to Augustine, the so-called saint and doctor of the Pauline Christian Church. He was in a relationship for over fifteen years, and the woman gave birth to his son Adeodatus, which means "Gift from God". In 385, Augustine ended his relationship with his common law wife in order to prepare to marry a teenaged heiress. (His motivation was money and not love.)

By the time he was able to marry her, however, he had decided to become a Catholic priest and the marriage did not happen.

Was Augustine in fact married according to the teachings of Jesus above? Certainly! But the Christian Church of his time obviously tried to cover up this fact because he was a key person in the Church and his teachings became part of the core teachings of the Pauline Christian Church.

Matthew 19:7 Then, they said to Him, why then did Moses command to give a bill of divorcement, and to put her away? He said to them, Moses for your hardness of Heart suffered you to put away your wives, but from the beginning it has not been so. And I say to you, whoever puts away his wife, except for fornication, and marries another, commits adultery. And he that marries her when she is put away commits adultery.

The disciples said to him, if the case of the man is so with his wife, it is not expedient to marry. But He said to them, not all men can receive this saying, but they to whom it is given. For there are eunuchs, that were so born from their mother's womb, and there are eunuchs, that were made eunuchs by men, and there are eunuchs, who made themselves eunuchs for the kingdom of Heaven's sake. He that is able to receive it, let him receive it.

This passage is somewhat redundant and in substance the same as Matthew 5:7, but it contains elements that are inconsistent with the Nature of God and elements that support celibacy (an idea that was promoted in the early Church and was probably influenced by the Essenes).

What is meant by the statement "but from the beginning it has not been so"? Does it mean from the beginning of time? Not likely! This is probably an insertion by the Gospel writers. Would Jesus go along with the male chauvinism of the Jews? Certainly not! The rules that can be applied to women should equally be applied to men.

And would Jesus allow for divorce in the event of infidelity? Absolutely not! And how would this reconcile with the teaching of Jesus to forgive a person who offends you seventy times seven times?

Matthew 19:16 And behold, one came to him and said, Teacher, what do I need to do, that I may have eternal life? And He said to him, why do you ask me concerning that which is good? One there is who is good, but if you want to enter into eternal life, keep the commandments.

He responded, which? And Jesus said, you shall not kill, you shall not commit adultery, you shall not steal, you shalt not bear false witness, honor your father, and mother, and love your neighbor as thyself.

The young man said to Him, all these things have I observed, what do I lack? Jesus said to him, if you would be perfect, go, sell what you have, and give to the poor, and you will have treasure in Heaven: and come, follow Me. But when the young man heard this, he went away sorrowful; for he was one that had great possessions.

This passage is at variance with Matthew 25:31 "And when the Son of man shall come in His majesty, and all the angels with Him, then shall He sit upon the seat of His majesty. And all nations shall be gathered together before Him, and He shall separate them one from another, as the shepherd separates the sheep from the goats. And He shall set the sheep on His right hand, but the goats on His left. Then shall the King say to them that shall be on His right hand: Come, you blessed of My

Father, possess the kingdom prepared for you from the foundation of the world. For I was hungry, and you gave me to eat; I was thirsty, and you gave me to drink; I was a stranger, and you took me in; naked, and you clothed Me: sick, and you took care of Me; I was in prison, and you came to Me. Then the just will ask Him, saying: Lord, when did we see You hungry and fed You; thirsty, and gave You a drink? And when did we see You a stranger, and took You in; or naked and clothed You? Or when did we see You sick or in prison, and assisted You? And the king will answer them saying: Amen I say to you, as long as you did it to one of these My least brethren, you did it to Me."

Matthew 25:31 is much more difficult to observe then the ten commandments. Unfortunately, the vast majority of Christians today observe the ten commandments but not the precepts of Matthew 25:31.

Matthew 19:16 indicates that only the observance of the ten commandments is necessary to obtain eternal life. While Matthew 25:31 makes no mention of the ten commandments. Is Matthew 19:16 the words of Jesus and only the words of Jesus? Or is this passage a fabrication?

This passage primarily shows what a Jew needs to do to have eternal life, that is, obey the Jewish commandments. And we are back to the audience of the Gospel writers, Jews.

Jesus became a human for all people and not just the Jews. Are we to assume that non-Jews who knew nothing of the Jewish Bible did not earn eternal life? And the statement "Jesus said to him, if you would be perfect, go, sell all that you have, and give to the poor, and you will have treasure in Heaven: and come, follow Me."

This is obviously a plug for the Essenes and the Pauline Christian Church, both of which held that perfection can only be attained by poverty, celibacy, and a rigorous penitential lifestyle and that implies that married individuals cannot attain to perfection. This is incorrect. Matthew 25:31 outlines what is necessary to attain perfection in this life, no matter whether you are married or single.

Matthew 19:23 And Jesus said unto his disciples, Verily I say unto you, it is hard for a rich man to enter into the kingdom of Heaven. It is easier for a camel to go through a needle's eye, than for a rich man to enter into the kingdom of God. And when the disciples heard it, they were astonished exceedingly, saying, who then can be saved?

The supposed response of the disciples "who then can be saved" is a very illogical statement regarding Jesus' comments on the difficulty of a rich man entering the kingdom of Heaven because his or her wealth is an obstacle in following the teachings of Jesus. The fact is that during the time of Jesus and in virtually every time period, the percentage of rich people is very small – often the percentage is estimated at one percent. So, if Jesus' statement involves only one percent of the population, then why would the disciples supposedly say, "who then can be saved"? Another fabrication inserted by the Gospel writers for literary effect.

Matthew 19:26 And Jesus looking upon them said to them, with men this is impossible; but with God all things are possible. Then answered Peter and said to him, Lord, we have left all, and followed you, what then shall we have? And Jesus said to them, Verily I say to you, that you who have followed me, in the regeneration when the Son of man shall sit on the throne of His glory, you also shall sit upon twelve thrones, judging the twelve tribes of Israel. And every one that has left houses, or brethren, or sisters, or father, or mother, or children, or lands, for My name's sake, shall receive a hundredfold, and shall inherit eternal life. But many who are first will be last, and many who are last will be first.

More psycho-babel on the part of the Gospel writers. Jesus came to teach people not to confuse people. The Gospel writers seem to delight in writing statements and putting them into the mouth of Jesus that support their theology and their objectives in writing. "In the regeneration when the Son of man shall sit on the throne of His glory, you also shall sit upon twelve thrones, judging the twelve tribes of Israel". Does that mean that Jesus is saying that only Jews will gain eternal life? Jesus would not have said this.

Matthew 20:17And as Jesus was going up to Jerusalem, He took the twelve disciples apart, and on the way He said to them, behold, we go up to Jerusalem; and the Son of man shall be delivered to the chief priests and scribes; and they shall condemn him to death, and shall deliver him unto the Gentiles to mock, and to scourge, and to crucify: and the third day He shall be raised up.

The Gospel writers repeat this again. Did Jesus really say these exact words, or did the writers knowing after the facts what would happen to Jesus, insert these lines in order to show that Jesus predicted exactly these things?

Matthew 21:1 And when they drew nigh unto Jerusalem, and came unto Bethphage, to the mount of Olives, then Jesus sent two disciples, saying to them, go into the village that is over against you, and straightway you shall find an ass tied, and a colt with her, loose them, and bring them to me. And if anyone says anything to you, say, the Lord has need of them, and straightway they will send them. Now this is come to pass, that it might be fulfilled which was spoken through the prophet, saying, tell you the daughter of Zion, behold, your King comes to you meek, and riding upon an ass, and upon a colt the foal of an ass.

Again, the Gospel writers are more interested in showing the link between so-called Jewish Bible prophecies or statements rather than presenting exactly what Jesus said and did. Did these things happen? Did Jesus say these things?

Jesus was God. God became human to teach humankind how to live, and how to be happy both in time and eternity. The Gospel writers were intent on preaching to the Jews and only the Jews and making Jesus the Messiah of only the Jews. This is wrong.

Matthew 21:18 Now in the morning as He returned to the city, He hungered. And seeing a fig tree by the wayside, He came to it, and found nothing thereon, but leaves only. And He said to it, let there be no fruit from you henceforward forever. And immediately the fig tree withered away. And when the disciples saw it, they marveled, saying, how did the fig tree immediately wither away? And Jesus answered and said to them, verily I say to you, if you have faith, and doubt not, you will not only do what has been done to this fig tree, but even if you shall say to this mountain, be taken up and cast into the sea, it will be done. And in all things, whatever you ask in prayer, believing, you will receive.

The passage regarding the fig tree is inconsistent with Jesus and His divine nature.

How could Jesus, Who was God Himself, express a human imperfection? This passage implies that Jesus became angry with the fig tree because He was supposedly hungry. In another passage it is stated that Jesus fasted for forty days and nights, so Jesus could control His hunger. Jesus would have known that it was not the season for figs to bear fruit, since He designed and sustains the Universe. It is actually absurd to think that Jesus would have even gone to the fig tree out of season looking for fruit. And the narrated anger of Jesus is childish and indicative of a person who cannot control his feelings. And then to imply that Jesus was so angry at a fig tree for being a fig tree that He cursed it and destroyed its life. The sentiments and actions of Jesus described in this passage are totally inconsistent with His Divine Nature.

This passage is not only untrue, but absolute fiction. Whoever wrote this passage was a theological idiot.

Matthew 24:3 And as He sat on the mount of Olives, the disciples came to him privately, saying, tell us, when shall these things be, what shall be the sign of your coming, and of the end of the world? And Jesus answered and said to them, take heed that no man leads you astray. For many will come in my name, saying, I am the Christ, and will lead many astray. And you will hear of wars and rumors of wars, but be not troubled, for these things need to happen, but the end is not near. For nation shall rise against nation, and kingdom against kingdom, and there will be famines and earthquakes in diverse places. But all these things are the beginning of travail. Then will they deliver you up to tribulation, and kill you, and you will be hated in all the nations for my name's sake. And then many will stumble, and will deliver up one another, and will hate one another. And many false prophets will arise and will lead many astray. And because iniquity will be multiplied, the love of the many will wax cold. But he that endures to the end, the same will be saved. And this gospel of the kingdom shall be preached in the whole world for a testimony to all the nations, and then shall the end come.

Matthew 24:15 When therefore you see the abomination of desolation, which was spoken of through Daniel the prophet, standing in the holy place (let he that reads this understand), then let them that are in Judaea flee unto the mountains, let him that is on the housetop not go down to take out things that are in his house, and let him that is in the field not return back to take his cloak. But woe to them that are with child and to them that give suck in those days! And pray you that your flight be not in the winter, neither on a sabbath. For then shall be great tribulation, such as hath not been from the beginning of the world until now, no, nor ever shall be. And except those days had been shortened, no flesh would have been saved, but for the elect's sake those days will be shortened. Then if any man says to you, lo, here is the Christ, or here, do not believe it. For there shall arise false Christs, and false prophets, and will show great signs and wonders, so as to lead astray, if possible, even the elect. Behold, I have told you beforehand. If therefore they say to you, behold, He is in the wilderness, do not go, behold, He is in the inner chambers, do not believe it. For as the lightning cometh forth from the east, and is seen even unto the west; so will be the coming of the Son of man. Wherever the carcass is, there will the vultures be gathered together.

But immediately after the tribulation of those days the sun shall be darkened, and the moon shall not give her light, and the stars shall fall from Heaven, and the powers of the Heavens shall be shaken. And then shall appear the sign of the Son of man in Heaven: and then shall all the tribes of the earth mourn, and they shall see the Son of man coming on the clouds of Heaven with power and great glory. And He shall send forth His angels with a great sound of a trumpet, and they shall gather together His elect from the four winds, from one end of Heaven to the other.

Now from the fig tree learn her parable: when her branch is now become tender, and puts forth its leaves, you know that the summer is near, even so you also, when you see all these things, know that He is near, even at the doors.

Verily I say to you, this generation will not pass away, until all these things are accomplished. Heaven and earth shall pass away, but My words shall not pass away. But of that day and hour no one knows, not even the angels of Heaven, neither the Son, but the Father only.

And as were the days of Noah, so shall be the coming of the Son of man. For as in those days which were before the flood they were eating and drinking, marrying, and giving in marriage, until the day that Noah entered into the ark, and they knew not until the flood came, and took them all away. So shall be the coming of the Son of man. Then shall two men be in the field; one is taken, and one is left, two women shall be grinding at the mill, one is taken, and one is left. Watch therefore, for you know not on what day your Lord cometh. But know this, that if the master of the house had known in what watch the thief was coming, he would have watched, and would not have suffered his house to be broken in to. Therefore, be you also ready; for in an hour that you think not the Son of man cometh.

First of all, these passages contain inconsistent sequencing and redundancy. The Gospel writers used multiple sources for the same events such as this one and instead of trying to construct what Jesus actually said, they threw everything on the document along with their own interpretation.

Secondly, these passages make very little sense. Is Jesus talking about the end of the world? If this is the sense of the words, then these are not the words of Jesus but the Gospel writers putting their words in the mouth of Jesus. Or is Jesus supposedly talking about the destruction of Jerusalem, and if so, it would also appear the Gospel writers put words into the mouth of Jesus since they had the vantage point of having experienced the destruction of Jerusalem during their lifetimes.

"Verily I say to you, this generation will not pass away, until all these things are accomplished. Heaven and earth shall pass away, but My words shall not pass away. But of that day and hour no one knows, not even the angels of Heaven, neither the Son, but the Father only."

This implies the end of the world would occur before the generation of the disciples who were hearing this passed – absurd!

Also, the phrase "neither the Son, but the Father only" betrays the lack of understanding of Who Jesus was and His relationship to His Father. This lack of understanding on the part of the Gospel writers could be excused, but it is their arrogance in trying to develop and teach their theology regarding God, Jesus, the mission of Jesus, and His teachings by putting their words in the mouth of Jesus trying to make the reader believe that these words are the words of Jesus and not their words, that is absolutely inexcusable.

The Book of Daniel originated as a collection of folk tales among the Jewish community in the late 4th to early 3rd centuries BC. It was modified by multiple individuals over three to four hundred years. "When therefore you see the abomination of desolation, which was spoken of through Daniel the prophet, standing in the holy place (let he that reads this understand)", how could this have been spoken by Jesus given the implication that a person is reading this passage "let he that reads this understand".

Christian eschatology, a major branch of study within Christian theology, deals with "last things". Such eschatology – the word derives from two Greek roots meaning "last" and "study" involves the study of "end things", whether of the end of an individual life, or of the end of the world. Eschatology was discussed during the time of Jesus, the time of Paul, and during the early Pauline Christine Church.

The last book of the so-called New Testament, The Book of Revelation, focuses entirely on eschatology indicating the wide-spread interest in this topic.

Again, with the reference to the so-called Book of Daniel, the Gospel writers were more intent in understanding/interpreting the so-called prophecies of the Jewish Bible than trying to understand the teachings of Jesus, the nature of God as reflected in the words and actions of Jesus, and the His mission.

It is also very dubious that so many passages in the Gospels seem to involve the so-called disciples only as though there were topics or teachings that were not meant for all people but only the special individuals referred to as disciples or apostles.

It is highly doubtful that these passages contain anything actually said by Jesus or if they do very, very little.

Jesus was intent on teaching people, all people, how to live their everyday lives and not focusing on tomorrow. Christian eschatology did not arise from ordinary people but from the highly educated individuals who became the influencers and leaders of the Pauline Christian Church and like all academics, they liked to propose and argue hypotheticals.

Lastly, does there even have to be an end to the world? God is infinite and eternal and there is no reason for the world to end and there is no reason why God creating people cannot go on for all eternity.

Matthew 25:31 And when the Son of man shall come in His majesty, and all the angels with Him, then shall He sit upon the seat of His majesty. And all nations shall be gathered together before Him, and He shall separate them one from another, as the shepherd separates the sheep from the goats. And He shall set the sheep on His right hand, but the goats on His left. Then shall the King say to them that shall be on His right hand: Come, you blessed of My Father, possess the kingdom prepared for you from the foundation of the world. For I was hungry, and you gave me to eat; I was thirsty, and you gave me to drink; I was a stranger, and you took me in; naked, and you clothed Me: sick, and you took care of Me; I was in prison, and you came to Me. Then the just will ask Him, saying: Lord, when did we see You hungry and fed You; thirsty, and gave You a drink? And when did we see You a stranger, and took You in; or naked and clothed You? Or when did we see You sick or in prison, and assisted You? And the king will answer them saying: Amen I say to you, as long as you did it to one of these My least brethren, you did it to Me.

Then He shall say to those on His left: Depart from Me, you cursed, into the everlasting fire which was prepared for the devil and his angels. For I was hungry, and you did not feed Me; I was thirsty, and you did not give me a drink. I was a stranger, and you did not take Me not in; naked and you did not clothe Me; sick and in prison, and you did not care for Me. Then they will ask Him, saying: Lord, when did we see You hungry, or thirsty, or a stranger, or naked, or sick, or in prison, and did not minister to You? Then He shall answer them, saying: Amen I say to you, as long as you did not do so to one of these least, neither did you do it to Me.

This is the summation of the teaching of Jesus, and the essence of the Christianity of Jesus. And it is most interesting that Jesus would have taught this just before the Passover and His death.

Christians have heard this passage from the bible many times. And yet, so few Christians understand its true meaning and even less apply this passage to their economic, business, and political lives. Who are the hungry, the thirsty, the naked, the strangers, the sick, and the imprisoned in modern society? Obviously, it is the homeless, the unemployed, those living in poverty, those who are underemployed, those who have had their homes repossessed, those who are physically, mentally, and emotionally sick; and all those imprisoned physically, financially, and emotionally.

Jesus identifies with these people and Christians are to see Jesus in these people. Do Christians see Jesus in the homeless, the unemployed, those living in poverty, those who are underemployed, those earning minimum wage, those who have had their homes repossessed, those who are physically, mentally, and emotionally sick; and all those imprisoned physically, financially, and emotionally? The vast majority do not. What is worse is that many people who call themselves Christian actually deride these people.

Christians claim to praise God in Church on Sunday but then they ignore and mistreat Him every day when they ignore and mistreat the homeless, the unemployed, those living in poverty, those who are underemployed, those who have had their homes repossessed, those who are physically, mentally, and emotionally sick; and all those imprisoned physically, financially, and emotionally. The following is a more contemporary expression of Matthew 25:31.

At the end of the world when God judges everyone, He will separate the good from the bad based on the commandment to 'love your neighbor as yourself'. He will say to the good, 'Come you blessed and inherit the kingdom prepared for you from the beginning of time.

For I was poor, and you helped Me out of poverty. I was unemployed and you helped Me to find a job, or you gave Me a job, or you created a job for Me. I did not have health insurance and you helped Me to obtain insurance. I was not making a living wage and you worked to have My employer pay a living wage. I was homeless and you helped me find a place to live. My house was in foreclosure, and you helped prevent it from being repossessed. I was old and you helped Me with a socially based income and health insurance. I was uneducated and you helped to educate Me. I was in prison, and you helped change the system from retribution based to restorative based. I was discriminated against, and you helped stop the discrimination.'

And the righteous will ask Him, 'Lord, when did we see You in poverty or unemployed or without insurance or making less than a living wage or homeless? When did we see Your home in foreclosure or You uneducated or old and without an income or health insurance? When did we see you in prison or being discriminated against?'

And God will answer, 'Whatever you did for any of my brothers or sisters (all people), you did for me.'

Then he will say to the others, 'Depart from me. For I was poor, and you ignored Me. I was unemployed and you did nothing but say that was My fault. I did not have health insurance and you resisted any means to provide Me with public health insurance. I was not making a living wage and you said that My employer should determine how much I was worth and that there should not be a minimum wage let alone a living wage. I was homeless and you crossed the street so that you would not have to walk by Me. My house was in foreclosure, and you did nothing. My house was repossessed, and you helped with My eviction. I was old and you worked to take away my government mandated pension and health insurance that I paid for. I was uneducated and you said that only those that can afford an education should be educated. I was in prison, and you threw away the key. I was discriminated against, and you did nothing to stop the discrimination.'

And the unrighteous will ask Him, 'Lord, when did we act this way to you?' And God will answer, 'What you did or did not do to your fellow human beings, you did to Me.'

Sixty-five percent of Americans identify themselves as Christians, so it would be logical to see a significant influence of Christianity within the US economy and political system. And yet, that is certainly not the case. With such a high percentage of Christians within the United States, there is obviously a very high percentage of so-called Christians within banking, the defense and weapons industry, the pharmaceutical industry, the chemical industry, the diversified manufacturing industry and within government (all levels and all branches).

And yet the Christians in these industries and within government make no effort to apply Christian principles within their jobs.

How could a Christian working within the banking industry support the foreclosure of over fifteen million homes and the repossession of over five million homes?

How could a Christian person working for the banking industry personally apply and enforce policies that took people's homes away knowing that this affected women, children, and senior citizens?

How could Christian sheriff or police officer forcefully evict a family from their home removing their belongings and placing the family's belongings on the street while the family watched?

How could a Christian help the corporation that they work for to outsource jobs to another country knowing that it results in the loss of employment for hundreds or thousands of employees and their families just to increase profits?

How can a Christian work for a company that manufactures military weapons that helps promote military conflicts so that the company can sell its products and services?

How can a Christian work for an employer who either directly or indirectly operate factories that employ young girls and even children paying them extremely low wages and making them work excessively long hours?

How can a Christian employer pay adults with families at the minimum wage rate or less than the minimum wage?

How can a Christian manager force employees to work without a break for ten or twelve hours at time?

How can a Christian manager lay off workers a day before a holiday so that the workers are not paid for the holiday?

How can a Christian work for a company that intentionally reduces the hours of its employees so that it does not have to provide health insurance?

How can a Christian work for a pay day loan company or a title loan company which has interest rates between 300 and 750 percent or higher?

How can a Christian work for a company that pays male workers much higher than it pays female workers for the exact same work?

How can a Christian work for a hospital or medical center which charges a person without insurance more than a person who has insurance because the insurance company gets a discount? (The person does not have insurance because they cannot afford insurance).

How can a Christian work for a company that discriminates against older applicants?

How can a Christian in government ignore the 9 million people who are unemployed, the 30 million people who are under-employed, the millions of people who have to work two jobs, the 90 million people who live from paycheck to paycheck, and the 46 million people living in poverty?

The current economic and political crises within the United States are the direct result of Christians not practicing their faith in their daily lives and this includes their business lives, their economic lives, and their political lives.

Unfortunately, the vast majority of Christians have closed their minds to the inconsistencies between their faith and the philosophies and practices of the business world which falsely claim that business is outside the realm of faith and morals as expressed in the statement 'it is neither right nor wrong, it is just business'. Good is to be done and promoted, and evil is to be avoided in all things including business and politics.

The commandment to love your neighbor as yourself does not stop when it comes to business and politics; it applies to every facet of a Christian's life. If the failure of Christians to practice their faith in their economic lives is the cause of the current economic and political crises, then the solution is the application of Christian principles to the US economy and political system by Christians living their faith.

And not the principles of Pauline Christianity but the principles of the Christianity of Jesus.

Matthew 26:1 And it came to pass, when Jesus had finished all these words, He said to his disciples, you know that within two days the Passover celebration will be here, and the Son of man will be delivered up to be crucified.

Then were gathered together the chief priests, and the elders of the people, in the court of the high priest, who was called Caiaphas, and they took counsel together that they might take Jesus by subtlety and kill him. But they said, not during the feast, less a tumult arises among people.

What is the source of this information on the discussion by the chief priests and elders regarding the decision to put Jesus to death? If this were true it would have to be someone who was there, otherwise this would be fiction.

Matthew 26:6 Now when Jesus was in Bethany, in the house of Simon the leper, there came to him a woman having an alabaster jar of exceedingly precious ointment, and she poured it upon His head as He sat dinner. But when the disciples saw it, they had indignation, saying, to what purpose is this waste? For this ointment might have been sold for much money and given to the poor. But Jesus hearing this said to them, why trouble the woman for she has wrought a good work upon me. For you have the poor always with you; but Me you have not always. For in pouring this ointment upon My body, she did it to prepare Me for burial. Verily I say unto you, wherever this gospel will be preached in the whole world, what this woman has done will be spoken of as a memorial of her.

This passage appears in all four Gospels but with variations regarding whose house this occurred in, who it was that anointed Jesus, and who was offended by this act and raised an objection regarding the use of such expensive ointment. Very strange that there could be these variations since it would seem that the latter Gospel writers would have read the earlier versions of the other Gospels and if this passage is true, there should not be any variations just the facts.

Would Jesus use the word gospel "wherever this gospel will be preached in the whole world" or was this a literary device to introduce the readers to the new idea of a gospel? The etymology of the word 'gospel' is based on the Old English word 'godspel', which means "god-story."

Matthew 26:14 Then one of the twelve, who was called Judas Iscariot, went to the chief priests, and said, what are you willing to give me if I deliver Him to you? And they gave him thirty pieces of silver. And from that time, he sought an opportunity to deliver Him to them.

What is the source of information for this passage? It would have to be either the chief priests, Judas himself, or some attendant to the chief priests, all of which are extremely doubtful. Also, why would the chief priests need the help of Judas in arresting Jesus? The chief priests like any leadership group since the beginning of government and politics would have soldiers who would operate as spies. It is most likely that the chief priests knew where Jesus was, what He was doing, and what He was saying at almost any time, and they had no need of Judas.

Matthew 26:17 Now on the first day of unleavened bread the disciples came to Jesus, saying, where do you want us to prepare for the Passover meal? And He said, go into the city to such a man, and say unto him, the teacher says, My time is at hand; I will keep the Passover at your house with My disciples. And the disciples did as Jesus appointed them; and they made ready the Passover.

Is this fact or fiction? The typical celebration of the Passover was a family event, attended by wives, children, and extended family. And the Passover meal was prepared by women not men. Would Jesus have intentionally excluded the families of the Apostles? Are we to accept that the wives and children were to have stayed home and either not celebrated Passover or celebrated it without the father of the family? And if these disciples or apostles were in Jerusalem with Jesus, where were their families? Were they back at home trying to support themselves because they were abandoned by their husbands?

This passage and the fabricated context of males only at the Last Supper is similar to the notion of chauvinistic gang mentality or the sanitized phrase boys' club mentality. Imagine Mary, who no doubt accompanied Jesus wherever He went and was in Jerusalem at this time, came to

Jesus and asked Him about Passover. Imagine Jesus responding that He was going to spend Passover with His boys (the so-called apostles), and that women, children, and family members were not invited because they were not part of His gang and that His gang was exclusive.

Sounds absurd, but there must have been some conversation between Jesus and Mary regarding this Passover and how did the conversation really go?

Neither Jesus nor the Apostles would have excluded the wives and children of the Apostles from the Last Supper and in fact, Mary, the mother of Jesus, was also present at the Last Supper. It would make no sense otherwise. Mary was obviously in Jerusalem during the time of the Last Supper, since she was present the next day at the crucifixion of Jesus. Would Jesus have left His Mother by herself for this last Passover celebration? Certainly not!

The Gospel writers intended to justify the existence and position of the Church organization and developed the Gospel narratives with this objective and intentionally left out information that did not support their views and objectives. Because the early Church organization which was developed by Paul and his school was based on the Christianity of Paul and not the Christianity of Jesus, it was necessary for the Gospel writers, and the Gospel school to try to establish some authenticity for the priesthood of the Church of Paul.

Paul wanted to create a new religious organization patterned after the religious organization of Judaism which had a hierarchy with priests. Paul's organization would have priests and very quickly a hierarchy of priests: deacons, priests, bishops, and a chief priest who would later be called the pope.

Judaism was created and developed by individuals like Paul and the Gospel writers who established Judaism based on alleged but really legendary figures like Abraham, Moses, and Melchizedek. Paul and the Gospel writers wanted to show that their organization consisting of priests and a priestly hierarchy was created by Jesus. Remember that the Gospel writers were not eyewitnesses to the events of Jesus' life and seemingly refused to use interviews and quote eyewitnesses.

Like the Jewish writers who developed Judaism, Paul and the Gospel writers used the gospels to supposedly prove that Jesus founded their Church and at the same time used their Church to claim that the gospels and the other writings of the so-called New Testament were the word of God, not just inspired by God but written by God. The Old Testament writers and the New Testament writers did this in order to actually coerce people into accepting both their writings and their institutions.

Of course, these arguments are logically incorrect. You cannot claim that the Church was instituted by Jesus using the gospels and at the same time claim that the gospels were written by God based on the authority of the Church. Their claim for the authority of the Church is based on the authority of the gospels and the authority of the gospels is based on the authority of the Church. While this is certainly illogical, yet why don't people see this?

Most people are aware of the teachings and position of the Church of Paul which developed into the Christian Church of today is that Jesus instituted the priesthood at the Last Supper. This is why in the gospel narratives it was necessary to exclude all other persons except the Apostles from the Last Supper. Not that the presence of other individuals such as the wives and children of the Apostles and Mary, the mother of Jesus, would have prevented Jesus from ordaining His Apostles as priests, but the presence of only the Apostles made the narrative so much more impressive.

The gospel narratives of the Last Supper which intentionally excluded people other than the Apostles shows the chauvinistic view of Paul and the gospel school regarding the superiority of men over women and their position that God in the person of Jesus regarded men as superior to women and the Apostles as superior to other men.

But is God chauvinistic? Was Jesus chauvinistic? Does God consider men superior to women? Did Jesus consider men superior to woman? Does God consider some men as superior to other men? Did Jesus consider some men as superior to other men? Does God hold that celibate people are superior to married people? (This view was promoted by Augustine because he considered that sex even within marriage other than specifically for bearing children was basically sinful and sex resulting in the conception of children the means for transmitting original sin.) Absolutely not!

The presence of woman at the Last Supper would have been an extreme conundrum for Paul and the Gospel writers as it is for present day Christian leaders especially within the Catholic Church. The Catholic Church holds that women cannot become priests primarily because Jesus supposedly chose only men to be His apostles and He only ordained men as priests at the Last Supper. As mentioned before, Paul and the gospel school wanted to establish an institution (the Church) which would be very similar to the Jewish institution.

Paul and the gospel school could not have accepted women at the Last Supper since this might imply that Jesus may have ordained some women as priests, something that they would not nor could not accept within their new institution since they felt that they as men were superior to women.

Of course, the idea that men are superior to women is contrary to the Nature of God and the teaching of Jesus that the relationship between God and humans is that of a parent and children. And God as a parent, loves all of His children equally.

How would the situation of women have been historically and currently different, if Jesus had ordained women and women had leadership roles within the Christian Church? No doubt, significantly better. And we can thank the bias of Mr. Paul of Tarsus and the misters who wrote the Gospels for likely having initiated and perpetuated this injustice because they knew better than God.

At Pentecost, the Holy Spirit descended on the disciples of Jesus, men and women. In Luke Chapter 24, the risen Jesus appeared to His disciples, both men and women.

Matthew 26:26 And as they were eating, Jesus took bread, and blessed, and broke it; and He gave to the disciples (and everyone who was celebrating this Passover meal with Him), and said, take, eat; this is my body. And He took a cup, and gave thanks, and gave to them, saying, all of you drink of this, for this is my blood of the covenant, which is poured out for many unto remission of sins. But I say to you, I shall not drink again of this fruit of the vine, until that day when I drink it new with you in my Father's kingdom.

This passage is considered to be the institution of the Eucharist. There is absolutely no reason why women and even children could not have participated in this first Eucharist.

"For this is my blood of the covenant, which is poured out for many unto remission of sins."

Paul wrote his epistles before the Gospels were written, so it can be assumed that his writings influenced in great part the Gospel writers. First Letter of Paul to the Corinthians 11:23-27 For I received from the Lord what I also passed on to you. The Lord Jesus, on the night He was betrayed, took bread, and when he had given thanks, he broke it and said, "This is my body, which is for you; do this in remembrance of me." In the same way, after supper he took the cup, saying, "This cup is the new covenant in my blood; do this, whenever you drink it, in remembrance of me." For whenever you eat this bread and drink this cup, you proclaim the Lord's death until he comes. So then, whoever eats the bread or drinks the cup of the Lord in an unworthy manner will be guilty of sinning against the body and blood of the Lord.

Given that the Gospel writers were Pauline Christians (that is they followed the theology of Paul on Jesus Christ) and Paul was intent on linking the Eucharist to the death of Jesus as a sacrifice to God for the sins of all humans past and present, it follows that the Gospel writers writing under the influence of the Pauline Christian Church would try to do the same even if Jesus did not state such things at the Last Supper.

It is also very interesting that the Eucharist narrative is not contained in the Gospel of John.

Matthew 26:29 "But I say to you, I shall not drink again of this fruit of the vine, until that day when I drink it new with you in my Father's kingdom." Very strange statement! Fact or fiction? Is this implying the Jesus will be drinking wine in Heaven with the disciples? What about the previous statement "drink of this, for this is my blood of the covenant", is it the blood of the new covenant, and if so, how is Jesus going to drink this in His Father's kingdom? Much of this makes no sense and is most likely an fabrication inserted by the Gospel writers.

Matthew 26:30 And after they sang a hymn, they went out to the mount of Olives.

Matthew 26:31Then Jesus said to them, all you shall be offended in me this night: for it is written, I will smite the shepherd, and the sheep of the flock shall be scattered abroad. But after I am raised up, I will go before you into Galilee. But Peter answered and said to Him, if all shall be offended in You, I will never be offended. Jesus said to him, truly I say to you, that this night, before the cock crows, you will deny Me three times. Peter said to Him, even if I must die with You, I will not deny You. Likewise, also said all the disciples.

Again, the Gospel writers wanted to link this back to some prophecy "for it is written, I will smite the shepherd, and the sheep of the flock shall be scattered abroad", but did Jesus actually say this or was it inserted by the Gospel writers?

"But after I am raised up, I will go before you into Galilee." This statement is rather confusing. How many individuals was Jesus talking to eleven, fifty, or a hundred? The implication from the Last Supper is that there were only twelve disciples and if Judas left, there would have only been eleven disciples at the Mount of Olives. Did these eleven disciples stay in Jerusalem after the resurrection of Jesus or did they return to Galilee? And if they returned to Galilee, why and when did they return to Jerusalem for the Ascension? As has been stated earlies, the Gospel writers did not intend to write a fact-based biography of Jesus, citing His travels, words, and actions. Rather, they were intent on writing a narrative based on their own views.

Obviously, most people would rather read a biography of Jesus, including His words and actions, and not someone else's interpretation. Unfortunately, the Gospel writers were 'spin doctors' who intentionally provided a biased interpretation of the life, teachings, words, and actions of Jesus to promote Pauline Christianity and the Pauline Christian Church.

Matthew 26:36 Then Jesus came with them unto a place called Gethsemane, and said to his disciples, sit here, while I go yonder and pray. And He took with him Peter and the two sons of Zebedee and began to be sorrowful and very troubled. Then He said to them, My soul is exceeding sorrowful, even unto death, stay here and watch with me. And He went forward a little, and fell on his face, and prayed, saying, My Father, if it be possible, let this cup pass away from Me, nevertheless, not as I will, but as You will. And He came to the disciples, and found them sleeping, and said to Peter, what, could you not watch with me one hour? Watch and pray, that do you do not enter into temptation, the spirit indeed is willing, but the flesh is weak. Again, a second time He went away, and prayed, saying, My Father, if this cannot pass away, except I drink it, Your will be done. And He came again and found them sleeping, for their eyes were heavy. And He left them again, and went away, and prayed a third time, saying again the same words. Then He came to the disciples, and said to them, sleep on now, and take your rest, behold, the hour is at hand, and the Son of man is betrayed into the hands of sinners. Arise, let us be going, behold, he is at hand that betrays Me.

If the disciples were sleeping, who captured these words of Jesus? And there would have not been any opportunity for Jesus to tell His disciples these words since he would be put to death? Fact or fiction.

Matthew 26:47 And while He was speaking, Judas, one of the twelve, came, and with him a great multitude with swords and staves, from the chief priest and elders of the people. Now he that betrayed Him gave them a sign, saying, whoever I kiss, that is He, take Him. And straightway He came to Jesus, and said, hail, Rabbi, and kissed him. And Jesus said to him, friend, why have you come? Then they came, grabbed Jesus and took him. And behold, one of them that were with Jesus stretched out his hand, and drew his sword, and struck the servant of the high priest, and cut off his ear. Then Jesus said to him, put away your sword, for all they that take the sword shall perish with the sword. Or do you think that I cannot ask my Father, and He shall even now send me more than twelve legions of angels? How then should the scriptures be fulfilled that thus it must be?

Matthew 26:55 In that hour said Jesus to the multitudes, Are you come out as against a robber with swords and staves to seize me? I sat daily in the temple teaching, and you took me not. But all this is come to pass, that the scriptures of the prophets might be fulfilled. Then all the disciples left Him and fled.

Does this passage imply that some of the chief priests and elders were present? It would seem that some of those who came to the garden had seen Jesus before, so was it necessary for Judas to show them which person was Jesus? The servant of the high priest indicates that the high priest had slaves. And if it is true that one of the disciples cut off the ear of the slave of the high priest with a sword, he obviously intended to strike the slaves head and kill him. This would violate the fifth commandment and the teachings of Jesus who taught non-violence. Fact or fiction. Obviously, this makes for a better story.

And when Jesus supposedly refers to twelve legions of angels, did He really say 'twelve'? The number twelve is a number used often in the Jewish Bible and the Gospel writers would have perhaps inserted the number twelve for linkage to the Jewish Bible.

"How then should the scriptures be fulfilled that thus it must be? In that hour said Jesus to the multitudes, have you come out as against a robber with swords and staves to seize me? I sat daily in the temple teaching, and you took me not. But all this is come to pass, that the scriptures of the prophets might be fulfilled."

Did Jesus really say this? Jesus did not become human to fulfill Jewish prophecies, except in the mind of Paul and Pauline Christianity. Jesus came for all people, to teach people of the nature of God, the relationship between God and humans (that of a parent and His children) and how people should live. The Gospel writers went to great lengths to de-emphasize and ignore the interactions of Jesus and non-Jews, since it did not fit their paradigm.

Matthew 26:57 And they that had taken Jesus led him away to the house of Caiaphas the high priest, where the scribes and the elders were gathered together. But Peter followed Him far off, to the court of the high priest, and entered in, and sat with the officers, to see the end.

While certainly possible, highly improbable that Peter was in the court of the high priest. In fact, Matthew 26:69 states that Peter was outside. How would Peter be allowed inside? Since some of the attendants would have been at the garden of Gethsemane, they would have recognized him and either prevented him from coming in or arrested him. And given that this is fiction that Peter was in the court of the high priest and witnessed the so-called trial, who then was able to record or memorize these proceedings?

Matthew 26:59 Now the chief priests and the whole council sought false witness against Jesus, that they might put him to death, they found nothing warranting death, though many false witnesses came. But afterward came two, and said, this man said, I am able to destroy the temple of God, and to build it in three days. And the high priest stood up, and said to Him, why don't you say anything regarding what these witnesses have testified against You? But Jesus remained silent. And the high priest said to him, I adjure You by the living God, that You tell us whether You are the Christ, the Son of God. Jesus said to him, you have said it, nevertheless I say to you, henceforth you shall see the Son of man sitting at the right hand of Power and coming on the clouds of Heaven. Then the high priest rent his garments, saying, He has spoken blasphemy: what further need have we of witnesses? Behold, now you have heard the blasphemy, what do you say? They answered and said, He is worthy of death. Then did they spit in his face and buffeted Him, and some struck Him with the palms of their hands, saying, prophesy to us, You Christ: who struck you? Now when morning came, all the chief priests and the elders of the people took counsel against Jesus to put him to death, and they bound him, and led him away, and delivered him up to Pilate the governor.

Matthew 27:3 Then Judas, who betrayed Him, when he saw that He was condemned, repented himself, and brought back the thirty pieces of silver to the chief priests and elders, saying, I have sinned in that I betrayed innocent blood. But they said, what is that to us, that is your problem. And He cast down the pieces of silver into the sanctuary and departed, and he went away and hanged himself. And the chief priests took the pieces of silver, and said, it is not lawful to put them into the treasury, since it is the price of blood. And they took counsel, and bought with them the potter's field, to bury strangers in. And to this day that field is called the field of blood. Then was fulfilled that which was spoken through Jeremiah the prophet, saying, and they took the thirty pieces of silver, the price of Him that was priced, whom certain of the children of Israel did price and they gave them for the potter's field, as the Lord appointed me.

Who recorded or memorized this interaction between Judas and the high priests and elders? Certainly not Judas and most likely not the chief priests and elders!

Most writers of the Pauline Church condemn Judas for what he supposedly did, denied that he repented of what he had done, and considered him damned to eternal Hell. It is also rather inconsistent that the Pauline Church writers blame Pilate for the death of Jesus, and while a few writers in history placed blame on the Jewish hierarchy of chief priests and elders, most writers place no blame on the Jewish hierarchy for the death of Jesus. And yet, any person considering these events objectively should place most of the blame on the Jewish leaders.

They had been looking for an opportunity to eliminate Jesus because He posed a threat to their power. They put Pilate in a very difficult position when they threatened a riot and threatened to tell Rome that Pilate was allowing the person of Jesus to be placed above the emperor.

Also, was the whole story of Judas fabricated to fulfill the so-called prophecy of Jeremiah?

Matthew 27:11 Now Jesus was brought before the governor, the governor asked him, saying, are you the King of the Jews? And Jesus said to him, it is as you say. And as He was accused by the chief priests and elders, He answered nothing. Then Pilate said to Him, do You hear the many things they witness against you? And He gave him no answer, not even to one word, and the governor marveled greatly. Now at the feast the governor usually released to the people one prisoner, whom they would ask for. And they had then a notable prisoner, called Barabbas.

Therefore, Pilate said to them, whom will you that I release unto you, Barabbas, or Jesus who is called Christ? For he knew that for envy they had delivered Him up. And while he was sitting on the judgment-seat, his wife sent a message to him, saying, have nothing to do with that righteous man, for I have suffered many things this day in a dream because of Him. Now the chief priests and the elders persuaded the multitudes that they should ask for Barabbas and destroy Jesus. But the governor answered and said to them, which of the two will you that I release? And they said, Barabbas. Pilate said to them, what then shall

I do with Jesus Who is called Christ? They all answered, let him be crucified. And he said, why, what evil has He done? But they cried out exceedingly, saying, let him be crucified. So, when Pilate saw that he prevailed nothing, but rather that a riot was arising, he took water, and washed his hands before the multitude, saying, I am innocent of the blood of this righteous man, you see to it. And all the people answered and said, His blood be on us, and on our children. Then he released to them Barabbas; but Jesus He scourged and delivered to be crucified.

In the Gospel of John 18:28 it is written that the Jewish leaders did not enter into the palace of Pilate, the Roman governor, in order to avoid ceremonial uncleanness because they wanted to be able to eat the Passover, so Pilate came out to them. And Pilate had Jesus brought into his palace to interview Jesus. This is obviously different from the passage above from Matthew as well as the corresponding passages of the Gospels of Mark and Luke.

But, why the inconsistency between the four gospels? It is impossible to find out about the life of Jesus, His actions, words, and teachings from any one of the Gospels. And even when comparing all four gospels, there is obviously so much missing because the Gospels writers did not want to write a biography of Jesus but rather commentaries. Why?

It really implies arrogance on the part of the Gospel writers and their sponsors (the Gospel writers had sponsors, individuals who supported them financially and politically) to take the position that their readers were too stupid to be able to understand Jesus, His mission, and teachings by themselves.

Matthew 27:37 Above his head they placed the written charge against him: this is Jesus, the king of the Jews. In the Gospel of John 19:19, it is stated that this sign was written in Aramaic, Latin and Greek indicating the cosmopolitan make-up of Jerusalem at that time. The chief priests of the Jews protested to Pilate, "Do not write 'The King of the Jews,' but that this man claimed to be king of the Jews." Pilate answered, "What I have written, I have written."

This and the presence of the high priests and elders at the crucifixion of Jesus where they taunted and mocked Him, shows the evil of these people, and they were the spiritual leaders of the Jews!

Matthew 27:50 And Jesus cried again with a loud voice and yielded up His spirit. And behold, the veil of the temple was rent in two from the top to the bottom, and the earth did quake, and the rocks were rent, and the tombs were opened, and many bodies of the saints that had fallen asleep were raised and coming forth out of the tombs after His resurrection they entered into the holy city and appeared to many. Zebedee.

While the Gospels of Mark and Luke also make the claim about the veil of the temple being ripped in two, they made no mention of the earthquake, the splitting of rocks, the opening of tombs, the resurrection of so-called saints, their appearances to people after the Resurrection. And the Gospel of John had none of these claims.

Also, it is rather strange that there is no mention of the presence of Mary, the mother of Jesus in the Gospels of Mark, Matthew, and Luke, yet in the Gospel of John Mary was said to be at the foot of the cross of Jesus. Was this intentional on the part of the writers of the Gospels of Mark, Matthew, and Luke? And why would the Gospel of John which was written decades after the Gospels of Mark, Matthew, and Luke were written have Mary at the Crucifixion and not the other Gospels?

Matthew 27:62 Now the next day, the chief priests and the Pharisees were gathered together before Pilate.

Previous passages indicated the chief priests and elders and no mention of the Pharisees, but now it is stated that the chief priests are joined by the Pharisees. True or does it just make for a better story?

Matthew 27:63 The chief priests and Pharisees spoke to Pilate saying, Sir, we remember that that deceiver said while He was still alive, after three days I rise again. Command therefore that the sepulcher be guarded until the third day, lest His disciples come and steal Him away, and say to the people, He is risen from the dead, and the last error will be worse than the first. Pilate said to them, you have a guard, go, make it as sure as you can. So they went, and made the sepulcher sure, sealing the stone, the guard being with them.

Was the guard under the authority of Pilate or the chief priests, and were they soldiers?

Matthew 28:1 Now late on the sabbath day, as it began to dawn toward the first day of the week, came Mary Magdalene and the other Mary to see the sepulcher. And behold, there was a great earthquake; for an angel of the Lord descended from Heaven, and came and rolled away the stone, and sat upon it. His appearance was as lightning, and his raiment white as snow. And for fear of him the guards did quake and became as dead men. And the angel answered and said unto the women, fear not, for I know that you seek Jesus, Who has been crucified. He is not here, for He is risen, even as He said. Come, see the place where the Lord lay. And go quickly, and tell His disciples, He is risen from the dead, and He goes before you into Galilee; there shall you see Him, lo, I have told you. And they departed quickly from the tomb with fear and great joy and ran to bring His disciples the news. And behold, Jesus met them, saying, All hail. And they came and took hold of His feet and worshipped him. Then Jesus said to them, fear not, go tell my brethren that should depart into Galilee, and there shall they see Me.

The writers of the Gospel of Matthew seem to like to embellish their story with amazing events. No other Gospel cites an earthquake, or an angel whose appearance was as lightning, and the guards becoming as dead men. The previous passage indicates one guard, now there are many guards.

Matthew 28:11 Now while they were going, behold, some of the guard came into the city, and told the chief priests all the things that were come to pass. And when they were assembled with the elders, and had taken counsel, they gave much money unto the soldiers, saying, tell the story that His disciples came by night, and stole Him away while we slept. And if this comes to the governor's ears, we will persuade him, and rid you of care. So, they took the money, and did as they were told, and this story was spread abroad among the Jews, and continues to this day.

Great story but not found in the other Gospels. Fact or fiction?

Matthew 28:16 But the eleven disciples went into Galilee, to the mountain where Jesus had appointed them. And when they saw Him, they worshipped Him; but some doubted. And Jesus came to them and spoke unto them, saying, all authority hath been given unto me in Heaven and on earth. Go you therefore, and make disciples of all the nations, baptizing them into the name of the Father and of the Son and of the Holy Spirit, teaching them to observe all things whatsoever I commanded you: and lo, I am with you always, even unto the end of the world.

The Gospel of John 20:19 states "That Sunday evening the disciples were meeting behind locked doors because they were afraid of the Jewish leaders. Suddenly, Jesus was standing there among them! "Peace be with you," He said. As He spoke, he showed them the wounds in His hands and His side. They were filled with joy when they saw the Lord!" This occurred in Jerusalem and not Galilee.

Which is true? They cannot both be true. Were the disciples in Galilee or Jerusalem?

And the statement "all authority hath been given unto me in Heaven and on earth. Go you therefore, and make disciples of all the nations, baptizing them into the name of the Father and of the Son and of the Holy Spirit, teaching them to observe all things whatsoever I commanded you: and lo, I am with you always, even unto the end of the world" is most certainly a fabrication to provide a basis for the Pauline Christian Church in that it was instituted by Jesus Himself.

But if Matthew and John were both written by earthly disciples of Jesus, why are they so very different, on all sorts of levels? Why do they contain so many contradictions? Why do they have such fundamentally different views of who Jesus was? In Matthew, Jesus comes into being when he is conceived, or born, of a virgin; in John, Jesus is the incarnate Word of God who was with God in the beginning and through whom the universe was made. In Matthew, there is not a word about Jesus being God; in John, that's precisely who he is. In Matthew, Jesus teaches about the coming kingdom of God and almost never about himself (and never that he is divine); in John, Jesus teaches almost exclusively about himself, especially his divinity. In Matthew, Jesus refuses to perform miracles in order to prove his identity; in John, that is practically the only reason he does miracles.

The gospel writers were influenced by Paul and his followers. They most likely lived outside of Palestine and may never have even visited Jerusalem.

There are Gospel passages that conflict with each other. This is due to the passages being written by two or more different individuals. The real dilemma arises because people have been led to believe that the Gospels (as well as the rest of the Bible; what is called the Old Testament and the New Testament) are the word of God – written by God or the writer or writers writing under the influence of God so that what was written was absolutely true. To deny what is in the Bible is to deny God.

This absurd notion which unfortunately has continued even to this day was and is meant to control the non-leadership people or members and prevent them objectively criticizing the leadership. As a result of this mindset that both passages are the word of God that is absolutely true and cannot be denied, the reader attempts in vain to reconcile two conflicting passages instead of realizing one of the passages is either only partially true or an intentional hyperbole written by one of the writers in order to make a point.

JUDAISM - INTRODUCTION

Judaism evolved starting in the Bronze Age (3300 BCE to 1200 BCE) from among the polytheistic Semitic religions. Semitic peoples were inhabitants of ancient southwestern Asia and included the Akkadians, Phoenicians, Hebrews, Canaanites, Arabs, and others. Judaism originated as a national and ethnic religion and evolved primarily out of the polytheistic ancient Canaanite religion. It co-existed with the Babylonian religion, and incorporated elements of Babylonian belief. The Hebrew Bible, which is also, called the Tanakh, contains myth narratives similar to the myth narratives of other religions which existed during its evolution.

Examples of myth narratives are fables, folktales, sagas, epics, and legends, all of which are traditional stories typically concerning the early history of a people. Myth narratives contain both facts and fiction, usually more fiction than facts, though some myth narratives are entirely fiction. They are written to persuade the reader to accept some idea as true in spite of virtually no evidence.

Judaism originated as a national and ethnic religion and has never changed as an ethnic and national religion (consider Israel today). The other major religions are universal and not ethnic and nationalistic at least in theory. And from a historical perspective, Judaism has been nationalistic first and ethnic second. This implies that the Jewish leaders have used Judaism to promote nationalism and the basis of the Jewish leadership power system. This means that Judaism has been subservient to the political and economic systems of the Jewish ruling elites. And the question must be asked, 'was Judaism created as a tool of the Jewish ruling elites?'

During the Iron Age I (1200 BCE to 550 BCE) Judaism became distinct from the Canaanite polytheism from which it evolved. The process began with the development of Yahwism, the monolatristic worship of Yahweh, one of the Canaanite gods.

Monolatrism is the recognition of the existence of many gods, but with the consistent worship of only one god. Later, this monolatristic belief changed into a strict monotheistic belief and worship of Yahweh alone, with the rejection of the existence of all other gods.

During the Babylonian captivity of the 6th and 5th centuries BCE, certain circles within the exiled Jewish people refined Jewish beliefs regarding Yahweh, the election of the Jewish People as Yahweh's chosen people, divine law, and the covenant between Yahweh and the Jewish People.

This was done to give hope to the exiled Jewish People and to create the idea of a Jewish nation with an identity as Yahweh's divinely selected nation with a mission to lead the Jewish People and the world to an age of justice and peace. More specifically the following new or refined tenets of Judaism were developed:

- God will redeem the Jewish people from the captivity of the Babylonian Exile and return the Jewish people to the Land of Israel

- God will restore the House of David and the Temple in Jerusalem

- God will raise up a leader from the House of David, the Jewish Messiah, to lead the Jewish people and the world to an age of justice and peace

- All nations will recognize that the God of Israel is the only true God

- God will resurrect the dead and will create a new heaven and a new earth at the end of time

The third bullet point above is certainly interesting. Was this new teaching only about the so-called Jewish Messiah or did this new teaching about leading the Jewish people and the world to an age of justice and peace apply to all Jews? That is, since that time was it incumbent on Jews to pursue justice and peace throughout the world?

If that was true and it has been a teaching of Judaism since the 5th century BCE that the Jewish people must promote justice and peace throughout the world, then Judaism has been an absolute failure. What has Judaism done to promote justice and peace throughout the world? Absolutely nothing!

In Judaism there are two sources of teachings supposedly handed down by God to certain Jewish individuals, oral and written. Both sources continue to this day, but is should be clear that the written teachings or scriptures were preceded by oral sources which were transmitted from the so-called original recipient of the teachings from God from individual to individual over hundreds of years.

The Tanakh, the Christian Old Testament, evolved over a very long period of time and obviously was not the result of one author but rather many, many authors and editors all of whom wrote during the evolution of Judaism. The objectives of the writers of the Tanakh were to persuade or rather coerce the reader or listener to accept the tenets of Judaism as supposedly derived by the interactions of God and the Jewish prophets as expressed in the biblical narratives involving the history of the Jewish People. The coercion was based on the assertion that the Tanakh was the written word of God, that is, dictated by God to the prophet or the activity of God directing the prophet what to write (or remember) through inspiration. Since the Tanakh was written by God, it contained no error and should not be doubted by anyone.

This coercion was obviously a scam perpetrated by the leadership of the Jews and Judaism, for Jewish scriptures contain more fiction (myths and legends) than facts, though it also, contains pious writings, that is, writings by pious individuals.

The analysis and commentary which follows is an attempt to:

- Allow the reader to realize that the Tanakh, the Old Testament to Christians, contains errors and therefore, the assertion by the leaders of Judaism and Christianity that the Tanakh is without error is absolutely false

- Allow the reader to question the self-proclaimed status of the Jewish people as God's Chosen people

- Allow the reader to question the laws incumbent on the Jewish people especially the 613 mitzvot commandments

- Allow the reader to decide if Judaism is a man-made religion or a God-made religion

The Tanakh is supposedly a narrative of the history of the Jewish people from the beginning of time that supposedly shows the interaction between God and the Jewish people and only the Jewish people as God's favorite nation or people before and above all other nations and people just because they are Jewish.

A significant amount of the writings in the Tanakh was based on Jewish mythology and legends (a story with perhaps some historical basis but greatly exaggerated). The writers weaved these narratives into a theme that portrayed the Jewish people as having a superior position relative to all other people and having special status with God. Almost all of the books of the Old Testament support this theme. In order to sell or market these religious themes regarding the Jewish people, the Jewish religious leadership and Jewish ruling elite promoted the idea that these writings were inspired by God. Some even taught that these writings were actually written or dictated by God.

To an uneducated society which was very subservient to their theocratic leadership, the majority of the Jewish people before, during and immediately after the time of Jesus Christ accepted this idea that the Torah was the word of God. Because early Christianity developed out of Judaism, the original leaders of the Christian Church adopted these writings and the idea that these writings were inspired by God. So, effective was this marketing tool (the Old Testament was inspired by God and was the 'word of God') in getting the regular Christians to submit to the Christian leaders, the Christian leaders applied the same idea to the writings which would be later called the New Testament.

Over the last 1900 years, many individuals took a more objective view of the Old Testament and subjected its writings to very critical analyses. The essence of the conclusions that these individuals came to is that the Old Testament has virtually no historical basis and is a fabricated collection of narratives. It is not necessary to read all the research of these scholars, for a casual, objective reading of the Old Testament shows inconsistencies between these stories and the very concept of God as well as the teachings of Jesus Christ. Some Old Testament stories even show a human such as Abraham as being more virtuous than God.

QUESTIONING THE BIBLE

Questions must be asked," Is the Old Testament really the word of God", "Is the Old Testament inspired by God", or is the Old Testament factual or pious fiction"? Unfortunately, the current leaders of the various Christian churches have no interest in honestly answering these questions since they would have to admit that they have been wrong for 2000 years. However, common people need to answer these questions for themselves even if it may put them at odds with the leaders of their church.

If a person does conclude that the Old Testament is not the "word of God", then other questions must also, be asked. If the story or stories about Abraham are fables and have no basis in history, then what about the claim of the Zionists that Palestine belongs to them because God gave these lands to Abraham and his posterity. The Zionists in Israel are intent on removing the Palestinians from their homeland because of this alleged promise by God. But if there was no Abraham, then there was no promise from God. And would God really approve of what Israel is doing to the Palestinian people supposedly in His name?

How can we limit our understanding of God based on the perspectives of people who lived thousands of years ago and who had limited understanding of philosophy, science, and human rights and who had a distorted view of leadership, kingship, parenting, and love?

The Jews like virtually every other religion, country and society at that time held the view that the king or leader or father of a family was an exalted and superior position such that any perceived act of disrespect was a punishable offense. This idea was even exaggerated to the point where it was held that an offense (any offense) against an infinite being was an infinite offense because of the infinite superiority of the infinite person even though the so-called offense was committed by a finite person. Sins or offenses against God were any acts committed by person which were against the so-called Laws of God which were for Jews the laws or rules ascribed to Moses. Note, that the historical existence of Moses is questioned (did Moses really exist or is Moses just a legend), and it is most probable that the so-called laws of Moses were laws or rules created by the leaders and authors of Judaism.

Lastly, the story of Abraham is the basis for the religion of Judaism. It is also one of the bases for Pauline Christian theology. But, what if the story of Abraham was a complete fabrication?

OLD TESTAMENT MYTHS

The story of the Tower of Babel attempts to explain the origin of different human languages. According to the story, which is recorded in Genesis everyone on earth spoke the same language. As people migrated from the east, they settled in the land of Mesopotamia. People there sought to make bricks and build a city and a tower with its top in the sky, to make a name for themselves, so, that they could not be scattered over the world. God came down to look at the city and tower, and remarked that as one people with one language, nothing that they sought would be out of their reach. God went down and confounded their speech, so, that they could not understand each other, and scattered them over the face of the earth, and they stopped building the city. Thus, the city was called Babel.

This story is so absurd that is can only be a myth and not even a legend since there is absolutely nothing true in it. Absolute fabrication by the authors and editors.

The Flood Myth has similarities to ancient flood stories told worldwide. One of the closest parallels is the Mesopotamian myth of a world flood, recorded in the Epic of Gilgamesh. In the Hebrew Bible flood story in Genesis, God decides to flood the world and start over, due to mankind's sinfulness. However, God sees that a man named Noah was righteous (because he walked with God) and blameless among the people. God instructs Noah to build an ark and directs him to bring at least two of every animal inside the boat, along with his family. The flood comes and covers the world. After a number of days, Noah sends a raven to check whether the waters have subsided, then a dove; after exiting the boat, Noah offers a sacrifice to God, who smells "the sweet savor" and promises never to destroy the earth by water again – making the rainbow a symbol of this promise.

Similarly, in the Mesopotamian Epic of Gilgamesh, the bustle of humanity disturbs the gods, who decide to send a flood. Warned by one of the gods, a man named Utnapishtim builds a boat and takes his family and animals inside. After the flood, Utnapishtim sends a dove, then a swallow, then a raven to check whether the waters have subsided. After exiting the boat, Utnapishtim offers a sacrifice to the gods, who smell "the sweet savor" and repent their choice to send the flood.

Searches for Noah's Ark have been made from at least the past 700 years up to this time without success. There is no scientific evidence Noah's Ark ever existed. Furthermore, there is no evidence of a global flood, and most scientists agree that such a ship and natural disaster would both be impossible.

Attacked by a lion, Samson grabbed it and ripped it apart. Using the jawbone of a donkey, he slew 1,000 Philistines. Fact or fiction?

The reading of any religious scripture of the major religious organizations, the Tanakh or Old Testament, the New Testament, the Quran, the Veda, and The Tripitaka should be done in a rather critical manner questioning passages that are contradictory to the nature of God and the Natural Law (a system of law based on values intrinsic to human nature that can be deduced and applied independently of the laws of the state and involve the natural or inherent rights of all people conferred by God.

Lastly, with respect to the Tanakh or Old Testament, the New Testament, and the Quran, there are two lies perpetrated by the original writers, original editors, and virtually every religious leader since the creation of these books until now and that is that these documents themselves contain lies and the second more egregious lie is that God is the author of these books.

GENESIS – THE CREATION MYTH

Genesis: In the beginning God created the heaven and the earth. Now the earth was unformed and void, and darkness was upon the face of the deep; and the spirit of God hovered over the face of the waters.

And God said: 'Let there be light' And there was light. And God saw the light, that it was good; and God divided the light from the darkness. And God called the light Day, and the darkness He called Night And there was evening and there was morning, one day.

And God said: 'Let there be a firmament in the midst of the waters, and let it divide the waters from the waters'. And God made the firmament and divided the waters which were under the firmament from the waters which were above the firmament; and it was so. And God called the firmament Heaven. And there was evening and there was morning, a second day.

And God said: 'Let the waters under the heaven be gathered together unto one place, and let the dry land appear' And it was so.

And God called the dry land Earth, and the gathering together of the waters the Seas; and God saw that it was good.

And God said: 'Let the earth put forth grass, herb yielding seed, and fruit-tree bearing fruit after its kind, wherein is the seed thereof, upon the earth' And it was so. And the earth brought forth grass, herb yielding seed after its kind, and tree bearing fruit, wherein is the seed thereof, after its kind; and God saw that it was good. And there was evening and there was morning, a third day.

And God said: 'Let there be lights in the firmament of the heaven to divide the day from the night; and let them be for signs, and for seasons, and for days and years; and let them be for lights in the firmament of the heaven to give light upon the earth'. And it was so. And God made the two great lights: the greater light to rule the day, and the lesser light to rule the night; and the stars. And God set them in the firmament of the heaven to give light upon the earth, and to rule over the day and over the night, and to divide the light from the darkness; and God saw that it was good. And there was evening and there was morning, a fourth day.

And God said: 'Let the waters swarm with swarms of living creatures and let fowl fly above the earth in the open firmament of heaven'. And God created the great sea-monsters, and every living creature that creeps, wherewith the waters swarmed, after its kind, and every winged fowl after its kind; and God saw that it was good. And God blessed them, saying: 'Be fruitful, and multiply, and fill the waters in the seas, and let fowl multiply in the earth'. And there was evening and there was morning, a fifth day.

And God said: 'Let the earth bring forth the living creature after its kind, cattle, and creeping thing, and beast of the earth after its kind' And it was so. And God made the beast of the earth after its kind, and the cattle after their kind, and everything that creeps upon the ground after its kind; and God saw that it was good.

And God said: 'Let us make man in our image, after our likeness; and let them have dominion over the fish of the sea, and over the fowl of the air, and over the cattle, and over all the earth, and over every creeping thing that creeps upon the earth'. And God created man in

His own image, in the image of God created him; male and female created them.

And God blessed them; and God said unto them: 'Be fruitful, and multiply, and replenish the earth, and subdue it; and have dominion over the fish of the sea, and over the fowl of the air, and over every living thing that creeps upon the earth'.

And God said: 'Behold, I have given you every herb yielding seed, which is upon the face of all the earth, and every tree, in which is the fruit of a tree yielding seed--to you it shall be for food; and to every beast of the earth, and to every fowl of the air, and to everything that creeps upon the earth, wherein there is a living soul, I have given every green herb for food' And it was so. And God saw everything that He had made, and behold, it was very good. And there was evening and there was morning, the sixth day.

Genesis: And the heaven and the earth were finished, and all the host of them. And on the seventh day God finished His work which He had made; and He rested on the seventh day from all His work which He had made. And God blessed the seventh day and hallowed it; because that in it He rested from all His work which God in creating had made.

These are the generations of the heaven and of the earth when they were created, in the day that the Lord God made earth and heaven. No shrub of the field was sprouted in the earth, and no herb of the field had sprung up; for the Lord God had not caused it to rain upon the earth, and there was not a man to till the ground; but there went up a mist from the earth and watered the whole face of the ground.

Then the Lord God formed man of the dust of the ground and breathed into his nostrils the breath of life; and man became a living soul.

Comments: Up to this point, there were no witnesses to what God had done, so, how was it recorded or captured to memory. Are we to assume that God later explained and described all of this to so-called Adam and perhaps to Eve?

The notion that it took God six days to create the universe and that He needed a day to rest is contrary to the nature of God. Again, we have this anthropomorphic description of God, that is, God having human characteristics. This was in fact the only view of God in all theologies and religions up to the time of Aristotle who defined God as the is divine Intellect, the unmoved Mover that stands as final cause responsible for the intelligible motion of the cosmos. According to Aristotle, the actuality of thought is life, and God is that actuality, and the essential actuality of God is life Infinitely good and eternal, and only One.

God does not need to rest. The writers were attempting to convince or persuade the readers that God established the Sabbath. While refraining from work and focusing on God for one day of the week is admirable, it was not ordained by God during the Creation.

So, if the Bible was written or dictated by God, how could it contain errors? Obviously, it could not contain errors if it was written by God, therefore, it was not written by God.

And later in Genesis, the passages refer to angels. When and how were they created?

Angels are intellects/persons without bodies. While humans acquire knowledge through initial sense perceptions and then grasp the essence of a thing, Angels do not need sense perceptions and grasp the essence of something directly and immediately. Angels communicate with humans through ideas imparted to the individual.

The Garden of Eden Myth Commentary

Genesis: And the Lord God planted a garden eastward, in Eden; and there He put the man whom He had formed. And out of the ground made the Lord God to grow every tree that is pleasant to the sight, and good for food, the tree of life also, in the midst of the garden, and the tree of the knowledge of good and evil.

And a river went out of Eden to water the garden; and from there it was parted and became four heads. The name of the first is Pishon, that is, it which compasses the whole land of Havilah, where there is gold; and the gold of that land is good; there is bdellium and the onyx stone. And the name of the second river is Gihon; the same is it that compasses the whole land of Cush. And the name of the third river is

Tigris; that is, it which goes toward the east of Asshur, and the fourth river is the Euphrates.

And the Lord God took the man and put him into the garden of Eden to dress it and to keep it. And the Lord God commanded the man, saying: 'Of every tree of the garden you may freely eat; but of the tree of the knowledge of good and evil, you shall not eat of it; for in the day that you eat of the fruit you will die.'

Comment: Again, how do we know that God created the garden in Eden with a supposed tree of life and a tree with the knowledge of good and evil? Also, would Adam have understood death?

Genesis: And the Lord God said: 'It is not good that the man should be alone; I will make him a helpmate for him.' And out of the ground the Lord God formed every beast of the field, and every fowl of the air; and brought them unto the man to see what he would call them; and whatever the man would call every living creature, that was to be the name thereof. And the man gave names to all cattle, and to the fowl of the air, and to every beast of the field; but for Adam there was not found a helpmate for him.

And the Lord God caused a deep sleep to fall upon the man, and he slept; and He took one of his ribs and closed up the place with flesh instead thereof. And the rib, which the Lord God had taken from the man, made He a woman, and brought her unto the man. And the man said: 'This is now bone of my bones, and flesh of my flesh; she shall be called Woman, because she was taken out of Man.'

Therefore, a man will leave his father and his mother, and will cleave unto his wife, and they shall be one flesh.

Comment: Who made this statement, God or Adam?

Genesis: Now the serpent was more subtle than any beast of the field which the Lord God had made. And he said unto the woman: Has God told you not to eat of any tree of the garden? And the woman said unto the serpent: 'Of the fruit of the trees of the garden we may eat, but of the fruit of the tree, which is in the middle of the garden, God has said, you should not eat of it, neither should you touch it, lest you die.'

Comments: First of all, we have a talking snake, or as most people will respond this is not a real snake but the devil who took the form of a snake. Up to this point, there has not been any mention of angels or devils, but the writers of the Tanakh or Old Testament assume that the readers or those hearing this read to them will understand about angels and devils.

Yet, why isn't there any mention of when and how the angels were created, what their nature was, and how devils were supposedly angels who sinned? And if a devil was able to take the form of a snake, then why aren't there any incidents in history up to this time of a devil taking the form of an animal? Fact or fiction?

Genesis: And the serpent said to the woman: 'You will surely not die, for God knows that in the day you eat the fruit, then your eyes will be opened, and you will be like God, knowing good and evil.'

Comment: How would Eve even know about death and how would the serpent know about death? The notion of death did not exist up to this time since death was and is a punishment for the sins of Adam and Eve.

And how would Eve understand good and evil since her only understanding was of good and God Who was good.

Genesis: And when the woman saw that the tree was good for food, and that it was a delight to the eyes, and that the tree was to be desired to make one wise, she took the fruit and ate it; and she also, gave some to her husband with her, and he also ate. And their eyes were opened, and they knew that they were naked, and they sewed fig leaves together, and made themselves clothes.

Comment: Obviously, we have to assume that Adam was not with Eve when she spoke with the serpent. But did Eve explain the words spoken by the serpent to Adam before he ate the fruit, or did he think that Eve was just giving him some fruit to eat? And why supposedly did the serpent tempt Eve and not Adam? Was this an attempt by the writers to show that women were less intelligent than men?

Genesis: And they heard the voice of the Lord God walking in the garden toward the cool of the day, and the man and his wife hid themselves from the presence of the Lord God amongst the trees of the garden. And the Lord God called to the man, and said to him, 'Where are you? And Adam said: 'I heard Your voice in the garden, and I was afraid, because I was naked, and I hid myself. And He said, who told you that you were naked? Have you eaten from the tree, that I told you not to eat from? And the man said: 'The woman whom you gave to be with me, she gave me of the tree, and I did eat.'

Comments: Now we have God taking on human characteristics, anthropomorphism, walking and talking and not knowing where Adam was. Inconsistent with the nature of God. And we have Adam placing all of the blame on Eve, not very manly.

Genesis: And the Lord God said to the woman, what have you done? And the woman said, the serpent deceived me. And the Lord God said to the serpent because you have done this, cursed are you from among all cattle, and from among all beasts of the field, upon your belly will you go, and you will eat dust all the days of your life. And I will put enmity between you and the woman, and between your seed and her seed, they will bruise your head, and you will bruise their heel.

Comment: Certainly, a snake could not have been responsible for deceiving Eve, then why would God punish all snakes for all time? Obviously, God would not do such a thing.

Genesis: To the woman God said, I will greatly multiply your pain and your labor, in pain you will bring forth children; and your desire will be to your husband, and he will rule over you.

Comments: The writers of the Tanakh or Old Testament are attempting to justify their male chauvinism as commanded by God. Absurd. God considers men and women as equals, His children, and He wants men to imitate Him and treat women as equals. The male chauvinism of both the Old and New Testaments has allowed the mistreatment of women by men all the way up to today. The notion that men are superior to women is not from God, but rather from the stupidity and bias of men.

And would Eve understand about children, and how babies are born? Good story, but unbelievable!

Genesis: And He said to Adam because you listened to your wife and have eaten of the tree which I commanded you not to eat of it, cursed is the ground for your sake; in toil will you eat of it all the days of your life. Thorns also and thistles will it bring forth to you, and you will eat the herb of the field. In the sweat of your face will you eat, until you return to the ground, for out of it you were you taken. For you are dust, and to dust you will return. And the man called his wife's name Eve because she was the mother of all living. And the Lord God made for Adam and for his wife garments of skins and clothed them.

Comments: Are we to assume that God killed animals to use their skins for clothes for Adam and Eve? Not likely!

Here we see the lack of understanding of the nature of God. God is not mean and vindicative, nor would he test Adam and Eve as described. God does not dole out punishments, that is something that earthly leaders do and the writers of the Tanakh or Old Testament viewed God like an earthly king with defects.

God is perfect, He is like a father, He only wishes what is best for His children.

Genesis: And the Lord God said, behold, the man is become as one of us, to know good and evil, and now, lest he put forth his hand, and take also of the tree of life, and eat, and live forever. Therefore, the Lord God sent him forth from the garden of Eden, to till the ground from where he was taken. So, He drove out the man, and He placed at the east of the garden of Eden the cherubim, and the flaming sword which turned every way, to keep the way to the tree of life.

Comments: Here we have the first reference to God speaking in the plural, "the man is become as one of us". Christians claim that this is a reference to the trinity of God. However, early Judaism was polytheistic and also, supposedly Yahweh had a female companion, Asherah.

Are we to assume that the creation narrative was passed on from generation to generation for thousands of years without any generation adding or removing things? And where is the garden of Eden which is guarded by angels and a flaming sword?

In the previous passages of Genesis, there are two creation narratives with two distinct perspectives. In the first, Adam and Eve (though not referenced by name) were created together in the image of God and jointly given instructions to multiply and to be stewards over everything else that God had made.

In the second narrative, God fashions Adam from dust and places him in the Garden of Eden where he is to have dominion over the plants and animals. God places the Tree of the Knowledge of Good and Evil in the garden which he prohibits Adam from eating the fruit of. Eve is later created from one of Adam's ribs to be Adam's companion. If this story is supposed to be true, why are there two narratives? The existence of two narratives implies that this story is a myth.

And what is this Tree of Life which would allow Adam and Eve to live forever. God does not need a tree to allow people to live forever and living forever has nothing to do with the body and eating something, rather it has to do with the soul.

Jewish mythology absorbed elements from pagan mythology. The narrative of the Forbidden Fruit is similar to the one forbidden thing popular in fairy tales and mythology such as the story of Pandora's box in Greek mythology.

CREATION MYTH – SUMMARY AND CONCLUSION

n summary, an objective reader of the Creation narrative in Genesis should conclude that the entire narrative is a fabrication, it is neither written by God nor inspired by God. That does not imply that God did not create the universe and does not sustain it, like the evolutionists claim.

Unfortunately, evolutionists and so-called scientists exclude the possibility of anything or any being that cannot be sensed or measured. This is certainly absurd in itself. Ideas and thoughts exist, but they cannot be sensed or measured? Scientists in limiting their study to only what can be sensed, measured, and experimented with prevent themselves from understanding the complete universe. And their attempts to explain the origin of the universe based on this limited view of things to only that which can be sensed and measured lead to absurd theories on the origin of the universe such as the big bang.

CAIN AND ABEL MYTH

FAbsolutely, absurd that God would not have respect for Cain's offering. Was it because it was fruit and not an animal. Are we to believe that God only desires animal sacrifices?

And Cain was very wroth, and his countenance fell. And the Lord said unto Cain: 'Why are you wroth and why is your countenance fallen? If you do well, it will be lifted up, and if you do not do well, sin waits at the door and to you is its desire, but you can overcome it.'

And Cain spoke to Abel his brother, 'Let's go out to the field.' And it came to pass, when they were in the field, Cain rose up against Abel his brother, and killed him. And the Lord said to Cain: 'Where is Abel your brother?' And he said: 'I do not know, am I my brother's keeper?' And He said, 'what have you done, the voice of your brother's blood cries to Me from the ground. And now cursed are you from the ground, which has opened her mouth to receive your brother's blood from your hand. When you till the ground, it will not from now on yield to you her strength, a fugitive and a wanderer will you be in the earth.' And Cain said to the Lord: 'My punishment is greater than I can bear. Behold, You have driven me out this day from the face of the land; and from Your face will I be hid, and I will be a fugitive and a wanderer in the earth and it will come to pass, that whoever finds me will kill me.'

And the Lord said to him: 'Whoever kills Cain, vengeance shall be taken on him sevenfold.' And the Lord set a sign for Cain, lest any finding him should smite him. And Cain went out from the presence of the Lord and lived in the land of Nod on the east of Eden.

Comments: This entire passage is certainly a fabrication by the writers of the Jewish Bible. God or Yahweh does not want offerings or sacrifices. The notion of offerings and sacrifices was common among most of the early religions, and they were intended to appease an angry or offended god.

But God does not get angry; anger is a human defect. And why would God prefer or accept Abel's offering and reject Cain's? God would not.

As a parent, God would gladly accept any gift from any of His children. And God does not punish, only humans punish. And the absurd statement that God cursed the earth because of what Cain supposedly did, is inconsistent with the nature of God.

And what is the supposed sign that God set upon Cain to prevent anyone from killing him? And why would anyone want to kill Cain? Supposedly there should have only been Adam and Eve, and perhaps some other brothers or sisters of Cain and Abel, so, where did these other people come from?

Genesis: And Cain knew his wife; and she conceived and bore Enoch, and he built a city, and called the name of the city after the name of his son Enoch. And to Enoch was born Irad, and Irad begot Mehujael and Mehujael begot Methushael and Methushael begot Lamech. And Lamech took for himself two wives, Adah and Zillah. And Adah bore Jabal; he was the father of such as dwell in tents and have cattle. And his brother's name was Jubal; he was the father of all such as handle the harp and pipe. And Zillah bore Tubal, the forger of every cutting instrument of brass and iron, and the sister of Tubal was Naamah.

Comments: Where did all of the wives come from? And since brass (an alloy of copper and zinc) was first known to exist in about 500 BCE and the Iron Age was a period between 1200   BCE and 600 BCE, it should be clear that this Tubal person could not have used brass or iron. What it does indicate is that the writers of this passage probably wrote this after 500 BCE.

And assuming that Genesis was written after the 5th Century BCE, it could not have been written by Moses who supposedly lived between 1391–1271 BCE.

Again, fabrication without any truth whatsoever!

The Generations of Adam Myth

Genesis: This is the book of the generations of Adam. In the day that God created man, in His likeness God made them, male and female created He them, and blessed them, and called their name mankind, in the day when they were created. And when Adam lived a hundred and thirty years, and begot a son in his own likeness, after his image; and called his name Seth. After Seth was born, Adam lived 800 more years and had other sons and daughters. Altogether, Adam lived a total of 930 years, and then he died.

Comment: What happened to Cain and Abel? And what about Eve? Genesis attempts to show the genealogy of Adam with his descendants (at the least the males) living up to 900 years. Unbelievable and absurd! How was all of this recorded, it certainly could not have been memorized and handed down from generation to generation?

Genesis: And Lamech lived a hundred eighty and two years and begot a son. And he called his name Noah, saying: 'This same shall comfort us in our work and in the toil of our hands, which comes from the ground which the Lord has cursed.'

NOAH AND THE FLOOD MYTH

Genesis: And Noah was five hundred years old and begot Shem, Ham, and Japheth.

Genesis: And it came to pass, when men began to multiply on the face of the earth, and daughters were born unto them, that the sons of God saw the daughters of men that they were fair, and they took them as wives whoever they chose.

Comments: What is this statement trying to convey, there are sons of God and there are men who are not sons of God who had attractive daughters? Did both the sons of God and the men who were not sons of God both descend from Adam and Eve? And how did the sons of God become the sons of God and why didn't the men who were not sons of God not become the sons of God?

Genesis: And the Lord said, 'My spirit will not abide in man forever for he also is flesh, therefore, his life will be limited to one hundred and twenty years.'

Genesis: And the Lord saw that the wickedness of man was great throughout the world and that every imagination of the thoughts of his heart was only evil continually. And Lord regretted that He had made man on the earth, and it grieved Him at His heart. And the Lord said: 'I will blot out man whom I have created from the face of the earth, man, and beast, and creeping thing, and fowl of the air, for I regret having made them'. But Noah found grace in the eyes of the Lord.

Comments: The story of Noah and the so-called Flood is perhaps the worse fairytale ever written. And yet adults believe this to be true.

The reader is to believe that:

- Every human other than Noah and this included babies who had not attained the age of reason were evil

- God regretted creating humans and animals

- Animals were also, somehow evil perhaps through association with the evil humans

- God was so, angry that He decided to kill all humans and animals

- God intentionally murdered all living humans and animals at that time except for Noah, his family, and the animals on the Ark

All of this is absolutely contrary to the nature of God! God could not write or dictate or inspire such an absurd narrative. People that read this should quickly conclude that this is not the Word of God and that those religious leaders (Jewish, Christian, and Islamic) who claim that this is the Word of God are liars and scam-artists.

Genesis: And God said unto Noah: 'The end of all flesh is come before Me; for the earth is filled with violence through them and I will destroy them with the earth. Make an Ark of gopher wood with rooms and pitch it inside and outside with pitch. But I will establish My covenant with you, and you will come into the ark, you, and your sons, and your wife, and your sons' wives with you.

Comments: Here is the first so-called covenant between God and humans. But why would God enter into a contract with humans? And why are these contracts always between God and the Jewish People? Given that the writers of the Jewish Bible were Jewish and one of their main objectives in writing it was to establish the Jewish People as God's Chosen People, who were supposedly God's special people, above all other people, and because of this destined to rule the world, it should be clear why God only has covenants with the Jewish People.

Yet, because the Noah/Flood narrative in Genesis is a complete fabrication, these was no and is no such covenant, it also, is a fabrication.

Genesis: And of every living thing of all flesh, take two of every sort into the ark, to keep them alive with you; they shall be male and female.

Genesis: Of the fowl after their kind, and of the cattle after their kind, of every creeping thing of the ground after its kind, two of every sort shall come with you, to keep them alive.

Comment: Given that there almost one million animal species, Noah would have had a great challenge to capture two million animals and bring them into the Ark.

Genesis: And take from all food that is eaten, and gather it, and it shall be for you and them.

Comment: An amazing amount of food! How could a person believe such a thing!

Genesis: And Noah built an altar to the Lord, and took of every clean beast, and of every clean fowl, and offered burnt offerings on the altar.

Comment: If these were two of every species, and Noah sacrificed one of each of them on the altar, how could any species survive after this? And, it certainly would have to have been a very large altar or it took a very long time.

Genesis: And the Lord smelled the sweet savor; and the Lord said in His heart 'I will not again curse the ground any more for man's sake; for the imagination of man's heart is evil from his youth; neither will I again smite any more everything living, as I have done. While the earth remains, seedtime and harvest, and cold and heat, and summer and winter, and day and night shall not cease.'

Comments: God does not smell, and He certainly does not appreciate nor approve of burnt flesh. If God said in His heart, 'I will not again....'. How did the writers find out about this? Did God speak to them? Certainly not! The notion that God admitted to Himself that he cursed the ground is inconsistent with the nature of God. And God smelled the sweet savor of burning flesh is inconsistent with the nature of God, Who does not condone sacrifice?

Genesis: And God blessed Noah and his sons, and said to them, 'be fruitful and multiply, and replenish the earth. And the fear of you and the dread of you shall be upon every beast of the earth, and upon every fowl of the air, and upon all wherewith the ground teems, and upon all the fishes of the sea: into your hand are they delivered. Every moving thing that lives will be food for you as well as the green herb have, I given you all. Only flesh with the life thereof, which is the blood thereof, you shall not eat. And surely your blood of your lives will I require; at the hand of every beast will I require it; and at the hand of man, even at the hand of every man's brother, will I require the life of man. Whoever sheds man's blood, by man shall his blood be shed; for in the image of God made He man.

Comment: Is this implying that God not only condones capital punishment but actually commands it? This is impossible since it is opposed to the nature of God.

Genesis: And the sons of Noah, that went forth from the ark, were Shem, and Ham, and Japheth, and Ham is the father of Canaan. These three were the sons of Noah, and of these was the whole earth overspread.

Comments: If everyone on the earth came from the three sons of Noah, then everyone is related to each other and this undermines the notion of Jew and gentile since everyone is a brother and sister to each other.

TOWER OF BABEL MYTH

Genesis: And the whole earth was of one language and of one speech. And it came to pass, as they journeyed east, that they found a plain in the land of Shinar, and they dwelt there. And they said one to another: 'Come, let us make brick, and burn them thoroughly.' And they had brick for stone, and slime had they for mortar. And they said: 'Come, let us build us a city, and a tower, with its top in heaven, and let us make us a name; lest we be scattered abroad upon the face of the whole earth.'

And the Lord came down to see the city and the tower, which the children of men built. And the Lord said: 'Behold, they are one people, and they have all one language; and this is what they begin to do; and now nothing will be withholden from them, which they purpose to do. Come, let us go down, and there confound their language, that they may not understand one another's speech.' So, the Lord scattered them abroad from thence upon the face of all the earth; and they left off to build the city. Therefore, was the name of it called Babel; because the Lord did there confound the language of all the earth; and from thence did the Lord scatter them abroad upon the face of all the earth.

Comment: Rather strange narrative! Why would God do this? The writers of the Bible are trying to explain the diversity of languages in spite of everyone having descended from Noah and his sons by stating that God did this intentionally. God would not have done such a thing. Another fabrication with absolutely no truth.

ABRAHAM LEGEND

Genesis: These are the generations of Shem. Shem was a hundred years old, and begot Arpachshad two years after the flood. And Terah lived seventy years, and begot Abram, Nahor, and Haran. Now these are the generations of Terah. Terah begot Abram, Nahor, and Haran; and Haran begot Lot. And Abram and Nahor took them wives: the name of Abram's wife was Sarai; and the name of Nahor's wife, Milcah, the daughter of Haran, the father of Milcah, and the father of Iscah. And Sarai was barren; she had no child.

Genesis: And Terah took Abram his son, and Lot the son of Haran, his son's son, and Sarai his daughter-in-law, his son Abram's wife; and they went forth with them from Ur of the Chaldees, to go into the land of Canaan; and they came unto Haran and dwelt there.

Genesis: Now the Lord said unto Abram: 'Get out of your country, and from your family, and from your father's house, and go to the land that I will show you. And I will make of you a great nation, and I will bless you, and make your name great, and I will bless them that bless you, and he that curses you I will curse, and in you shall all the families of the earth be blessed.'

Comments: Why would God choose a person like Abram? There were obviously other men at the time. And why wouldn't God choose a woman? God does not prefer men over women, but the Jewish writers of the Jewish Bible did hold that men were superior to women, and they wanted to provide a basis for this position by implying that God also, preferred men over women.

This narrative of Abram (Abraham) is fictional. It is either a myth or a legend where there may have been a person named Abram, but the whole scenario of him being more just than God, passing a supposed test by God regarding his obedience, and the establishment of the Covenant between God and Abraham was totally fabricated.

Also, it will be shown later below, Moses is either a myth or a legend where there may have been a person called Moses, but the actions and events related to Moses are totally fabricated. Most specifically, the so-called Moses if he did exist did not write the Pentateuch.

The Jewish Bible was written mostly during the Babylonian exile (6th to 5th centuries BCE) and was edited continuously over the following 300 years. It was also, during this time that the idea of a Messiah was further developed from the writings of Isaiah.

THE JEWISH MESSIAH

The idea of a Messiah who is supposed to be an actual person from the house of David will reign over the world during what is called a Messianic Era. This Messianic Era will be one of global peace and harmony, free of all conflict, hardship, and social injustice. From the words of Isaiah: They shall beat their swords into plowshares and their spears into pruning hooks; nation will not lift sword against nation, and they will no longer study warfare.

Isaiah: The wolf will live with the lamb, the leopard will lie down with the goat, the calf and the lion and the yearling together; and a little child will lead them. The cow will feed with the bear, their young will lie down together, and the lion will eat straw like the ox. The infant will play near the hole of the cobra, and the young child put his hand into the viper's nest. They will neither harm nor destroy on all my holy mountain, for the earth will be full of the knowledge of the Lord as the waters cover the sea.

Comments: The main objective of the writers of the Jewish Bible (the Old Testament) was to provide a history of the Jewish People, their relationship with God, and their favored status with God. Unfortunately, these writers got caught up in the ultra-nationalist view of the Jewish nation, ignored the role that the Jewish People could have played in bringing about the Messianic Age without an actual person as the Messiah.

Unfortunately, the current state of Israel is the antithesis to the words of Isaiah above regarding the Messianic Age and implicitly the role that the Jewish People should be playing in bringing about the Messianic Age.

Genesis: So, Abram went, as the Lord had told him; and Lot went with him, and Sarai his wife, and all their substance that they had gathered, and the souls that they had gotten in Haran; and they went forth to go into the land of Canaan.

Genesis: And Abram passed through the land to the place of Shechem, into the terebinth of Moreh. And the Canaanites were then in the land. And the Lord appeared to Abram and said: 'to your seed will I give this land'; and he built an altar to the Lord. And Abram journeyed, going on still toward the South. And there was a famine in the land, and Abram went down into Egypt to sojourn there for the famine was extreme in the land.

Genesis: And it came to pass, when he was nearing Egypt, that he said to Sarai his wife, 'Now, I know that you are a fair woman to look upon. And it will come to pass, when the Egyptians will see you, that they will say: this is his wife; and they will kill me, but you they will keep alive. Say, I pray you, that you are my sister that it may be well with me for your sake, and that my soul may live because of you.' And it came to pass, that, when Abram was came into Egypt, the Egyptians saw the woman that she was very fair.

And the princes of Pharaoh saw her, and praised her to Pharaoh, and the woman was taken into Pharaoh's house. And he dealt well with Abram for her sake; and he had sheep, and oxen, and donkeys and male slaves, and female slaves and camels. And the Lord plagued Pharaoh and his house with great plagues because of Sarai Abram's wife.

Comments: Very incredulous story! Egypt was a very large country. Why would Abram supposedly go the city where the Pharaoh lived? And while he was afraid of being killed for being the husband of Sarai, he had absolutely no concern for what could happen to his wife – not a very virtuous man!

And Abram being rewarded for being the supposed brother of Sarai with slaves shows that Abram had no concern for his fellow human beings. And how did Egypt get so many people four to five hundred years after the Great Flood since all humans should have descended from Noah and his sons according to Genesis?

And lastly, God would not have plagued Pharaoh and his house with great plagues for this is inconsistent with the nature of God, for what did Pharaoh supposedly do?

And the storyline that all of this happened because Sarai was a beautiful woman sounds like a romance novel. And lastly these plagues seem to be similar to the supposed plagues also, inflicted on Egypt during the Moses narrative.

Genesis: And Pharaoh called Abram, and said: 'what is this that you have done to me, why didn't you tell me that she was your wife? Why did you say, she is my sister, so, that I took her to be my wife? Now therefore, take your wife and go your way.'

Comment: Pharaoh appears to be is far more just than Abram.

Genesis: And Pharaoh gave men charge concerning him, and they brought him on the way, and his wife, and all that he had. (Including the slaves)

Genesis: And Abram went up out of Egypt, he, and his wife, and all that he had, and Lot with him, into the South. And Abram was very rich in cattle, in silver, and in gold.

Comments: And how did Abram get all of this wealth, was it the wealth that he was given from the Pharaoh? And what happened to the so-called famine?

Genesis: And he went on his journeys from the South even to Bethel, to the place where his tent had been at the beginning, between Bethel and Ai to the place of the altar, which he had made there earlier where Abram called on the name of the Lord.

And Lot also, who went with Abram, had flocks, and herds, and tents. And the land was not able to bear them, that they might dwell together; for their substance was great, so, that they could not dwell together.

Genesis: And there was a strife between the herdsmen of Abram's cattle and the herdsmen of Lot's cattle. And Abram said to Lot, 'let there be no strife, I pray you, between me and you, and between my herdsmen and your herdsmen for we are brethren. Is not the whole land before you, if go to the left I will go to the right, or if you go to the right I will go to the left'?

Comments: Were the so-called herdsmen of Abram and Lot slaves? It would seem so. And, how in the four to five hundred years from Noah to Abram did slavery enter into society in which virtually all people were brethren of Abram since they all descended from Noah and his sons?

Illogical, inconsistent, and obviously a fabrication of the writers of the Jewish Bible.

Genesis: And Lot lifted up his eyes, and beheld all the plain of the Jordan, that it was well watered everywhere, before the Lord destroyed Sodom and Gomorrah, like the garden of the Lord, like the land of Egypt. So, Lot chose for himself all the plain of the Jordan, and journeyed east, and they separated themselves the one from the other. Abram dwelt in the land of Canaan, and Lot dwelt in the cities of the Plain, and moved his tent as far as Sodom.

Genesis: Now the men of Sodom were wicked and sinners against the Lord exceedingly.

Genesis: And the Lord said to Abram, after that Lot was separated from him: 'Lift up now your eyes, and look from the place where you are, northward and southward and eastward and westward; for all the land which you see, I will give to you and to your offspring forever. And I will make your descendants like dust of the earth; so, that if a man can number the dust of the earth, then shall your seed also, be numbered. Arise, walk through the land in the length of it and in the breadth of it; for to you will I give it.' And Abram moved his tent, and came and dwelt by the terebinths of Mamre, which are in Hebron, and built there an altar to the Lord.

Comments: Are we to assume that this land was totally uninhabited? Or were there people dwelling on this land already having made claim to it earlier and having worked the land for themselves and their families? If there were people on this land, God would not have given this land to Abram for it would be stealing this land from the current owners, something that is inconsistent with the nature of God, that is, to steal. In like manner God does not condone what the Israelis are doing to the Palestinians.

Genesis: And there went out the king of Sodom, and the king of Gomorrah, and the king of Admah, and the king of Zeboiim, and the king of Bela--the same is Zoar; and they set the battle in array against them in the valley of Siddim; against Chedorlaomer king of Elam, and Tidal king of Goiim, and Amraphel king of Shinar, and Arioch king of Ellasar; four kings against the five. Now the valley of Siddim was full of slime pits; and the kings of Sodom and Gomorrah fled, and they fell there, and they that remained fled to the mountain. And they took all the goods of Sodom and Gomorrah, and all their food and went their way.

Genesis: And they took Lot, Abram's brother's son, who dwelt in Sodom, and his goods, and departed. And there came one that had escaped and told Abram the Hebrew. And when Abram heard that his brother's son had taken captive, he led forth his trained men, born in his house, three hundred and eighteen, and pursued as far as Dan.

And he divided himself against them by night, he and his servants (slaves), and smote them, and pursued them unto Hobah, which is on the left hand of Damascus. And he brought back all the goods, and also, brought back his brother Lot, and his goods, and the women also, and the people.

Genesis: And Melchizedek king of Salem brought forth bread and wine; and he was priest of God the Most High. And he blessed him and said: 'Blessed be Abram of God Most High, Maker of heaven and earth, and blessed be God the Most High, who has delivered your enemies into your hand.' And he gave him a tenth of all.

Comments: Within just four or five hundred years after the supposed flood, there is a king who is also a high priest. This seems to fit the ideal picture of Judaism; a king and high person in one person.

Genesis: And the king of Sodom said to Abram: 'give me the persons, and take the goods to yourself.' And Abram said to the king of Sodom: 'I have lifted up my hand to the Lord, God Most High, Maker of heaven and earth, that I will not take a thread nor a shoe latchet nor anything that is yours, less you should say: I have made Abram rich, save only that which the young men have eaten, and the portion of the men which went with me, let them take their portion.'

Genesis: After these things the word of the Lord came unto Abram in a vision, saying: 'Fear not, Abram, I am your shield, your reward shall be exceeding great.' And Abram said: 'O Lord God, what will You give me, seeing that I go childless, and he that will be possessor of my house is Eliezer of Damascus?' And Abram said: 'Behold, to me You have given me no offspring, and no one born in my house is to be my heir.'

And behold, the word of the Lord came to him, saying: 'This man shall not be your heir, but he that shall come forth out of your own bowels shall be your heir.' And He said unto him: 'I am the Lord that brought you out of Ur of the Chaldees, to give you this land to inherit it.'

Genesis: And it came to pass, that, when the sun was going down, a deep sleep fell upon Abram, and a dread, even a great darkness, fell upon him. And God said to Abram: 'Know for sure that your seed shall be a stranger in a land that is not theirs and shall serve them; and they shall afflict them four hundred years, and also, that nation, whom they shall serve, will I judge; and afterward shall they come out with great substance. But you will go to your fathers in peace; you shall be buried in a good old age.

In that day the Lord made a covenant with Abram, saying: 'to your seed have I given this land, from the river of Egypt unto the great river, Euphrates.

Genesis: Now Sarai Abram's wife bore him no children; and she had a handmaid, an Egyptian, whose name was Hagar. And Sarai said to Abram: 'Behold now, the Lord has restrained me from bearing; go in, I pray you, to my handmaid (slave); it may be that I will be built up through her.' And Abram hearkened to the voice of Sarai. And Sarai Abram's wife took Hagar the Egyptian, her handmaid (slave), after Abram had dwelt ten years in the land of Canaan and gave her to Abram her husband to be his wife. And he went in to Hagar, and she conceived; and when she saw that she had conceived, her mistress was despised in her eyes.

Comments: Abraham does not appear to be very virtuous. If Sarai could not have any children, then Abram should have accepted this and not sought out a child with a slave.

Genesis: And Sarai said unto Abram: 'My wrong be upon you: I gave my handmaid into your bosom; and when she saw that she had conceived, I was despised in her eyes: the Lord judge between me and you.' But Abram said to Sarai: 'Behold, your maid is in your hands; do to her that which is good in your eyes.' And Sarai dealt harshly with her, and she fled from her face.

Comments: Abram and Sarai are certainly not virtuous people. Hagar is now the second wife of Abram and the mother of his child. She should now no longer be considered a slave. And God could never condone such actions.

Genesis: And the angel of the Lord found her by a fountain of water in the wilderness, by the fountain in the way to Shur. And he said: 'Hagar, Sarai's handmaid, from where did you come and where are you going?' And she said: 'I fled from the face of my mistress Sarai.' And the angel of the Lord said unto her: 'Return to your mistress and submit your self under her hands.' And the angel of the Lord said to her: 'I will greatly multiply your seed, that it shall not be numbered for multitude.

Comments: How does this supposed angel have the ability to 'greatly multiply the offspring of Hagar? And no good angel would tell a slave to return to their slave master. And again, how is Hagar a slave? She was the wife of Abram, so, she should be an equal to Sarai.

Genesis: And the angel of the Lord said to her: 'Behold, you are with child, and will bear a son; and you will call his name Ishmael, because the Lord has heard your affliction. And he shall be a wild ass of a man: his hand shall be against every man, and every man's hand against him; and he shall dwell in the face of all his brethren.' And she called the name of the Lord that spoke to her, you are a God of seeing; for she said: 'Have I even here seen Him that sees Me?'

Genesis: And Hagar bore Abram a son; and Abram called the name of his son, whom Hagar bore, Ishmael. And Abram was fourscore and six years old, when Hagar bore Ishmael to Abram.

Genesis: And when Abram was ninety years old and nine, the Lord appeared to Abram, and said to him: 'I am God Almighty; walk before Me and be wholehearted. And I will make My covenant between Me and you and will multiply you exceedingly.' And Abram fell on his face; and God talked with him, saying: 'As for Me, behold, My covenant is with you, and you will be the father of a multitude of nations. Neither will your name any more be Abram, but your name will be Abraham; for the father of a multitude of nations have I made you.

Comments: The father of a multitude of nations? Abram was not a good person, so, why would God make such a promise? The answer is, God would not. God did not make such a promise to Abram, rather the writers of the Jewish Bible made the promise in God's name for they wanted to instill patriotism in the hearts and minds of their readers. Complete fiction! The entire story of Abram is fiction and a myth.

Genesis: And I will make you exceedingly fruitful, and I will make nations from you, and kings shall come out of you. And I will establish My covenant between Me and you and your seed after you throughout their generations for an everlasting covenant, to be a God to you and to your seed after you. And I will give to you, and to your seed after you, the land of your sojourning, all the land of Canaan, for an everlasting possession; and I will be their God.'

Comments: Here God establishes a covenant with Abram and his descendants not distinguishing between the descendants from Abram's wife Sarai and the descendants from Abram's wife Hagar. But later supposedly God does make a distinction between the two based on the bias of free over slave. God would not and could not make such a distinction. God considers all people equal regardless of social status. The bias of the Jewish People and the Jewish writers of the Jewish Bible hold that bias that so-called free women are somehow superior to woman who is a slave, but God does not. Implying that God makes such a distinction clearly shows that these passages are not from God but rather from man, the Jewish writers. And the son of Hagar should be equal to the son of Sarai.

Genesis: And God said unto Abraham: 'And as for you, you must keep My covenant, and your seed after you throughout their generations. This is My covenant, which you shall keep, between Me and you and your seed after you, every male among you shall be circumcised. And you shall be circumcised in the flesh of your foreskin; and it shall be a token of a covenant between Me and you. And he that is eight days old shall be circumcised among you, every male throughout your generations, he that is born in the house, or bought with money of any foreigner, that is not of your seed. He that is born in your house, and he that is bought with your money, must needs be circumcised, and My covenant shall be in your flesh for an everlasting covenant. And the uncircumcised male who is not circumcised in the flesh of his foreskin, that soul shall be cut off from his people for he has broken My covenant.'

Comments: Truly an absurd set of statements supposedly made by God. God would not require the practice of circumcision, nor would He refer to slaves (he that is bought with your money) in an acceptable manner, nor would He propose that a person who is not circumcised be cut off from his people. The notion of circumcision is part of the rather extreme position of Judaism regarding 'cleanliness' that was made mandatory by the rules created by the writers of Leviticus.

Judaism did not begin the practice of infant, male circumcision until the 5th Century BCE around the same time that Genesis and Exodus were written. Obviously, the writers of Genesis and Exodus inserted this passage in an attempt to show that circumcision came from God, which it did not.

Genesis: And God said to Abraham, 'As for Sarai your wife, you will not call her Sarai, but Sarah will be her name. And I will bless her, and moreover I will give you a son from her; I will bless her, and she will be a mother of nations and kings of peoples will be of her.' Then Abraham fell upon his face, and laughed, and said in his heart: 'Shall a child be born to him that is a hundred years old, and shall Sarah, that is ninety years old, bear a child?' And Abraham said to God: 'Oh that Ishmael might live before You!' And God said: "No, but Sarah your wife shall bear you a son; and you shall call his name Isaac; and I will establish My covenant with him for an everlasting covenant for his seed after him.

Genesis: And as for Ishmael, I have heard you; behold, I have blessed him, and will make him fruitful, and will multiply him exceedingly; twelve princes shall he beget, and I will make him a great nation. But My covenant will I establish with Isaac, whom Sarah shall bear to you at this set time in the next year.' And He left off talking with him, and God went up from Abraham.

Genesis: And Abraham took Ishmael his son, and all that were born in his house, and all that were bought with his money (slaves?), every male among the men of Abraham's house, and circumcised the flesh of their foreskin on the same day as God had said to him. And Abraham was ninety-nine years old, when he was circumcised in the flesh of his foreskin. And Ishmael his son was thirteen years old, when he was circumcised in the flesh of his foreskin. In the same day was Abraham circumcised, and Ishmael his son, and all the men of his house, those born in the house, and those bought with money of a foreigner, were circumcised with him.

Genesis: And the Lord appeared to him by the terebinths of Mamre, as he sat in the tent door in the heat of the day; and he lifted up his eyes and looked, and, lo, three men stood over against him; and when he saw them, he ran to meet them from the tent door, and bowed down to the earth, and said: 'My Lord, if now I have found favor in your sight, pass not away, I pray you, from your servant.

Comment: Was this God or three men or three angels?

Genesis: Let now a little water be fetched, and wash your feet, and recline yourselves under the tree. And I will fetch a morsel of bread, and stay here, after that you can on, for you have come to your servant.' And they said: 'So, do, as you have said.'

Genesis: And Abraham hurried into the tent to Sarah and said: 'make ready quickly three measures of fine meal, knead it, and make cakes.' And Abraham ran unto the herd, and fetched a calf tender and good, and gave it unto the servant; and he hurried to dress it. And he took curd, and milk, and the calf which he had dressed, and set it before them; and he stood by them under the tree, and they did eat. And they said unto him: 'Where is Sarah your wife?' And he said: 'Behold, in the tent.' And He said: 'I will certainly return to you when the season comes around, and Sarah your wife shall have a son.' And Sarah heard in the tent door, which was behind him. Now, Abraham and Sarah were old, and well stricken in age; it had ceased to be with Sarah after the manner of women. And Sarah laughed within herself, saying: 'After I am waxed old shall I have pleasure, my Lord being old also?' And the Lord said unto Abraham, 'Wherefore did Sarah laugh, saying: will I of a surety bear a child, who am old? Is anything too hard for the Lord. At the set time I will return unto you, when the season comes round, and Sarah shall have a son.' Then Sarah denied, saying: 'I laughed not'; for she was afraid. And He said: 'No, but you did laugh.'

Genesis: And the men rose up from there and looked out toward Sodom; and Abraham went with them to bring them on the way. And the Lord said: 'Shall I hide from Abraham that which I am going to do seeing that Abraham shall surely become a great and mighty nation, and all the nations of the earth shall be blessed in him? For I have known him, to the end that he may command his children and his household after him, that they may keep the way of the Lord, to do righteousness and justice; to the end that the Lord may bring upon Abraham that which He hath spoken of him.'

Comments: Absurd statements concerning God and Abraham. It almost seems like Abraham is the supreme being and God is inferior to and subordinate to Abraham. Certainly, this is the work of the writers, and it is not from God, that is, God did not write nor dictate nor inspire this.

Genesis: And the Lord said: 'Truly, the cry of Sodom and Gomorrah is great, and their sin is exceeding grievous. I will go down now and see whether they have done altogether according to the cry of it, which is come to Me; and if not, I will know.'

Comments: God does not know what is happening in Sodom and Gomorrah. Does the writer not know that God is omniscient, certainly not? Again, the writers do not understand the nature of God!

Genesis: And the men turned from there and went toward Sodom; but Abraham stood outside before the Lord. And Abraham drew near, and said: 'Will You indeed sweep away the righteous with the wicked? What if there are fifty righteous people within the city; will You indeed sweep away and not forgive the place for the fifty righteous that are therein? That be far from You to do after this manner, to slay the righteous with the wicked, that so, the righteous should be as the wicked; be that far from You; shall not the judge of all the earth do justly?' And the Lord said: 'If I find in Sodom fifty righteous within the city, then I will forgive all the place for their sake.'

And Abraham answered and said: 'Behold now, I have taken upon me to speak unto the Lord, who am but dust and ashes. What if there shall lack five of the fifty righteous; wilt You destroy all the city for lack of five?' And He said: 'I will not destroy it if I find there forty and five.' And he spoke to Him again and said: 'what if there are forty found there.' And He said: 'I will not do it for the forty's sake.' And he said: 'Oh, let not the Lord be angry, and I will speak. What if there are thirty be found there.' And He said: 'I will not do it if I find thirty there.' And he said: 'Behold now, I have taken upon me to speak unto the Lord. What if there are twenty found there.' And He said: 'I will not destroy it for the twenty's sake.' And he said: 'Oh, let not the Lord be angry, and I will speak but this once. What if ten are found there.' And He said: 'I will not destroy it for the ten's sake.' And the Lord went His way, as soon as He had left off speaking to Abraham, and Abraham returned unto his place.

Comments: Absolutely, unbelievable. How can any objective reader with an understanding of the nature of God accept this as the Word of God, that is, that Abram is more just and forgiving than God? But this represents a conundrum for the current leaders of the Jewish and the Christian organizations? For their predecessors have taken the position that everything in the Bible is the Word of God; either directly written by God and handed to Moses or dictated by God to Moses or inspired by God. To take the contrary position now would mean to claim that the previous leaders were wrong.

Genesis: And the two angels came to Sodom at evening; and Lot sat in the gate of Sodom; and Lot saw them, and rose up to meet them; and he fell down on his face to the earth, and he said: 'Behold now, my Lords, turn aside, I pray you, into your servant's house, and stay all night, and wash your feet, and you shall rise up early, and go on your way.' And they said: 'No; but we will abide in the broad place all night.' And he urged them greatly; and they turned in to him and entered into his house; and he made them a feast, and did bake unleavened bread, and they did eat. But before they lay down, the men of the city, even the men of Sodom, compassed the house round, both young and old, all the people from every quarter. And they called unto Lot and said to him: 'Where are the men that came to you this night bring them out unto us, that we may know them.' And Lot went out unto them to the door and shut the door after him. And he said: 'I pray you, my brethren, do not so, wickedly. Behold now, I have two daughters that have not known man; let me, I pray you, bring them out to you, and do to them as is good in your eyes; only to these men do nothing, forasmuch as they are come under the shadow of my roof.'

Comments: What a story? Certainly, written by the writers and not by God – and certainly a fabrication. And Lot is certainly not a virtuous individual to offer up his daughters, who had husbands.

Genesis: And they said: 'Stand back.' And they said: 'This one fellow came to sojourn, and he will needs play the judge; now will we deal worse with you, than with them.' And they pressed upon the man, even Lot, and drew near to break the door. But the men put forth their hand, and brought Lot into the house to them, and the door they shut. And they smote the men that were at the door of the house with blindness, both small and great; so, that they wearied themselves to find the door. And the men said to Lot: 'Do you have anyone here besides yourself, son-in-law, and sons, daughters, and whoever you have in the city; bring them out of the place for we will destroy this place, because the cry of them is waxed great before the Lord; and the Lord hath sent us to destroy it.'

Comments: God, nor angels murder people. And it is extremely difficult to believe that all people in Sodom and Gomorrah, including children and babies were guilty and deserving of death. Unbelievable story. It is a fabricated story, not from God.

Genesis: And Lot went out, and spoke to his sons-in-law, who married his daughters, and said, 'get up and out of this place; for the Lord will destroy the city.' But he seemed unto his sons-in-law as one that jested. And when the morning arose, then the angels told Lot, saying: 'arise, take your wife, and your two daughters that are here; less you be swept away in the iniquity of the city.' But he lingered; and the men laid hold upon his hand, and upon the hand of his wife, and upon the hand of his two daughters; the Lord being merciful to him. And they brought him and set him outside the city. And it came to pass, when they had brought them forth that he said: 'Escape for your life; look not behind, neither stay you in all the Plain; escape to the mountain, lest you be swept away.'

And Lot said to them: 'Oh, not so, my Lord, behold now, your servant has found grace in your sight, and you have magnified your mercy, which you have shown to me in saving my life; and I cannot escape to the mountain, less the evil overtakes me, and I die. Behold now, this city is near to flee to, and it is a little one; oh, let me escape thither—is it not a little one? --and my soul shall live.' And He said to him: 'See, I have accepted you concerning this thing also, that I will not overthrow the city of which you have spoken. Hurry now, escape from here; for I cannot do anything until you have left.'

Genesis: Then the Lord caused to rain upon Sodom and upon Gomorrah brimstone and fire from the Lord out of heaven, and He overthrow those cities, and all the Plain, and all the inhabitants of the cities, and that which grew upon the ground. But his wife looked back from behind him, and she became a pillar of salt.

Genesis: And Abraham got up early in the morning to the place where he had stood before the Lord. And he looked out toward Sodom and Gomorrah, and toward all the land of the Plain, and beheld the smoke of the land went up as the smoke of a furnace. And it came to pass, when God destroyed the cities of the Plain, that God remembered Abraham, and sent Lot out of the midst of the overthrow, when He overthrew the cities in which Lot dwelled.

Genesis: And Abraham journeyed from theree toward the land of the South and dwelt between Kadesh and Shur; and he sojourned in Gerar. And Abraham said of Sarah his wife: 'She is my sister.' And Abimelech king of Gerar sent and took Sarah. But God came to Abimelech in a dream of the night, and said to him: 'Behold, you will die, because of the woman whom you have taken; for she is a man's wife.' Now Abimelech had not come near her; and he said: Lord, will You kill even a righteous nation? He told me, she is my sister, and she even she herself said: He is my brother. In the simplicity of my heart and the innocence of my hands have I done this.'

Genesis: And God said unto him in the dream: I know that in the simplicity of your heart you have done this, and I also, kept from sinning against Me. Therefore, I did not allow you to touch her. Now therefore, restore the man's wife, for he is a prophet, and he shall pray for you, and you will live; and if you do not restore her, know that you shall surely die, you, and all that are yours.'

Comments: This is certainly not from God. God would not kill Abimelech for a lie from Abraham and Sarah. Nor would God kill Abimelech's family or everyone in his kingdom (and all that is yours) for a stupid reason and Abimelech is not even guilty. We have another ridiculous example (the first involved the Pharaoh of Egypt) where Abraham lies about his wife and hands her over to become the wife or mistress of the supreme ruler. Total fabrication and not true at all.

Genesis: And Abimelech rose early in the morning, and called all his servants, and told all these things in their ears; and the men were sorely afraid. Then Abimelech called Abraham and said to him: 'What have you done to us, and how have I sinned against you, that you have brought on me and on my kingdom a great sin? You have done deeds to me that ought not to have been done.' And Abimelech said to Abraham: 'What say you, that you have done this thing?' And Abraham said: 'because I thought, Surely the fear of God is not in this place; and they will slay me for my wife's sake. And moreover, she is indeed my sister, the daughter of my father, but not the daughter of my mother; and so, she became my wife. And it came to pass, when God caused me to wander from my father's house, that I said to her: This is your kindness which you will show me, at every place we go, say of me, He is my brother.' And Abimelech took sheep and oxen, and men servants (slaves) and women servants (slaves), and gave them to Abraham, and restored him Sarah his wife. And Abimelech said, 'behold, my land is before you: dwell where it pleases you.' And to Sarah he said: 'behold, I have given your brother a thousand pieces of silver, it is for you a covering of the eyes to all that are with you; and before all men you are righted.' And Abraham prayed to God, and God healed Abimelech, and his wife, and his maid servants (slaves) and they bore children. For the Lord had closed up all the wombs of the house of Abimelech, because of Sarah Abraham's wife.

Genesis: And the Lord remembered Sarah as He had said, and the Lord did unto Sarah as He had spoken. And Sarah conceived, and bore Abraham a son in his old age, at the set time of which God had spoken to him. And Abraham called the name of his son that was born unto him, whom Sarah bore to him, Isaac.

Genesis: And the child grew and was weaned. And Abraham made a great feast on the day that Isaac was weaned. And Sarah saw the son of Hagar the Egyptian, whom she had borne unto Abraham, playing sports. Wherefore, she said unto Abraham: 'Cast out this bondwoman and her son; for the son of this bondwoman shall not be heir with my son, even with Isaac.' And the thing was very grievous in Abraham's sight on account of his son. And God said unto Abraham: 'Let it not be grievous in your sight because of the lad, and because of your slave woman; in all that Sarah said to you, listen to her voice; for in Isaac shall seed be called to you. And also, of the son of the slave woman will I make a nation, because he is your seed.'

Genesis: And Abraham arose up early in the morning, and took bread and a bottle of water, and gave it to Hagar, putting it on her shoulder, and the child, and sent her away; and she departed, and strayed in the wilderness of Beersheba.

Comments: Are we to think that Abraham is a good and virtuous person? Certainly not! He is a most corrupt and sinful person. The writers think that the readers are stupid to believe such a story.

Genesis: And it came to pass after these things, that God did prove Abraham, and said to him, 'Abraham'; and he said: here I am.' And He said: 'Take now your son, your only son, whom you love, even Isaac, and get you to the land of Moriah; and offer him there for a burnt offering upon one of the mountains which I will tell you of.'

Comments: Truly absurd! Any parent hearing a voice telling him to sacrifice his son would not consider the voice to be that of God. In addition, God would not tell a person to sacrifice their son. This idea of God testing Abraham's obedience is from men and not from God. This is contrary to the nature of God. God does not go around testing people in such a way. Parents don't do that, and God is a parent to all people, His children.

Genesis: And Abraham rose early in the morning, and saddled his ass, and took two of his young men with him, and Isaac his son; and he cleaved the wood for the burnt offering, and rose up, and went unto the place of which God had told him. On the third day Abraham lifted up his eyes and saw the place afar off.

And Abraham said unto his young men: 'Abide you here with the ass, and I and the lad will go yonder; and we will worship and come back to you.' And Abraham took the wood of the burnt offering and laid it on Isaac his son; and he took in his hand the fire and the knife; and they went both of them together. And Isaac spoke to Abraham his father and said: 'My father.' And he said: 'Here I am son.' And he said: 'Behold the fire and the wood; but where is the lamb for a burnt offering?' And Abraham said: 'God will provide Himself the lamb for a burnt–offering, my son.' So, they went both of them together. And they came to the place which God had told him of; and Abraham built the altar there, and laid the wood in order, and bound Isaac his son, and laid, him on the altar, upon the wood.

And Abraham stretched forth his hand and took the knife to slay his son. And the angel of the Lord called to him out of heaven, and said: 'Abraham, Abraham.' And he said: 'Here am I.' And he said: 'Lay not your hand upon the lad, neither do anything to him; for now, I know that you are a God- fearing man, seeing you did not withhold your son, your only son, from Me.'

Comment: In one sentence, the voice from heaven is an angel, and in the next sentence it is God speaking. Which is it?

Genesis: And Abraham lifted up his eyes, and looked, and behold behind him a ram caught in the thicket by his horns. And Abraham went and took the ram and offered him up for a burnt offering in the place of his son. And the angel of the Lord called unto Abraham a second time out of heaven, and said: 'by myself have I sworn, says the Lord, because you have done this thing, and have not withheld your son, your only son, that in blessing I will bless you, and in multiplying I will multiply your seed as the stars of the heaven, and as the sand which is upon the seashore; and your seed shall possess the gate of his enemies, and in your seed shall all the nations of the earth be blessed; because you have hearkened to My voice.'

Genesis: And there was a famine in the land, beside the first famine that was in the days of Abraham. And Isaac went unto Abimelech king of the Philistines to Gerar. And the Lord appeared to him and said: 'Go not down unto Egypt; dwell in the land which I shall tell you. Stay there in this land, and I will be with you, and will bless you, for to you, and to your seed, I will give all these lands, and I will establish the oath which I swore to Abraham your father, and I will multiply your seed as the stars of heaven, and will give to your seed all these lands, and by your seed will all the nations of the earth bless themselves, because that Abraham hearkened to My voice, and kept My charge, My commandments, My statutes, and My laws.' And Isaac dwelt in Gerar. And the men of the place asked him of his wife; and he said: 'She is my sister'; for he feared to say: 'My wife'; 'les the men of the place should kill me for Rebekah, because she is fair to look upon.'

Comments: First of all, this passage shows Isaac, like father like son in so far as he, Isaac, tried to pass off his wife as his sister. Ridiculous!

The stories of Abraham and Isaac are either complete fabrications with absolutely no historical basis or legends where there were some individuals such as Abraham and Isaac but these stories in the book of Genesis were created by individuals over time and finalized during the Babylonian captivity in the 5th Century BCE.

The myths or legends of Abraham and Isaac provided a very convenient opportunity for the writers of the final narratives to create the theme that the Jewish People have a special status with God that no other people have. But God has no favorite children, for all of God's children are equal in His eyes.

THE BOOK OF EXODUS MYTH

The Book of Exodus narrates the story of the Exodus, in which the Israelites leave supposed slavery in Biblical Egypt. The Israelites then journey with the supposed prophet Moses to Mount Sinai, where Yahweh (God) gives them the ten commandments and they enter into a covenant with Yahweh, who promises to make them a "holy nation, and a kingdom of priests" on condition of their faithfulness. He gives them their laws and instructions to build the Tabernacle, the means by which he will come from heaven and dwell with them and lead them in a holy war to possess the land of Canaan (the "Promised Land").

Traditionally it was said to be written by Moses. However, modern scholars see its initial composition as a product of the Babylonian exile (5th century BCE), based on earlier written sources and oral traditions. The consensus among modern scholars is that the story in the Book of Exodus is best understood as a myth. In summary:

- The actual exodus of the Jews from Egypt is a myth

- Not all of the Hebrews living in Egypt were slaves.

- Passage of the Jews through the Red Sea is a great storyline but there is no truth to it

- The passage of God appearing to Moses as a burning bush and commanding him to return to Egypt and bring His People out of bondage and into the Promised Land is a great storyline but there is no truth to it

- Supposedly during the journey, God tried to kill Moses, but Zipporah saved his life.

- It is against the nature of God to kill people, so, this is fiction.

- Moses returned to carry out God's command, but God caused the Pharaoh to refuse, and only after God had subjected Egypt to punishments (plagues) did the Pharaoh relent.

- 'God caused the Pharoah to refuse to leave' – absurd notion. And God would not inflict Egypt with plagues, for the Egyptians were God's people as all people are God's children.

- Moses led the Israelites to the border of Egypt, but there, God hardened the Pharaoh's heart once again, so, that he could destroy the Pharaoh.

- Absurd notion that God would destroy people. It is against His nature.

From Egypt, Moses led the Israelites to Mount Sinai, where he was given Ten Commandments from God, written on stone. Later at Mount Sinai, Moses and the elders entered into a covenant, by which Israel would become the people of Yahweh, obeying his laws, and Yahweh would be their god. Moses delivered the laws of God to Israel, instituted under the sons of Moses' brother Aaron, and destroyed those Israelites who fell away from his worship. After forty years had passed, Moses eventually led the Israelites into the Land of Canaan.

Fabrication. First of all, the substance of the Ten Commandments is part of the Natural Law, that is, these so-called commandments can be deduced by reason. Secondly, the so-called laws of God contained in the Book of Leviticus did not come from God, especially given the ridiculousness of many of these so-called laws as will be shown in the below commentary on the Mitzvot. Lastly, God would not destroy or kill those who did not follow such ridiculous, man-made rules.

Lastly scholars no longer accept the biblical Exodus account as history because there is absolutely no archeological evidence.

EXODUS COMMENTARY

Exodus: And the children of Israel brought forth fruit and increased in abundance, and were multiplied, and were exceeding mighty, so, that the land was full of them. Then there rose up a new King in Egypt, who knew not Joseph. And he said to his people, 'behold, the people of the children of Israel are greater and mightier than we. Come, let us work wisely with them, lest they multiply, and it come to pass, that if there be war, they join themselves also, unto our enemies, and fight against us, and get them out of the land. Therefore, they set taskmasters over them, to keep them under with burdens. And they built the cities Pithom and Raamses for the treasures of Pharaoh. But the more they vexed them, the more they multiplied and grew. Therefore, they were more grieved against the children of Israel. Wherefore, the Egyptians by cruelty caused the children of Israel to serve. Thus, they made them weary of their lives by sore labor in clay and in brick, and in all work in the field, with all manner of bondage, which they laid upon them most cruelly.

Comments: Did the king really consider the Hebrews as a threat to his kingdom, or do we just have a good story? The Jews were in Egypt supposedly for over 400 years. In that amount of time, they would have assimilated themselves into Egyptian society. And how many Hebrews could there have been 400 years after coming to Egypt? Certainly, not enough to be a threat. Some of the Jews in Egypt may have slaves, but not all of them.

Exodus: Moreover, the King of Egypt commanded the midwives of the Hebrew women, (of which the one's name was Shiphrah, and the name of the other Puah.) And he said, when you do the office of a midwife to the women of the Hebrews, and see them on their stools, if it be a son, then kill him; but if it be a daughter, then let her live. However, the midwives feared God, and did not as the King of Egypt commanded them but preserved alive the men children. Then the King of Egypt called for the midwives, and said to them, why have you done thus, and have preserved alive the men children? And the midwives answered Pharaoh, because the Hebrew women are not as the women of Egypt, for they are lively, and are delivered before the midwives come at them.

Comments: Only two midwives? If this is true, it would indicate the small population of Hebrews living in Egypt.

Exodus: God therefore, prospered the midwives, and the people multiplied, and were very mighty. And because the midwives feared God, therefore, he made them houses. Then Pharaoh charged all his people, saying, every man child that is born, cast into the river, but reserve every maid child alive.

Comments: God made houses for the midwives! Where were they living before? And God does not build houses for people. He could, but He does not. This would be the first time in the history of humankind.

Exodus: Then there went a man of the house of Levi, and took to wife a daughter of Levi, and the woman conceived and bare a son, and when she saw that he was fair, she hid him three months. But when she could no longer hide him, she took for him an ark made of reed, and daubed it with slime and with pitch, and laid the child therein, and put it among the bulrushes by the river's brink. Now his sister stood afar off, to watch what would come of him. Then the daughter of Pharaoh came down to wash her in the river, and her maidens walked by the river's side; and when she saw the ark among the bulrushes, she sent her maid to fetch it. Then she opened it, and saw it was a child: and the baby wept, so, she had compassion on it, and said, this is one of the Hebrew's children. Then his said his to Pharaoh's daughter, shall I go and call for you a nurse of the Hebrew women to nurse you the child? And Pharaoh's daughter said to her, go. So, the maid went and called the child's mother, to whom Pharaoh's daughter said, take this child away, and nurse it for me, and I will reward you. Then the woman took the child and nursed him. Now the child grew, and she brought him to Pharaoh's daughter, and he was as her son, and she called his name Moses, because, said she, I drew him out of the water.

Comments: What a story! How did Pharoah's daughter explain the child to her father? Are we supposed to assume that Pharoah was stupid? Or is the reader who believes this story stupid?

Exodus: And in those days, when Moses was grown, he went forth to his brethren, and looked on their burdens, he also, saw an Egyptian hitting a Hebrew, one of his brethren. And he looked round about, and when he saw no man, he slew the Egyptian, and hid him in the sand.

Comments: Was Moses practicing 'an eye for an eye'? He kills the Egyptian for having struck a Hebrew. While this was written to motivate Jews to hate Egyptians and admire Moses, Moses is guilty of murder. Are not all people your neighbors? And should not Moses love his neighbor as himself. In addition, it would appear that all people descended from Noah and his sons, both Hebrews and Egyptians. So, the Egyptians were relatives of the Hebrews.

Exodus: Again, he came forth the second day, and saw two Hebrew's fighting; and he said to him that did the wrong, why did you strike your fellow Hebrew? And he answered, who made you a man of authority, and a judge over us? I think to myself, you killed an Egyptian and you are criticizing me? Then, Moses feared and said, certainly this thing is known. Now, Pharaoh heard about this matter and sought to slay Moses. Therefore, Moses fled from Pharaoh, and dwelt in the land of Midian, and he sat down by a well. And the Priest of Midian had seven daughters, which came and drew water, and filled the troughs to water their father's sheep. Then the shepherds came and drove them away, but Moses rose up and defended them, and watered their sheep. And when they came to Reuel their father he said, how did things go for you today? And they said, A man of Egypt delivered us from the hand of the shepherds, and also, he drew us water, and watered the sheep. Then he said to his daughters, 'where is he'? Why have you left the man? Call him that he may eat bread. And Moses agreed to dwell with the man, who gave to Moses Zipporah his daughter, and she bore him a son, whose name he called Gershom, for he said, I have been a stranger in a strange land.

Comment: Notice how the narrative makes Moses the 'good guy' and the Pharoah the 'bad guy'. And where does this information come from? That is, who captured and recorded this information?

Exodus: Then in process of time, the King of Egypt died, and the children of Israel sighed for their bondage and cried; and their cry for the bondage came up unto God. Then God heard their moan, and God remembered his covenant with Abraham, Isaac, and Jacob.

Comments: God remembered His covenant! As though God is human and can forget things. The writers of Exodus have an incorrect idea of the nature of God. If Abraham, Isaac, and Jacob were legends, there was no covenant. In addition, God treats all people the same, and there is no reason for a covenant with one people for all people are equal in the eyes of God. The notion of a covenant was a fabrication devised by the writers to inspire the Jewish people. There was no covenant with Noah, nor one with Abraham.

Exodus: So, God looked upon the children of Israel, and God had respect for them. When Moses kept the sheep of Jethro his father-in-law, Priest of Midian, and drove the flock to the backside of the desert, and came to the Mountain of God, Horeb. Then the Angel of the Lord appeared to him in a flame of fire, out of the middle of a bush; and he looked, and behold, the bush burned with fire, but the bush was not consumed. Therefore, Moses said, I will turn aside now, and see this great sight, why the bush does not burn. And when the Lord saw that he turned aside to see, God called unto him out of the midst of the bush, and said, Moses, Moses.

Comment: Was an angel in the bush or God?

Exodus: And he answered, I am here. Then He said, do not come here, take your shoes off, for the place where you stand is holy ground.

Comment: What does wearing shoes have to do with a holy site?

Exodus: Moreover, He said, I am the God of your father, the God of Abraham, the God of Isaac, and the God of Jacob. Then Moses hid his face, for he was afraid to look upon God. Then the Lord said, I have surely seen the trouble of my people, which are in Egypt, and have heard their cry, because of their taskmasters, for I know their sorrows. Therefore, I am come down to deliver them out of the hand of the Egyptians, and to bring them out of that land into a good and large land, into a land that flows with milk and honey, even into the place of the Canaanites, and the Hittites, and the Amorites, and the Perizzites, and the Hivites, and the Jebusites. And now, the cry of the children of Israel is come to me, and I have also, seen the oppression wherewith the Egyptians oppress them. Come now Therefore, I will send you to Pharaoh, that you may bring my people the children of Israel out of Egypt. But Moses said to God, who am I, that I should go to Pharaoh, and that I should bring the children of Israel out of Egypt? And he answered, I will be with you, and this shall be a token to you, that I have sent you, after that you have brought the people out of Egypt, you shall serve God upon this mountain. Then Moses said to God, behold, when I shall come to the children of Israel, and shall say to them, the God of your fathers has sent me to you. If they say to me, what is his Name? What shall I say to them? And God answered Moses, 'I am that I am'. Also, He said, thus shall you say to the children of Israel, I AM hath sent me to you. And God spoke further to Moses, thus shall you say to the children of Israel, The Lord of your fathers, the God of Abraham, the God of Isaac, and the God of Jacob has sent me unto you. This is my Name forever, and this is my memorial unto all ages. Go and gather the Elders of Israel together, and you shall say to them, The Lord God of your fathers, the God of Abraham, Isaac, and Jacob appeared to me, and said, I have surely remembered you, and that which is done to you in Egypt. Therefore, I did say, I will bring you out of the affliction of Egypt to the land of the Canaanites, and the Hittites, and the Amorites, and the Perizzites, and the Hivites, and the Jebusites, to a land that flows with milk and honey. Then shall they obey your voice, and you and the Elders of Israel shall go to the King of Egypt, and say to him, The Lord God of the Hebrews has met with us; we pray you now Therefore, let us go three days journey in the wilderness, that we may sacrifice to the Lord, our God. But, I know, that the King of Egypt will not let you go, but by a strong hand. Therefore, will I stretch out my hand and smite Egypt with all my wonders, which I will do in the midst thereof; and after that he will let you go. And I will make this people to be favored of the Egyptians; so, that when you go, you shall not go empty. For every woman shall ask of her neighbor, and of her that stays in her house, jewels of silver and jewels of gold and raiment, and you shall put them on your sons, and on your daughters, and shall spoil the Egyptians.

Comments: Good guy, bad guy. Good people, bad people. Motivating story for the naïve reader. First of all, the idea that God's essence is existence ('I am Who am') was borrowed from Aristotle who lived after the Babylonian Captivity and shows the editing or revising of the Pentateuch after it was first written during the Babylonian Captivity. Secondly, God would not promise the so-called Israelites with someone else's land ('I will bring you out of the affliction of Egypt unto the land of the Canaanites, and the Hittites, and the Amorites, and the Perizzites, and the Hivites, and the Jebusites, unto a land that flows with milk and honey'). All people are God's children, and He does not have favorites, this is fiction on the part of the writers and the Jewish Leaders.

Exodus: Then Moses answered, and said, 'but, they will not believe me, nor listen to my voice, for they will say, The Lord has not appeared to you'. And the Lord said unto him, what is that in your hand? And he answered, a rod. Then said he, cast it on the ground. So, he cast it on the ground, and it was turned into a serpent, and Moses fled from it. Again, the Lord said to Moses, put forth your hand, and take it by the tail. Then he put forth his hand and caught it, and it was turned into a rod in his hand. Do this that they may believe that the Lord God of their fathers, the God of Abraham, the God of Isaac, and the God of Jacob has appeared to you.

Comments: If someone turned a rod into a snake in front of you, would you believe that it was God acting through the person? And if so, is a magician such as David Copperfield acting on behalf of God?

Exodus: And the Lord said further to him, Thrust now your hand to your bosom. And he thrust his hand into his bosom, and when he took it out again, his hand was leprous as snow. Moreover, He said, Put your hand into your bosom again. So, he put his hand into his bosom again, and plucked it out of his bosom, and it was turned again as his other flesh. So, if they will not believe you, nor obey the voice of the first sign, you should try second sign. But if they will not believe these two signs, nor obey your voice, then you should take water from the river, and pour it upon the dry land; and the water which you shall take out of the river will be turned to blood upon the dry land. But Moses said to the Lord, I am not eloquent, and never have been, and I am slow of speech and slow of tongue. Then the Lord said to him, who has given the mouth to man? Or who hath made the dumb, or the deaf, or him that sees, or the blind? Have not I the Lord? Therefore, go now, and I will be with your mouth, and will teach you what to say. But he said, Lord, send, I pray you, by the hand of him, whom you would send. Then the Lord was very angry with Moses, and said, do not I know Aaron your brother the Levite, that he himself shall speak? For he comes also, to meet you, and when he sees you, he will be glad in his heart. Therefore, you shall speak to him, and put the words in his mouth, and I will be with your mouth, and with his mouth, and will teach you what you ought to do. And he shall be your spokesman to the people; and he shall be, even he shall be as your mouth, and you shall be to him as God. Moreover, you shall take this rod in your hand, and perform miracles.

Comment: God does not get angry; it is against His nature. And again, how was this discussion between God and Moses captured. Also, it seems very strange that God has to coax and persuade Moses.

Exodus: Therefore, Moses went and returned to Jethro his father-in-law, and said to him, I pray you, let me go, and return to my brethren, which are in Egypt, and see whether are still alive. Then Jethro said to Moses, go in peace. (For the Lord had said to Moses in Midian, go, return to Egypt, for they are all dead who wanted about to kill you.) Then Moses took his wife and his sons, and put them on an ass, and returned toward the land of Egypt. And Moses took the rod of God in his hand. And the Lord said to Moses, when you have entered and come into Egypt again, see that you do all the wonders before Pharaoh, which I have put in your hand; but I will harden his heart, and he shall not let the people go. Then you shall say to Pharaoh, thus, says the Lord, Israel is my son, even my firstborn. Wherefore I say to you, let my son go, that he may serve me; if you refuse to let him go, I will slay your son, even your firstborn.

Comments: First of all, nowhere is it explained how Moses came to know that he was a Hebrew and not an Egyptian. Secondly, God would not harden Pharaoh's heart, that is something the person must do. Thirdly, Israel is not God's firstborn son, that is, God does not give preference to any people, nation, or race; God loves everyone equally and considers all people equal. Another example of the writers not understanding the nature of God. Lastly, God would not kill anyone, again the failure of the writers to understand the true nature of God. Incredulous and absurd statements.

Exodus: And as he was by the way in the inn, the Lord met him, and would have killed him. Then Zipporah took a sharp knife, and cut away the foreskin of her son, and cast it at his feet, and said, you are indeed a bloody husband to me. So, he departed from him. Then she said, O bloody husband (because of the circumcision.)

Comments: Absurd to state that 'the Lord met him (Moses) and would have killed him'. It implies that God was walking along the same road as Moses. God is a spirit and does not have a body. Also, God would not kill anyone, and this statement implies that God was going to kill Moses with His own hands – ridiculous. Again, the failure of the writers to understand the true nature of God. And Moses failed to circumcise his sons, and yet he is favored by God? Lastly, the wife of Moses circumcised her son because the most favored and obedient instrument of God, Moses, did not do so in spite of God's supposed commandment. What an absurd and unbelievable story!

Exodus: Then the Lord said to Aaron, go meet Moses in the wilderness. And he went and met him in the Mount of God and kissed him. Then Moses told Aaron all the words of the Lord, who had sent him, and all the signs wherewith he had charged him. So, went Moses and Aaron, and gathered all the Elders of the children of Israel. And Aaron told all the words, which the Lord had spoken to Moses, and he did the miracles in the sight of the people, and the people believed. And when they heard that the Lord had visited the children of Israel, and had looked upon their tribulation, they bowed down, and worshipped.

Comments: It seems that God supposedly spoke to Aaron as well. But how did God speak to Aaron and how did Aaron know that it was God who was speaking? Seems like fiction and provides for a good storyline.

Exodus: Moses and Aaron gave their message to Pharaoh, who did not let the people of Israel depart, but oppressed them more and more. They cried out to Moses and Aaron, and Moses complained to God. Then afterwards, Moses and Aaron went and said to Pharaoh, thus says the Lord God of Israel, let my people go, that they may celebrate a feast to me in the wilderness. And Pharaoh said, who is the Lord, that I should hear His voice, and let Israel go? I do not know the Lord, neither will I let Israel go. And they said, we worship the God of the Hebrews. We pray you, let us go three days journey in the desert, and sacrifice to the Lord our God, less He bring upon us the pestilence or sword. Then said the King of Egypt to Moses and Aaron, why cause the people to cease from their works? Get you to your burdens. Pharaoh said furthermore, behold, many people are now in the land, and you make them leave their work Therefore, Pharaoh gave the commandment the same day to the taskmasters of the people, and to their officers, saying, you shall give the people no more straw, to make brick (as in time past) but let them go and gather them straw themselves. Notwithstanding, lay upon them the number of bricks, which they made in time past, diminish nothing thereof, for they be idle, Therefore, they cry, saying, let us go to offer sacrifice unto our God. Lay more work upon the men, and cause them to do it, and let them not regard vain words.

Comments: Great story of good guys versus bad guys. One of the objectives of the writers is to denigrate the Egyptians and glorify the Jewish people. Poetic license and not true. Seems to be a recurring theme in the Pentateuch, conflict with the Egyptians.

Exodus: Then the officers of the children of Israel came, and cried to Pharaoh, saying, how do you deal with your servants? There is no straw given to your servants, and they say to us, Make brick! And your servants are beaten, and your people are blamed. But he said, you are too idle, and say, let us go to offer sacrifice to the Lord. Go now and work, for there will be no straw given to you, and you shall deliver the whole quota of brick. Then the officers of the children of Israel saw themselves in an evil case because it was said, you shall diminish nothing of your brick, nor of every day's task.

Comment: The writers of the Book of Exodus make Pharoah out to be a typical capitalist but was he since there is no historical evidence to substantiate these claims.

Exodus: And they met Moses and Aaron, which stood in their way as they came out from Pharaoh, to whom they said, The Lord looks upon you and judge, for you have made our savor to stink before Pharaoh and before his servants, in that you have put a sword in their hand to slay us. Wherefore Moses returned to the Lord, and said, Lord, why have You afflicted this people? Why have you sent me? For since I came to Pharaoh to speak in Your Name, he has vexed this people, and You have not delivered your people. Then the Lord said unto Moses, now, you will see, what I will do unto Pharaoh; for by a strong hand shall he let them go, and even be constrained to drive them out of his land. Moreover, God spoke to Moses, and said to him, I am the Lord. And I appeared to Abraham, to Isaac, and to Jacob by the Name of Almighty God, but by my Name Jehovah was I not known to them.

Comments: Totally fabricated by the writers. God has no favorite children, and the Jewish people are no more special in the eyes of God than any other people. And there is no covenant between God and the Jewish people. Total propaganda! And why has not God destroyed all those in history who have treated the Jewish people unjustly. God did not save the Jews from the Nazis. Of course, the Jewish people want God to destroy all of those who treat them unjustly. What about loving your neighbor as yourself?

Exodus: So, Moses told the children of Israel this, but they did not listen to Moses, because of anguish of spirit and for cruel bondage. Then the Lord spoke to Moses, saying, go speak to Pharaoh King of Egypt, that he let the children of Israel go out of his land. But Moses spoke to the Lord, saying, the children of Israel do not listen to me, how will the Pharaoh hear me, which is of uncircumcised lips? Then the Lord spoke to Moses and Aaron and charged them to go to the children of Israel and to Pharaoh King of Egypt, to bring the children of Israel out of the land of Egypt. These be the heads of their fathers' houses. The sons of Reuben the firstborn of Israel are Hanoch and Pallu, Hezron and Carmi, these are the families of Reuben. Also, the sons of Simeon: Jemuel and Jamin, and Ohad, and Jachin, and Zoar, and Shaul the son of a Canaanitish woman, these are the families of

Simeon. These also are the names of the sons of Levi in their generations Gershon and Kohath and Merari. The sons of Gershon were Libni and Shimi by their families. And the sons of Kohath were Amram and Izhar, and Hebron, and Uzziel. The sons of Merari were Mahali and Mushi. And Amram took Jochebed his father's sister to his wife, and she bore him Aaron and Moses. The sons of Izhar were Korah, and Nepheg, and Zichri. The sons of Uzziel were Mishael, and Elzaphan, and Sithri. Aaron took Elisheba daughter of Amminadab, who bore him Nadab, and Abihu, Eleazar and Ithamar. The sons of Korah were Assir, and Elkanah, and Abiasaph. Eleazar Aaron's son took him one of the daughters of Putiel to be his wife who which bore him Phinehas. These are the principal fathers of the Levites throughout their families. These are Aaron and Moses to whom the Lord said, bring the children of Israel out of the land of Egypt, according to their armies.

Comments: It certainly seems like a very small group of people. And how would the writers know their names 700 years later? The Jews supposedly stayed in Egypt for 430 years. And did all of the Hebrews leave Egypt or just some of them.

Exodus: Then Moses said to the Lord, Behold, I am of uncircumcised lips, and how shall Pharaoh hear me?

Comments: Does this imply that Moses was uncircumcised? Or are we to apply this to Pharaoh. But if we do, then does that mean that Pharaoh is incapable of understanding Moses because he is uncircumcised. And if so, are only circumcised men capable of understanding?

Exodus: God hardened Pharaoh's heart.

Comments: God would not do this. It is against His nature.

Exodus: You shall speak all that I commanded you, and Aaron your brother shall speak to Pharaoh so that he allows the children of Israel to go out of his land. But I will harden Pharaoh's heart and multiply my miracles and my wonders in the land of Egypt. And Pharaoh will not listen to you, that I may lay my hand upon Egypt, and bring out my armies, even my people, the children of Israel out of the land of Egypt, by great judgments. Then the Egyptians shall know that I am the Lord, when I stretch forth my hand upon Egypt, and bring out the children of Israel from among them.

Comments: This is an amazingly contrived paragraph with absolutely no truth to it. This is against God's nature. God would not harden the heart of Pharaoh, nor arbitrarily punish Egyptians, and God does not have any armies 'that I may lay my hand upon Egypt and bring out my armies'.

Exodus: So, Moses and Aaron did as the Lord commanded them. Now Moses was fourscore years old, and Aaron fourscore and three, when they spoke to Pharaoh. And the Lord spoke to Moses and Aaron, saying, if Pharaoh speaks to you, saying, show me a miracle, then you shall say to Aaron, take your rod, and cast it before Pharaoh, and it shall be turned into a serpent. Then went Moses and Aaron to the Pharaoh and did as the Lord had commanded; and Aaron cast forth his rod before Pharaoh and before his servants, and it was turned into a serpent. Then Pharaoh also, called for the wise men and sorcerers, and those charmers also, of Egypt did in like manner with their enchantments, for they cast down every man his rod, and they were turned into serpents. But Aaron's rod devoured their rods. So, Pharaoh's heart was hardened, and he did not listen to them, as the Lord had said. The Lord then said to Moses, Pharaoh's heart is obstinate, he refuses to let the people go. Go to Pharaoh in the morning, he will come forth to the water and you shall stand and meet him by the river's brink, and the rod, which was turned into a serpent, shall you take in your hand. And you shall say to him, The Lord God of the Hebrews has sent me to you, saying, let My people go, that they may serve Me in the wilderness. And behold, you would not hear.

Comments: God is the Lord of all people, not just the Hebrews. Extremely arrogant statement.

Exodus: Thus says the Lord, in this you shall know that I am the Lord: behold, I will smite with the rod that is in my hand upon the water that is in the river, and it shall be turned to blood. And the fish that are in the river shall die, and the river shall stink, and it shall grieve the Egyptians to drink of the water of the river.

Comment: God would not do this; it is against His nature. The Egyptians were God's people since all people are God's people. And the Egyptians were equal to the Hebrews since all people are equal in the eyes of God, all people are the children of God.

Exodus: The Lord then spoke to Moses, say to Aaron, take your rod, and stretch out your hand over the waters of Egypt, over their streams, over their rivers, and over their ponds, and over all pools of their waters, and they shall be blood, and there shall be blood throughout all the land of Egypt, both in vessels of wood, and of stone.

Comments: Truly absurd! God was speaking to Moses while Moses was in the presence of Aaron and the Pharaoh. And God would not change all drinkable water to blood impacting innocent children.

Exodus: Moses and Aaron did as the Lord commanded. And he lifted up the rod and smote the water that was in the river in the sight of Pharaoh, and in the sight of his servants, and all the water that was in the river, was turned into blood. And the fish that was in the river died, and the river stank, so, that the Egyptians could not drink of the water of the river. And there was blood throughout all the land of Egypt. And the enchanters of Egypt did likewise with their sorceries; and the heart of Pharaoh was hardened, so, that he did not listen to them, as the Lord had said. Then Pharaoh returned, and went again into his house, neither did this enter into his heart. All the Egyptians then dug round about the river for waters to drink, for they could not drink of the water of the river. And this continued fully seven days after the Lord had smitten the river.

Exodus: Afterward the Lord said to Moses, go to Pharaoh, and tell him, thus says the Lord, let My people go, that they may serve Me; And if you will not let them go, behold, I will smite all your country with frogs; and the river shall crawl full of frogs, which shall go up and come into your house, and into your chamber, where you sleep, and upon your bed, and into the house of your servants (slaves), and upon your people, and into your ovens, and into your kneading troughs. The frogs shall climb up upon you, and on your people, and upon all your servants. Also, the Lord said to Moses, say to Aaron, stretch out your hand with your rod upon the streams, upon the rivers, and upon the ponds, and cause frogs to come up upon the land of Egypt. Then Aaron stretched out his hand upon the waters of Egypt, and the frogs came up, and covered the land of Egypt. And the sorcerers did likewise with their sorceries and brought frogs up upon the land of Egypt. Then Pharaoh called for Moses and Aaron, and said, pray to the Lord, that he may take away the frogs from me, and from my people; and I will let the people go, that they may do sacrifice to the Lord.

Comment: God would not send plagues on the Egyptian people. This is the stuff of fairy tales. Again, such actions would be against God's nature.

Exodus: And Moses said to Pharaoh, concerning me, even command when I shall pray for you, and for you servants, and for your people, to destroy the frogs from you and from your houses, that they may remain in the river only. Then he said, tomorrow. And he answered, be it as you have said, that you may know, that there is none like the Lord our God. So, the frogs shall depart from you, and from your houses, and from your servants, and from your people; only they shall remain in the river. Then Moses and Aaron went out from Pharaoh; and Moses cried unto the Lord concerning the frogs, which he had sent to Pharaoh. And the Lord did according to the saying of Moses, so, the frogs died in the houses, in the towns, and in the fields. And they gathered them together by heaps, and the land stank of them.

Comments: When in all of recorded history, not fabricated history, has something similar happened? And why did God not do something similar during the holocaust? If God did not save people from the Holocaust, neither did He save the Jews from the Egyptians. For the Holocaust was far worse than supposed slavery under the Pharaoh. Obviously, this is all a total fabrication by the writers to instill nationalism and a false notion that the Jews are more esteemed by God than other people. All people are equal in God's eyes.

Exodus: But when Pharaoh saw that he had been given rest, he hardened his heart, and did not listen to them, as the Lord had said. Again, the Lord said to Moses, say to Aaron, stretch out your rod, and smite the dust of the earth, that it may be turned to lice throughout all the land of Egypt. And they did so; for Aaron stretched out his hand with his rod, and smote the dust of the earth, and lice came upon man and upon beast.

Comment: God would not send lice on children and animals; it is against His nature.

Exodus: All the dust of the earth was lice throughout all the land of Egypt. Now the enchanters saw and did likewise with their enchantments to bring forth lice, but they could not. So, the lice were upon man and upon beast. Then said the enchanters to Pharaoh, this is the finger of God. But Pharaoh's heart remained obstinate, and he hearkened not to them, as the Lord had said. Moreover, the Lord said to Moses, rise up early in the morning, and stand before Pharaoh (lo, he will come forth to the water) and say to him, thus says the Lord, let My people go, that they may serve Me. Else, if you will not let My people go, behold, I will send swarms of flies both upon you, and upon your servants, and upon your people, and into your houses; and the houses of the Egyptians shall be full of swarms of flies, and the ground also, whereon they are. But the land of Goshen, where my people are, will I cause to be wonderful in that day, so, that no swarms of flies shall be there, that you may know that I am the Lord in the middle of the earth. And I will make a deliverance of my people from your people. Tomorrow shall this miracle be. And the Lord did so. For there came great swarms of flies into the house of Pharaoh, and into his servant's houses, so, that through all the land of Egypt, the earth was corrupt by the swarms of flies.

Comments: Rather absurd! It is hard to believe that God would play such games with people, and this has never been repeated, that is, it only happened once if you believe this story. There are two lies perpetrated by the writers and editors of the book of Exodus and that is that this book lies (fabrications) and the second more egregious lie is that God is the author of the book of Exodus.

Exodus: Then Pharaoh called for Moses and Aaron, and said, go, do sacrifice to your God in this land. But Moses answered, it is not right for us to do so, for then we should offer to the Lord our God that, which is an abomination to the Egyptians. Can we sacrifice the abomination of the Egyptians before their eyes, and they not stone us? Let us go three days journey in the desert, and sacrifice unto the Lord our God, as he has commanded us. And Pharaoh said, I will let you go, that you may sacrifice to the Lord your God in the wilderness; but go not far away; pray for me. And Moses said, I will go out from you, and pray to the Lord, that the swarms of flies may depart from Pharaoh, from his servants, and from his people tomorrow; but let Pharaoh from henceforth deceive no more, in not suffering the people to sacrifice to the Lord. So, Moses went out from Pharaoh and prayed to the Lord. And the Lord did according to the saying of Moses, and the swarms of flies departed from Pharaoh, from his servants, and from his people, and there remained not one. Yet Pharaoh hardened his heart at this time also and did not let the people go.

Exodus Then the Lord said to Moses, go to Pharaoh, and tell him, thus says the Lord God of the Hebrews, let My people go, that they may serve me. But if you refuse to let them go, and will hold them still, behold, the hand of the Lord will upon your flock which is in the field, for upon the horses, upon the asses, upon the camels, upon the cattle, and upon the sheep shall be a mighty great disease. And the Lord shall do wonderfully between the beasts of Israel, and the beasts of Egypt, so, that there shall nothing die of all, that pertains to the children of Israel. And the Lord appointed a time, saying, Tomorrow the Lord shall finish this thing in this land. So, the Lord did this thing the next day, and all the cattle of Egypt died; but of the cattle of the children of Israel did not die. Then Pharaoh sent, and behold, there was not one of the cattle of the Israelites dead.

Comments: Again, these supposed actions by God are against the nature of God. God would not destroy animals for the mistakes of people. Pure fairytale material! Totally fabricated by the writers. While most people see the ridiculousness of these supposed chastisements and threats by God against the Egyptians, they force themselves to accept them because they have been told that this was written by God Himself, the greatest scam by the leaders of Judaism and Pauline Christianity in all of history.

Exodus: And the heart of Pharaoh was obstinate, and he did not let the people go. And the Lord said to Moses and to Aaron, take your handful of ashes of the furnace, and Moses shall sprinkle them toward the heaven in the sight of Pharaoh. And they shall be turned to dust in all the land of Egypt, and it shall be as a scab breaking out into blisters upon man, and upon beast, throughout all the land of Egypt. Then, they took ashes of the furnace, and stood before Pharaoh; and Moses sprinkled them toward the heaven, and there came a scab breaking out into blisters upon man, and upon beast. And the sorcerers could not stand before Moses, because of the scab, for the scab was upon the enchanters, and upon all the Egyptians.

Comments: God would not do this. He never has and never will torture non-guilty people and animals. God is incapable of torture, only humans are.

Exodus: And the Lord hardened the heart of Pharaoh, and he hearkened not to them, as the Lord had said to Moses. Also, the Lord said to Moses, rise up early in the morning, and stand before Pharaoh, and tell him, thus says the Lord God of the Hebrews, let My people go, that they may serve me. For I will at this time to send all my plagues upon your heart, and upon your servants, and upon your people, that you may know that there is none like Me in all the earth.

Comments: God does not have to prove Himself to anyone. Nor does God threaten anyone. That would indicate an imperfection on the part of God.

Exodus: For now, I will stretch out my hand, that I may smite you and your people with the pestilence, and you shall perish from the earth. And indeed, for this cause have I appointed you, to show My power in you, and to declare my Name throughout all the world. Behold, tomorrow this time I will cause to rain a mighty great hail, such as was not in Egypt since the foundation thereof was laid to this time. Go now, and gather the cattle, and all that you have in the field, for upon all the men, and the beasts, which are found in the field, and not brought home, the hail shall fall upon them, and they shall die.

Comments: Absurd! How can anyone believe that God Who is Love itself would destroy His children (all people are God's children) and innocent animals. How can anyone believe such nonsense and how can anyone follow religions that promote such nonsense.

Exodus: Such then as feared the word of the Lord among the servants of Pharaoh, made his servants and his cattle flee into the houses. But such as regarded not the word of the Lord, left his servants, and his cattle in the field. And the Lord said to Moses, stretch forth your hand toward heaven, that there may be hail in all the land of Egypt, upon man, and upon beast, and upon all the herbs of the field in the land of Egypt. Then Moses stretched out his rod toward heaven, and the Lord sent thunder and hail, and lightning upon the ground. And the Lord caused hail to rain upon the land of Egypt. So, there was hail, and fire mingled with the hail, so, grievous, as there was none throughout all the land of Egypt since it was a nation. And the hail smote throughout all the land of Egypt all that was in the field, both man and beast; also, the hail smote all the herbs of the field, and broke to pieces all the trees of the field. Only in the land of Goshen (where the children of Israel were) was no hail. Then Pharaoh sent and called for Moses and Aaron, and said to them, I have now sinned; the Lord is righteous, but I and my people are wicked. Pray you unto the Lord (for it is enough) that there be no more mighty thunders and hail, and I will let you go, and you shall tarry no longer. Then Moses said unto him, as soon as I am out of the city, I will spread my hands unto the Lord, and the thunder shall cease, neither shall there be any more hail, that you may know that the earth is the Lord's. As for you and your servants, I know before I pray you will fear before the face of the Lord God. (And the flax and the barley were smitten, for the barley was eared, and the flax was bolled. But the wheat and the rye were not smitten, for they were hid in the ground.) Then Moses went out of the city from Pharaoh, and spread his hands to the Lord, and the thunder and the hail ceased, neither rained it upon the earth. And when Pharaoh saw that the rain and the hail and the thunder were ceased, he sinned again, and hardened his heart, both he, and his servants. So, the heart of Pharaoh was hardened, neither would he let the children of Israel go, as the Lord had said by Moses.

Exodus: Again the Lord said unto Moses, Go to Pharaoh, for I have hardened his heart, and the heart of his servants, that I might work these my miracles in the midst of his realm, And that you may declare in the ears of your son, and of your son's son, what things I have done in Egypt, and My miracles, which I have done among them; that you may know that I am the Lord. Then came Moses and Aaron unto Pharaoh, and they said to him, Thus, says the Lord God of the Hebrews, how long wilt you refuse to humble yourself before me, let my people go, that they may serve Me. But if you refuse to let my people go, behold, tomorrow will I bring grasshoppers into your coasts. And they shall cover the face of the earth, that a man cannot see the earth. And they shall eat the residue which remains to you, and has escaped from the hail, and they shall eat all your trees that bud in the field. And they shall fill your houses, and all your servant's houses, and the houses of all the Egyptians, as neither your fathers, nor your father's fathers have seen, since the time they were upon the earth unto this day. So, he returned, and went out from Pharaoh. Then Pharaoh's servants said unto him, how long shall he be an offence to us? Let the men go, that they may serve the Lord their God. Will you first know that Egypt is destroyed? So, Moses and Aaron were brought again unto Pharaoh, and he said unto them, go, serve the Lord your God, but who are they that shall go? And Moses answered, we will go with our young and with our old; with our sons and with our daughters, with our sheep and with our cattle will we go, for we must celebrate a feast unto the Lord.

Comments: If the Jews were slaves in Egypt, how could they own sheep and cattle. Owning sheep and cattle implies that these Hebrews were not slaves which undermines the veracity of Exodus.

Exodus: And he said unto them, let the Lord so, be with you, as I will let you and your children go! Behold, for evil is before your face. It shall not be so! Now go you that are men, and serve the Lord, for that was your desire. Then they were thrust out from Pharaoh's presence. After, the Lord said to Moses, stretch out your hand upon the land of Egypt for the grasshoppers, that they may come upon the land of Egypt, and eat all the herbs of the land, even all that the hail hath left. Then Moses stretched forth his rod upon the land of Egypt, and the Lord brought an East wind upon the land all that day, and all that night; and in the morning the East wind brought the grasshoppers. So, the grasshoppers went up upon all the land of Egypt and remained in all quarters of Egypt, so, grievous were the grasshoppers, like never before or after them. For they covered all the face of the earth, so, that the land was dark; and they did eat all the herbs of the land, and all the fruits of the trees, which the hail had left, so, that there was no green thing left upon the trees, nor among the herbs of the field throughout all the land of Egypt. Therefore, Pharaoh called for Moses and Aaron, and said, I have sinned against the Lord your God, and against you. And now forgive me my sin only this once, and pray to the Lord your God, that he may take away from me this death only. Moses then went out from Pharaoh and prayed to the Lord. And the Lord turned a mighty strong West wind, and took away the grasshoppers, and violently cast them into the Red Sea, so, that there remained not one grasshopper in all the coasts of Egypt. But the Lord hardened Pharaoh's heart, and he did not let the children of Israel go. Again, the Lord said unto Moses, stretch out your hand toward heaven, that there may be upon the land of Egypt darkness, even darkness that may be felt. Then Moses stretched forth his hand toward heaven, and there was a black darkness in all the land of Egypt three days. No man saw another, neither rose up from the place where he was for three days, but all the children of Israel had light where they dwelled. Then Pharaoh called for Moses, and said, Go, serve the Lord; only your sheep and your cattle shall abide, and your children shall go with you. And Moses said, you must give us also, sacrifices, and burnt offerings that we may do sacrifice unto the Lord our God. Therefore, our cattle also, shall go with us; there shall not a hoof be left, for thereof must we take to serve the Lord our God. Neither do we know how we shall serve the Lord, until we come thither. (But the Lord hardened Pharaoh's heart, and he would not let them go.) And Pharaoh said unto him, Go away from me! Look you, see my face no more, for whenever you come in my sight, you shall die. Then Moses said, you have said correctly; from henceforth will I see your face no more. Now the Lord had said to Moses, yet will I bring one plague more upon Pharaoh, and upon Egypt; after that, he will let you go hence. When he lets you go, he shall at once chase you. Speak you now to the people, that every man requires of his neighbor, and every woman of her neighbor, jewels of silver, and jewels of gold. And the Lord gave the people favor in the sight of the Egyptians. Also, Moses was very great in the land of Egypt, in the sight of Pharaoh's servants, and in the sight of the people.) Also, Moses said, thus says the Lord, at midnight will I go out into the middle of Egypt. And all the firstborn in the land of Egypt shall die, from the firstborn of Pharaoh that sits on his throne, to the firstborn of the maidservant, that is at the mill, and all the firstborn of beasts. Then there shall be a great cry throughout all the land of Egypt, such as was never none like, nor shall be. But against none of the children of Israel shall a dog move his tongue, neither against man nor beast, that you may know that the Lord puts a difference between the Egyptians and Israel.

Comments: Absolutely contrary to the nature of God to kill innocent children (the firstborns) and animals. And God would not (put a difference between the Egyptians and the Israelites since both are His children and God does not have favorite children.

Exodus: And all these your servants shall come down to me, and fall before me, saying, get out, and all the people that are at your feet, and after this will I depart. So, he went out from Pharaoh very angry. And the Lord said to Moses, Pharaoh shall not hear you, that my wonders may be multiplied in the land of Egypt. So, Moses and Aaron did all these wonders before Pharaoh; but the Lord hardened Pharaoh's heart, and he did not let the children of Israel to go out from his land. Then the Lord spoke to Moses and to Aaron in the land of Egypt, saying, this month shall be for you the beginning of months; it shall be to you the first month of the year. Speak to all the congregation of Israel, saying, In the tenth of this month let every man take unto him a lamb, according to the house of the fathers, a lamb for a house. And if the household be too little for the lamb, he shall take his neighbor, which is next unto his house, according to the number of the persons; every one of you, according to his eating shall make your count for the lamb. Your lamb shall be without blemish, a male of a year old; you shall take it of the lambs, or of the kids. And you shall keep it until the fourteenth day of this month, then all the multitude of the Congregation of Israel shall kill it at eleven. After, they shall take of the blood, and strike it on the two posts, and on the upper door post of the houses where they shall eat it. And they shall eat the flesh that same night, roasted with fire; and unleavened bread with sour herbs they shall eat it. Eat not thereof raw, boiled nor sodden in water, but roast with fire, both his head, his feet, and his inner organs. And you shall reserve nothing of it until the morning; but that, which remains of it until the morrow, shall you burn with fire. And you shall eat it with your loins girded, your shoes on your feet, and your staves in your hands; and you shall eat it in haste. For it is the Lord's Passover.

Comments: God would never give such instructions, obviously fabricated by the writers and editors of Exodus.

Exodus: For I will pass through the land of Egypt the same night and will kill all the firstborn in the land of Egypt, both man and beast, and I will execute judgment upon all the gods of Egypt. I am the Lord. And the blood shall be a token for you upon the houses where you are; so, when I see the blood, I will pass over you, and the plague shall not be upon you to destruction, when I smite the land of Egypt. And this day shall be to you a remembrance, and you shall keep it a holy feast unto the Lord; throughout your generations, you shall keep it holy by an ordinance forever. Seven days shall you eat unleavened bread, and in any case, you shall put away leaven the first day out of your houses; for whosoever eats leavened bread from the first day until the seventh day, that person shall be cut off from Israel.

Comments: God would never kill innocent babies or animals. And later God supposedly gave Moses the 10 commandments one of which is 'you shall not kill'. How could God tell people not to kill when He kills. Impossible! God does not kill. And it is absurd to describe the event as God going from house to house killing the firstborn humans and animals! And God would not know an Egyptian home from a Jewish home except for blood on the door? Absolutely, absurd, and contrary to the nature of God. The writers had the same false understanding of God that virtually every other religion at the time had. And lastly, it would appear the Jewish homes were mixed among Egyptian homes, strange for supposed slaves. All of this is a fabricated myth.

It is amazing how people are like sheep who follow their leaders, political and religious, blindly even off a cliff. The Passover is a complete myth fabricated by the writers and Jewish leaders who commissioned the writers.

Exodus: And in the first day shall be a holy assembly, also, in the seventh day shall be a holy assembly for you; no work shall be done in them, except for that which every man must eat, that only you may do. You shall also, keep the feast of unleavened bread, for that same day I will bring your armies out of the land of Egypt; Therefore, you shall observe this day, throughout your posterity, by an ordinance forever. In the first month and the fourteenth day of the month in the evening, you shall eat unleavened bread to the one and twentieth day of the month I the evening. For seven days shall no leaven be found in your houses, for whoever eats leavened bread, that person shall be cut off from the Congregation of Israel, whether he be a stranger, or born in the land. You shall eat no leavened bread; but in all your habitations shall you eat unleavened bread.

Comments: God would not propose such rituals, this is a fabrication of the Jewish writers.

Exodus: Then Moses called all the Elders of Israel, and said to them, choose out and take you for every of your households a lamb, and kill for the Passover.

Comment: How would the Elders understand the word 'Passover'?

Exodus: And take a bunch of hyssops and dip it in the blood that is in the basin, and strike the lintel, and the door cheeks with the blood that is in the basin and let none of you go out at the door of his house, until the morning. For the Lord will pass by to smite the Egyptians; and when he sees the blood upon the lintel and on the two door cheeks, the Lord will pass over the door, and will not suffer the destroyer to come into your houses to plague you. Therefore, shall you observe this thing as an ordinance, both for you and your sons forever. And when you shall come into the land, which the Lord will give you, as he has promised, then you shall keep this service. And when your children ask you, what service is this you keep? Then you shall say, it is the sacrifice of the Lord's Passover, which passed over the houses of the children of Israel in Egypt, when he killed the Egyptians, and preserved our houses. Then the people bowed themselves and worshipped. So, the children of Israel went, and did as the Lord had commanded Moses and Aaron. Now at midnight, the Lord killed all the firstborns in the land of Egypt, from the firstborn of Pharaoh that sat on his throne, to the firstborn of the captive that was in prison, and all the firstborn of beasts. And Pharaoh rose up in the night, he, and all his servants, and all the Egyptians, and there was a great cry in Egypt, for there was no house where there was not one dead. And he called to Moses and to Aaron by night, and said, rise up, get you out from among my people, both you, and the children of Israel, and go serve the Lord as you have said. Also, take your sheep and your cattle as you have said, and depart, and bless me also. And the Egyptians did force the people because they would send them out of the land in haste, for they said, we will all die. Therefore, the people took their dough before it was leavened, even their dough bound in clothes upon their shoulders. And the children of Israel did according to the saying of Moses, and they asked of the Egyptians jewels of silver and jewels of gold, and raiment. And the Lord gave the people favor in the sight of the Egyptians, and they granted their request. So, they spoiled the Egyptians.

Comments: This passage implies that God smited or murdered the firstborn males of the Egyptians. God would not murder anyone because God loves everyone equally. And spoiled the Egyptians' or defrauded them? God would certainly not be a part of this, that is against His nature. "They asked of the Egyptians jewels of silver and jewels of gold, and raiment"?

Again, it is obvious that the writers and editors of the Book of Exodus has a very incorrect understanding of the nature of God. And God could not have been the author of such an incorrect and outrageous text about Himself.

Exodus: Then the children of Israel took their journey from Rameses to Succoth about six hundred thousand men of foot, beside children. And a great multitude of sundry sorts of people went out with them, and sheep, and beeves, and cattle in great abundance.

Comment: An amazing number of people given that they were only in Egypt for 430 years starting from a small number at the time of Joseph?

Exodus: And they baked the dough which they brought out of Egypt and made unleavened cakes; for it was not leavened, because they were thrust out of Egypt, neither could they tarry, nor prepare themselves food. So, the dwelling of the children of Israel, while they dwelled in Egypt, was four hundred and thirty years. And when the four hundred and thirty years were expired, even the selfsame day departed all the hosts of the Lord out of the land of Egypt. It is a night to be kept holy to the Lord because He brought them out of the land of Egypt; this is that night of the Lord, which all the children of Israel must keep throughout their generations. Also, the Lord said unto Moses and Aaron, this is the Law of the Passover: no stranger shall eat thereof. But every servant that is bought for money, when you have circumcised him, then shall he eat thereof. A stranger or a hired servant shall not eat thereof. In one house shall it be eaten, you shall carry none of the flesh out of the house, neither shall you break a bone thereof. All the Congregation of Israel shall observe it. But if a stranger dwell with you, and will observe the Passover of the Lord, let him circumcise all the males, that belong unto him, and then let him come and observe it; and he shall be as one that is born in the land. For no uncircumcised person shall eat thereof. One law shall be to him that is born in the land, and to the stranger that dwells among you.

Comments: Ridiculous claim that God distinguishes people based on circumcision. God does not care if a male has foreskin on his penis.

And God would not propose a celebration every year based on His (that is God) killing or rather murdering the firstborns of the Egyptians and their animals. Fabrication, fabrication, fabrication. Outrageous, outrageous, outrageous!

Exodus: And the Lord spoke to Moses, saying, sanctify to Me all the firstborn, that is, everyone that first opens the womb among the children of Israel, as well of man as of beast; for it is mine.

Comment: How is the firstborn to be preferred to the second born or third born. This is against the nature of God. God considers everyone equal. This appears to be an attempt to show that the cultural prejudice of Judaism for the firstborn was ordered by God.

Exodus: Then Moses said to the people, remember this day in the which you came out of Egypt, out of the house of bondage; for by a mighty hand the Lord brought you out from thence. Therefore, no leavened bread shall be eaten. This day come you out in the month of Abib. Now when the Lord hath brought you into the land of the Canaanites, and Hittites, and Amorites, and Hivites, and Jebusites (which he swore to your fathers, that he would give you, a land flowing with milk and honey) then you shall keep this service in this month. Seven days shall you eat unleavened bread, and the seventh day shall be the feast of the Lord. Unleavened bread shall be eaten seven days, and there shall no leavened bread be seen with you, nor be seen with you in all your quarters. And you shall show your son in that day, saying, this is done, because of that which the Lord did to me, when I came out of Egypt. And it shall be a sign to you upon your hand, and for a remembrance between your eyes, that the Law of the Lord may be in your mouth; for by a strong hand the Lord brought you out of Egypt. Keep therefore, this ordinance in his season appointed from year to year. And when the Lord shall bring you into the land of the Canaanites, as he swore unto you and to your fathers, and shall give it you. Then you shall set apart to the Lord all that first opens the womb, also, everything that first does open the womb, and comes forth of your beast; the males shall be the Lord's. But every first foal of an ass, you shall redeem with a lamb, and if you redeem him not, then you shall break his neck, likewise all the firstborn of man among your sons shall you buy out. And when your son shall ask you tomorrow, saying, what is this? you shall then say to him, with a mighty hand the Lord brought us out of Egypt, out of the house of bondage. For when Pharaoh was hard hearted against our departing, the Lord then killed all the firstborn in the land of Egypt, from the firstborn of man even to the firstborn of beast. Therefore, I sacrifice to the Lord all the males that first open the womb, but all the firstborn of my sons I redeem. And it shall be as a token upon your hand, and as frontlets between thine eyes, that the Lord brought us out of Egypt by a mighty hand.

Comments: God does not discriminate between males and females ('the males shall be the Lord's'). The statement 'the Lord then killed all the firstborn in the land of Egypt' shows the ignorance of the writers of the Book of Exodus regarding the nature of God. At the time of the writing of Exodus, the 5th Century BCE (Exodus was not written by the mythical or legendary figure of Moses), people ascribed human-like attributes to God including defects. While this ignorance can perhaps be excused for the writers in the 5Th Century, it cannot be applied to the leaders of Judaism and the Pauline Christian Church over the last 2000 years up to this day. And it is inexcusable for the current Jewish and Pauline Christine Church leaders not to condemn such passages in Exodus. Shame on them. They don't want to admit that Exodus and the rest of the Old Testament was not written by God.

Exodus: Now when Pharaoh had let the people go, God carried them not by the way of the Philistines' country, though it was nearer; (for God said, lest the people repent when they see war, and turn again to Egypt.) But God made the people to go about by the way of the wilderness of the Red Sea; and the children of Israel went up armed out of the land of Egypt… And the Lord went before them by day in a pillar of a cloud to lead them the way, and by night in a pillar of fire to give them light, that they might go both by day and by night. He took not away the pillar of the cloud by day, nor the pillar of fire by night from before the people.

Comments: Has this been done any time in history 'And the Lord went before them by day in a pillar of a cloud to lead them the way, and by night in a pillar of fire to give them light' or for that matter any similar type of action on the part of God? Never! Complete fabrication.

Exodus: Then the Lord spoke to Moses, saying, speak to the children of Israel, that they return and camp before Pihahiroth, between Migdol and the Sea, over against Baalzephon, about it shall you camp by the Sea. For Pharaoh will say of the children of Israel, they are tangled in the land, the wilderness has shut them in. And I will harden Pharaoh's heart that he shall follow after you; so, I will get Myself honor from Pharaoh, and from all his host, the Egyptians also, shall know that I am the Lord.

Comments: This passage implies that God was setting up the Egyptians so, that He could kill them in the Red Sea. Perhaps, the writers in the 5th century BCE thought that God had human imperfections like people thought in other countries during that time. But God does not have human imperfections, He could not set up and kill people, it is against His nature.

Exodus: And they did so. Then it was to the told the King of Egypt, that the people fled, and the heart of Pharaoh and of his servants was turned against the people, and they said, why have we this done, and have let Israel go out of our service? And he made ready his chariots and took his people with him. And took six hundred chosen chariots, and all the chariots of Egypt, and captains over every one of them. (For the Lord had hardened the heart of Pharaoh the King of Egypt, and he followed after the children of Israel, but the children of Israel went out with a high hand.) And the Egyptians pursued after them, and all the horses and chariots of Pharaoh, and his horsemen and his host overtook them camping by the Sea, beside Pihahiroth, before Baalzephon. And when Pharaoh drew nigh, the children of Israel lifted up their eyes, and behold, the Egyptians marched after them, and they were afraid, wherefore the children of Israel cried to the Lord. And they said to Moses, have you brought us to die in the wilderness, because there were no graves in Egypt? Why have you served us thus, to carry us out of Egypt? Did not we tell you this in Egypt, saying, let us be in rest, that we may serve the Egyptians? For it had been better for us to serve the Egyptians, than that we should die in the wilderness.

Comments: Does this imply that the majority of Jews did not want to leave Egypt, but it was only God and Moses that wanted them to leave? Rather bizarre!

Exodus: Then Moses said to the people, fear not, stand still, and behold the salvation of the Lord which he will show to you this day. For the

Egyptians whom you have seen this day, you shall never see them again. The Lord shall fight for you; Therefore, hold your peace.

Comments: Does this imply that Moses knew God's plan to kill the Egyptians and that Moses was okay with this plan? And Moses did not warn the Egyptians?

Exodus: And the Lord said to Moses, why do you cry to me? Speak to the children of Israel, that they go forward. And lift up your rod and stretch out your hand upon the Sea and divide it and let the children of Israel go on dry ground through the midst of the Sea. And I, behold, I will harden the heart of the Egyptians, that they may follow them, and I will get me honor upon Pharaoh, and upon all his host, upon his chariots, and upon his horsemen. Then the Egyptians shall know that I am the Lord, when I have gotten me honor upon Pharaoh, upon his chariots, and upon his horsemen. (And the Angel of God, which went before the host of Israel, removed, and went behind them; also, the pillar of the cloud went from before them, and stood behind them. And came between the camp of the Egyptians and the camp of Israel; it was both a cloud and darkness, it gave light by night, so, that all the night long the one came not at the other.) And Moses stretched forth his hand upon the Sea, and the Lord caused the Sea to run back by a strong East wind all the night, and made the Sea dry land, for the waters were divided. Then the children of Israel went through the midst of the Sea upon the dry ground, and the waters were a wall unto them on their right hand, and on their left hand. And the Egyptians pursued and went after them to the midst of the Sea, even all Pharaoh's horses, his chariots, and his horsemen. Now in the morning watch, when the Lord looked unto the host of the Egyptians, out of the fiery and cloudy pillar, he struck the host of the Egyptians with fear. For he took off their chariot wheels, and they drove them with much ado; so, that the Egyptians everyone said, I will flee from the face of Israel, for the Lord fights for them against the Egyptians. Then the Lord said to Moses, stretch your hand upon the Sea, that the waters may return upon the Egyptians, upon their chariots and upon their horsemen. Then Moses stretched forth his hand upon the Sea, and the Sea returned to his force early in the morning, and the Egyptians fled against it; but the Lord overthrew the Egyptians in the midst of the Sea. So, the water returned and covered the chariots and the horsemen, even all the host of Pharaoh that came into the Sea after them; there remained not one of them. But the children of Israel walked upon dry land through the midst of the Sea, and the waters were a wall unto them on their right hand, and on their left. Thus, the Lord saved Israel the same day out of the hand of the Egyptians, and Israel saw the Egyptians dead upon the Sea bank. And Israel saw the mighty power, which the Lord showed upon the Egyptians, so, the people feared the Lord, and believed the Lord, and his servant Moses.

Comments: People that read this and believe this do not understand the nature of God but like blind sheep believe what they are told. They cannot claim ignorance because God gave them an intellect to understand and a will to follow the truth. This is not the truth but fiction. This whole passage is a myth. It did not happen; it was made up to deceive the Jews into thinking that somehow, they are better than other and that they are special in the eyes of God. God has no favorites. Who believes that two babies, one Jewish and one non-Jewish when born that the Jewish baby is more special in the eyes of God? They are both God's children and equal.

Exodus: Then sang Moses and the children of Israel this song to the Lord, and said in this manner, I will sing to the Lord, for he has triumphed gloriously. The horse and him that rode upon him has been thrown into the Sea. The Lord is my strength and praise, and he is become my salvation; he is my God, and I will prepare him a tabernacle; he is my father's God, and I will exalt him. The Lord is a man of war, His Name is Jehovah. Pharaoh's chariots and his host hath he cast into the Sea; his chosen captains also, were drowned in the Red Sea. The depths have covered them, they sank to the bottom as a stone. Your right hand, O Lord, is glorious in power, your right hand, O Lord, hath bruised the enemy. And in your great glory you have overthrown them that rose against you; you send forth your wrath, which consumed them as the stubble. And by the blast of your nostrils the waters were gathered, the floods stood still as a heap, the depths congealed together in the heart of the Sea.

Comments: 'The Lord is a man of war'? God is the Prince of Peace not war. Anyone who delights and sings to the deaths of others is not favored in the eyes of God. Sick writers and sick religious leaders who directed the writers.

Exodus: The enemy said, I will pursue, I will overtake them, I will divide the spoil, my lust shall be satisfied upon them, I will draw my sword, my hand shall destroy them. You blew with your wind, the Sea covered them, they sank as lead in the mighty waters. Who is like to You, O Lord, among the gods!

Comment: Does this imply that the Jews believed in more than one God or were they Henotheists, individuals who believe in and worship one single, supreme god while accepting the existence or other lesser gods?

Exodus: Then Moses brought Israel from the Red Sea, and they went three days in the wilderness and found no water... Then the people murmured against Moses, saying, what shall we drink? And he cried unto the Lord, and the Lord showed him a tree, which when he had cast into the waters, the waters were sweet. There he made them an ordinance and a law, and there he proved them, And said, if you will diligently listen, O Israel, to the voice of the Lord your God, and will do that which is right in His sight, and will give ear to His commandments, and keep all His ordinances, then will I put none of these diseases upon you, which I brought upon the Egyptians; for I am the Lord that heals you. And they came to Elim, where were twelve fountains of water, and seventy palm trees, and they camped there by the waters.

Comments: Strange passage! God speaking and referring to Himself first in the third person and then in the first person. Such inconsistency implies the poor quality of writing and also that God did not write this.

Exodus: And the whole Congregation of the children of Israel murmured against Moses and against Aaron in the wilderness. For the children of Israel said to them, oh that we had died by the hand of the Lord in the land of Egypt, when we sat by the flesh pots, when we ate bread our bellies full; for you have brought us out into this wilderness, to kill this whole company with famine.

Comments: The statement 'when we sat by the flesh pots, when we ate bread our bellies full' implies that the Hebrews while in Egypt were well fed. Does that mean that they were not really slaves of the Egyptians?

Exodus: Then said the Lord to Moses, I will rain from heaven to you, and the people shall go out, and gather that which is sufficient for every day, that I may prove them, whether they will walk in my Law or not. But the sixth day they shall prepare that, which they shall bring home, and it shall be twice as much as they gather daily. Then Moses and Aaron said unto all the children of Israel. At evening, you shall know, that the Lord brought you out of the land of Egypt. And in the morning, you shall see the glory of the Lord, for he has heard your complaints against the Lord, and what are we that you have murmured against us? Again, Moses said, at evening shall the Lord give you flesh to eat, and in the morning your fill of bread; for the Lord hath heard your murmurings, which you murmur against Him. For what are we? Your murmurings are not against us, but against the Lord.

Comments: The writers are trying to create the basis of Judaism as though its beliefs, rules and practices supposedly came from God.

Exodus: You have seen what I did to the Egyptians, and how I carried you upon eagles' wings, and have brought you to me. Now, therefore, if you will hear my voice indeed, and keep my covenant, then you shall be My chief treasure above all people, though all the earth be mine. You shall be to me also, a kingdom of Priests, and a holy nation. These are the words which you shall speak to the children of Israel.

Comment: God has no special people; all people are equal in the eyes of God. It is against His nature to have favorites. Again, the writers are trying to create the basis of Judaism as though its beliefs, rules and practices supposedly came from God. Judaism is a man-made religion.

Exodus: Moses then came and called for the Elders of the people, and proposed to them all these things, which the Lord commanded him. And the people answered all together, and said, all that the Lord has commanded, we will do. And Moses reported the words of the people to the Lord.

Comment: Would not God know how the Jews responded? God knows all things; it is His nature. Another example of the writers of Exodus not understanding the nature of God and the fact that Exodus was not written by God but by ignorant men.

Exodus: And the Lord said to Moses, I come to you in a thick cloud, that the people may hear while I talk with you, and that they may also, believe you forever. (For Moses had told the words of the people to the

Lord). Moreover, the Lord said to Moses, go to the people, and sanctify them today and tomorrow, and let them wash their clothes. And let them be ready on the third day, for the third day the Lord will come down in the sight of all the people upon mount Sinai. And you shall set marks unto the people round about, saying, take heed to yourselves that you go not up to the mount, nor touch the border of it; whoever touches the mount, will surely die. No hand shall touch it, but he shall be stoned to death, or stricken through with darts; whether it be beast or man, he shall not live.

Comment: Does this imply that God will kill anyone who enters the mount, absurd? God would never do that nor say such a thing.

Exodus: When the horn blows long, they shall come up into the mountain. Then Moses went down from the mount to the people, and sanctified the people, and they washed their clothes. And he said to the people, be ready on the third day, and come not with your wives.

Comments: What does washing their clothes have to do with the narrative? And 'come not with your wives' mean? Is this just another example of the cultural chauvinism of the Jews against women?

Exodus: And the third day, when it was morning, there was thunder and lightnings, and a thick cloud upon the mount, and the sound of the trumpet exceeding loud, so, that all the people that were in the camp was afraid. Then Moses brought the people out of the tents to meet with God, and they stood in the nether part of the mount. And mount Sinai was on smoke, because the Lord came down upon it in fire, and the smoke thereof ascended, as the smoke of a furnace, and all the mount trembled exceedingly. And when the sound of the trumpet blew long, and waxed louder and louder, Moses spoke, and God answered him by voice. (For the Lord came down upon mount Sinai on the top of the mount.) And when the Lord called Moses up to the top of the mount, Moses went up. Then the Lord said to Moses, go down, charge the people, that they break not their bounds, to go up to the Lord to gaze, less many of them perish. And let the Priests also, which come to the Lord be sanctified, less the Lord destroy them. And Moses said to the Lord, the people cannot come up into the mount Sinai, for you have charged us, saying, set marks on the mountain, and sanctify it. And the Lord said to him, go down, and come up, you, and

Aaron with you, but do not let the Priests and the people break their bounds to come up unto the Lord, lest He destroy them. So, Moses went down unto the people, and told them.

Comment: Again, does this imply that God will kill anyone who enters the mount, absurd? God would never do that nor say such a thing.

Exodus: Then God spoke all these words, saying, I am the Lord your God, which have brought you out of the land of Egypt, out of the house of bondage. You shall have none other gods before Me. You shall make no graven image, neither any similitude of things that are in heaven above, neither that are in the earth beneath, nor that are in the waters under the earth. You shall not bow down to them, neither serve them; for I am the Lord your God, a jealous God, visiting the iniquity of the fathers upon the children, upon the third generation and upon the fourth of them that hate me. And, showing mercy to you to them that love me, and keep my commandments. You shall not take the Name of the Lord your God in vain, for the Lord will not hold him guiltless that takes his Name in vain. Remember the Sabbath day, to keep it holy. Six days shall you labor and do all your work. But the seventh day is the Sabbath of the Lord your God, in it you shall not do any work, you, nor your son, nor your daughter, your manservant, nor your maid, nor your beast, nor your stranger that is within your gates. For in six days the Lord made the heaven and the earth, the sea, and all that in them is, and rested the seventh day, therefore, the Lord blessed the Sabbath day, and hallowed it. Honor your father and your mother, that your days may be prolonged upon the land, which the Lord your God gives you. You shall not kill. You shall not commit adultery. You shall not steal. You shall not bear false witness against your neighbor. You shall not covet your neighbor's house, neither shall you covet your neighbor's wife, nor his manservant, nor his maid, nor his ox, nor his ass, neither anything that is your neighbor's.

Comments: God gave to all humans the precepts of the Ten Commandments through His Natural Law. God did not give the so-called Ten Commandments to Moses according to the above narrative, that is a myth. This is part of the attempt by the writers to create Judaism and also, as a segway to all of the laws and rules in Leviticus. Could it be that the writers of Exodus were also the writers of Leviticus?

Exodus: And all the people saw the thunder and the lightnings, and the sound of the trumpet, and the mountain smoking; and when the people saw it, they fled and stood far off. And they said to Moses, talk to, and we will hear, but do not let God talk to us, less we die. Then Moses said to the people, fear not, for God is come to prove you, and that His fear may be before you, that you sin not. So, the people stood afar off, but Moses drew near unto the darkness where God was. And the Lord said unto Moses, you shall say to the children of Israel, you have seen that I have talked with you from heaven. You shall not make therefore, with me gods of silver, nor gods of gold; you shall make you none. An altar of earth you shall make to me, and thereon shall offer your burnt offerings, and your peace offerings, your sheep, and your oxen; in all places, where I shall put the remembrance of my Name, I will come to you, and bless you. But if you will make me an altar of stone, you shall not build it of hewn stones, for if you lift up your tool upon them, you have polluted them. Neither shall you go up by steps to my altar, that your filthiness be not discovered thereon.

Comments: Fabrication by the writers who were creating Judaism and wanted the reader to think or believe that rules, laws, and practices that were being created by the writers were actually dictated by God. Absolute nonsense.

Exodus: Now these are the laws, which you shall set before them, if you buy a Hebrew servant, he shall serve six years, and in the seventh he shall go out free for nothing. If he came himself alone, he shall go out himself alone; if he were married, then his wife shall go out with him. If his master has given him a wife, and she hath born him sons or daughters, the wife and her children shall be her masters, but he shall go out himself alone. But if the servant says, I love my master, my wife, and my children, I will not go out free. Then his master shall bring him to the Judges, and set him to the door, or to the post, and his master shall bore his ear through with a awl, and he shall serve him forever. Likewise, if a man sells his daughter to be a servant, she shall not go out as the menservants do. If she please not her master, who hath betrothed her to himself, then shall he cause to buy her. He shall have no power to sell her to a strange people, seeing he despised her.

Comments: Again, fabrications by the writers who were creating Judaism and wanted the reader to think or believe that rules, laws, and practices that were being created by the writers were actually dictated by God. Absolute nonsense. God would never give rules regarding slaves since in the eyes of God everyone is equal and there is no right to own some else. And the idea that 'if a man sells his daughter to be a servant' is certainly not of or from God. Anyone who accepts this is as ignorant of the nature of God as the writers of Exodus.

Exodus: But if he has betrothed her to his son, he shall deal with her according to the custom of the daughters. If he takes himself another wife, he shall not diminish her food, her raiment, and recompense of her virginity. And if he does not do these three things to her, then she shall go out free, paying no money. He that hits a man, and he dies, shall die the death. And if a man has not laid wait, but God has offered him into his hand, then I will appoint you a place where he shall flee. But if a man come presumptuously upon his neighbor to slay him with guile, you shall take him from My altar, that he may die. Also, he that strikes his father or his mother, shall die the death. And he that steals a man, and sells him, if it be found with him, shall die the death. And he that curses his father or his mother, shall die the death. When men also, strive together, and one strike another with a stone, or with the fist, and he does not die, but lies in bed. If he rises again and walks without a staff, then shall he that stroke him go quit, save only he shall bear his charges for his resting, and shall pay for his healing. And if a man strikes his servant, or his maid with a rod, and he die under his hand, he shall be surely punished. But if he continues a day or two days, he shall not be punished; for he is his money. Also, if men strive and hurt a woman with child, so, that her child depart from her, and death follow not, he shall be surely punished, according as the woman's husband shall appoint him, or he shall pay as the Judges determine. But if death follow, then you shall pay life for life, eye for eye, tooth for tooth, hand for hand, foot for foot, burning for burning, wound for wound, stripe for stripe. And if a man strikes his servant in the eye, or his maid in the eye, and hath perished it, he shall let him go free for his eye. Also, if he strikes out his servant's tooth, or his maid's tooth, he shall let him go out free for his tooth. If an ox gores a man or a woman, and they die, the ox shall be stoned to death, and his flesh shall not be eaten; but the owner of the ox shall go quit. If the ox were wont to push in times past, and it hath been told his master, and he hath not kept him, and after he kills a man or a woman, the ox shall be stoned, and his owner shall die also. If there be set to him a sum of money, then he shall pay the ransom of his life, whatsoever shall be laid upon him. Whether he hath gored a son, or gored a daughter, he shall be judged after the same manner. If the ox gores a servant or a maid, he shall give unto their master thirty shekels of silver, and the ox shall be stoned. And when a man shall open a well, or when he shall dig a pit and cover it not, and an ox or an ass fall therein. The owner of the pit shall make it good, and give money to the owner thereof, but the dead beast shall be his. And if a man's ox hurt his neighbor's ox and he dies, then they shall sell the live ox, and divide the money thereof, and the dead ox also, they shall divide. Or if it be known that the ox has used to push in times past, and his master hath not kept him, he shall pay ox for ox, but the dead shall be his own.

Comments: None of this is from God, totally fabricated by the writers in the process of creating Judaism. Very extreme fabricated morality. Certainly, inconsistent with 'love your neighbor as yourself' and forgiving someone who harms you. An eye for eye, tooth for tooth, hand for hand, foot for foot, burning for burning, wound for wound, stripe for stripe is against the nature of God and opposed to how God wants people to treat each other.

Exodus: If a man steals an ox or a sheep, and kills it or sell it, he shall restore five oxen for the ox, and four sheep for the sheep. If a thief be found breaking in, and be struck that he dies, no blood shall be shed for him. But if it be in the daylight, blood shall be shed for him, for he should make full restitution. If he does not have the means to pay, then should he be sold for his theft. If the theft be found with him alive, (whether it be ox, ass, or sheep) he shall restore the double. If a man does hurt to a field, or vineyard, and puts in his beast to feed in another man's field, he shall recompense of the best of his own field, and of the best of his own vineyard. If fire break out, and catch in the thorns, and the stacks of corn, or the standing corn, or the field be consumed, he that kindled the fire shall make full restitution. If a man delivers his neighbor money or stuff to keep, and it be stolen out of his house, if the thief be found, he shall pay double. If the thief be not found, then the master of the house shall be brought unto the Judges to swear, whether he hath put his hand on his neighbor's goods, or not. In all manner of trespass, whether it be for oxen, for ass, for sheep, for raiment, or for any manner of lost thing, which another person challenges to be his, the cause of both parties shall come before the Judges, and whom the Judges condemn, he shall pay the double unto his neighbor.

Comments: The writers are attempting to create the theocratic government of Judaism (judges) as though it was designed by God. It was not.

Exodus: If a man delivers to his neighbor to keep ass, or ox, or sheep, or any beast, and it dies, or is hurt, or taken away by enemies, and no man sees it. An oath of the Lord shall be between them, that he has not put his hand to his neighbor's goods, and the owner of it shall take the oath, and he shall not make it good. But if it be stolen from him, he shall make restitution to the owner thereof. If it be torn in pieces, he shall bring record, and shall not make that good, which is devoured. And if a man borrows from his neighbor, and it be hurt, or else die, the owner thereof not being by, he shall surely make it good. If the owner thereof be by, he shall not make it good; for if it be a hired thing, it came for his hire. And if a man entices a maid that is not betrothed, and lies with her, he shall endow her, and take her to be his wife. If her father refuses to give her to him, he shall pay money according to the dowry of virgins. You shall not suffer a witch to live. Whoever lies with a beast, shall die the death. He that offers to any gods, except to the Lord only, shall be slain. Moreover, you shall not do injury to a stranger, neither oppress him, for you were strangers in the land of Egypt. You shall not trouble any widow, nor fatherless child. If you vex or trouble such, and so, cries to me, I will surely hear his cry. Then shall my wrath be kindled, and I will kill you with the sword, and your wives shall be widows, and your children fatherless.

Comments: God does not become angry ('my wrath be kindled') and God does not kill ('I will kill you with the sword'), that is against His nature.

Exodus: If you lend money to my people, that is, to the poor with you, you shall not be as a usurer to him, you shall not oppress him with usury.

Comment: Does this imply that God does not allow usury to a fellow Jew, but it is allowed for a non-Jew? God's Natural Law does not allow usury for any people.

Exodus: If you take your neighbor's raiment to pledge, you shall restore it to him before the sun go down, and that is his only covering; and this is his garment for his skin. Wherein shall he sleep? Therefore, when he cries to me, I will hear him, for I am merciful. You shall not complain about Judges, neither speak evil of the ruler of your people.

Comment: God's Natural Law dictates that the natural type of government is a democracy which was unknown to the writers/creators of Judaism.

Exodus: Your abundance and your liquor shall you not keep back. The firstborn of your sons shall you give me. Likewise, shall you do with your oxen and with your sheep. Seven days it shall be with his dam, and the eighth day you shall give it me. You shall be a holy people to me, neither shall you eat any flesh that is torn of beasts in the field; you shall cast it to the dog.

Comment: Judaism being created through the writers of Exodus.

Exodus: You shall not receive a false tale, neither shall you put your hand with the wicked, to be a false witness. You shall not follow a multitude to do evil, neither agree in a controversy to decline after many and overthrow the truth. You shall not esteem a poor man in his cause. If you meet your enemy's ox, or his ass going astray, you shall bring him to him again. If you see thine enemy's ass lying under his burden, wilt you cease to help him? You shall help him up again with it. You shall not overthrow the right of your poor in his suit. You shall keep you far from a false matter, and you shall not slay the innocent and the righteous, for I will not justify a wicked man. You shall take no gift, for the gift blinds the wise, and perverts the words of the righteous. You shall not oppress a stranger, for you know the heart of a stranger, seeing you were strangers in the land of Egypt. Moreover, six years you shall sow your land, and gather the fruits thereof. But the seventh year you shall let it rest and lie still, that the poor of your people may eat; and what they leave, the beasts of the field shall eat. In like manner you shall do with your vineyard, and with thine olive trees. Six days you shall do your work, and in the seventh day you shall rest, that thine ox, and thine ass may rest, and the son of your maid, and the stranger may be refreshed. And you shall take heed to all things that I have said to you, and you shall make no mention of the name of other gods, neither shall it be heard from your mouth. Three times you shall keep a feast to me in the year. You shall keep the feast of unleavened bread; you shall eat unleavened bread seven days, as I commanded you, in the season of the month of Abib, for in it you came out of Egypt. And none shall appear before me empty. The feast also, of the harvest of the first fruits of your labors, which you have sown in the field; and the feast of gathering fruits in the end of the year, when you have gathered in your labors out of the field. These three times in the year shall all your men children appear before the Lord Jehovah. You shall not offer the blood of my sacrifice with leavened bread; neither shall the fat of my sacrifice remain until the morning. The first of the first fruits of your land, you shall bring into the house of the Lord your God. You shall you not seethe a kid in his mother's milk. Behold, I send an Angel before you, to keep you in the way, and to bring you to the place which I have prepared. Beware of him, and hear his voice, and provoke him not; for he will not spare your misdeeds, because my Name is in him. But if you hearken unto his voice, and do all that I speak, then I will be an enemy unto thine enemies, and will afflict them that afflict you. For my Angel shall go before you, and bring you to the Amorites, and the Hittites, and the Perizzites, and the Canaanites, the Hivites, and the Jebusites, and I will destroy them. You shall not bow down to their gods, neither serve them, nor do after the works of them; but utterly overthrow them and break in pieces their images. For you shall serve the Lord your God, and he shall bless your bread and your water, and I will take all sickness away from the midst of you. There shall none cast their fruit, nor be barren in your land; the number of your days will I fulfill. I will send my fear before you and will destroy all the people among whom you shall go, and I will make all thine enemies turn their backs unto you. And I will send hornets before you, which shall drive out the Hivites, the Canaanites, and the Hittites from your face. I will not cast them out from your face in one year, lest the land grow to a wilderness, and the beasts of the field multiply against you. By little and little I will drive them out from your face, until you increase, and inherit the land. And I will make your coasts from the Red Sea to the sea of the Philistines, and from the desert to the river; for I will deliver the inhabitants of the land into your hand, and you shall drive them out from your face. You shall make no covenant with them, nor with their gods. Neither shall they dwell in your land, lest they make you sin against me; for if you serve their gods, surely it shall be your destruction.

Comments: None of this came from God. Again, these rules were created by the creators of Judaism, and they wanted to deceive and coerce the Jewish People into accepting these rules supposedly because they came from God. But these rules were created by men, not God!

Exodus: Moses was forty days and forty nights in the Mountain. Now the Lord said to Moses, come up to the Lord, you, and Aaron, Nadab, and Abihu, and seventy of the Elders of Israel, and you shall worship from far off. And Moses himself alone shall come near to the Lord, but they shall not come near, neither shall the people go up with him. Afterward Moses came and told the people all the words of the Lord, and all the Laws; and all the people answered with one voice, and said, All the things which the Lord has said, will we do. And Moses wrote all the words of the Lord, and rose up early, and set up an altar under the mountain, and twelve pillars according to the twelve tribes of Israel. And he sent young men of the children of Israel, which offered burnt offerings of beef, and sacrificed peace offerings to the Lord. Then Moses took half of the blood, and put it in basins, and half of the blood he sprinkled on the altar. After he took the book of the covenant, and read it in the audience of the people, who said, all that the Lord has said, we will do, and be obedient. Then Moses took the blood, and sprinkled it on the people, and said, behold, the blood of the covenant, which the Lord has made with you concerning all these things.

Comments: God does not want sacrifices of animals or people. And how many so-called covenants did God supposedly make with the Jewish people?

Exodus: Then went up Moses, and Aaron, Nadab, and Abihu, and seventy of the Elders of Israel. And they saw the God of Israel, and under his feet was as it were a work of a Sapphire stone, and as the very heaven when it is clear. And upon the nobles of the children of Israel he laid not his hand; also, they saw God, and did eat and drink.

Comment: They saw God? God is a spirit or intellect Who has no body or physical attributes to see. Obviously, the writers had an incorrect understanding of God. And God would not be standing on a sapphire. What a false description!

Exodus: And the Lord said to Moses, come up to me into the mountain, and be there, and I will give you tablets of stone, and the Law, and the Commandment, which I have written, for to teach them.

Comments: The writers of Exodus are trying to imply that their laws and the Ten Commandments came directly from God. This is fiction and a marketing tool to coerce the reader to accept their writings, their concocted rules, and their concocted laws.

Exodus: Then Moses rose up, and his minister Joshua, and Moses went up into the mountain of God. And he said to the Elders, stay here, until we come again unto you. And behold, Aaron, and Hur are with you; whoever has any matters, let him come to them. Then Moses went up to the mount, and the cloud covered the mountain. And the glory of the Lord abode upon mount Sinai, and the cloud covered it six days; and the seventh day he called unto Moses out of the midst of the cloud. And the sight of the glory of the Lord was like consuming fire on the top of the mountain, in the eyes of the children of Israel. And Moses entered into the midst of the cloud and went up to the mountain; and Moses was in the mount forty days and forty nights.

Comment: Extraordinary, fabricated narrative with continued use of the special numbers of seven and forty. Also, the statement regarding Moses being up on the mountain for forty days was repeated twice. Was Moses supposedly up on the mountain twice or is this an error because there were multiple writers of Exodus?

Exodus: Then the Lord spoke to Moses, saying, speak to the children of Israel, that they receive an offering for me; of every man, whose heart giveth it freely, you shall take the offering for me. And this is the offering which you shall take of them, gold, and silver, and brass, And blue silk, and purple, and scarlet, and fine linen, and goat's hair, And rams' skins colored red, and the skins of badgers, and the wood Shittim, Oil for the light, spices for anointing oil, and for the perfume of sweet savor, Onyx stones, and stones to be set in the Ephod, and in the breastplate. Also, they shall make me a Sanctuary, that I may dwell among them.

Comments: God does not want gifts from people and God would not dictate what gifts He wants from people. God is not selfish and self-serving. Another example of the writers not understanding the nature of God but rather considering the selfish characteristics of human kings.

Exodus: According to all that I show you, even so, shall you make the form of the Tabernacle, and the fashion of all the instruments thereof. They shall also, make an Ark of Shittim wood, two cubits and a half long, and a cubit and a half broad, and a cubit and a half high. And you shall overlay it with pure gold inside and outside, and they shall also, make upon it a crown of gold. And you shall cast four rings of gold for it, and put them in the four corners thereof, that is, two rings shall be on the one side of it, and two rings on the other side thereof. And you shall make bars of Shittim wood and cover them with gold. Then you shall put the bars in the rings by the sides of the Ark, to bear the Ark with them. The bars shall be in the rings of the Ark; they shall not be taken away from it. So, you shall put in the Ark the Testimony, which I shall give you. Also, you shall make a Mercy seat of pure gold, two cubits and a half long, and a cubit and a half broad. And you shall make two Cherubims of gold; of work beaten out with the hammer shall you make them at the two ends of the Mercy seat. And the one Cherub shall you make at the one end, and the other Cherub at the other end; of the matter of the Mercy seat shall you make the Cherubims, on the two ends thereof. And the Cherubims shall stretch their wings on high, covering the Mercy seat with their wings, and their faces one to another; to the Mercy seat ward shall the faces of the Cherubims be. And you shall put the Mercy seat above upon the Ark, and in the Ark you shall put the Testimony, which I will give you, And there I will declare myself to you, and from above the Mercy seat between the two Cherubims, which are upon the Ark of the Testimony, I will tell you all things which I will give you in commandments to the children of Israel. You shall also, make a Table of Shittim wood, of two cubits long, and one cubit broad, and a cubit and a half high. And you shall cover it with pure gold and make thereto a crown of gold round about. You shall also, make unto it a border of four fingers round about; and you shall make a golden crown round about the border thereof. After, you shall make for it four rings of gold, and shall put the rings in the four corners that are in the four feet thereof. Over the border shall the rings be for places for bars, to bear the Table. And you shall make the bars of Shittim wood, and shall overlay them with gold, that the Table may be borne with them. You shall make also, dishes for it, and incense cups for it, and coverings for it, and goblets, wherewith it shall be covered, even of fine gold shall you make them. And you shall set upon the Table shewbread before me continually. Also, you shall make a Candlestick of pure gold; of work beaten out with the hammer shall the Candlestick be made, his shaft, and his branches, his bowls, his knops, and his flowers shall be of the same. Six branches also, shall come out of the sides of it: three branches of the Candlestick out of the one side of it, and three branches of the Candlestick out of the other side of it. Three bowls like unto almonds, one knop and one flower in one branch, and three bowls like almonds in the other branch, one knop and one flower; so, throughout the six branches that come out of the Candlestick. And in the shaft of the Candlestick shall be four bowls like unto almonds, his knops, and his flowers. And there shall be a knop under two branches made thereof, and a knop under two branches made thereof, and a knop under two branches made thereof, according to the six branches coming out of the Candlestick. Their knops and their branches shall be thereof; all this shall be one beaten work of pure gold. And you shall make the seven lamps thereof; and the lamps thereof shall you put thereon, to give light toward that which is before it. Also, the snuffers and snuff dishes shall be of pure gold. Of a talent of fine gold shall you make it with all these instruments. Look therefore, that you make them after their fashion, that was showed you in the mountain.

Comments: Is this Moses speaking or God speaking? It certainly cannot be God. God would not specify such exact requirements for worshipping Him. God is not self-serving and only wishes to be served by people serving other people.

What fabrication! Again, God is not self-serving and selfish. He would never tell people to worship Him in such a specific way. In fact, God does not want to be worshipped. Rather, He wants people, His children, to get along – no wars, no fighting, helping each other. God is Love. Love is patient and kind; love does not envy or boast; it is not arrogant or rude. It does not insist on its own way; is not selfish or self-serving; it does not rejoice at wrongdoing but rejoices with the truth.

Again, God does not want to be worshipped. Like a parent, God only wants what is good for His children and He does not want to be praised.

THE 613 MITZVOT COMMANDMENTS

The 613 mitzvot commandments were created by extracting precepts from the Torah. They did not come from God. It was an attempt by Jewish leadership to provide a more formal structure to Judaism. They can be divided into positive commandments and negative commandments. Many of these commandments are not followed by Jews because they violate the Natural Law. These laws or rules are part of the man-made creation of the religion of Judaism. Below are some of these rules that require comments because of their inconsistency with the Natural Law and the nature of God.

• Not to blaspheme, the penalty for which is death.

Comments: Rather extreme! Seems to contradict the fifth of the Ten Commandments, 'you shall not kill.'

• To love God.

• To fear Him reverently.

Comment: Love of God and fear of God are incompatible.

- Not to put the word of God to the test.

- To love other Jews.

- To love converts.

- Not to hate fellow Jews

Comment: People should cleave or love all people not just those who know God. And all people should be loved not just other Jews.

- To circumcise the male offspring.

Comment: As said earlier, this commandment does not come from God. God does not care whether a male has foreskin on his penis, Absurd.

- To burn a city that has turned to idol worship.

- Not to rebuild it as a city.

- Not to derive benefit from it.

Comment: To burn a city with children and babies – God would not command this.

- Not to missionize an individual to idol worship.

- Not to love the missionary.

- Not to cease hating the missionary.

- Not to save the missionary.

- Not to say anything in his defense.

- Not to refrain from incriminating him.

Comment: God does not command hate.

- To put tzitzit on the corners of clothing.

- To bind tefillin on the head.

- To bind tefillin on the arm.

- To affix the mezuzah to the doorposts and gates of your house.

Comment: What does this have to do with God? This is certainly not from God. God does not care what a person wears or what is on the doorposts and gates of your house.

- Not to listen to a false prophet.

- Not to be afraid of killing the false prophet.

Comment: Again, rather extreme! Seems to contradict the fifth of the Ten Commandments, 'you shall not kill.'

- Not to erect a pillar in a public place of worship.

- Not to bow down on smooth stone.

- Not to plant a tree in the Temple courtyard.

Comment: What does this have to do with serving God. God is love, and serving God is serving and propagating love of neighbor in word and act.

- To love all human beings who are of the covenant.

Comment: Does this imply there is no obligation to love all human beings, that is human beings who are not of the so-called covenant, that is, non-Jews?

- Not to put any Jew to shame.

- Not to curse any other Israelite.

Comment: Why do these only apply to Jews and not all people.

- Not to gather the imperfect clusters of the vineyard.

- Not to gather grapes that have fallen to the ground.

- To leave the single grapes of the vineyard for the poor.

- Not to intermarry with gentiles.

- To exact the debt of an alien.

- To lend to an alien at interest.

Comments: Different rules for Jews and non-Jews. Non-Jews equal aliens. To exact the debt of a non-Jew and charge the non-Jew interest, these things are not from God because all people are God's children.

- That a eunuch shall not marry a daughter of Israel.

Comment: Why would the Jews have eunuchs in the first place? Did they intentionally castrate men to make them eunuchs? This is certainly not from God.

- That a mamzer shall not marry the daughter of a Jew.

Comment: A mamzer, or a child born to Jewish parents whose relationship is incestuous or otherwise forbidden by Jewish law (e.g., an unmarried man and a married woman) has no guilt because of his parents. And did this commandment only apply to males?

- That an Ammonite or Moabite shall never marry the daughter of an Israelite.

Comment: The Moabites were hated by the Jews because of their supposed maltreatment of Israel and for engaging Balaam to curse the children of Israel, while they journeyed in the wilderness. The Jews carried this grudge for generations even to those who were never involved in their supposed maltreatment of Israel, while they journeyed in the wilderness.

- That the woman suspected of adultery shall be dealt with as prescribed in the Torah.

Comment: Should this not apply to both men and women?

- That a widow whose husband died childless must not be married to anyone but her deceased husband's brother.
- To marry the widow of a brother who has died childless.
- That the widow formally releases the brother-in-law (if he refuses to marry her).

Comments: Shouldn't this also apply to widowers?

- Not to indulge in familiarities with relatives, such as kissing, embracing, winking, skipping, which may lead to incest.
- Not to have intercourse with a woman during her menstrual period. When a woman has her regular flow of blood, the impurity of her monthly period will last seven days, and anyone who touches her will be unclean till evening. Anything she lies on during her period will be unclean, and anything she sits on will be unclean.

Comment: The Jewish leaders were obviously 'clean freaks', though this is not from God. How is a woman considered impure due to her menstrual cycle?

- To remove chametz on the Eve of Passover.

Comment: Chametz were foods with leavening agents. What does this have to do with serving God?

- That no chametz be in the Israelite's possession during Passover.

- Not to eat any food containing chametz on Passover

- Not to eat chametz on Passover.

- That chametz shall not be seen in an Israelite's home during Passover.

- Not to eat chametz after mid-day on the fourteenth of Nissan.

Comments: Who can really believe that God commands people to not eat food with yeast? God does not care about what food people eat – food with yeast, pork, etc.

- To examine the marks in cattle.

- Not to eat the flesh of unclean beasts.

- To examine the marks in fishes so as to distinguish the clean from the unclean.

- Not to eat unclean fish.

- To examine the marks in fowl, so as to distinguish the clean from the unclean.

- Not to eat unclean fowl.

- To examine the marks in locusts, so as to distinguish the clean from the unclean.

- Not to eat a worm found in fruit.

- Not to eat of things that creep upon the earth.

- Not to eat any vermin of the earth.

- Not to eat things that swarm in the water.

- Not to eat of winged insects.

- Not to eat the flesh of a beast that is torn.

- Not to eat the flesh of a beast that died of itself.

- To slay cattle, deer, and fowl according to the laws of shechitah if their flesh is to be eaten.

- Not to eat a limb removed from a living beast.

- Not to eat the flesh of an ox that was condemned to be stoned.

- Not to boil meat with milk.

- Not to eat flesh with milk.

- Not to eat the of the thigh-vein which shrank.

- Not to eat tallow-fat.

- Not to eat blood.

Comments: How can anyone believe these commandments are from God? In Genesis 9:3 God says, "Every creature that lives shall be yours to eat." Isn't this a contradiction?

- Not to do wrong in buying or selling.

- Not to make a loan to an Israelite on interest.

Comments: There is a previous commandment to charge usurious interest to a non-Jew but here there is a commandment not to charge interest to a Jew. Surely, this is not from God. And why is there a distinction between Jews and non-Jews. If interest is wrong, it is wrong for everyone. Unfortunately, usury has been a significant societal evil for thousands of years, and Jews have been involved in money lending for thousands of years. Is this partially to blame?

- Not to take in pledge utensils used in preparing food.

- Not to exact a pledge from a debtor by force.

- Not to keep the pledge from its owner at the time when he needs it.

- To return a pledge to its owner.

- Not to take a pledge from a widow.

Comment: Do these commandments regarding a pledge or collateral apply also to non-Jews?

- Not to delay payment of a hired man's wages.

- That the hired laborer shall be permitted to eat of the produce he is reaping.

- That the hired laborer shall not take more than he can eat.

- That a hired laborer shall not eat produce that is not being harvested.

- To pay wages to the hired man at the due time.

Comment: Does this also apply to non-Jewish laborers?

- To deal judicially with the Hebrew bondman in accordance with the laws appertaining to him.

- Not to compel the Hebrew servant to do the work of a slave.

Comment: This implies that Jews could own slaves and slavery is wrong since all people are equal in the eyes of God.

- Not to sell a Hebrew servant as a slave.

- Not to treat a Hebrew servant rigorously.

Comment: Why does this only apply to a Hebrew?

- Not to permit a gentile to treat harshly a Hebrew bondman sold to him.

Comment: The Jews obviously bought and sold slaves.

- Not to send away a Hebrew bondman servant empty handed when he is freed from service.

- To bestow liberal gifts upon the Hebrew bondsman at the end of his term of service, and the same should be done to a Hebrew bondwoman.

- To redeem a Hebrew maidservant.

- Not to sell a Hebrew maidservant to another person.

- To espouse a Hebrew maidservant.

- To keep the Canaanite slave forever.

- Not to surrender a slave, who has fled to the land of Israel, to his owner who lives outside Palestine.

- Not to wrong such a slave.

Comments: Strange distinction between servant and slave. Servants and slaves are opposed to the nature of God. God would not create rules or laws regarding servants and slaves, especially 'to keep the Canaanite slave forever'. After the Jews left Egypt, they fought a series of wars against the Canaanites (and other groups), which led to them taking over most of the Canaanites' land. There are stories which say that those Canaanites who survived had to do forced labor. Very strange given that Jews and Canaanites had common ancestors, so they were actually related.

- That a man should fulfill whatever he has uttered.

- Not to swear needlessly.

- Not to violate an oath or swear falsely.

- To decide in cases of annulment of vows, according to the rules set forth in the Torah.

- Not to break a vow.

Comment: Isn't divorce a vow?

- To release debts in the seventh year.

- Not to demand return of a loan after the Sabbatical year has passed.

Comments: Does this apply also to non-Jews? And how is this applied today?

- That a transgressor shall not testify.

- That the court shall not accept the testimony of a close relative of the defendant in matters of capital punishment.

Comment: The accused cannot testify on his own behalf? It would appear that Judaism does not consider a person innocent until proven guilty.

- Not to slay an innocent person.

Comment: What about not killing any person. Does the 5th commandment 'you shall not kill' only apply to innocent people?

- That the Court shall pass sentence of death by decapitation with the sword.

- That the Court shall pass sentence of death by strangulation.

- That the Court shall pass sentence of death by burning with fire.

- That the Court shall pass sentence of death by stoning.

- To hang the dead body of one who has incurred that penalty.

Comment: What about the 5th Commandment 'you shall not kill'. And what does 'to hang the dead body' mean, display the dead body in public?

- To exile one who committed accidental homicide.

- To establish six cities of refuge for those who committed accidental homicide.

- Not to accept ransom from an accidental homicide, so as to relieve him from exile.

Comment: This certainly is not from God. An accident is unintentional. This is a very extreme commandment. Is it still followed today, so that a person in Israel who accidentally kills a person in a car accident is exiled from Israel?

- To decapitate the heifer in the manner prescribed in expiation of a murder on the road, the perpetrator of which remained undiscovered.

- Comment: What does the cow have to do with the murder? And does killing the cow bring the murdered person back to life?

- Not to plow nor sow the rough valley in which a heifer's neck was broken.

- To adjudge a thief to pay compensation or in certain cases suffer death.

Comment: Capital punishment for stealing? This is not from God.

- To heed the call of every prophet in each generation, provided that he neither adds to, nor takes away from the Torah.

Comment: Who is a prophet, and are there any prophets today?

- Not to prophesy falsely.

- Not to refrain from putting a false prophet to death nor to be in fear of him.

Comment: How do you determine who is a false prophet and isn't death an extreme punishment?

• Not to give up hating the enticer to idolatry.

Comment: Does God allow hate?

• Not to remove the entire beard, like the idolaters.

• Not to round the corners of the head, as the idolatrous priests do.

• Not to tattoo the body like the idolaters.

Comment: Tattoos, beards, and sideburns, sideboards, or side whiskers have nothing to do with serving God.

• Not to make a covenant with the seven Canaanite, idolatrous nations.

Comments: Again, total unforgiveness for the Canaanites in perpetuity. Not from God!

• To slay the inhabitants of a city that has become idolatrous and burn that city.

Comments: Very extreme, does this apply to children and babies as well? This would not come from God.

• That a person with a physical blemish shall not serve in the Sanctuary.

• That a priest with a temporary blemish shall not serve there.

• That a person with a physical blemish shall not enter the Sanctuary further than the altar.

• That a priest who is unclean shall not serve in the Sanctuary.

- To send the unclean out of the Camp of the Shechinah, that is, out of the Sanctuary.

- That a priest who is unclean shall not enter the courtyard.

Comments: What does a blemish have to do with serving God?

- Not to build an altar of hewn stone.

Comment: What does this have to do with serving God?

- That a priest shall not enter the Sanctuary with disheveled hair.

- That a priest shall not enter the Sanctuary with torn garments.

- That the priest shall not leave the Courtyard of the Sanctuary, during service.

Comments: This is certainly not from God. God does not care about such superficial things, He only cares what is in a person's heart.

- Not to offer up leaven or honey.

- That every sacrifice be salted.

- Not to offer up any offering unsalted.

- Not to allow the remainder of the meal offerings to become leavened.

Comment: What does salt, or honey or leaven have to do with God?

- That a woman after childbirth shall bring an offering when she is clean.

- That the leper shall bring a sacrifice after he is cleansed.

- That a man having an issue shall bring a sacrifice after he is cleansed of his issue.

- That a woman having an issue shall bring a sacrifice after she is cleansed of her issue.

Comment: How do these things make a person unclean? And does this matter to God? And what about handicapped people?

- Not to sanctify blemished cattle for sacrifice on the altar.

- That every animal offered up shall be without blemish.

- Not to inflict a blemish on cattle set apart for sacrifice.

- Not to eat of the unblemished firstling outside Jerusalem.

- Not to offer up a beast that has a temporary blemish.

- Not to slaughter blemished cattle as sacrifices.

- Not to burn the limbs of blemished cattle upon the altar.

- Not to sprinkle the blood of blemished cattle upon the altar.

- Not to offer up a blemished beast that comes from non-Israelites.

Comment: Again, some Jewish leaders were clean freaks and they deprived people of their God-given rights because of a blemish.

- That eight species of creeping things defile by contact.

- That foods become defiled by contact with unclean things.

- That anyone who touches the carcass of a beast that died of itself shall be unclean.

- That a lying-in woman is unclean like a menstruating woman in terms of uncleanness.

- That a leper is unclean and defiles.

- That the leper shall be universally recognized as such by the prescribed marks. So too, all other unclean persons should declare themselves as such.

- That a leprous garment is unclean and defiles.

- That a leprous house defiles.

- That a man, having a running issue, defiles.

- That the seed of copulation defiles.

- That purification from all kinds of defilement shall be affected by immersion in the waters of a mikvah.

- Not to have sexual relations with a menstrually impure woman.

- That a menstruating woman is unclean and defiles others.

- That a woman, having a running issue, defiles.

- That a corpse defiles.

Comment: Defiled means to make unclean or impure, how is a leper or menstruating woman impure?

- To anoint a special priest to speak to the soldiers in a war.

- In a permissive war as distinguished from obligatory ones, to observe the procedure prescribed in the Torah.

Comments: God is opposed to all war. All people are God's children, and He does not want His children to fight.

- Not to keep alive any individual of the seven Canaanite nations.

- To exterminate the seven Canaanite nations from the land of Israel.

Comments: What about the 5th Commandment 'you shall not kill'. And such a bitter hared of the Canaaites. The Canaaites were in fact distant relatives of the Hebrews.

- Not to destroy fruit trees wantonly or in warfare.

- To deal with a beautiful woman taken captive in war in the manner prescribed in the Torah.

- Not to sell a beautiful woman taken captive in war.

- Not to degrade a beautiful woman taken captive in war to the condition of a bondwoman.

- Not to offer peace to the Ammonites and the Moabites before waging war on them, as should be done to other nations.

- Always to remember what Amalek did.

- That the evil done to us by Amalek shall not be forgotten.

- To destroy the seed of Amalek.

Comments: This is certainly not from God. What happened to 'you shall not kill'. Does that only apply to Jews?

- A judge must not have mercy on the poor man at the trial.

Comment: God is all people's Parent and wants people to show mercy to each other.

- To break the neck of the donkey if the owner does not intend to redeem it.

- Observe the laws of impurity caused by a dead beast.

Comment: Rather absurd!

- Observe the laws of impurity concerning liquid and solid foods.

- Every impure person must immerse himself in a Mikveh to become pure.

Comment: Also, rather absurd!

COMMENTARY ON THE TORAH CONCLUSION

The first five books of the Jewish Bible were first written during the Babylonian Captivity (6th Century BCE to the 5th Century BCE). They were edited and refined for the next 300 years before taking their final forms around the 2nd Century BCE.

These books constitute the basis for Judaism and because of their nature show Judaism to be a man-made religion. It is quite unfortunate that the leaders of Judaism, Pauline Christianity, and Islam cannot admit that these books are myths and legends and that there is no truth to these stories. Also, these leaders should admit that the writers of these books misled and intentionally tried to deceive their readers. It is amazing how gullible people are. People need to think for themselves and not blindly follow their so-called leaders whether it be in government or the religious organization to which they belong.

The supposed creator of the religion of Islam is said to be Muhammed. Though similar to Abraham, Moses, and Paul of Tarsus; the claimed creators of Judaism and Pauline Christianity; those individuals who wrote about Muhammed, Abraham, Moses, and Paul may have in fact been the creators of Islam, Judaism, and Pauline Christianity and not Muhammed, Abraham, Moses, and Paul.

Like Pauline Christianity which holds an almost reverence for Paul, the creator of the religion Pauline Christianity, and Abraham and Moses, the supposed creators of the religion of Judaism, who are held in reverence by the followers of Judaism; Muhammed, the supposed creator of Islam, is held in reverence by the followers of Islam. In a similar manner, Siddhartha Gautama (the "Buddha"), the founder of Buddhism is held in reverence by the followers of Buddhism. Hinduism has no one founder, being a blend of various beliefs.

MUHAMMED, THE FOUNDER OF ISLAM

The followers of Islam hold Muhammed in such reverence that they have killed individuals who have defamed him. Do these people who hold such reverence consider that they may have been misled? Over centuries, extreme leaders of Islam have proposed to Muslims that Muhammed is almost like a god. But is that true?

Was Muhammed a holy, devout, and righteous man, and what kind of religion is Islam? Was Muhammed really chosen by Allah (God)? Having been founded 1500 years ago, is the world a better place today because of Muhammed and Islam? Is there peace in predominantly Muslim countries? Are all people treated equally including woman in predominantly Muslim countries? What about all of the Muslim terrorist groups seeking to topple governments throughout the Middle East, Africa, and Asia? Are they inspired by Islam and Muhammed?

What about Sharia Law, is it good or bad, and is it at variance with the Natural Law? And what about Jihad? 'Jihad' is mentioned in the Quran twenty-nine times and numerous times in the Hadiths. However, it is the modern and current notion of jihad that has been used over the last thirty years especially in the context of what we call terrorism, and the Muslims call Jihad primarily in the examples of suicide bombers that undermine Islam as a peaceful religion and one that is approved by God.

It is certainly strange that almost immediately after the death of Muhammed, Islam was broken into two different factions; the Sunnis and the Shias, based on politics regarding the leadership of Islam. Obviously, these factions existed before the death of Muhammed and Muhammed did nothing to bring them together. Was this intentional on the part of Muhammed? And how was this a good thing? Certainly, Allah does not consider this a good thing. And even today, the conflicts between Sunnis and Shias (prompted by the United States) are not approved by Allah. For God/Allah/Yahweh/Braham is the God of Love and Peace for all people and not just believers or adherents of certain religions.

There is almost no historical evidence of and information about Muhammed. Most information comes from biographies written about him such as the Sīrah (Sira) in addition to the Quran and Hadiths. Unfortunately, because the Sira was composed over a hundred years after the death of Muhammed and the Hadiths were composed over two hundred years after his death, the accuracy of the facts or statements contained in these works are questionable because they are not based on individuals who knew Muhammed personally and witnessed the actual events of his life.

It would appear that Muhammed was a monotheistic Arab before starting Islam. Probably influenced by Jews and possibly Christians who lived in the Arabian Peninsula at the time of Muhammed, Muhammed probably transitioned from a polytheistic Arab to a monotheistic one, adopting many of the beliefs of Judaism though not converting to either Judaism or Christianity. Muhammed was probably a member of the Hanif group, a group of Arabs that believed that they descended "from Ishmael and Hagar" and practiced some Jewish rules such as not eating pork and extreme cleanliness. Hanif is mentioned twelve times in the Quran.

Muhammed was also involved in political groups that wanted to unite all of the tribes within the Arabian Peninsula religiously, politically, and economically. And Muhammed seemed to have merged the ideas of the

Hanifs and these political groups and became not only a very fervent follower but a leader as well.

In addition, Muhammed was a businessperson who managed his wife's trading business and with almost any businessperson wanted to expand and eliminate competitors.

Within this context, Muhammed developed Islam. Was Muhammed's purpose in developing Islam to promote the ideas of Hanif and to promote the union of the various tribes within the Arabian Peninsula, to eliminate the polytheistic Arabs and to eliminate his competitors? Given that Muhammed was considered both a prophet and a general who waged wars, battles, and attacks, his motivation in creating Islam has to be questioned. If Muhammed's motivation in establishing Islam was strictly religious and moral, he would not have engaged in warfare and terrorism.

Is Islam a religion of peace or of war. Allah (God) wants peace among all people and not war. Muhammed promoted war and terrorism. He condemned retreating during battle, and taught that if you die in battle, you will go to Heaven. This is not from Allah (God). It is from men who promote war. While Muhammed was supposedly a prophet, he was also a warrior general and while he was supposedly dictating the Quran, fought eight major battles, led eighteen raids, and planned another thirty-eight military campaigns.

Additional criticism of Muhammad involves his marriages, his ownership of slaves, and his cruelty in his treatment of his enemies.

Muhammad's life can be divided into two periods, Meccan and Medinan. In the Meccan period of his life, Muhammed appeared to be a sincere person. However, after his emigration to Medina with a small number of followers, power, greed, and arrogance took over his personality and his vision of himself as the messenger of God and the final Prophet of God after Abraham, Moses, and Jesus obscured his grasp of reality. Muhammed's so-called visions from God also changed. In Mecca, his visions were more religious in nature, while after fleeing to Medina his visions were more political, directed to his personal vision of himself as God's prophet, condemnation of those who did not believe and submit to him, and justification for his attacks on his enemies. It appears that the old saying 'power corrupts' applies to Muhammed's life after moving to Medina.

Muhammed was a brilliant strategist and used both military methods and nonmilitary methods to establish his leadership and control. These nonmilitary methods included alliances, assassination, bribery, and butchery. He was both a revolutionary and a guerrilla leader who used his newly created religion to support his political, social, and economic objectives.

The history of Islam is replete with wars, and Islam spread in great part has been due to its military conquests. Major battles in the early history of Islam were the Battle of Badr in 624 CE, the battle in Uhud 625 CE, the battle in Khandaq 627 CE, the battle in Mecca 630 CE and the battle in Hunayn also in 630 CE, all during the lifetime of Muhammed.

In relating the battle of Badr, the Quran states that Allah sent an "unseen army of angels" that helped the Muslims defeat the Meccans.

Since God would not send angels to fight humans (it is against both the nature of God and the nature of angels), this claim was intended to tell people that Islam wars were supported by Allah. This was a marketing tool by Muhammed and the writers and/or editors of the Quran.

Muslims have fought against Arabs, Jews, Christians, and other Muslims since the founding of Islam fifteen hundred years ago all of which have been supported by the leadership of Islam.

Besides military conquests, Islam spread through trade, pilgrimages, and missionaries. Most of the significant expansion occurred during the reign of the Rashidun from 632 to 661 CE, which was the reign of the first four successors of Muhammad. During a period of a few hundred years, Islam spread from the Arabian Peninsula to modern Spain in the west and northern India in the east. Within two decades, they created a massive Arab Muslim empire spanning three continents. The Arab Muslim rulers were not solely motivated by religion, they were also motivated by political and economic objectives.

The caliphate, a new Islamic political structure, evolved during the Umayyad and Abbasid caliphates. The Umayyads did not actively encourage conversion, and most subjects remained non-Muslim. Because non-Muslim subjects were required to pay a special tax, the Umayyads were able to subsidize their political expansion. However, many people converted to Islam in order to avoid the taxes levied on non-Muslims.

The basic religious text on Islam is the Quran, which is not biographical in nature, and it tells practically nothing about Muhammad. In fact, Muhammed is mentioned only five times in the Quran while Jesus is mentioned twenty-five times.

This raises an interesting point regarding the presence of statements regarding Jesus, Abraham, and Moses in the Quran. Given that the Quran was supposedly given by Allah through the angel Gabriel to Muhammed in order to start a new religion, and given that Allah is the same as Yahweh Who was the founder of Judaism and also the same as God Who was the founder of Christianity, did Allah/Yahweh/God really want to create three separate religions? Since Allah/Yahweh/God is the father of all humans, it would seem like He would create only one true religion.

Or perhaps, Judaism, Pauline Christianity, and Islam are man-made religions, and the Quran is a man-made creation (not from Allah/ Yahweh/God) and has references to the Jewish and Christian Bibles in order to market it to its readers, just like the Jewish Bible and Christian Bible are man-made documents created to market its religions to its followers.

The Hadiths are supposed collections of sayings and deeds of Muhammad written with the objective of explaining what a Muslim should do in a given situation based on the so-called teachings and life of Muhammed. Therefore, there is no detailed historical source written within a century of the prophet of Islam, and no source trusted by the majority of Muslims within two centuries. This gap of time undermines knowing almost anything at all about Muhammad's life and whether he was a good person or not.

Muhammad was supposedly born in Mecca around 570 AD. His father died before he was born, and his mother died when he was about six years old. Not much is known about Muhammad prior to the time he started receiving his so-called revelations at the age of forty other than he married at twenty-five and ran his wife's trading business. It is likely that during this time and during his business travels, he was exposed to Christianity and Judaism.

Supposedly, when Muhammed was forty years of age (interesting that forty is a special Jewish number), he was visited by the angel Gabriel. How Gabriel appeared to or spoke to Muhammed is unknown given that angels are immaterial spirits. Gabriel supposedly brought him the command of God. "He came to me," said Muhammed, "while I was asleep, with a coverlet of brocade whereon was some writing, and said, 'Read!' I said, 'What shall I read?' He pressed me with it so tightly that I thought it was death; then he let me go and said, 'Read!' I said, 'What shall I read?' He pressed me with it again so that I thought it was death; then he let me go and said 'Read!' I said, 'What shall I read?' He pressed me with it the third time so that I thought it was death and said 'Read!' I said, 'What shall I read?'—and this last time I said only to deliver myself from him, less he should do the same to me again. He said: 'Read in the name of your Lord Who created man of blood coagulated.

Strange statement, 'your Lord Who created man of blood coagulated.'

'Read in the name of thy Lord who creates, creates man from a clot, read that your Lord is most generous, Who taught by the pen, taught man what he did not know. No, man is surely inordinate, because he looks upon himself as self-sufficient. Surely to your Lord is the return. Have you seen Him Who forbids a servant when he prays? See if he is on the right way, or enjoins observance of duty? Sees if He denies and turns away? Do you not know that Allah sees everything? No, if he resists, we will seize him by the forelock, a lying, sinful forelock! Then let him summon his council. We will summon the braves of the army. No! Obey him not, but prostrate yourself, and draw close to Allah. Read! Your Lord is the most beneficent, Who taught by the pen, taught that which they knew not unto men.'

What does this mean that Allah taught by the pen? And what does it mean that God created man from a clot?

Muhammed replied, "I cannot read." Then the Angel read out five verses to him. And Muhammed awoke from his sleep, with the words written on his heart. He then returned home, and he was so overcome by this incident that he asked his wife to cover him.

Is this fact or fiction? This event is somewhat similar to the conversion of Paul (it is possible and probable that Muhammed or his scribes heard the story of Paul's conversion). In the case of Paul, Paul probably fabricated his story of his conversion to Christianity to make it appear that God chose him personally to be an Apostle and to authenticate Paul's teachings. Muhammed might have employed the same logic to make it appear that he was a prophet and messenger of Allah (God).

Also, it is rather interesting that Muhammed could not read. Are we to believe that Muhammed ran a successful business without being able to read? Or was this inserted by the writers and editors of the Quran and his biographers to make the narrative much more interesting?

Muhammad was frightened by what happened to him. He thought it was a bad dream or even the devil. After telling his wife, she convinced him that he was a prophet of God, and that he had met the angel Gabriel in the cave.

It is interesting that Muhammed did not realize what supposedly appeared to him in his sleep was an angel and specifically the angel Gabriel, the same angel who supposedly appeared to Mary, the mother of Jesus. It is also interesting that Muhammed did not think that he was chosen to be a prophet. Did these ideas come from his wife? And is she the creator of Islam and not Muhammed? Could she read and write, and did she begin writing or fabricating the Quran by herself and the scribes that actually wrote the Quran?

A serious question must be asked, is the Quran the Word of God or a man-made work? Muslims have been told by their religious leaders that it is, but that is also the same for the members of Judaism and Pauline Christianity with respect to their bibles. And it has been shown earlier in this book, that the Jewish and Christian Bibles were not written, nor dictated, nor inspired by God.

Jews, Christians, and Muslims are afraid to question the Quran, the Tanakh, and the New Testament because they have been told that they were written, dictated by, or inspired by Allah, Yahweh, or God? But what if that is not true and they are victims of scams.

And would God or Allah or Yahweh (different names for the same Being) really create three separate sets of documents in order to create three separate religions. Does God really want three different religions? Certainly not! God is One, and there is only one truth.

Supported and promoted by his wife, Muhammad spent the next twelve years preaching after his dream with the angel, Gabriel, first in private, and then in public. What did Muhammed preach and where did he get the material that he preached on? People assume that Muhammed was preaching about Islam, but where did these teachings come from? Did Muhammed develop his teachings or did his wife develop his teachings or a combination of both him and his wife?

Through his preaching, Muhammed gained followers and the assumption is that these first followers were the first Muslims or adherents of Islam.

Because Muhammed's new religion was not accepted by many people in Mecca, in 622, Muhammad and many of his followers moved to what is now Medina.

From his base in Medina, Muhammad and his followers began a series of raids against the Meccan caravans. The first six failed, but the seventh raid called the Nakhla raid was a success. In the Nakhla raid the Muslims attacked during a holy month in which everyone had agreed not to fight. In addition, an innocent man was killed during the raid. Can anyone claim that this was commanded by Allah?

First of all, how can this new religion created to serve Allah engage in raids and military engagements? The two seem to be incompatible. Were these raids and military engagements meant to promote his business or were they just revenge against the Meccans for having rejected Muhammed's new religion?

Also, isn't this considered 'dirty fighting'. If those guarding the caravans assumed that there would be no fighting or attacking because it was a holy month, wouldn't it be morally wrong to attack the caravans during this time? And what was the moral basis for attacking these caravans? Was Muhammed a righteous religious leader or a typical political leader intent on power and conquering competitors and those who opposed him? Attacking a caravan was not a defensive act but an offensive act and an act of terror for future caravans. If this is true, how can this this be reconciled with the supposed peaceful message of Muhammed and Islam? And how can Muslims consider these actions as being approved by Allah?

Also, it is interesting that Muhammed and his followers started attacking caravans. Instead of attacking their supposed enemies in Mecca, they are attacking caravans from Mecca. Muhammed started out as a merchant, and after working for several years as a merchant, he was hired by Khadija, a wealthy widow whom he would later marry, to guard her caravans. After his so-called initial revelation, it is not known what Muhmmed did to support his family. It is rather interesting that he directed raids on caravans. Were these caravans owned and managed by his competitors? And if so, these attacks on his competitor's caravans had nothing to do with his role as the leader of Islam but rather his greedy attempt to eliminate his competition. This would undermine his image as a virtuous man who was Allah's prophet.

Mecca sent 1000 guards to protect their next caravan. The Muslims attacked with a smaller force, and they won what came to be known as the Battle of Badr. For the next ten years until Muhammad's death in 632 CE, the Muslims never stopped fighting. Muhammad fought several more key battles against Mecca (the Battle of Uhud and the Battle of the Trench), finally taking the city in 630.

How can anyone claim that Islam is a peaceful religion founded by Allah (God)?

Muhammad attacked other groups as well. In 629, Muslims attacked a Jewish settlement in the oasis of Khaybar in Northwestern Arabia. Shortly after the conquest of Mecca, Muhammad supposedly received Surah 9:29, which ordered Muslims to fight non-Muslims (including Christians and Jews) until they submitted to Islam. Supposedly in obedience to this command, Muhammad marched an army against the Byzantine Empire, though the Byzantines chose not to fight. After this battle, Muhammad became sick and died shortly thereafter.

Surah 9:29 states, 'fight against those who do not believe in Allah, nor in the Last Day, nor those who do not follow the commandments of Allah and His Messenger, Muhammed, and those who do not acknowledge Islam, unless they pay the Jizyah (tax) with willing submission and feel themselves subdued.'

Surah 9:29 certainly did not come from Allah.

Unfortunately, Muslims focus entirely on the supposed good actions of their prophet, and completely ignore his bad actions. When Muslims started attacking trading caravans, greed became one of the primary factors in people's rapid conversion to Islam. Muhammad deliberately used the spoils of war (goods and women) to lure people to convert to Islam. When he was criticized for the way he distributed his newfound wealth, he replied, "Are you disturbed in mind because of the good things of this life by which I win over a people that they may become Muslims while I entrust you to your Islam?"

Muhammad patiently endured persecution in Mecca supposedly because of his monotheistic beliefs and teachings, but his attitude changed with the increase in the number of his followers. When this happened, he would not tolerate any criticism of himself and Islam whatsoever (and this intolerance of criticism of Islam has continued until today).

One incident during the life of Muhammed involved a man who was more than a hundred years old and who wrote a poem criticizing people for converting to Islam. Muhammad ordered that he be killed, and the elderly poet was murdered in his sleep.

When a woman heard that Muslims had killed such an elderly man, she wrote a poem calling for people to take a stand against Islam. When Muhammed heard what the woman had said, he said, "who will rid me of Marwan's daughter?" One of his companions who was with him and heard him, he went to her house and killed her. In the morning the murderer came to Muhammed and told him what he had done, and Muhammed said, "You have helped God and His apostle!"

Since this involved Muhammed and the earlier followers of Islam, it is questionable whether Muhammed was a virtuous and holy man and whether violence was found in Islam from the beginning. It does appear that Islam spread so fast and wide because of its conquest of neighbors. This is inconsistent with Natural Law and how God wants people to treat each other.

Muhammad's violence was directed towards non-Arabs as well. It is claimed that Muhammad once said to his followers, "I will expel the Jews and Christians from the Arabian Peninsula and will not leave any but Muslims."

The Banu Qurayza were a Jewish tribe which lived in northern Arabia, close to what is now as Medina, the stronghold of Muhammed and his first followers. The Jews of Qurayza resisted Muhammad and attempted to form an alliance against him. When the alliance failed, Muhammed's armies surrounded them and besieged them for twenty-five nights until they were conquered and surrendered. An arbiter was chosen, and he gave his decision that the men should be killed, all property divided, and the women and children taken as slaves as per Jewish law". Muhammad approved of the decision, calling it similar to the judgment in the Torah, and all male members of the tribe who had reached puberty were beheaded. Muhammad divided the women, children, and property among his men taking a fifth of the spoils for himself.

Continuing to conquer and spread Islam, Muslim armies raided town after town, and they captured many women, who would often be sold or traded. The Muslim men asked for guidance from Allah through Muhammed regarding their female captives. It wasn't long before Muhammad supposedly received a revelation from Allah allowing the soldiers to sleep with the female captives.

The verses of the Quran (4:24,23:1-6; 33:50; 70:22-30), granted Muslims the right to have sex with their female captives and slave girls, even those who were still married or who were going to be sold or traded. In addition, Muslims could have sex with girls who hadn't even reached puberty.

Muhammad himself had sex with a nine-year-old, Aisha. Supposedly, Muhammad had a dream about her, which led him to believe that God wanted him to marry Aisha.

God would not want a forty-year-old or a fifty-year-old man to marry a nine-year-old girl!

Aisha was six or seven years old at the time of her marriage, and nine at the time of consummation. She played an important role in early Islam, especially after Muhammed's death.

Muslims believe that Muhammad was morally perfect, and that he was Allah's prophet. Actual evidence shows that Muhammad was not morally perfect, and there are good reasons to believe that he was not Allah's prophet. There is the Muhammed of history and the Muhammad of faith, and they are significantly different.

Islam spread through military conquest, trade, pilgrimage, and missionaries. Arab Muslim forces conquered vast territories and built imperial structures over time. Over a few hundred years, Islam spread from its origin in the Arabian Peninsula all the way to Spain in the west and northern India in the east.

Concerns over Muhammad's morality, his marriages, his ownership of slaves, his cruelty towards his enemies and his critics, and his acquisitions of the spoils of war (money, goods, and slaves) undermine Muhmmed's image as a virtuous and holy person and a spokesperson for God.

His ultimate goal, the transformation of Arab society through the spread of a new religion, was strategic in concept. Muhammad's application of force and violence was always directed at this goal. The question must be asked, was Islam just a tool created by Muhammed to promote his political and economic aspirations of uniting the disconnected tribes within Arabia and establishing a new powerful country?

Dogs in Islam, as they are in Rabbinic Judaism, are conventionally thought of as ritually impure. This idea taps into a long tradition that considers even the mere sight of a dog during prayer to have the power to nullify a pious Muslim's supplications. Was this because Muhammed did not like dogs?

In Islam, cats are viewed as holy animals. Above all, they are admired for their cleanliness. They are thought to be ritually clean which is why they're allowed to enter homes and even mosques. According to authentic narrations, one may make ablution for prayer with the same water that a cat has drunk from. Is this because Muhammed liked cats?

God loves both dogs and cats equally.

INTRODUCTION TO THE QURAN

The Quran is the central religious document of Islam, believed by Muslims to be a revelation from God.

Muslims believe that the Quran was orally revealed by God to the final prophet, Muhammad, through the archangel Gabriel incrementally over a period of twenty- two years beginning when Muhammad was forty years old and concluding in 632, the year of his death. Muslims believe the Quran is the final message from God starting with the revelations of the Torah (to Adam, Abraham, and Moses) and continuing with the New Testament.

The Quran is thought by Muslims to be not simply divinely inspired, but the literal word of God. Muhammad did not write it because he did not know how to write. Supposedly, Muhammad had scribes, who wrote down the revelations, the first of which happened while Muhammed was asleep.

Whether all of the so-called revelations received by Muhammed were received by him in his sleep is unknown.

Muhammed could not read or write, so he had a large group of scribes who wrote down his words and activities.

After the prophet's death, the Quran was compiled by individuals, who supposedly had written down or memorized parts of it. No doubt some one person or group of people had to oversee this collaborative effort. And it is likely that the Quran was edited and made to conform to the objectives of its promoters.

But is the Quran the literal word of God? If one reads the Quran, does it really appear to be the word of God? Jews are taught to believe that the Torah is the word of God. Pauline Christians are taught to believe that the Gospels are the words of God. Are they all correct or are they all incorrect?

Inconsistencies, inaccuracies, and contradictions to the Natural Law and the nature of God that are contained in the Torah, the New Testament, and the Quran undermine the claims that these works are the literal words of God. The claims that these documents were the words of God were an attempt (really a marketing attempt) to persuade or rather coerce people to accept these documents without question.

And so great was this marketing on the parts of the leaders and clerics of these three major religions, that their adherents fear criticizing or denying an element of the supposed documents written by, or dictated by, or inspired by God (God = Yahweh = Allah).

There is no historical evidence of the Quran until 691, fifty-nine years after the death of Muhammad's death. So, it is not known when it was actually written and edited and by whom.

Supposedly, the Quran was written down by Muhammad's companions while he was alive, but since there were multiple writers or scribes (supposedly up to forty-three) someone had to compile all of the different snippets from the different scribes into one integrated document. Any whoever did this, certainly would have done some editing. And if Muhammed had forty-three scribes, he must have been very wealthy and influential to have so many scribes working for him.

But who were these writers and who were the editors of the Quran? And what were the objectives of the writers of the Quran? While there were many objectives of the various writers and editors of the Quran, the main objective of the Quran was to establish Islam as the final religion and only true way to serve God. It is possible that another objective was for Jews and Christians to accept Islam.

The following section contains verses from the Quran and comments. The reader is asked to decide after reading honestly, and objectively it whether the Quran is the Word of Allah (God) dictated by Him and contains no mistakes or contains no inconsistencies with His nature. After reading each verse, the reader should ask himself or herself, 'if this God speaking or the work of men?'.

THE QURAN COMMENTARY

(Translated by Talal Itani published in May of 2012 at www. ClearQuran.com provided under the Creative Commons License and there is no copyright to the translation.)

Quran: It is Allah who ridicules them and leaves them bewildered in their transgression.

Comment: Allah (God) does not ridicule anyone. And if this is the word of Allah, why is it in the 3rd person?

Quran: Those who violate Allah's covenant after its confirmation, and sever what Allah has commanded to be joined, and commit evil on earth. These are the losers.

Comments: What is this so-called covenant? It is a new covenant between God and the Muslims? And is it an attempt to replace the so-called covenants between God and Abraham and Moses just like the Christians claimed that their New Covenant replaced these Jewish covenants. But does there really have to be any covenants between God and humans?

Quran: He said, "O Adam, tell them their names." And when he told them their names, He said, "Did I not tell you that I know the secrets of the heavens and the earth, and that I know what you reveal and what you conceal?" And We said to the angels, "Bow down to Adam." They bowed down, except for Satan. He refused, was arrogant, and was one of the disbelievers. We said, "O Adam, inhabit the Garden, you and your spouse, and eat from it freely as you please, but do not approach this tree, lest you become wrongdoers."

Comments: Sounds like a copy of the Creation myth of the Torah. Given that the narrative of Creation in the book of Genesis involves a myth (not even a legend), the Quran is repeating the same myth narrative copying from Genesis. Even the change back and forth between the first-person singular 'I' and the first-person plural 'We' referring to God, is right from Genesis.

Quran: And recall that We delivered you from the people of Pharaoh. They inflicted on you terrible persecution, killing your sons and sparing your women. This was a tremendous trial from your Lord. And recall that We parted the sea for you, and We saved you, and We drowned the people of Pharaoh as you looked on. And recall that We appointed for Moses forty nights. Then you took to worshiping the calf after him, and you turned wicked. Then We pardoned you after that, so that you might be grateful. And recall that We gave Moses the Scripture and the Criterion, so that you may be guided. And recall that Moses said to his people, "O my people, you have done wrong to yourselves by worshiping the calf. So, repent to your Maker, and kill your egos. That would be better for you with your Maker." So, He turned to you in repentance. He is the Accepter of Repentance, the Merciful. And recall that you said, "O Moses, we will not believe in you unless we see Allah plainly." Thereupon the thunderbolt struck you, as you looked on. Then We revived you after your death, so that you may be appreciative. And We shaded you with clouds, and We sent down for you to eat manna and quails: "Eat of the good things We have provided for you." They did not wrong Us, but they used to wrong their own souls. And recall that We said, "Enter this town, and eat plentifully from it whatever you wish; but enter the gate humbly, and say, 'Pardon.' We will forgive your sins and give increase to the virtuous." And recall when Moses prayed for water for his people. We said, "Strike the rock with your staff." Thereupon twelve springs gushed out from it, and each tribe recognized its drinking-place. "Eat and drink from Allah's provision, and do not corrupt the earth with disobedience."

Comments: These passages appear to be copied and modified from the Torah, not from God.

Quran: And you surely knew those of you who violated the Sabbath. We said to them, "Be despicable apes!"

Comment: God (Allah) would never use the phrase 'be despicable apes'. And we are supposed to believe that the Quran is the Word of Allah with such statements attributed to God, nonsense.

Quran: As for those who believe and do righteous deeds, these are the inhabitants of Paradise, wherein they will dwell forever.

Comments: This is the teaching of Paul regarding Pauline Christianity, that belief and good works are necessary to attain to eternal life in Heaven or Paradise, not just good works but beliefs as well. Both Pauline Christianity and Islam claim that believing in their doctrines are necessary for eternal life. And for unbelievers, there is only eternal damnation. However, this is contrary to the nature of God. These are just other marketing tools to get people to accept their religions.

Quran: Thus, they incurred wrath upon wrath. And there is a demeaning punishment for the disbelievers.

Comment: Similar to Pauline Christianity which asserts that a person must be a believer to enter into Heaven and that disbelievers are damned? Did Islam copy this idea from Pauline Christianity?

Quran: Whoever is hostile to Allah, and His angels, and His messengers, and Gabriel, and Michael Allah is hostile to the faithless.

Comment: Is Allah hostile to those who do not have faith but yet live good lives: doing good and avoiding evil, loving their neighbor as themselves, and treating all other as equals.

Quran: We have revealed to you clear signs, and none rejects them except the sinners.

Comment: A person who rejects a myth or a legend is a sinner?

Quran: The Jews and the Christians will not approve of you unless you follow their creed. Say, "Allah's guidance is the guidance." Should you follow their desires, after the knowledge that has come to you, you will have in Allah neither guardian nor helper.

Comment: Does this mean that only the creed of Islam is correct and not the creeds of Judaism and Pauline Christianity. And also, if a Muslim leaves Islam and converts to Judaism or Pauline Christianity, that God will not help them?

Quran: Those to whom We have given the Scripture follow it, as it ought to be followed these believe in it. But as for those who reject it, these are the losers.

Comment: This cannot be from God or Allah. The so-called Scriptures of Judaism and Pauline Christianity did not come from God, they were composed by men with the specific purpose of promoting their respective religious organizations by tying to show that they were established by God.

Quran: And We made the House a focal point for the people, and a sanctuary. Use the shrine of Abraham as a place of prayer. And We commissioned Abraham and Ishmael, "Sanctify My House for those who circle around it, and those who seclude themselves in it, and those who kneel and prostrate."

Comments: The writers of the Quran establishing Ishmael, the first son of the mythical person Abraham, as a prophet equal to Abraham. If Abraham did not exist, neither would Ishmael. Obviously, this is an attempt by the writers to link Islam and Judaism based on the fabricated narrative of Abraham. How could this have come from God since the Torah was fabricated by men and there is no historical evidence for Adam, Eve, Noah, Abraham, and Moses?

Quran: He said, "And whoever disbelieves, I will give him a little enjoyment, then I will consign him to the punishment of the Fire; how miserable the destiny!"

Comments: If the Quran is the literal Word of God, why would God be speaking in the third person 'He said'? And God does not damn to eternal fire (the Fire) people who do not believe in Islam, or Judaism, or Pauline Christianity. And God does not play with people 'I will give him a little enjoyment, then I will consign him to the punishment of the Fire'.

Quran: Our Lord, and make us submissive to You, and from our descendants a community submissive to You. And show us our rites and accept our repentance. You are the Acceptor of Repentance, the Merciful. Our Lord, and raise up among them a messenger, of themselves, who will recite to them Your revelations, and teach them the Book and wisdom, and purify them. You are the Almighty, the Wise."

Comments: Again, if the Quran is the literal Word of God, how is it that the above has someone speaking to Allah and who is this? And the so-called messengers of God, Abraham, Moses, and Muhammed, were all self-appointed and not identified by a petition of people.

Quran: Who would forsake the religion of Abraham, except he who fools himself? We chose him in this world, and in the Hereafter, he will be among the righteous. And Abraham exhorted his sons, and Jacob, "O my sons, Allah has chosen this religion for you, so do not die unless you have submitted." Or were you witnesses when death approached Jacob, and he said to his sons, "What will you worship after Me?" They said, "We will worship your God, and the God of your fathers, Abraham, Ishmael, and Isaac; One God; and to Him we submit."

Comments: The writers and editors of the Quran are equating Yahweh and Allah as the same person, so, why doesn't Islam just use the name Yahweh instead of Allah? And God or Yahweh or Allah (different names for the same person) has never and never will choose a religion for people like Judaism or Islam or Pauline Christianity. These religions are man-made, not God-made.

Quran: And they say, "Be Jews or Christians, and you will be guided." Say, "rather, the religion of Abraham, the Monotheist; he was not an idolater." Say, "We believe in Allah; and in what was revealed to us; and in what was revealed to Abraham, and Ishmael, and Isaac, and Jacob, and the Patriarchs; and in what was given to Moses and Jesus; and in what was given to the prophets from their Lord. We make no distinction between any of them, and to Him we surrender."

Comments: Equating Abraham, Ishmael, Jacob, Moses, and Jesus, and claiming that all of their teachings are equivalent in spite of the fact that there are significant differences between their teachings. This was perhaps intended by the writers and editors of the Quran to facilitate the conversion of Jews and Christians to Islam.

Quran: Thus, We made you a moderate community, that you may be witnesses to humanity, and that the Messenger may be a witness to you. We only established the direction of prayer, which you once followed, that We may distinguish those who follow the Messenger from those who turn on their heels. It is indeed difficult, except for those whom Allah has guided. But Allah would never let your faith go to waste. Allah is Kind towards the people, Merciful.

Comments: These verses show the intention of the writers and editors of the Quran that Islam be a universal religion, 'that you may be witnesses to humanity' and to establish Muhammed, the Messenger, as the premier prophet of God.

Quran: We have seen your face turned towards the heaven. So, We will turn you towards a direction that will satisfy you. So, turn your face towards the Sacred Mosque. And wherever you may be, turn your faces towards it. Redundant, similar verses 'And wherever you come from, turn your face towards the Sacred Mosque. This is the truth from your Lord, and Allah is not heedless of what you do. And wherever you come from, turn your face towards the Sacred Mosque. And wherever you may be, turn your faces towards it'.

Comments: Are these verses meant to establish the commandment that Muslims pray facing Mecca as though it is ordained by Allah? The Great Mosque in Mecca was built in 638 CE, six years after the death of Muhammed. If the Quran was dictated by Allah to Gabriel to Muhammed to his scribes, and Muhammed died before the Great Mosque was built, it would appear that these verses came from the writers and editors of the Quran, who wrote it and edited it after the death of Muhammed rather than from Muhammed and Gabriel and Allah.

Quran: Just as We sent to you a messenger from among you, who recites Our revelations to you, and purifies you, and teaches you the Book and wisdom, and teaches you what you did not know. So, remember Me, and I will remember you. And thank Me, and do not be ungrateful.

Comments: First of all, again there is one verse where supposedly Allah is speaking in the first-person plural, 'We', and then there is the verse where Allah is speaking in the first person singular. How is this to be interpreted. Also, Islam denies the Christianity belief in the trinity or persons in the One God, so to use the first-person plural, 'We' is a contradiction.

Also, the writers are trying to show that Allah chose Muhammed to be His messenger.

The statement 'remember Me, and I will remember you, seems to imply that Allah will only remember a person if they remember Him. This is opposed to the nature or God, Who considers all humans as His children.

And lastly, the statement 'and thank Me, and do not be ungrateful' certainly is not from Allah or God. God does not look for thanks from His children. He does what He does out of pure, unconditional, unrequited love.

Quran: And do not say of those who are killed in the cause of Allah, "Dead." Rather, they are alive, but you do not perceive.

Comment: 'Killed in the cause of Allah', God does not have any cause where people die. This could not have been dictated by Allah (God).

Quran: We will certainly test you with some fear and hunger, and some loss of possessions and lives and crops. But give good news to the steadfast.

Comments: This is a typical exhortation by a superior for sub-ordinate to sacrifice for the desires of the superior.

Quran: Safa and Marwa are among the rites of Allah. Whoever makes the Pilgrimage to the House, or performs the Umrah, commits no error by circulating between them. Whoever volunteers good, Allah is Appreciative and Cognizant.

Comments: Again, these verses can only have been written by individuals after the death of Muhammed trying to establish these practices as part of Islam and commanded by Allah. Allah (God) is not self-serving, and He does not dictate any religious rituals and practices.

Quran: Those who suppress the proofs and the guidance We have revealed, after We have clarified them to humanity in the Scripture, those Allah curses, and the cursers curse them.

Comment: Allah (God) does not curse anyone. It is against His nature.

Quran: Except those who repent, and reform, and proclaim. Those I will accept their repentance. I am the Acceptor of Repentance, the Merciful. But as for those who reject faith, and die rejecting, upon them is the curse of Allah, and of the angels, and of all humanity. They will remain under it forever, and the torment will not be lightened for them, and they will not be reprieved. Your God is one God. There is no god but Him, the Benevolent, the Compassionate.

Comments: These verses sound like they came from Paul of Tarsus and Pauline Christianity. There is the implication that all people are sinners who must repent, reform themselves and proclaim and accept faith in the proposed religion. And if they do not, they will be cursed by Allah, the angels, all humanity and damned for all eternity in Hell. And yet, supposedly Allah (God) claims to be the Benevolent and the Compassionate. God did not say this. It is contrary to His nature. It appears that the writers and editors were copying ideas from Pauline Christianity in creating the doctrines of Islam. Also, these same writers and editors are using coercion in trying to get people to accept Islam – convert to Islam or be damned for all eternity. From the playbook of Pauline Christianity.

Quran: Yet among the people are those who take other than Allah as equals to Him. They love them as the love of Allah. But those who believe have greater love for Allah. If only the wrongdoers would realize, when they see the torment, that all power is Allah's, and that Allah is severe in punishment.

Comments: More coercive verses. And there is the implication that one who does not believe is a wrongdoer. A person should be drawn to God or Yahweh or Allah through love and not fear.

Quran: Those who followed will say, "If only we can have another chance, we will disown them, as they disowned us." Thus, Allah will show them their deeds, as regrets to them, and they will not come out of the Fire.

Comment: It is debatable whether God sends people to an eternal punishment. The idea of Hell was created to instill in people a fear for not adhering to the teachings of a proposed man-made religion.

Quran: He has forbidden you carrion, and blood, and the flesh of swine, and what was dedicated to other than Allah. But if anyone is compelled, without desiring or exceeding, he commits no sin. Allah is Forgiving and Merciful.

Comments: Islam borrowing rules from Judaism on forbidden foods. This is not from God but from Judaism.

Quran: Those who conceal what Allah revealed in the Book, and exchange it for a small price, they swallow nothing but fire into their bellies. And Allah will not speak to them on the Day of Resurrection, nor will He purify them, and they will have a painful punishment. It is they who exchange guidance for error, and forgiveness for punishment. But why do they insist on the Fire? That is because Allah has revealed the Book in truth; and those who differ about the Book are in deep discord. Righteousness does not consist of turning your faces towards the East and the West. But righteous is he who believes in Allah, and the Last Day, and the angels, and the Scripture, and the prophets.

Comments: A person does not intentionally choose to be damned to eternal punishment. And a person chooses not to accept 'what Allah revealed in the Book' because they do not believe that it was Allah who actually revealed this but rather these things were fabricated by men. And righteousness has nothing to do with beliefs and faith.

Quran: O you who believe! Retaliation for the murdered is ordained upon you: the free for the free, the slave for the slave, the female for the female. But if he is forgiven by his kin, then grant any reasonable demand, and pay with good will. This is a concession from your Lord, and a mercy. But whoever commits aggression after that, a painful torment awaits him. There is life for you in retaliation, O people of understanding, so that you may refrain.

Comments: Retaliation is not from God.

Quran: O you who believe! Fasting is prescribed for you, as it was prescribed for those before you, that you may become righteous. For a specified number of days. But whoever among you is sick, or on a journey, then a number of other days. For those who are able: a ransom of feeding a needy person. But whoever volunteers goodness, it is better for him. But to fast is best for you if you only knew. Ramadan is the month in which the Quran was revealed. Guidance for humanity, and clear portents of guidance, and the Criterion. Whoever of you witnesses the month, shall fast it. But whoever is sick, or on a journey, then a number of other days. Allah desires ease for you, and does not desire hardship for you, that you may complete the number, and celebrate Allah for having guided you, so that you may be thankful.

Comments: Islam borrowing from Pauline Christianity the notion of fasting and perhaps even the notion of Lent. Both of these Pauline Christian practices and the Islamic corresponding practices are not from God or Allah, but man-made.

Quran: Permitted for you is intercourse with your wives on the night of the fast. They are a garment for you, and you are a garment for them. Allah knows that you used to betray yourselves, but He turned to you and pardoned you. So, approach them now, and seek what Allah has ordained for you, and eat and drink until the white streak of dawn can be distinguished from the black streak. Then complete the fast until nightfall. But do not approach them while you are in retreat at the mosques. These are the limits of Allah, so do not come near them. Allah thus clarifies His revelations to the people, that they may attain piety.

Comments: It appears that the writers and editors of the Quran are borrowing from the Judaistic norms regarding Passover with respect to Ramadan.

Quran: And kill them wherever you overtake them and expel them from where they had expelled you. Oppression is more serious than murder. But do not fight them at the Sacred Mosque unless they fight you there. If they fight you, then kill them. Such is the retribution of the disbelievers.

Comments: Killing disbelievers is not the words of Allah but the men who wrote and edited the Quran.

Quran: And fight them until there is no oppression, and worship becomes devoted to Allah alone. But if they cease, then let there be no hostility except against the oppressors.

Comments: And what is oppression meant by here, is it perceived oppression? And is financial oppression included?

Quran: The sacred month for the sacred month, and sacrilege calls for retaliation. Whoever commits aggression against you, retaliate against him in the same measure as he has committed against you. And be conscious of Allah and know that Allah is with the righteous.

Comment: Very similar to 'an eye for an eye, and a tooth for a tooth'.

Quran: And carry out the Hajj and the Umrah for Allah. But if you are prevented, then whatever is feasible of offerings. And do not shave your heads until the offering has reached its destination. Whoever of you is sick, or has an injury of the head, then redemption of fasting, or charity, or worship. When you are secure: whoever continues the Umrah until the Hajj, then whatever is feasible of offering. But if he lacks the means, then fasting for three days during the Hajj and seven when you have returned, making ten in all. This is for whose household is not present at the Sacred Mosque. And remain conscious of Allah and know that Allah is stern in retribution. The Hajj is during specific months. Whoever decides to perform the Hajj, there shall be no sexual relations, nor misconduct, nor quarrelling during the Hajj.

Comments: First of all, Allah (God) is not stern in retribution. In fact, God does not seek retribution or retaliation. That is contrary to His nature.

Quran: Fighting is ordained for you, even though you dislike it. But it may be that you dislike something while it is good for you, and it may be that you like something while it is bad for you. Allah knows, and you do not know.

Comment: 'Fighting is ordained for you, even though you dislike it.'? God does not order fighting. And to try to show that this is coming from God, 'Allah know, and you do not know', even though fighting is against God's nature is insulting to both God and the reader.

Quran: And persecution is more serious than killing. They will not cease to fight you until they turn you back from your religion if they can. Whoever among you turns back from his religion, and dies a disbeliever, those are they whose works will come to nothing, in this life, and in the Hereafter. Those are the inmates of the Fire, abiding in it forever.

Comments: These verses are attempting to divide believers from unbelievers promoting animosity between the two. Allah or God would not do this and therefore these verses could not have come from Allah.

Quran: Those who believed, and those who migrated and fought for the sake of Allah, those look forward to Allah's mercy. Allah is Forgiving and Merciful.

Comments: Fight for Allah! God is opposed to fighting, wars, conflicts since all people are the children God and He want all of His children to treat each peacefully.

Quran: They ask you about intoxicants and gambling. Say, "There is gross sin in them, and some benefits for people, but their sinfulness outweighs their benefit." Do not marry idolatresses unless they have believed. A believing maid is better than an idolatress, even if you like her. And do not marry idolaters unless they have believed. A believing servant is better than an idolater, even if you like him. These call to the Fire, but Allah calls to the Garden and to forgiveness, by His leave. He makes clear His communications to the people, that they may be mindful. And they ask you about menstruation: say, "It is harmful, so keep away from women during menstruation. And do not approach them until they have become pure. Once they have become pure, approach them in the way Allah has directed you." Allah loves the repentant, and He loves those who keep clean."

Comments: These verses are copied from the Jewish mitzvot and the Jewish notion of super cleanliness. Menstruating women are not impure or unclean. And why are dogs considered by Jews and Muslims to be avoided? The incidents of dog's absolute faithfulness to humans is without question even to the point of sacrificing their lives for their human companions.

Quran: Your women are cultivation for you; so, approach your cultivation whenever you like, and send ahead for yourselves. And fear Allah and know that you will meet Him. And give good news to the believers.

Comment: This implies that women are only good for breeding and that is not from God.

Quran: Allah does not hold you responsible for your unintentional oaths, but He holds you responsible for your intentions. Allah is forgiving and forbearing.

Comment: Like Judaism which has one set rules for Jews and another set of rules for non-Jews, this implies that Allah (God) is only forgiving and forbearing to Muslims, and from other verses He is not forgiving and forbearing to non-believers, or non-Muslims. This is certainly not from God for all people are equal in God's eyes.

Quran: Those who vow abstinence from their wives must wait for four months. But if they reconcile, Allah is Forgiving and Merciful. And if they resolve to divorce—Allah is Hearing and Knowing. Divorced women shall wait by themselves for three periods. And it is not lawful for them to conceal what Allah has created in their wombs if they believe in Allah and the Last Day. Meanwhile, their husbands have the better right to take them back if they desire reconciliation. And women have rights similar to their obligations, according to what is fair. But men have a degree over them. Allah is Mighty and Wise.

Comment: This verse implying that men are superior to women and women must submit to men is not from God for men and women are equal in the eyes of God.

Quran: Divorce is allowed twice. Then, either honorable retention, or setting free kindly. It is not lawful for you to take back anything you have given them, unless they fear that they cannot maintain Allah's limits. If you fear that they cannot maintain Allah's limits, then there is no blame on them if she sacrifices something for her release. These are

Allah's limits, so do not transgress them. Those who transgress Allah's limits are the unjust.

Comments: First of all, this is not from God but the writers and editors of the Quran and possibly the leaders of Islam when the Quran was written. These rules on divorce are favorable to men and not to women. And there is the implication that men can divorce their wives, but wives cannot divorce their husbands. Is there no sanctity in marriage within Islam? In addition, by allowing two divorces this rule undermine faithfulness and is totally contrary to the permanence of marriage as expressed in the phare' until death do us part'.

Quran: If he divorces her, she shall not be lawful for him again until she has married another husband. If the latter divorces her, then there is no blame on them for reuniting, provided they think they can maintain Allah's limits. These are Allah's limits; He makes them clear to people who know. When you divorce women, and they have reached their term, either retain them amicably, or release them amicably. But do not retain them to hurt them and commit aggression. Whoever does that has wronged himself. And do not take Allah's revelations for a joke. When you divorce women, and they have reached their term, do not prevent them from marrying their husbands, provided they agree on fair terms. Thereby, it is advised whoever among you believes in Allah and the Last Day.

Comments: Are the above verses considered to be from Allah? Certainly not! God would not specify such chauvinistic rules.

Quran: Mothers may nurse their infants for two whole years, for those who desire to complete the nursing-period. It is the duty of the father to provide for them and clothe them in a proper manner. No soul shall be burdened beyond its capacity. No mother shall be harmed on account of her child, and no father shall be harmed on account of his child. The same duty rests upon the heir. If the couple desire weaning, by mutual consent and consultation, they commit no error by doing so. You commit no error by hiring nursing mothers, as long as you pay them fairly.

Comments: These verses are not from Allah, but from the leaders of Islam who want to control every aspect of a Muslim's life. Decisions regarding nursing, weaning, engaging a wet-nurse, are all decisions solely at the discretion of the parents and the government and its leaders must leave parents alone to make these decisions on their own.

Quran: As for those among you who die and leave widows behind, their widows shall wait by themselves for four months and ten days. When they have reached their term, there is no blame on you regarding what they might honorably do with themselves. Allah is fully acquainted with what you do.

Comments: Widows must wait four months and ten days – God would not dictate such an arbitrary period of time. Surely, this is not from Allah, but from the writers and editors of the Quran and possibly leaders within the Muslim community that again, are trying to mandate rules in areas in which they have no business. And what is the sense of stating that there is no blame on the dead husband regarding what his widow does after his death. This makes absolutely no sense whatsoever. Once a person has died, he or she is not to blame for anything done by the living.

Quran: You commit no error by announcing your engagement to women, or by keeping it to yourselves. Allah knows that you will be thinking about them. But do not meet them secretly unless you have something proper to say. And do not confirm the marriage tie until the writing is fulfilled. And know that Allah knows what is in your souls, so beware of Him. And know that Allah is Forgiving and Forbearing.

Comments: These rules, mandates, and admonitions are man-made and not from Allah.

Quran: You commit no error by divorcing women before having touched them, or before having set the dowry for them. And compensate them, the wealthy according to his means, and the poor according to his means, with a fair compensation, a duty upon the doers of good.

Comments: Allah would never mandate a dowry. The idea of a dowry implies that the man and his family are buying the woman from her family. Does this imply that the man now somehow owns his wife? Allah (God) is opposed to all buying and selling of people and God is absolutely against slavery and any kind of servitude.

Quran: If you divorce them before you have touched them, but after you had set the dowry for them, give them half of what you specified, unless they forego the right, or the one in whose hand is the marriage contract foregoes it. But to forego is nearer to piety. And do not forget generosity between one another. Allah is seeing of everything you do.

Comments: The mention of the marriage contract and that this contract could be owned by someone other than the man sounds like marriage in Islam is a business transaction where goods are exchanged, a woman for a dowry. And Allah does not consider marriage to be a business transaction. This are certainly man-made verses.

Quran: Have you not considered those who fled their homes, by the thousands, fearful of death? Allah said to them, "die." Then He revived them.

Comments: Allah would never say to people 'die'. And if the Quran is the literal word of God speaking through Gabriel through Muhammed to the writers of the Quran, why does God sometimes speak in first-person singular, sometimes first-person plural, and not third person referring to Himself as 'Allah'. Such inconsistencies undermine the claim that Allah is the author of the Quran.

Quran: Fight in the cause of Allah and know that Allah is Hearing and Knowing. Have you not considered the notables of the Children of Israel after Moses? When they said to a prophet of theirs, "Appoint a king for us, and we will fight in the cause of Allah." He said, "Is it possible that, if fighting was ordained for you, you would not fight?" They said, "Why would we not fight in the cause of Allah, when we were driven out of our homes, along with our children?" But when fighting was ordained for them, they turned away, except for a few of them. But Allah is aware of the wrongdoers.

Comments: 'Fight in the cause of Allah'. First of all, Allah would never say this because it is opposed to His nature. Secondly, who will determine when and how people should fight in the cause of Allah. Obviously, the leaders of the people would tell their submissive followers when to fight. Since the spread of Islam was due in great part to military conquests, these verses could be used to justify the leader's call for war, claiming that this war is in the cause of Allah, and such a mandate appears in the Quran. This supports Muslim leadership and not Allah and is another example of why the authorship of the Quran is men and not Allah (God).

Quran: When Saul set out with the troops, he said, "Allah will be testing you with a river. Whoever drinks from it does not belong with me. But whoever does not drink from it, does belong with me, except for whoever scoops up a little with his hand." But they drank from it, except for a few of them. Then, when he crossed it, he and those who believed with him, they said, "We have no strength to face Goliath and his troops today." But those who knew that they would meet Allah said, "How many a small group has defeated a large group by Allah's will. Allah is with the steadfast." And when they confronted Goliath and his troops, they said, "Our Lord, pour down patience on us, and strengthen our foothold, and support us against the faithless people." And they defeated them by Allah's leave, and David killed Goliath, and Allah gave him sovereignty and wisdom, and taught him as He willed.

Comments: It is rather interesting how the writers of the Quran know the Jewish Scripture and make use of these Scripture to develop Islamic teachings. Does this imply that one of the objectives of the writers of the Quran was to motivate Jews to accept Islam?

Quran: These are Allah's revelations, which We recite to you in truth. You are one of the messengers. These messengers: We gave some advantage over others. To some of them Allah spoke directly, and some He raised in rank. We gave Jesus, son of Mary, the clear miracles, and We strengthened him with the Holy Spirit. Had Allah willed, those who succeeded them would not have fought one another, after the clear signs had come to them; but they disputed; some of them believed, and some of them disbelieved. Had Allah willed, they would not have fought one another; but Allah does whatever He desires.

Comments: Again, these verses intersperse the word Allah with the first-person plural 'We'. Who does 'We' refer to? Does 'We' refer to the angel, Gabriel. And is Gabriel supposedly speaking to Muhammed, 'You are one of the messengers'? And if so, are these verses implying that Gabriel gave Jesus the clear miracles and strengthened him with the Holy Spirit? And what is the meaning of 'Had Allah willed, those who succeeded them would not have fought one another, after the clear signs had come to them; but they disputed; some of them believed, and some of them disbelieved.'? And who is the Holy Spirit?

Quran: Allah is the Lord of those who believe; He brings them out of darkness and into light. As for those who disbelieve, their lords are the evil ones; they bring them out of light and into darkness, these are the inmates of the Fire, in which they will abide forever.

Comments: This is coercing people to believe because if they do not, they will go to Hell. Allah is a loving parent, not a despotic king.

Quran: Or like him who passed by a town collapsed on its foundations. He said, "How can Allah revive this after its demise?" Thereupon Allah caused him to die for a hundred years, and then resurrected him. He said, "For how long have you tarried?" He said, "I have tarried for a day, or part of a day." He said, "No. You have tarried for a hundred years. Now look at your food and your drink, it has not spoiled, and look at your donkey. We will make you a wonder for mankind. And look at the bones, how We arrange them, and then clothe them with flesh." So, when it became clear to him, he said, "I know that Allah has power over all things."

Quran: The parable of those who spend their wealth in Allah's way is that of a grain that produces seven spikes; in each spike is a hundred grains. Allah multiplies for whom He wills. And the parable of those who spend their wealth seeking Allah's approval, and to strengthen their souls, is that of a garden on a hillside. If heavy rain falls on it, its produce is doubled; and if no heavy rain falls, then dew is enough.

Comments: Are these verses referring to parables copying from the Pauline Christian Gospels which claim that Jesus spoke in parables.

Quran: Satan promises you poverty and urges you to immorality, but Allah promises you forgiveness from Himself, and grace.

Comments: Satan does not promise poverty. Does this imply that a person in poverty is immoral and has been misled by Satan? Poverty only arises due to the exploitation of the lower class by the upper class supported by the leaders in government.

Quran: If you give charity openly, that is good. But if you keep it secret, and give it to the needy in private, that is better for you. It will atone for some of your misdeeds.

Comment: Somewhat similar instruction to Matthew 6:1-4 (did the writers of the Quran copy the idea?). Matthew 6:1-4 "Be careful not to practice your righteousness in front of others to be seen by them. If you do, you will have no reward from your Father in heaven. So, when you give to the needy, do not announce it with trumpets, as the hypocrites do in the synagogues and on the streets, to be honored by others. Truly I tell you, they have received their reward in full. But when you give to the needy, do not let your left hand know what your right hand is doing, so that your giving may be in secret. Then your Father, who sees what is done in secret, will reward you." However, in Matthew 6: 1-4, giving in public may be wrong if the motive is to appear generous and charitable to other.

Quran: Allah condemns usury, and He blesses charities. Allah does not love any sinful ingrate. Those who believe, and do good deeds, and pray regularly, and give charity, they will have their reward with their Lord; they will have no fear, nor shall they grieve.

Comments: Islam has failed with respect to this commandment since Financial Institutions in Muslim counties today, do charge interest through workarounds. Islam could have been an example to the rest of the world if Muslim countries followed this commandment.

Quran: O you who believe! Fear Allah, and forgo what remains of usury, if you are believers. If you do not, then take notice of a war by Allah and His Messenger. But if you repent, you may keep your capital, neither wronging, nor being wronged.

Comments: What does this mean? Will Allah and Muhammed wage war on those who practice usury? That did not nor ever has happened. And does the statement regarding 'capital' imply that Islam promoted capitalism? Muhammed was a trader. Was he a capitalist? Did he practice usury? Usury was practiced in Mecca during the life of Muhammed. Given that Muhammed was a business, it is likely that his friends and business practiced usury. In addition, in Mecca there were only two classes of people, the wealthy, business class, which constituted the upper class which controlled the governments, and the poor, working class, which was the lower class. They were uneducated and did not participate in the various governments and branches of government. Muhammed, because of his wife, belonged to the upper class.

Quran: But if he is in hardship, then deferment until a time of ease. But to remit it as charity is better for you if you only knew. O you who believe! When you incur debt among yourselves for a certain period of time, write it down. And have a scribe write in your presence, in all fairness. And do not think it too trivial to write down, whether small or large, including the time of repayment. That is more equitable with Allah, and stronger as evidence, and more likely to prevent doubt, except in the case of a spot transaction between you, then there is no blame on you if you do not write it down. And let there be witnesses whenever you conclude a contract, and let no harm be done to either scribe or witness. If you are on a journey, and cannot find a scribe, then a security deposit should be handed over. But if you trust one another, let the trustee fulfill his trust, and let him fear Allah, his Lord. And do not conceal testimony. Whoever conceals it is sinner at heart. Allah is aware of what you do.

Comment: While not wrong, these verses involve business transactions, contracts, and lending. Obviously, contracts, lending, and capitalism existed during Muhammed's life and were part of the economic life of the people of his time. But they cannot be attributed to God for God would not assign such rules or laws.

Quran: Allah does not burden any soul beyond its capacity. To its credit is what it earns, and against it is what it commits. "Oh Lord, do not condemn us if we forget or make a mistake. Oh Lord, do not burden us as You have burdened those before us. Oh Lord, do not burden us with more than we have strength to bear; and pardon us, and forgive us, and have mercy on us. You are our Lord and Master, so help us against the disbelieving people."

Comments: These verses show a lack of understanding of the nature of God. God does not condemn His children for making a mistake. And why does the last verse imply that disbelieving people are out to harm believers.

Quran: Allah, there is no god but He, the Living, the Eternal. He sent down to you the Book with the Truth, confirming what came before it; and He sent down the Torah and the Gospel. Aforetime, as guidance for mankind; and He sent down the Criterion. Those who have rejected Allah's signs will have a severe punishment. Allah is Mighty, Able to take revenge.

Comments: Allah (God) does not take revenge, that is opposed to His nature. Revenge is a human defect. God is a God of forgiveness, not revenge. Are we to assume by this statement that Islam does not condemn revenge.

Quran: As for those who disbelieve, neither their wealth nor their children will avail them anything against Allah. These will be fuel for the Fire. Like the behavior of Pharaoh's people and those before them. They rejected Our signs, so, Allah seized them for their sins. Allah is Strict in retribution. Say to those who disbelieve, "You will be defeated, and rounded up into Hell—an awful resting-place."

Comments: Allah is not strict in retribution, but rather great in forgiveness.

Quran: Religion with Allah is Islam. Those to whom the Scripture was given differed only after knowledge came to them, out of envy among themselves. Whoever rejects the signs of Allah, Allah is quick to take account. If they argue with you, say, "I have surrendered myself to Allah, and those who follow me." And say to those who were given the Scripture, and to the unlearned, "Have you surrendered?" If they have surrendered, then they are guided; but if they turn away, then your duty is to convey.

Comments: Does this imply that Muslims are supposed to proselytize, and try to convert Jews and Christians to Islam?

Quran: Believers are not to take disbelievers for friends instead of believers. Whoever does that has nothing to do with Allah, unless it is to protect your own selves against them. Allah warns you to beware of Him.

Comments: All people are Gods' (Allah's) children not just believers. And the best way to proselytize is to show friends by example. God (Allah) would not say this.

Quran: Say, "Obey Allah and the Messenger." But if they turn away, Allah does not love the faithless.

Comments: If Allah said this, why would He refer to Himself in the third person as 'Allah'. And here the writers and editors of the Quran are trying to show that God (Allah) is commanding people to listen to Allah and if they do not, they are not loved by God. God loves all people, for all people are His children. God (Allah) will not stop loving someone because they do not follow Muhammed.

Quran: Allah chose Adam, and Noah, and the family of Abraham, and the family of Imran (Joachim, the father of Mary, the mother of Jesus), over all mankind. Offspring one of the other. The wife of Imran said, "My Lord, I have vowed to You what is in my womb, dedicated, so accept from me; You are the Hearer and Knower." And when she delivered her, she said, "My Lord, I have delivered a female," and Allah was well aware of what she has delivered, "and the male is not like the female, and I have named her Mary, and have commended her and her descendants to Your protection, from Satan the outcast."

Comments: Allah could not have chosen Adam, Noah. and Abraham over all mankind. First of all, there is no historical evidence that these people ever existed, their narratives were myths. Second, God (Allah) has no favorite children, for God (Allah) loves all of His children equally. The verses regarding Mary, the mother of Jesus, and her parents are based on noncanonical sources and are legends. While the story of Joachim and Anne first appears in the apocryphal Gospel of James. This account appears to be a copy of the Old Testament story of the barren Hannah and her conception of Samuel (1 Samuel 1). The writers of Quran were obviously trying to influence Pauline Christians.

Quran: Her Lord accepted her with a gracious reception, and brought her a beautiful upbringing, and entrusted her to the care of Zechariah. Whenever Zechariah entered upon her in the sanctuary, he found her with provision. He said, "O Mary, where did you get this from?" She said, "It is from Allah; Allah provides to whom He wills without reckoning."

Thereupon Zechariah prayed to his Lord; he said, "My Lord, bestow on me good offspring from Your presence; You are the Hearer of Prayers." Then the angels called out to him, as he stood praying in the sanctuary: "Allah gives you good news of John; confirming a Word from Allah, and honorable, and moral, and a prophet; one of the upright." He said, "My Lord, how will I have a son, when old age has overtaken me, and my wife is barren?" He said, "Even so, Allah does whatever He wills." He said, "My Lord, give me a sign." He said, "Your sign is that you shall not speak to the people for three days, except by gestures.

Comments: This narrative mixes the apocryphal legends of Mary's parents and the parents of John the Baptist. The writers and editors of the Quran are trying to gain favor with Pauline Christians but fail with respect to accuracy. Certainly, not from God.

Quran: The angels said, "O Mary, Allah has chosen you, and has purified you. He has chosen you over all the women of the world. "O Mary, be devoted to your Lord, and bow down, and kneel with those who kneel." The Angels said, "O Mary, Allah gives you good news of a Word from Him. His name is the Messiah, Jesus, son of Mary, well-esteemed in this world and the next, and one of the nearest. He will speak to the people from the crib, and in adulthood, and will be one of the righteous." She said, "My Lord, how can I have a child, when no man has touched me?" He said, "It will be so. Allah creates whatever He wills. To have anything done, He only says to it, 'Be,' and it is." And He will teach him the Scripture and wisdom, and the Torah and the Gospel.

Comments: How is God supposed to teach Jesus the Gospel before it is even written. In addition, as shown earlier, the Gospels were not written as an objective account of the actions and words of Jesus but rather in order to convert Jews to Pauline Christianity and convince them that Jesus was the Messiah.

Quran: When Jesus sensed disbelief on their part, he said, "Who are my allies towards Allah?" The disciples said, "We are Allah's allies; we have believed in Allah, and bear witness that we submit." "Our Lord, we have believed in what You have revealed, and we have followed the Messenger, so count us among the witnesses." Allah said, "O Jesus, I am terminating your life, and raising you to Me, and clearing you of those who disbelieve. And I will make those who follow you superior to those who disbelieve, until the Day of Resurrection. Then to Me is your return; then I will judge between you regarding what you were disputing. As for those who disbelieve, I will punish them with a severe punishment, in this world and the next, and they will have no helpers.

Comments: These verses are certainly a fabrication by the writers and editors of the Quran. Where did the so-called statements of Jesus come from? And where in the Gospels is there any mention of 'Allah'? And where is there any evidence of a conversation between God and the allies of Jesus ("Our Lord, we have believed in what You have revealed, and we have followed the Messenger, so count us among the witnesses." And where is there any evidence of the conversation between Allah and Jesus?

Quran: O People of the Book! Why do you argue about Abraham, when the Torah and the Gospel were not revealed until after him? Will you not reason? Abraham was neither a Jew nor a Christian, but he was a Monotheist, a Muslim. And he was not of the Polytheists. Among the People of the Book is he, who, if you entrust him with a heap of gold, he will give it back to you. And among them is he, who, if you entrust him with a single coin, he will not give it back to you, unless you keep after him. That is because they say, "We are under no obligation towards the gentiles." They tell lies about Allah, and they know it.

Comments: Do these verses imply interactions between a Jew and a non-Jew and the stingy Jews who say, "we are under no obligation towards the gentiles." Tell lies about Allah? And the statement 'we are under no obligation towards the gentile' is very interesting. Does it represent an attitude or rule of the Jews at the time when the Quran was written?

Quran: Say, "We believe in Allah, and in what was revealed to us; and in what was revealed to Abraham, and Ishmael, and Isaac, and Jacob, and the Patriarchs; and in what was given to Moses, and Jesus, and the prophets from their Lord. We make no distinction between any of them, and to Him we submit." Whoever seeks other than Islam as a religion, it will not be accepted from him, and in the Hereafter, he will be among the losers.

Comments: Does this imply that all people need to seek Islam as a religion? And does this mean that Islam is supposedly the only true religion. Judaism and Pauline Christianity state the same regarding their religions.

Quran: Their penalty is that upon them falls the curse of Allah, and of the angels, and of all mankind. Remaining in it eternally, without their punishment being eased from them, and without being reprieved.

Comments: Allah (God) does not curse anyone, nor do angels. And it is debatable whether people will be punished eternally.

Quran: As for those who disbelieve and die disbelievers, even the earth full of gold would not be accepted from any of them, were he to offer it for ransom. These will have a painful torment and will have no saviors.

Comments: Belief is not a criterion as to whether a person is good or bad.

Quran: The first house established for mankind is the one at Mecca; blessed, and guidance for all people.

Comments: This implies that Islam with Mecca as its center is the only religion for all people. Is this really the teachings of Islam? And if so, only Muslims are pleasing to Allah (God). Marketing on the part of the writers and editors to coerce people into converting to Islam.

Quran: You are the best community that ever emerged for humanity: you advocate what is moral, and forbid what is immoral, and believe in Allah. Had the People of the Scripture believed it would have been better for them. Among them are the believers, but most of them are sinners.

Comments: Are these verses referring to Jews and Christians?

Quran: O you who believe! Do not befriend outsiders who never cease to wish you harm. They love to see you suffer. Hatred has already appeared from their mouths, but what their hearts conceal is worse. We have made the messages clear for you if you understand.

Comment: 'Do not befriend outsiders.' Does this imply that Muslims should not love their non-Muslim neighbors? And do all so-called outsiders wish harm to Muslims? Certainly, not!

Quran: Remember when you left your home in the morning, to assign battle-positions for the believers. Allah is Hearing and Knowing. When two groups among you almost faltered, but Allah was their Protector. So, in Allah let the believers put their trust. Allah had given you victory at Badr when you were weak. So, fear Allah, that you may be thankful.

Comment: Allah (God) does not give victory to a war or battle between humans. He does not condone fighting or wars.

Quran: When you said to the believers, "Is it not enough for you that your Lord has reinforced you with three thousand angels, sent down?" It is, but if you persevere and remain cautious, and they attack you suddenly, your Lord will reinforce you with five thousand angels, well trained.

Comments: Well-trained angels? Allah (God) would not send angels to battle with humans. Nor is it within the nature of angels to fight humans,

Quran: Allah made it but a message of hope for you, and to reassure your hearts thereby. Victory comes only from Allah the Almighty, the Wise.

Quran: To Allah belongs everything in the heavens and the earth. He forgives whom He wills, and He punishes whom He wills.

Comment: Allah (God) forgives all and does not punish.

Quran: O you who believe! Do not feed on usury, compounded over and over, and fear Allah, so that you may prosper.

Comment: Interesting statement! It implies that usury was common at the time of the writing of the Quran.

Quran: So that Allah may prove those who believe and eliminate the disbelievers.

Comment: Allah does not eliminate the disbelievers; it is against His nature.

Quran: Muhammad is no more than a messenger.

Comment: This implies that a person needs to accept everything in the Quran because it supposedly was dictated by Muhammed (the Quran was actually written by others and not by Muhmmed) and Muhammed was the messenger of Allah. Rather coercive!

Quran: Those of you who turned back on the day when the two armies clashed, it was Satan who caused them to backslide, on account of some of what they have earned. But Allah has forgiven them. Allah is Forgiving and Prudent.

If you are killed in the cause of Allah, or die, forgiveness and mercy from Allah are better than what they hoard. If you die, or are killed, to Allah you will be gathered up.

Comments: Is Islam a religion of peace or of war. Allah (God) wants peace among all people and not war. These verses promote war, condemning retreat during battle, and claim that if you die in battle, you will go to Heaven. This is not from Allah (God). It is from men who promote war. Did this come from Muhammed, the so-called Prophet, who was also a warrior general and while he was supposedly dictating the Quran, fought eight major battles, led eighteen raids, and planned another thirty-eight military campaigns. Would Allah (God) really choose a warmonger to be His prophet and leader of a new religion? Doubtful!

Quran: Is someone who pursues Allah's approval the same as someone who incurs Allah's wrath, and his refuge is Hell—the miserable destination? They have different ranks with Allah, and Allah is Seeing of what they do. Allah has blessed the believers, as He raised up among them a messenger from among themselves, who recites to them His revelations, and purifies them, and teaches them the Scripture and wisdom, although before that they were in evident error.

Comments: Promoting Muhammed?

Quran: And that He may know the hypocrites. And it was said to them, "Come, fight in the cause of Allah, or contribute." They said, "If we knew how to fight, we would have followed you." On that day they were closer to infidelity than they were to faith. They say with their mouths what is not in their hearts, but Allah knows what they hide. Those who said of their brethren, as they stayed behind, "Had they obeyed us, they would not have been killed." Do not consider those killed in the cause of Allah as dead. In fact, they are alive, at their Lord, well provided for. So, they came back with grace from Allah, and bounty, and no harm having touched them. They pursued what pleases Allah. Allah possesses immense grace.

Comments: Fighting in the cause of Allah – Allah has no cause that required fighting.

Quran: Those who withhold what Allah has given them of his bounty should not assume that is good for them. In fact, it is bad for them. They will be encircled by their hoardings on the Day of Resurrection.

Comments: These verses are coercing people to contribute to Islam. People should contribute based on their own choice and not be coerced into giving. Contributing out of coercion is not a good thing.

Quran: O people! Fear your Lord, who created you from a single soul, and created from it its mate, and propagated from them many men and women.

Comment: Allah (God) creates from nothing. The verse above about the Lord creating mankind from one first, single soul is fabricated by the writers of the Quran, it is not from God.

Quran: If you fear you cannot act fairly towards the orphans, then marry the women you like, two, or three, or four. But if you fear you will not be fair, then one, or what you already have. That makes it more likely that you avoid bias.

Comments: These verses imply that Islam allows polygyny, but polygyny implies a superiority of males over females which God opposes. Since all people, male and female, rich and poor, educated and uneducated are equal in the eyes of God.

Quran: Allah instructs you regarding your children: The male receives the equivalent of the share of two females. If they are daughters, more than two, they get two-thirds of what he leaves. If there is only one, she gets one-half. As for the parents, each gets one-sixth of what he leaves if he had children. If he had no children, and his parents inherit from him, his mother gets one-third. If he has siblings, his mother gets one-sixth. After fulfilling any bequest and paying off debts. You get one-half of what your wives leave behind if they had no children. If they had children, you get one-fourth of what they leave. They get one-fourth of what you leave behind if you have no children. If you have children, they get one-eighth of what you leave. If a man or woman leaves neither parents nor children, but has a brother or sister, each of them gets one-sixth. If there are more siblings, they share one third. These are the bounds set by Allah. Whoever obeys Allah and His Messenger, He will admit him into Gardens beneath which rivers flow, to abide therein forever. That is the great attainment.

Comments: These verses seem to imply that the writers are proposing rules or laws to be followed similar to the mitzvot rules and commandments of Judaism. The element of coercion is used very often, that is, you must follow these rules, otherwise you will not see Paradise.

Quran: Those of your women who commit lewdness, you must have four witnesses against them, from among you. If they testify, confine them to the homes until death claims them, or Allah makes a way for them.

Comments: Peculiar verses! People who testify against a supposed women must be confined to their homes for the rest of their lives. These verses are certainly not from Allah.

Quran: O you who believe! It is not permitted for you to inherit women against their will. And do not coerce them in order to take away some of what you had given them unless they commit a proven adultery. And live with them in kindness. If you dislike them, it may be that you dislike something in which Allah has placed much good. If you wish to replace one wife with another, and you have given one of them a fortune, take nothing back from it. Would you take it back fraudulently and sinfully? And how can you take it back, when you have been intimate with one another, and they have received from you a solid commitment? Do not marry women whom your fathers married, except what is already past. That is improper, indecent, and a bad custom. Forbidden for you are your mothers, your daughters, your sisters, your paternal aunts, your maternal aunts, your brother's daughters, your sister's daughters, your foster mothers who nursed you, your sisters through nursing, your wives' mothers, and your stepdaughters in your guardianship, born of wives you have gone into, but if you have not gone into them, there is no blame on you. And the wives of your genetic sons and marrying two sisters simultaneously. And all married women, except those you rightfully possess. This is Allah's decree, binding upon you.

Comments: 'Replace one wife with another'. How could this have come from God through Gabriel through Muhammed. And what about replacing a husband with another, should all rules and advice apply equally to both men and women.

Quran: If any of you lack the means to marry free believing women, he may marry one of the believing maids under your control. Allah is well aware of your faith. You are from one another. Marry them with the permission of their guardians, and give them their recompense fairly, to be protected, neither committing adultery, nor taking secret lovers. When they are married, if they commit adultery, their punishment shall be half that of free women.

Comments: These verses imply that slavery is allowed in Islam ('believing maids under your control'). This is implied in the verse, 'When they are married, if they commit adultery, their punishment shall be half that of free women. God does not condone slavery in any form. It is against His nature. It is obvious that Muhammed, the writers of the Quran, and the editors of the Quran did not understand the nature of God.

Quran: Men are the protectors and maintainers of women, as Allah has given some of them an advantage over others, and because they spend out of their wealth. The good women are obedient, guarding what Allah would have them guard. As for those from whom you fear disloyalty, admonish them, and abandon them in their beds, then strike them.

Comments: These verses imply that men are superior to women and also that men can physically punish their wives ('then strike them').

Quran: O you who believe! Do not approach the prayer while you are drunk, so that you know what you say; nor after sexual orgasm, unless you are travelling, until you have bathed. If you are sick, or traveling, or one of you comes from the toilet, or you have had intercourse with women, and cannot find water, find clean sand, and wipe your faces and your hands with it.

Comment: These verses on cleanliness are very similar to the rules of Judaism in the Mitzvot commandments.

 Quran: Among the Jews are some who take words out of context, and say, "We hear, and we disobey", and "Hear without listening", and "Observe us," twisting with their tongues and slandering the religion. Had they said, "We hear, and we obey", and "Listen", and "Give us your attention," it would have been better for them, and more upright. But Allah has cursed them for their disbelief; they do not believe except a little.

Comment: Is this a condemnation of Jews?

Quran: O you who believe! Take your precautions, and mobilize in groups, or mobilize altogether. Among you is he who lags behind. Then, when a calamity befalls you, he says, "Allah has favored me, that I was not martyred with them." But when some bounty from Allah comes to you, he says as if no affection existed between you and him, "If only I had been with them, I would have achieved a great victory."

Comment: Are these verses implying mobilization for war?

Quran: Whoever fights in the cause of Allah, and then is killed, or achieves victory, We will grant him a great compensation.

And why is the first-person plural used here to refer to God? God would not endorse war and reward a person killed in a war.

Quran: And why would you not fight in the cause of Allah, and the helpless men, and women, and children, cry out, "Our Lord, deliver us from this town whose people are oppressive, and appoint for us from

Your Presence a Protector, and appoint for us from Your Presence a Victor."

Comments: These verses seem to refer to the battles between the early Muslims and the polytheistic Arab who discriminated against them, promoted, directed, and commanded by Muhammed. These verses attempt to show that such military engagements are directed by God.

Quran: Those who believe fight in the cause of Allah, while those who disbelieve fight in the cause of Evil. So, fight the allies of the Devil. Whoever obeys the Messenger is obeying Allah.

Comment: This verse is obviously trying to coerce people into obeying Muhammed because what he commands is what God commands. This is certainly an outrageous claim.

Quran: So, fight in the cause of Allah; you are responsible only for yourself. They would love to see you disbelieve, just as they disbelieve, so you would become equal. So do not befriend any of them unless they emigrate in the way of Allah. If they turn away, seize them, and execute them wherever you may find them; and do not take from among them allies or supporters.

Comments: 'Execute them wherever you may find them'. If whoever obeys Muhammed, obeys God. Does God support executing people even if they are disbelievers? Certainly not! And 'fight in the cause of Allah'? Who decides if a cause is the cause of Allah – Muhammed?

Quran: You will find others who want security from you, and security from their own people. But whenever they are tempted into civil discord, they plunge into it. So, if they do not withdraw from you, nor offer you peace, nor restrain their hands, seize them and execute them wherever you find them. Against these, We have given you clear authorization.

Comments: These verses again contain the mandate to execute non-Muslims and also contains the statement, 'We have given you clear authorization'. God would never give any authorization to execute someone, so Muhammed does not speak for God, and Muslims should question what Muhammed says.

Quran: Never should a believer kill another believer, unless by error. Anyone who kills a believer by error must set free a believing slave, and pay compensation to the victim's family, unless they remit it as charity. If the victim belonged to a people who are hostile to you, but is a believer, then the compensation is to free a believing slave. If he belonged to a people with whom you have a treaty, then compensation should be handed over to his family, and a believing slave set free. Anyone who lacks the means must fast for two consecutive months, by way of repentance to Allah.

Comments: These verses imply that there were Muslim slaves. How can Islam claim to have been founded by Allah while allowing one Muslim to own another Muslim?

Quran: Whoever kills a believer deliberately, the penalty for him is Hell, where he will remain forever. And Allah will be angry with him, and will curse him, and will prepare for him a terrible punishment.

Comments: Allah (God) does not get angry, nor curse, nor condemn. These things are against the Nature of God.

Quran: When you travel in the land, there is no blame on you for shortening the prayers, if you fear that the disbelievers may harm you. The disbelievers are your manifest enemies. When you are among them, and you stand to lead them in prayer, let a group of them stand with you, and let them hold their weapons. Then, when they have done their prostrations, let them withdraw to the rear, and let another group, that have not prayed yet, come forward and pray with you; and let them take their precautions and their weapons. Those who disbelieve would like you to neglect your weapons and your equipment, so they can attack you in a single assault. Indeed, Allah has prepared for the disbelievers a demeaning punishment.

Comments: Does Islam allow weapons while praying and in a house of worship? Does mean that Muslims carry weapons to pray?

Quran: And do not falter in the pursuit of the enemy.

Comment: 'Do not falter in the pursuit of the enemy' implies that the so-called enemy must be pursued even while they, the enemy, is retreating. Is this virtuous?

Quran: Whoever does that, seeking Allah's approval, We will give him a great compensation.

Comment: Again, literally in the same verse, Allah is referred to in the third person and then in the first-person plural (We). If this is Allah speaking, then why is He doing this? Or is Allah not speaking?

Quran: Whoever makes a breach with the Messenger, after the guidance has become clear to him, and follows other than the path of the believers, We will direct him in the direction he has chosen, and commit him to Hell, what a terrible destination!

Comment: Another example of coercion. A person must follow Muhammed and do what he says or be damned to Hell.

Quran: And who is better in religion than he who submits himself wholly to Allah, and is a doer of good, and follows the faith of Abraham the Monotheist? Allah has chosen Abraham for a friend.

Comments: Muhammed and the Muslims think that they are descendants of Abraham who supposedly lived 2700 years before Muhammed. Muhammed would not have known the narrative of Abraham was a myth and that there is no historical evidence to prove his existence. Obviously, Muhammed and the writers and editors of the Quran relied completely on the Jewish Bible for this information.

Quran: They ask you for a ruling about women. Say, "Allah gives you a ruling about them, and so does what is stated to you in the Book about widowed women from whom you withhold what is decreed for them, yet you desire to marry them, and about helpless children: that you should treat the orphans fairly." You will not be able to treat women with equal fairness, no matter how much you desire it.

Comments: 'You will not be able to treat women with equal fairness'. Does this imply that Islam has a rule from Allah that women should not be treated as equals to men? If that is what this is implying, then this is certainly not from God because men and women are equal in the eyes of God.

Quran: O you who believe! Believe in Allah and His messenger, and the Book He sent down to His messenger, and the Book He sent down before. Whoever rejects Allah, His angels, His Books, His messengers, and the Last Day, has strayed far in error.

Comments: More coercive verses forcing people to believe in Muhammed. These verses state that believing in Muhammed is like believing in God Himself. How can anyone objectively accept this. These verses are not from God, but from men.

Quran: He has revealed to you in the Book that when you hear Allah's revelations being rejected, or ridiculed, do not sit with them until they engage in some other subject. Otherwise, you would be like them. Allah will gather the hypocrites and the disbelievers, into Hell, altogether.

Comments: Allah will not send disbelievers to Hell just because they disbelieve in the teachings of Muhammed.

Quran: Those who disbelieve in Allah and His messengers, and want to separate between Allah and His messengers, and say, "We believe in some, and reject some," and wish to take a path in between. These are the unbelievers, truly. We have prepared for the unbelievers a shameful punishment.

Quran: The People of the Scripture challenge you to bring down to them a book from the sky. They had asked Moses for something even greater. They said, "Show us Allah plainly." The thunderbolt struck them for their wickedness. Then they took the calf for worship, even after the clear proofs had come to them. Yet We pardoned that, and We gave Moses a clear authority. And We raised the Mount above them in accordance with their covenant, and We said to them, "Enter the gate humbly", and We said to them, "Do not violate the Sabbath", and We received from them a solemn pledge. But for their violation of their covenant, and their denial of Allah's revelations, and their killing of the prophets unjustly, and their saying, "Our minds are closed." In fact, Allah has sealed them for their disbelief, so they do not believe, except for a few. And for their faithlessness, and their saying against Mary a monstrous slander. And for their saying, "We have killed the Messiah, Jesus, the son of Mary, the Messenger of Allah." In fact, they did not kill him, nor did they crucify him, but it appeared to them as if they did. Indeed, those who differ about him are in doubt about it. They have no knowledge of it, except the following of assumptions. Certainly, they did not kill him. Rather, Allah raised him up to Himself.

Comments: These verses are trying to connect Judaism, Christianity, and Islam as though God established them all. But can there be three different, true religions established by God for people to follow? And are there implications that the Jews broke their covenant with God? And what about the statement that the Jews did not kill Jesus, nor did they crucify him, but it appeared to them as if they did?

Quran: Due to wrongdoing on the part of the Jews, We forbade them good things that used to be lawful for them; and for deterring many from Allah's path. And for their taking usury, although they were forbidden it, and for their consuming people's wealth dishonestly. We have prepared for the faithless among them a painful torment.

Comments: These verses seem to continue the claim that the Jews strayed from the path to God. The verses condemning the Jews for practicing usury is very interesting. The Jews were forbidden from practicing usury with a fellow Jew but not with non-Jews. But this claim and the claim that the Jews consumed people's wealthy dishonestly probably indicated the reputation at the time of Muhammed and the founding of Islam of the Jews engaging in usury and other dishonest business practices. These claims are probably true, but these claims are coming from Muhammed, the writers of the Quran, and the editors of the Quran and not Allah through Gabriel.

Quran: We have inspired you, as We had inspired Noah and the prophets after him. And We inspired Abraham, and Ishmael, and Isaac, and Jacob, and the Patriarchs, and Jesus, and Job, and Jonah, and Aaron, and Solomon. And We gave David the Psalms. Some messengers We have already told you about, while some messengers We have not told you about. And Allah spoke to Moses directly.

Comments: The writers of the Quran were certainly familiar with the Tanakh and the Gospels. Again, who is the 'We' in these verses who inspired these so-called messengers? The Tanakh implies that God (Allah) spoke directly to the Jewish messengers, and, and the Gospels imply that God spoke directly to Jesus and that Jesus was God. If the 'We' is the angel, Gabriel, then the Quran is the first time that such a claim has been made. Or is this just a fabrication to connect Judaism, Christianity, and Islam?

Quran: O people! The Messenger has come to you with the truth from your Lord, so believe, that is best for you.

Comments: Coercive! Who is claiming that the Messenger, Muhammed, has come to people from the Lord. This is coercive because it insinuates that everything that Muhammed says is from the Lord and is best for people. Actually, this is a rather arrogant and outrageous claim.

Quran: O People of the Scripture! Do not exaggerate in your religion, and do not say about Allah except the truth. The Messiah, Jesus, the son of Mary, is the Messenger of Allah, and His Word that He conveyed to Mary, and a Spirit from Him. So, believe in Allah and His messengers, and do not say, "Three." Refrain, it is better for you. Allah is only one God. Glory be to Him that He should have a son. To Him belongs everything in the heavens and the earth, and Allah is a sufficient Protector.

Comments: These verses attempt to discredit the Christian belief in a triune God.

Quran: The Messiah does not disdain to be a servant of Allah, nor do the favored angels. Whoever disdains His worship and is too arrogant— He will round them up to Himself altogether.

Comments: Does this imply that Islam considers Jesus to be the Messiah?

Quran: They ask you for a ruling. Say, "Allah gives you a ruling concerning the person who has neither parents nor children." If a man dies, and leaves no children, and he had a sister, she receives one-half of what he leaves. And he inherits from her if she leaves no children. But if there are two sisters, they receive two thirds of what he leaves. If the siblings are men and women, the male receives the share of two females." Allah makes things clear for you, less you err. Allah is Aware of everything.

Comments: Similar rules or guidance was contained in earlier verses, most likely a mistake on the part of the writers, but such a mistake could not have come from God Who makes no mistakes. This mistake undermines the claim that the Quran was dictated by God to Gabriel to Muhammed.

Quran: O you who believe! Fulfill your commitments. Livestock animals are permitted for you, except those specified to you; but not wild game while you are in pilgrim sanctity. Allah decrees whatever He wills. Prohibited for you are carrion, blood, the flesh of swine, and animals dedicated to other than Allah; also, the flesh of animals strangled, killed violently, killed by a fall, gored to death, mangled by wild animals, except what you rescue, and animals sacrificed on altars; and the practice of drawing lots. For it is immoral. Today, those who disbelieve have despaired of your religion, so do not fear them, but fear Me. Today I have perfected your religion for you, and have completed My favor upon you, and have approved Islam as a religion for you.

Comments: Again, copying rules from the Jewish Mitzvot.

Quran: They ask you what is permitted for them. Say, "Permitted for you are all good things, including what trained dogs and falcons catch for you." You train them according to what Allah has taught you. So, eat from what they catch for you, and pronounce Allah's name over it. And fear Allah. Allah is swift in reckoning.

Comment: Training dogs and falcons according to what Allah taught. What document contains the directions from God how to train dogs and falcons? And God would never give specific directions on how to train does and falcons.

Quran: Today all good things are made lawful for you. And the food of those given the Scripture is lawful for you, and your food is lawful for them. So are chaste believing women, and chaste women from the people who were given the Scripture before you, provided you give them their dowries, and take them in marriage, not in adultery, nor as mistresses. But whoever rejects faith, his work will be in vain, and in the Hereafter, he will be among the losers.

Comment: These verses allow marriage with Jewish and Christian women, indicating the mixed society within the Arabian Peninsula at the time of the writing of the Quran. Many verses are concluded with statements such as,' But whoever rejects faith, his work will be in vain, and in the Hereafter, he will be among the losers.' This is another example of coercion on the part of the writers who are trying to coerce the people into accepting this rule or guidance because it is part of faith in God and if a person does not believe and submit, they will be damned to Hell.

Quran: O you who believe! When you rise to pray, wash your faces and your hands and arms to the elbows, and wipe your heads, and your feet to the ankles. If you had intercourse, then purify yourselves. If you are ill, or travelling, or one of you returns from the toilet, or you had contact with women, and could not find water, then use some clean sand and wipe your faces and hands with it. Allah does not intend to burden you, but He intends to purify you, and to complete His blessing upon you, that you may be thankful.

Comments: Similar verses are found earlier in the Quran, and this is another example of the writer repeating the same thing twice. A human writer would do so, but not God. And the Jewish idea that a person is unclean, and Allah wants them to be purified by washing due to physical actions is actually contrary to the nature of God. God does not care whether a person is physically clean or dirty.

Quran: Allah received a pledge from the Children of Israel, and We raised among them twelve chiefs. Allah said, "I am with you; if you perform the prayer, and pay the alms, and believe in My messengers and support them, and lend Allah a loan of righteousness; I will remit your sins and admit you into Gardens beneath which rivers flow. But whoever among you disbelieves afterwards has strayed from the right way."

Comments: God would never say that a person needs to perform the prayer or believe in His so-called, self-proclaimed messengers in order to merit Heaven.

Quran: Because of their breaking their pledge, We cursed them, and made their hearts hard. They twist the words out of their context, and they disregarded some of what they were reminded of. You will always witness deceit from them, except for a few of them. But pardon them and overlook. Allah loves the doers of good.

Comments: Another condemnation of most Jews! God or

Gabriel would never curse anyone and make their hearts hard. It is against their natures. And the statement that, 'You will always witness deceit from them, except for a few of them.' is very interesting. Is this a comment on how the Jews of the period when the Quran was written really were, that is, deceitful?

Quran: And from those who say, "we are Christians," We received their pledge, but they neglected some of what they were reminded of. So, we provoked enmity and hatred among them until the Day of Resurrection; Allah will then inform them of what they used to craft. O People of the Book! Our Messenger has come to you, clarifying for you much of what you kept hidden of the Book, and overlooking much. A light from Allah has come to you, and a clear Book.

Comments: First the Quran condemns most Jews, and now most Christians. Is this intended by the writers to imply that Islam is preferred by God over Judaism and Christianity?

Quran: They disbelieve those who say, "Allah is the Christ, the son of Mary." Say, "Who can prevent Allah, if He willed, from annihilating the Christ son of Mary, and his mother, and everyone on earth?"

Comments: This is obviously a condemnation of the Christian belief that Jesus Christ is the Son of God and equal to God and an attempt to dissuade people from becoming Christians.

Quran: The Jews and the Christians say, "We are the children of Allah, and His beloved." Say, "Why then does He punish you for your sins?" In fact, you are humans from among those He created. He forgives whom He wills, and He punishes whom He wills.

Comments: Who is the beloved of Allah in these verses, Muhammed? In fact, Jews, Christians, polytheists, and all people are the children of Allah. Are these verses trying to lead people to conclude that only Muslims are the children of Allah? These verses are certainly not from Allah to Gabriel to Muhammed.

Quran: The punishment for those who fight Allah and His Messenger, and strive to spread corruption on earth, is that they be killed, or crucified, or have their hands and feet cut off on opposite sides or be banished from the land. That is to disgrace them in this life; and in the Hereafter they will have a terrible punishment.

Comments: Islam has engaged in many wars and military engagements since the time of Muhammed and included Muhammed who commanded and led multiple wars and military engagements. Are these verses a condemnation of anyone who dares to resist Islam and their military efforts and an implication that anyone who resists Islam is spreading corruption and should be killed or crucified or have their hands and feet cutoff? This is certainly not from Allah, nor from Gabriel, but fabricated by the human writers and editors of the

Quran: But whoever repents after his crime, and reforms, Allah will accept his repentance. Allah is Forgiving and Merciful. As for the thief, whether male or female, cut their hands as a penalty for what they have reaped, a deterrent from Allah. Allah is Mighty and Wise.

Comments: Allah (God) would never command this practice. But if these verses are not from God, then they must be from Muhammed or the writers and editors of the Quran. Unfortunately, even today in Saudi Arabia and Sudan this practice exists.

Quran: Do you not know that to Allah belongs the kingdom of the heavens and the earth? He punishes whom He wills, and He forgives whom He wills. And Allah is Capable of everything.

Comments: God forgives but does not punish. He will allow people to suffer the consequences of their own decisions. And God is only capable of doing good and whatever is not opposed to His nature.

Quran: Messenger! Do not let those who are quick to disbelief grieve you, from among those who say with their mouths, "We believe," but their hearts do not believe; and from among the Jews, listeners to lies, listeners to other people who did not come to you. They distort words from their places, and they say, "If you are given this, accept it, but if you are not given it, beware." Whomever Allah has willed to divert you have nothing for him from Allah. Those are they whose hearts Allah does not intend to purify. For them is disgrace in this world, and for them is a great punishment in the Hereafter.

Comments: Are these verses an instruction to Muhammed, 'Messenger! Do not let those who are quick to disbelief grieve you, from among those who say with their mouths, "We believe," but their hearts do not believe; and from among the Jews, listeners to lies, listeners to other people who did not come to you. They distort words from their places, and they say, "If you are given this, accept it, but if you are not given.'

Quran: And We wrote for them in it: a life for a life, an eye for an eye, a nose for a nose, an ear for an ear, a tooth for a tooth, and an equal wound for a wound; but whoever forgoes it in charity, it will serve as atonement for him. Those who do not rule according to what Allah revealed are the evildoers.

Comments: 'A life for a life, an eye for an eye, a nose for a nose, an ear for an ear, a tooth for a tooth, and an equal wound for a wound; but whoever forgoes it in charity, it will serve as atonement for him.' Are these verses trying to justify the absurd notion from the Book of Exodus (in the Jewish Bible) which allows for retaliation? The law of retaliation is not from God. God demands forgiveness, not retaliation.

Quran: In their footsteps, We sent Jesus son of Mary, fulfilling the Torah that preceded him; and We gave him the Gospel, wherein is guidance and light, and confirming the Torah that preceded him, and guidance and counsel for the righteous. So let the people of the Gospel rule according to what Allah revealed in it. Those who do not rule according to what Allah revealed are the sinners.

Comments: Jesus did not fulfill or confirm the Torah. And who is the 'We' who gave him the Gospels, the Gospels were written by men and not inspired or dictated by God. These verses were written by men and not by Allah.

Quran: O you who believe! Do not take the Jews and the Christians as allies; some of them are allies of one another. Whoever of you allies himself with them is one of them. Allah does not guide the wrongdoing people.

Comments: Another condemnation of the Jews and the Christians. And the statement, 'Whoever of you allies himself with them is one of them. Allah does not guide the wrongdoing people.' Is the implication that Jews and Christians are the wrongdoing people or those that are allies or friends of Jews and Christians or both?

Quran: Your allies are Allah, and His Messenger, and those who believe, those who pray regularly, and give charity, and bow down. Whoever allies himself with Allah, and His Messenger, and those who believe, surely the Party of Allah is the victorious.

Quran: Say, "O People of the Scripture! Do you resent us only because we believe in Allah, and in what was revealed to us, and in what was revealed previously; and most of you are sinners?" Say, "Shall I inform you of worse than that for retribution from Allah? He whom Allah has cursed, and with whom He became angry; and He turned some of them into apes, and swine, and idol worshipers. These are in a worse position, and further away from the right way."

Comment: God does not become angry and when did God ever turn people into apes or swine?

Quran: Why do the rabbis and the priests do not prevent them from speaking sinfully and from consuming forbidden wealth? Evil is what they have been doing.

Comments: Are these verses another condemnation of Judaism and Christianity? And now the claim of consuming forbidden wealth, usury and dishonest business and economic practices, are made against both the Jews and the Christians. Muhammed, being a businessperson, would know about dishonest and unethical business practices, even among the Jews and Christians. Perhaps, there is some truth to these claims and the warnings against such practices.

Quran: The Jews say, "Allah's hand is tied." It is their hands that are tied, and they are cursed for what they say. In fact, His hands are outstretched; He gives as He wills. Certainly, what was revealed to you from your Lord will increase many of them in defiance and blasphemy. And We placed between them enmity and hatred, until the Day of Resurrection. Whenever they kindle the fire of war, Allah extinguishes it. And they strive to spread corruption on earth. Allah does not love the corrupters. Had the People of the Scripture believed and been righteous, We would have remitted their sins, and admitted them into the Gardens of Bliss. Had they observed the Torah, and the Gospel, and what was revealed to them from their Lord, they would have consumed amply from above them, and from beneath their feet. Among them is a moderate community, but evil is what many of them are doing.

Comments: These verses appear to condemn the Jews and Christians for being adversaries and threatening war. Historically, it appears that Muslims initiated war with Jews and Christians.

Quran: Say, "O People of the Scripture! You have no basis until you uphold the Torah, and the Gospel, and what is revealed to you from your Lord." But what is revealed to you from your Lord will increase many of them in rebellion and disbelief, so do not be sorry for the disbelieving people. Those who believe, and the Jews, and the Sabeans, and the Christians, whoever believes in Allah and the Last Day, and does what is right, they have nothing to fear, nor shall they grieve. We made a covenant with the Children of Israel, and We sent to them messengers. Whenever a messenger came to them with what their souls did not desire, some of them they accused of lying, and others they put to death. They assumed there would be no punishment, so they turned blind and deaf. Then Allah redeemed them, but then again many of them turned blind and deaf. But Allah is Seeing of what they do. They disbelieve those who say, "Allah is the Messiah the son of Mary." But the Messiah himself said, "O Children of Israel, worship Allah, my Lord and your Lord. Whoever associates others with Allah, Allah has forbidden him Paradise, and his dwelling is the Fire. They disbelieve those who say, "Allah is the third of three." But there is no deity except the One God. If they do not refrain from what they say, a painful torment will befall those among them who disbelieve.

Comments: These verses imply that many Jews, Sabeans, and Christians are among the disbelievers. Obviously, any Jewish or Sabian or Christian teaching that is at variance with Islamic teaching renders a person a disbeliever. Note the condemnation again of the Christian doctrines of the trinity of God and of the divinity of Jesus.

Quran: The Messiah, son of Mary was only a messenger, before whom other Messengers had passed away, and his mother was a woman of truth. They both used to eat food. Note how We make clear the revelations to them; then note how deluded they are.

Comments: Mary, the mother of Jesus, is recorded in the Gospels as having spoken very little, yet these verses say she was a woman of truth. The verse that states that 'they both used to eat food' implies that both Jesus and Mary were human and not divine. And the 'We' states that despite having made clear revelations to them, they were deluded, a rather strange assertion.

Quran: You will find that the people most hostile towards the believers are the Jews and the polytheists. And you will find that the nearest in affection towards the believers are those who say, "We are Christians." That is because among them are priests and monks, and they are not arrogant. And when they hear what was revealed to the Messenger, you see their eyes overflowing with tears, as they recognize the truth in it. They say, "Our Lord, we have believed, so count us among the witnesses."

Comments: Do these verses imply that there are few Jewish converts to Islam, but many Christian ones?

Quran: But as for those who disbelieve and deny Our signs, these are the inmates of the Fire.

Comment: More coercion! If you do not believe, you will go to Hell. Allah does not coerce.

Quran: Allah does not hold you accountable for your unintended oaths, but He holds you accountable for your binding oaths. The atonement for it is by feeding ten needy people from the average of what you feed your families, or by clothing them, or by freeing a slave. Anyone who lacks the means shall fast for three days. That is the atonement for breaking your oaths when you have sworn them. So, keep your oaths.

Comments: Freeing a slave, a fellow human being, and a child of God, is the same as feeding ten needy people. Slavery is not from God, but obviously, it is allowed in Islam.

Quran: Know that Allah is severe in retribution, and that Allah is Forgiving and Merciful. The Messenger's sole duty is to convey. Allah knows what you reveal and what you conceal.

Comments: God is not capable of retribution; it is against His nature. It is doubtful that Muhammed conveyed anything from God, rather he fabricated everything on his own with the assistance of the writers of the Quran.

Quran: When Allah will say, "O Jesus, son of Mary, recall My favor upon you and upon your mother, how I supported you with the Holy Spirit. You spoke to the people from the crib, and in maturity. How I taught you the Scripture and wisdom, and the Torah and the Gospel. And recall that you molded from clay the shape of a bird, by My leave, and then you breathed into it, and it became a bird, by My leave. And you healed the blind and the leprous, by My leave; and you revived the dead, by My leave. And recall that I restrained the Children of Israel from you when you brought them the clear miracles. But those who disbelieved among them said, `This is nothing but obvious sorcery.' And when I inspired the disciples: `Believe in Me and in My Messenger.' They said, `We have believed, so bear witness that We have submitted. 'And when the disciples said, 'O Jesus, son of Mary, is your Lord able to bring down for us a feast from heaven?' He said, 'Fear Allah, if you are believers. '"They said, "We wish to eat from it, so that our hearts may be reassured, and know that you have told us the truth, and be among those who witness it." Jesus, son of Mary said, "O Allah, our Lord, send down for us a table from heaven, to be a festival for us, for the first of us, and the last of us, and a sign from You; and provide for us; You are the Best of providers." Allah said, "I will send it down to you. But whoever among you disbelieves thereafter, I will punish him with a punishment the like of which I never punish any other being." And Allah will say, "O Jesus, son of Mary, did you say to the people, `Take me and my mother as gods rather than Allah?' 'He will say, "Glory be to You! It is not for me to say what I have no right to. Had I said it, You would have known it. You know what is in my soul, and I do not know what is in your soul. You are the Knower of the hidden.

Comments: 'And Allah will say, "O Jesus, son of Mary, did you say to the people, `Take me and my mother as gods rather than Allah?' What a fabricated statement! For a person not familiar with Christianity, they may be led to believe such a statement. Were the writers of these verses trying to mislead the reader?

Quran: Say, "What thing is more solemn in testimony?" Say, "Allah is Witness between you and me. This Quran was revealed to me, that I may warn you with it, and whomever it may reach. Do you indeed testify that there are other gods with Allah?" Say, "I myself do not testify." Say, "He is but One God, and I am innocent of your idolatry."

Comments: 'This Quran was revealed to me'. Muhammed could not write, so the writers of the Quran are putting words in the mouth of Muhammed.

Quran: Who does greater wrong than someone who fabricates lies against Allah, or denies His revelations? The wrongdoers will not succeed.

Comments: More coercive verses! What is the basis for believing in these revelations, the word of Muhmmed. These are fear tactics. These are the same tactics used by the leaders of Judaism and the leaders of Christianity to get people to accept their leadership and teachings.

Quran: Among them are those who listen to you; but We place covers over their hearts, to prevent them from understanding it, and heaviness in their ears. Even if they see every sign, they will not believe in it. Until, when they come to you, to argue with you, those who disbelieve will say, "These are nothing but myths of the ancients." If only you could see, when they are made to stand before the Fire; they will say, "If only we could be sent back, and not reject the revelations of our Lord, and be among the faithful."

Comments: There are many myths and legends, and those who take a myth or legend for fact are deceived by the authors of the myths and legends.

Quran: Those who reject Our revelations are deaf and dumb, in total darkness. Whomever Allah wills, He leaves astray; and whomever He wills, He sets on a straight path. But as for those who reject Our revelations, torment will afflict them because of their defiance.

Comment: This is coercive. Do these verses imply that "Our revelations' are God's revelations? And do people who reject the so-called revelations reject them because they truly doubt that they came from God.

Quran: Say, "He is able to send upon you an affliction, from above you, or from under your feet. Or He can divide you into factions, and make you taste the violence of one another.

Comment: Who is the 'He' in these verses? It certainly cannot be Allah, since He would never 'and make you taste the violence of one another.'

Quran: When you encounter those who gossip about Our revelations, turn away from them, until they engage in another topic. But should Satan make you forget, do not sit after the recollection with the wicked people.

Comment: Is it not allowed to question the authenticity of the revelations to Muhammed? There is absolutely no evidence that Allah or God wrote the Quran, it is only the words of Muhammed, the writers, and the editors who tell people that the Quran is the word of God and was revealed by God to Muhammed. Why should they be believed?

Quran: And We gave him Isaac and Jacob, each of them We guided. And We guided Noah previously, and from his descendants David, and Solomon, and Job, and Joseph, and Moses, and Aaron. Thus, We reward the righteous. And Zechariah, and John, and Jesus, and Elias, every one of them was of the upright. And Ishmael, and Elijah, and Jonah, and Lot, We favored each one of them over all other people.

Comments: Unfortunately, all of the individuals mentioned in these verses were mythical characters, there is no evidence that they ever existed.

Quran: "O assembly of jinn and humans, did there not come to you messengers from among you, relating to you My revelations, and warning you of the meeting of this Day of yours?" They will say, "We testify against ourselves." The life of the world seduced them. They will testify against themselves that they were disbelievers.

Comments: Jinns were supposedly some kind of created being whose nature was between angels and humans. What messengers were sent to these jinns? And these beings don't exist in Jewish or Christian books, so where did they come from some middle-Eastern myth?.

Quran: And they say, "What lies in the wombs of these animals is exclusively for our males and prohibited to our wives." But if it is stillborn, they can share in it. He will surely punish them for their allegations. He is Wise and Knowing. Lost are those who kill their children foolishly, with no basis in knowledge, and forbid what Allah has provided for them—innovations about Allah. They have gone astray. They are not guided.

Comments: These are rather bizarre verses and could not have come from God to Gabriel to Muhammed. And the statement, 'Lost are those who kill their children foolishly', that this imply that it is okay to kill children if it is not foolishly?

Quran: How many a town have We destroyed? Our might came upon them by night, or while they were napping.

Comments: Who is the 'We' in these verses. It cannot be God, for God does not destroy towns and people in them. It is against His nature. Nor could it be angels, for destruction and murder are also against their nature. Does the word 'We' refer to Muhammed? He was responsible for destroying towns and killing people whom he considered his enemies. 'We' could also apply to the early leaders of Islam who also destroyed towns and killed people whom they considered as their enemies.

Quran: We created you, then We shaped you, then We said to the angels, "Bow down before Adam;" so they bowed down, except for Satan; he was not of those who bowed down. He said, "What prevented you from bowing down when I have commanded you?" He said, "I am better than he; You created me from fire, and You created him from mud." He said, "Get down from it! It is not for you to act arrogantly in it. Get out! You are one of the lowly!"

Comments: These verses indicate that Allah (God) is speaking using the first-person plural 'We'. And while there is some similarity to the Genesis creation myth, there are some differences. These differences may have come from other Creation myths, or they may have been the products of the writers of the Quran acting as 'spin doctors', adding text to serve their purposes and objectives. Also, the verse including the statement, 'Bow down before Adam', was given in a previous set of verses in the Quran. If this was God speaking, would He repeat Himself? No!

Quran: And you, Adam, inhabit the Garden, you and your wife, and eat whatever you wish; but do not approach this tree, lest you become sinners." But Satan whispered to them, to reveal to them their nakedness, which was invisible to them. He said, "Your Lord has only forbidden you this tree, lest you become angels, or become immortals." And he swore to them, "I am a sincere advisor to you." So, he lured them with deceit. And when they tasted the tree, their nakedness became evident to them, and they began covering themselves with the leaves of the Garden. And their Lord called out to them, "Did I not forbid you from this tree, and say to you that Satan is a sworn enemy to you?" They said, "Our Lord, we have done wrong to ourselves. Unless You forgive us, and have mercy on us, we will be among the losers." He said, "Fall, some of you enemies to one another. On earth you will have residence and livelihood for a while." He said, "In it you will live, and in it you will die, and from it you will be brought out." O children of Adam! We have provided you with clothing to cover your bodies, and for luxury. But the clothing of piety, that is best. These are some of Allah's revelations, so that they may take heed.

Comments: This is a variation of the Jewish Creation Myth. The writers of the Quran must have been very familiar with Jewish documents. And how would Adam make the statement, 'we will be among the losers' since it was only him and Eve at the time. Fabrication!

Quran: O Children of Adam! When messengers from among you come to you, relating to you My revelations, whoever practices piety and reforms, upon them shall be no fear, nor shall they grieve. But as for those who reject Our revelations, and are too proud to accept them, these are the inmates of the Fire, where they will remain forever. Who does greater wrong than he who invents lies about Allah, or denies His revelations?

Comments: More coercive statements. If the so-called revelations are in fact man-made and not revelations from God, it is coercive and misleading to state that a person must believe these statements because they came from God when in fact, they did not come from God but rather from men.

Quran: He will say, "Join the crowds of jinn and humans who have gone into the Fire before. Those who reject Our revelations and are too arrogant to uphold them, the doors of Heaven will not be opened for them, nor will they enter Paradise, until the camel passes through the eye of the needle.

Comments: Another verse about the jinn, but what did they do to merit Hell? And the statement about 'until the camel passes through the eye of the needle seems like of copy of the Gospel of Matthew 19:24.

Quran: And the inhabitants of the Garden will call out to the inmates of the Fire, "We found what our Lord promised us to be true; did you find what your Lord promised you to be true?" They will say, "Yes." Thereupon a caller will announce in their midst, "The curse of Allah is upon the wrongdoers." "Those who hinder from the path of Allah, and seek to distort it, and who deny the Hereafter." And between them is a partition, and on the Elevations are men who recognize everyone by their features. They will call to the inhabitants of the Garden, "Peace be upon you." They have not entered it, but they are hoping. And when their eyes are directed towards the inmates of the Fire, they will say, "Our Lord, do not place us among the wrongdoing people." And the dwellers of the Elevations will call to men they recognize by their features, saying, "Your hoardings did not avail you, nor did your arrogance." "Are these the ones you swore Allah will not touch with mercy?" "Enter the Garden; you have nothing to fear, and you will not grieve." The inmates of the Fire will call on the inhabitants of the Garden, "Pour some water over us, or some of what Allah has provided for you." They will say, "Allah has forbidden them for the disbelievers."

Comments: These verses seem to be copied from the Gospel of Luke 16:19-31 and the narrative of the rich man and Lazarus, the beggar. Again, it appears that the writers and editors of the Quran were very knowledgeable of Christian literature as well as Jewish literature. But the question must be asked, what was the reason for copying some things from Jewish and Christian literature into the Quran? Was it to make it appear that the Quran was consistent with Judaism and Christianity with respect to so-called revelations from God? Or was it meant to facilitate conversion of Jews and Christians to Islam?

Quran: And Lot, when he said to his people, "Do you commit lewdness no people anywhere have ever committed before you?" "You lust after men rather than women. You are an excessive people." And his people's only answer was to say, "Expel them from your town; they are purist people." But We saved him and his family, except for his wife; she was of those who lagged behind. And We rained down on them a rain; note the consequences for the sinners.

Comments: Again, the writers of the Quran are borrowing from Jewish literature. This may have made sense when the Quran was written, but now that is seems most likely that the Jewish book of Genesis was based on multiple myths, including this myth in the Quran undermines the claim that the Quran was dictated by God to the angel, Gabriel, who dictated it to Muhammed. In other words, this is not from God.

Quran: The elite of his people who disbelieved said, "If you follow Shuaib, you will be losers." Thereupon, the quake struck them; and they became lifeless bodies in their homes. Those who rejected Shuaib, as if they never prospered therein. Those who rejected Shuaib, it was they who were the losers.

Comments: Shuaib was a supposed prophet and the most revered prophet in the Druze faith, though the narratives surrounding him are questionable. The writers of the Quran were trying to compare Shuaib and Muhammed and how people who do not accept Muhammed will suffer the supposed same fate as those who did not accept Shuaib.

Quran: Then, after them, We sent Moses with Our miracles to Pharaoh and his establishment, but they denounced them. So, consider the end of the evildoers. Moses said, "O Pharaoh, I am a messenger from the Lord of the Worlds." "It is only proper that I should not say about Allah anything other than the truth. I have come to you with clear evidence from your Lord, so let the Children of Israel go with me." He said, "If you brought a miracle, then present it, if you are truthful." So, he threw his staff, and it was an apparent serpent. And He pulled out his hand, and it was white to the onlookers. The notables among Pharaoh's people said, "This is really a skilled magician." "He wants to evict you from your land, so what do you recommend?" They said, "Put him off, and his brother, and send heralds to the cities." "And let them bring you every skillful magician." The magicians came to Pharaoh, and said,

"Surely there is a reward for us, if we are the victors." He said, "Yes, and you will be among my favorites." They said, "O Moses! Either you throw, or we are the ones to throw." He said, "You throw!" And when they threw, they beguiled the eyes of the people, and intimidated them, and produced a mighty magic. And We inspired Moses: "Throw your staff." And at once, it swallowed what they were faking. So, the truth came to pass, and what they were producing came to nothing. There they were defeated, and utterly reduced. And the magicians fell to their knees. They said, "We have believed in the Lord of the Worlds." "The Lord of Moses and Aaron." Pharaoh said, "Did you believe in Him before I have given you permission? This is surely a conspiracy you schemed in the city, in order to expel its people from it. You will surely know." "I will cut off your hands and your feet on opposite sides; then I will crucify you all." They said, "It is to our Lord that we will return." "You are taking vengeance on us only because we have believed in the signs of our Lord when they have come to us." "Our Lord! Pour out patience upon us and receive our souls in submission." The chiefs of Pharaoh's people said, "Will you let Moses and his people cause trouble in the land, and forsake you and your gods?" He said, "We will kill their sons, and spare their women. We have absolute power over them." Moses said to his people, "Seek help in Allah, and be patient. The earth belongs to Allah. He gives it in inheritance to whomever He wills of His servants, and the future belongs to the righteous." They said, "We were persecuted before you came to us, and after you came to us." He said, "Perhaps your Lord will destroy your enemy, and make you successors in the land; then He will see how you behave." And We afflicted the people of Pharaoh with barren years, and with shortage of crops, that they may take heed. When something good came their way, they said, "This is ours." And when something bad happened to them, they ascribed the evil omen to Moses and those with him. In fact, their omen is with Allah, but most of them do not know. And they said, "No matter what sign you bring us, to bewitch us with, we will not believe in you." So, We let loose upon them the flood, and the locusts, and the lice, and the frogs, and blood, all explicit signs, but they were too arrogant. They were a sinful people. Whenever a plague befell them, they would say, "O Moses, pray to your Lord for us, according to the covenant He made with you. If you lift the plague from us, we will believe in you, and let the Children of Israel go with you." But when We lifted the plague from them, for a term they were to fulfill, they broke their promise. So, We took vengeance on them, and drowned them in the sea because they rejected Our signs, and paid no heed to them. And We made the oppressed people inherit the eastern and western parts of the land, which We had blessed. Thus, the fair promise of your Lord to the Children of Israel was fulfilled, because of their endurance. And We destroyed what Pharaoh and his people had built, and what they had harvested. And We delivered the Children of Israel across the sea.

Comments: These verses are a copy from the Jewish book of Exodus with some changed text to emphasize certain points.

Quran: Those who follow the Messenger, the Unlettered Prophet, whom they find mentioned in the Torah and the Gospel in their possession. He directs them to righteousness, and deters them from evil, and allows for them all good things, and prohibits for them wickedness, and unloads the burdens and the shackles that are upon them. Those who believe in him, and respect him, and support him, and follow the light that came down with him, these are the successful.

Comments: These verses seem to try to link the Messengers of Judaism and Christianity with Muhammed, the Messenger of Islam in order to persuade people to accept Muhammed.

Quran: Evil is the metaphor of the people who reject Our signs and wrong themselves. Whomever Allah guides is the guided one. And whomever He sends astray, these are the losers. We have destined for Hell multitudes of jinn and humans. They have hearts with which they do not understand. They have eyes with which they do not see. They have ears with which they do not hear. Among those We created is a community, they guide by truth, and do justice thereby. As for those who reject Our messages, We will gradually lead them from where they do not know. Whomever Allah misguides has no guide. And He leaves them blundering in their transgression.

Comments: These verses imply that whoever follows Muhammed, follows Allah. In addition, it appears that these verses claim that predestination from God is true. God does not predestine anyone for Hell, it is against His nature.

Quran: When the Quran is recited, listen to it, and pay attention, so that you may experience mercy. And remember your Lord within yourself, humbly and fearfully, and quietly, in the morning and the evening, and do not be of the neglectful.

Comments: And do these verses imply that a person who does not listen to and pay attention to the Quran will not experience mercy and only Muslims will merit Heaven and no one else?

Quran: That is because they opposed Allah and His Messenger. Whoever opposes Allah and His Messenger, Allah is severe in retribution. "Here it is, so taste it." For the disbelievers there is the suffering of the Fire.

Comments: These verses coerce people into believing that Muhmmed is the Messenger of Allah and failure to believe Muhammed will merit Hell.

Quran: It was not you who killed them, but it was Allah who killed them. And it was not you who launched when you launched, but it was Allah who launched. That He may bestow upon the believers an excellent reward. Such is the case. Allah will undermine the strategy of the disbelievers. If you desire a verdict, the verdict has come to you. And if you desist, it would be best for you. And if you return, We will return; and your troops, however numerous, will not benefit you. Allah is with the believers.

Comments: Allah (God) does not kill, it is against His nature. Nor does God take sides in a military conflict.

Quran: O you who believe! Do not betray Allah and the Messenger, nor betray your trusts, while you know. When the disbelievers plotted against you, to imprison you, or kill you, or expel you. They planned, and Allah planned, but Allah is the Best of planners. Fight them until there is no more persecution, and religion becomes exclusively for Allah. But if they desist, Allah is Seeing of what they do.

Comments: 'Fight them until there is no more persecution, and religion becomes exclusively for Allah.' Does this imply that Islam is the only legitimate religion and the only way to serve God?

Quran: O you who believe! When you meet a force, stand firm, and remember Allah much, so that you may prevail. And obey Allah and His Messenger, and do not dispute, lest you falter and lose your courage. And be steadfast. Allah is with the steadfast.

Comments: Obviously motivating people to fight for and obey Muhammed, the Messenger, because Muhammed speaks for God. This idea is both arrogant and absurd. No one speaks for God, and He has no representative on earth.

Quran: If only you could see, as the angels take away those who disbelieve, striking their faces and their backs: "Taste the agony of the Burning." Like the behavior of the people of Pharaoh, and those before them. They rejected the signs of Allah, so Allah seized them for their sins. Allah is Powerful, Severe in punishment. Such was the case with the people of Pharaoh, and those before them. They denied the signs of their Lord, so We annihilated them for their wrongs, and We drowned the people of Pharaoh—they were all evildoers.

Comments: Allah is not severe in punishment. He is all-loving. And who is the 'We' who annihilated and drowned the people of Pharaoh? Certainly, not God!

Quran: The worst of creatures in Allah's view are those who disbelieve. They have no faith. Those of them with whom you made a treaty, but they violate their agreement every time. They are not righteous. If you confront them in battle, make of them a fearsome example for those who follow them, that they may take heed.

Comments: 'The worst of creatures in Allah's view are those who disbelieve.' This is absolutely false. All people are God's children and among His children are those who misbehave and who mistreat others and engage in war. God does not want His children to engage so-called disbelievers in battle and make a fearsome example of them.

Quran: Let not the disbelievers assume that they are ahead. They will not escape. And prepare against them all the power you can muster, and all the cavalry you can mobilize, to terrify thereby Allah's enemies and your enemies, and others besides them whom you do not know, but Allah knows them. Whatever you spend in Allah's way will be repaid to you in full, and you will not be wronged.

Comments: These verses equate the enemies of Islam as disbelievers who are also enemies of Allah, and they must be destroyed and made an example of. But God has no enemies and all people, both believers and non-believers are children of God.

Quran: O prophet! Count on Allah, and on the believers who have followed you. O prophet! Rouse the believers to battle. If there are twenty steadfast among you, they will defeat two hundred; and if there are a hundred of you, they will defeat a thousand of those who disbelieve; because they are a people who do not understand.

Comments: Do these verses sound like they are coming from a religious leader or a political leader who is trying to imply that Allah (God) supports their military efforts? Allah (God) does not support nor condone wars or battles or military engagements or even fighting, for all people are the children of God and God wants all of His children to get along with each other, love each other, and help each other.

Quran: If there are a hundred steadfast among you, they will defeat two hundred; and if there are a thousand of you, they will defeat two thousand by Allah's leave. Allah is with the steadfast. It is not for a prophet to take prisoners before he has subdued the land. Were it not for a predetermined decree from Allah, an awful punishment would have afflicted you for what you have taken. So, consume what you have gained, legitimate and wholesome; and remain conscious of Allah.

Comments: These verses are a repeat from the verses before, God does not repeat Himself. And what is meant by a prophet should not take prisoners before he has subdued the land. A holy person should never take prisoners. And the statements 'Were it not for a predetermined decree from Allah, an awful punishment would have afflicted you for what you have taken. So, consume what you have gained, legitimate and wholesome; and remain conscious of Allah.' Are these statements referring to the spoils of war where the conquering army takes the possessions from the vanquished, materials, land, and even women? God does not approve of the spoils of war and would never provide a predetermined decree allowing such a thing. This is made-up by Mohammed and the writers of the Quran to motivate the armies of Islam to fight and pillage and plunder without impunity.

Quran: A declaration of immunity from Allah and His Messenger to the polytheists with whom you had made a treaty. So, travel the land for four months, and know that you cannot escape Allah, and that Allah will disgrace the disbelievers. And a proclamation from Allah and His Messenger to the people on the day of the Greater Pilgrimage, that Allah has disowned the polytheists, and so did His Messenger. If you repent, it will be better for you. But if you turn away, know that you cannot escape Allah. And announce to those who disbelieve a painful punishment.

Comments: God does not disown anyone. And is the implication that disbelievers will experience a painful punishment anyone who does not accept Islam and its teachings?

Quran: When the Sacred Months have passed, kill the polytheists wherever you find them. And capture them, and besiege them, and lie in wait for them at every ambush. But if they repent, and perform the prayers, and pay the alms, then let them go their way. How can there be a treaty with the polytheists on the part of Allah and His Messenger, except for those with whom you made a treaty at the Sacred Mosque? As long as they are upright with you, be upright with them.

Comments: 'Kill the polytheists wherever you find them. And capture them, and besiege them, and lie in wait for them at every ambush.' This is certainly not from God, but from people who hate. God does not hate and does not promote hatred.

Quran: Will you not fight a people who violated their oaths, and planned to exile the Messenger, and initiated hostilities against you? Do you fear them? It is Allah you should fear if you are believers. Fight them. Allah will punish them at your hands, and humiliate them, and help you against them, and heal the hearts of a believing people.

Comments: More verses inciting Muslims to fight whoever the Messenger deems an enemy and for them to believe that this is Allah's will.

Quran: It is not for the polytheists to attend Allah's places of worship while professing their disbelief. These, their works are in vain, and in the Fire they will abide. The only people to attend Allah's places of worship are those who believe in Allah and the Last Day, and pray regularly, and practice regular charity, and fear none but Allah.

Comments: These verses indicate lack of charity and perhaps, hatred. If Allah's place of worship belongs to Allah, these places are open to all.

Quran: O you who believe! Do not ally yourselves with your parents and your siblings if they prefer disbelief to belief. Whoever of you allies himself with them, these are the wrongdoers. Say, "If your parents, and your children, and your siblings, and your spouses, and your relatives, and the wealth you have acquired, and a business you worry about, and homes you love, are dearer to you than Allah, and His Messenger, and the struggle in His cause, then wait until Allah executes His judgment." Allah does not guide the sinful people.

Comments: These verses are similar to the Gospel of Luke 14:26.

Quran: Then Allah sent down His serenity upon His Messenger, and upon the believers; and He sent down troops you did not see; and He punished those who disbelieved. Such is the recompense of the disbelievers.

Comments: Do these verses imply that God bestows peace on Muhammed and his followers in this life and punishes those who do not believe Muhammed and his teachings in this life?

Quran: O you who believe! The polytheists are polluted, so let them not approach the Sacred Mosque after this year of theirs. And if you fear poverty, Allah will enrich you from His grace, if He wills. Allah is Aware and Wise. Fight those who do not believe in Allah, nor in the Last Day, nor forbid what Allah and His Messenger have forbidden, nor abide by the religion of truth from among those who received the Scripture, until they pay the due tax, willingly or unwillingly.

Comments: 'If you fear poverty, Allah will enrich you from His grace'? God does not make such a promise, but rather someone who is trying to manipulate you. And 'Fight those who do not believe in Allah', implies that Islam teaches what God wants, but to fight against people who do not believe in Islam implies that Islam is a religion of hate and not of love. But God is Love.

Quran: The Jews said, "Ezra is the son of Allah," and the Christians said, "The Messiah is the son of Allah." These are their statements, out of their mouths. They emulate the statements of those who blasphemed before. May Allah assail them! How deceived they are! They have taken their rabbis and their priests as lords instead of Allah, as well as the Messiah son of Mary. Although they were commanded to worship none but The One God. There is no god except Him.

Comments: More verses condemning Judaism and Christianity. Neither Judaism nor Christianity consider their rabbis or priests as lords instead of God. But then what about Muslim clerics?

Quran: They want to extinguish Allah's light with their mouths, but Allah refuses except to complete His light, even though the disbelievers dislike it. It is He who sent His Messenger with the guidance and the religion of truth, in order to make it prevail over all religions, even though the idolaters dislike it.

Comments: How can anyone seriously believe that God chose Muhammed to establish a new religion that prevailed over all other religions. The first so-called revelation to Muhammed occurred in a dream and Muhammed did not consider it a revelation from God until his wife convince him so. And what historical evidence is there that proves that Muhammed had any actual revelations from God and that he did not fabricate these so-called revelations to promote himself and his political and economic objectives.

Quran: O you who believe! Many of the rabbis and priests consume people's wealth illicitly and hinder from Allah's path. Those who hoard gold and silver, and do not spend them in Allah's cause, inform them of a painful punishment. On the Day when they will be heated in the Fire of Hell, then their foreheads, and their sides, and their backs will be branded with them: "This is what you hoarded for yourselves; so, taste what you used to hoard."

Comments: The writers of the Quran seem to have a great dislike for rabbis and priests, yet don't the Quran also classify Islam Imams in this same category as rabbis and priests?

Quran: The number of months, according to Allah, is twelve months, in the decree of Allah, since the Day He created the heavens and the earth, of which four are sacred. This is the correct religion. So do not wrong yourselves during them. And fight the polytheists collectively, as they fight you collectively, and know that Allah is with the righteous.

Comments: Julius Caesar's astronomers were the first to propose that there are twelve months in a year. And when did God decree that there are four holy months? This seems like a fabrication on the part of the writers of the Quran.

Quran: O you who believe! What is the matter with you, when it is said to you, "Mobilize in the cause of Allah," you cling heavily to the earth? Do you prefer the present life to the Hereafter? The enjoyment of the present life, compared to the Hereafter, is only a little. Unless you mobilize, He will punish you most painfully, and will replace you with another people, and you will not harm Him at all. Allah has power over all things. Mobilize, light or heavy, and strive with your possessions and your lives in the cause of Allah. That is better for you, if you only knew.

Comments: Mobilization is the process of preparing individuals to become soldier and prepare for war. 'Mobilize in the cause of Allah', is another example that shows that Islam is a religion to support and promote political and economic objectives and not support and promote the peace that God wants among all of His children.

Quran: Those who believe in Allah and the Last Day do not ask you for exemption from striving with their possessions and their lives. Allah is fully aware of the righteous. Only those who do not believe in Allah and the Last Day ask you for exemption. Their hearts are full of doubts, so they waver in their doubts. Had they wanted to mobilize, they would have prepared for it; but Allah disliked their participation, so he held them back, and it was said, "Stay behind with those who stay behind." Had they mobilized with you, they would have added only to your difficulties, and they would have spread rumors in your midst, trying to sow discord among you. Some of you are avid listeners to them. Allah is Aware of the wrongdoers.

Comments: And among them are those who insult the Prophet, and say, "He is all ears." Say, "He listens for your own good. He believes in Allah, and trusts the believers, and is mercy for those of you who believe." Those who insult the Messenger of Allah will have a painful penalty. They swear to you by Allah to please you. But it is more proper for them to please Allah and His Messenger if they are believers. Do they not know that whoever opposes Allah and His Messenger, will have the Fire of Hell, abiding in it forever?

Quran: Allah has promised the hypocrite men and hypocrite women, and the disbelievers, the Fire of Hell, abiding therein forever. It is their due. And Allah has cursed them. They will have a lasting punishment.

Comment: These verses group hypocrite men and hypocrite women, and the disbelievers together and condemn them to Hell. God does not condemn anyone to Hell, so how can these verses have come from God?

Quran: Have they not heard the stories of those before them? The people of Noah, and Aad, and Thamood; and the people of Abraham, and the inhabitants of Median, and the Overturned Cities? Their messengers came to them with the clear proofs.

Comments: First of all, there are no messengers of God. The phrase 'messenger of God' is a fabricated phrase to try to make people believe in what the pseudo messenger of God is teaching. Secondly, and because of the previous two sentences, there are NO clear proofs – another false claim by the self-proclaimed messengers of God.

Quran: Allah promises the believers, men and women, gardens beneath which rivers flow, abiding therein forever, and fine homes in the Gardens of Eden. But approval from Allah is even greater. That is the supreme achievement. O Prophet! Strive against the disbelievers and the hypocrites and be stern with them. Their abode is Hell, what a miserable destination!

Comments: In these verses, who is stating that the Prophet, presumably Mohammed, should be stern with disbelievers, non-believers in Islam.

Quran: They swear by Allah that they said nothing; but they did utter the word of blasphemy, and they renounced faith after their submission. And they plotted what they could not attain. They were resentful only because Allah and His Messenger have enriched them out of His grace. If they repent, it would be best for them; but if they turn away, Allah will afflict them with a painful punishment, in this life and in the Hereafter, and they will have on earth no protector and no savior.

Comments: Do these verses imply that anyone who does not submit fully and completely to all of the doctrines of Islam will be punished in Hell. And does the verse 'Allah and His Messenger have enriched them out of His grace' imply that Muhammed enriches people with the grace of God?

Quran: You are never to pray over anyone of them who dies, nor are you to stand at his graveside. They rejected Allah and His Messenger and died while they were sinners.

Comments: It is virtuous and charitable to pray for everyone without distinction even after they have died. To do otherwise indicated bias and hatred.

Quran: But the Messenger and those who believe with him struggle with their possessions and their lives. These have deserved the good things. These are the successful. Allah has prepared for them gardens beneath which rivers flow, wherein they will abide forever. That is the great victory.

Comment: Obviously, the writers of the Quran are trying to persuade readers to follow Muhammed.

Quran: They present excuses to you when you return to them. Say, "Do not offer excuses; we do not trust you; Allah has informed us of you. And Allah will watch your actions, and so will the Messenger; then you will be returned to the Knower of the Invisible and the Visible, and He will inform you of what you used to do."

Comments: Very strange verses. Who is 'us', it is not Allah nor Muhammed, do these verses represent a different writing style from other verses?

Quran: Among the Desert-Arabs around you there are some hypocrites, and among the inhabitants of Medina too. They have become adamant in hypocrisy. You do not know them, but We know them. We will punish them twice; then they will be returned to a severe torment.

Others have confessed their sins, having mixed good deeds with bad deeds. Perhaps Allah will redeem them. Allah is Forgiving and Merciful.

Comment: Again, who is the 'We' who punish them twice? It cannot be God or angels for that is against their nature.

Quran: Then there are those who establish a mosque to cause harm, and disbelief, and disunity among the believers, and as an outpost for those who fight Allah and His Messenger. They will swear: "Our intentions are nothing but good." But Allah bears witness that they are liars. Do not stand in it, ever.

Comment: These verses imply that Islam does not like any competition from Arab religions.

Quran: Allah has purchased from the believers their lives and their properties in exchange for Paradise. They fight in Allah's way, and they kill and get killed. It is a promise binding on Him in the Torah, and the Gospel, and the Quran. And who is truer to his promise than Allah? So, rejoice in making such an exchange. that is the supreme triumph.

Comments: Believers in God do not fight in God's way, killing and getting killed. This is contrary to the nature of God. Is the Quran promoting a peaceful religion, or a political organization that uses religion to coerce its adherents into following the political and nationalistic aspirations of its leaders?

Quran: It is not for the Prophet and those who believe to ask forgiveness for the polytheists, even if they are near relatives, after it has become clear to them that they are people of Hellfire. Abraham asked forgiveness for his father only because of a promise he had made to him. But when it became clear to him that he was an enemy of Allah, he disowned him. Abraham was kind and clement.

Comments: All people are God's children. and He wants everyone to help one another, including praying for one another if they have fallen away from God. These verses show that Islam has contempt for non-Muslims or non-believers. And the statement that 'Abraham was kind and clement' is certainly false and misleading. It attempts to make believers follow this ridiculous guidance that a person should not pray for non-believers.

Quran: Allah has redeemed the Prophet, and the Emigrants, and the Supporters, those who followed him in the hour of difficulty, after the hearts of some of them almost swerved.

Comment: Does God only redeem Muslims and only forgive the sins (mistakes) of Muslims? All people are God's children and God treats all people equally.

Quran: O you who believe! Fight those of the disbelievers who attack you, and let them find severity in you, and know that Allah is with the righteous.

Comment: Fight the disbelieves of Islam, how is this from God?

Quran: There has come to you a messenger from among yourselves, concerned over your suffering, anxious over you. Towards the believers, he is compassionate and merciful.

Comment: The messenger, Muhammed, is only compassionate and merciful to his believers?

Quran: We destroyed generations before you when they did wrong. Their messengers came to them with clear signs, but they would not believe. Thus, We requite the sinful people. Then We made you successors on earth after them, to see how you would behave. And when Our clear revelations are recited to them, those who do not hope to meet Us say, "Bring a Quran other than this, or change it." Say, "It is not for me to change it of my own accord. I only follow what is revealed to me. I fear, if I disobeyed my Lord, the torment of a terrible Day."

Comment: 'We destroyed generations before you when they did wrong.' Who is making this statement, certainly not God nor angels. It is fabricated by the writers. And there are no 'clear revelations.' Implying that the so-called revelations claimed by Muhammed are clear and must be accepted is coercive and false.

Quran: Who does greater wrong than someone who fabricates lies about Allah, or denies His revelations? The guilty will never prosper. This Quran could not have been produced by anyone other than Allah. In fact, it is a confirmation of what preceded it, and an elaboration of the Book. There is no doubt about it, it is from the Lord of the Universe.

Comments: These verses are coercive and demeaning to the reader. The writers are browbeating the readers or hearers of the Quran and forcing them to accept based on their claim alone.

Quran: And they said, "Allah has taken a son." Be He glorified. He is the Self-Sufficient. His is everything in the heavens and everything on earth. Do you have any proof for this? Or are you saying about Allah what you do not know? Say, "Those who fabricate lies about Allah will not succeed."

Comments: A criticism of the divinity of Jesus as the Son of God and a criticism of the Christian Church.

Quran: And relate to them the story of Noah, when he said to his people, "O my people, if my presence among you and my reminding you of Allah's signs is too much for you, then in Allah I have put my trust. So come to a decision, you, and your partners, and do not let the matter perplex you; then carry out your decision on me, and do not hold back." But they denounced him, so We saved him and those with him in the Ark, and We made them successors, and We drowned those who rejected Our signs. So, consider the fate of those who were warned. Then, after them, We sent Moses and Aaron with Our proofs to Pharaoh and his dignitaries. But they acted arrogantly. They were sinful people. And do not be of those who deny Allah's revelations, lest you become one of the losers.

Comments: These verses are attempting to establish that God has sent messengers and people must accept these so-called revelations.

Quran: Had your Lord willed, everyone on earth would have believed. Will you compel people to become believers? No soul can believe except by Allah's leave; and He lays disgrace upon those who refuse to understand.

Comments: God created and creates people with a free will. People are free to believe or not to believe.

Quran: Then We save Our messengers and those who believe. It is binding on Us to save the believers. Say, "O people, if you are in doubt about my religion, I do not serve those you serve apart from Allah. But I serve Allah, the one who will terminate your lives. And I was commanded to be of the believers." And dedicate yourself to the true religion, a monotheist, and never be of the polytheists. If Allah afflicts you with harm, none can remove it except Him. And if He wants good for you, none can repel His grace.

Comments: Who is the 'We' and the 'US'? And which religion is meant in the expression 'if you are in doubt about my religion'?

Quran: Who does greater wrong than he who fabricates lies about Allah? These will be presented before their Lord, and the witnesses will say, "These are they who lied about their Lord." Indeed, the curse of Allah is upon the wrongdoers. "I do not say to you that I possess the treasures of Allah, nor do I know the future, nor do I say that I am an angel. Nor do I say of those who are despicable in your eyes that Allah will never give them any good.

Comments: Who is speaking in these verses?

Quran: Thus, We revealed it an Arabic code of law. Were you to follow their desires, after the knowledge that has come to you, you would have neither ally nor defender against Allah. We sent messengers before you, and We assigned for them wives and offspring. No messenger could bring a sign except with the permission of Allah. For every era is a scripture. Allah abolishes whatever He wills, and He affirms. With Him is the source of the Scripture.

Comments: Again, who is speaking in these verses? It is not Allah.

Quran: Do you not see how Allah presents a parable? A good word is like a good tree, its root is firm, and its branches are in the sky. It yields its fruits every season by the will of its Lord. Allah presents the parables to the people, so that they may reflect. And the parable of a bad word is that of a bad tree, it is uprooted from the ground; it has no stability.

Quran: It is We who give life and cause death, and We are the Inheritors. And We know those of you who go forward, and We know those who lag behind. It is your Lord who will gather them together.

He is the Wise, the Knowing. We created the human being from clay, from molded mud. And the jinn We created before, from piercing fire. Your Lord said to the angels, "I am creating a human being from clay, from molded mud." "When I have formed him, and breathed into him of My spirit, fall down prostrating before him." So, the angels prostrated themselves, all together. Except for Satan. He refused to be among those who prostrated themselves. He said, "O Satan, what kept you from being among those who prostrated themselves?" He said, "I am not about to prostrate myself before a human being, whom You created from clay, from molded mud." He said, "Then get out of here, for you are an outcast". "And the curse will be upon you until the Day of Judgment." He said, "My Lord, reprieve me until the Day they are resurrected." He said, "You are of those reprieved." "Until the Day of the time appointed." He said, "My Lord, since You have lured me away, I will glamorize for them on earth, and I will lure them all away." "Except for Your sincere servants among them." He said, "This is a right way with Me." "Over My servants you have no authority, except for the sinners who follow you." And Hell is the meeting-place for them all. "It has seven doors; for each door is an assigned class." But the righteous will be in gardens with springs. "Enter it in peace and security." And We will remove all ill-feelings from their hearts, brothers, and sisters, on couches facing one another. No fatigue will ever touch them therein, nor will they be asked to leave it. Inform My servants that I am the Forgiver, the Merciful. And that My punishment is the painful punishment.

Comments: These verses are a rewrite of the Creation myths. And who captured the supposed conversation between God and Satan? Sound like a fabrication and part of one of the myths.

Quran: And inform them of the guests of Abraham. When they entered upon him, and said, "Peace." He said, "We are wary of you." They said, "Do not fear; we bring you good news of a boy endowed with knowledge." He said, "Do you bring me good news, when old age has overtaken me? What good news do you bring?" They said, "We bring you good news in truth, so do not despair." He said, "And who despairs of his Lord's mercy but the lost?" He said, "So what is your business, O envoys?" They said, "We were sent to a sinful people." "Except for the family of Lot; we will save them all." "Except for his wife." We have determined that she will be of those who lag behind. And when the envoys came to the family of Lot. He said, "You are a people unknown to me." They said, "We bring you what they have doubts about." "We bring you the truth, and we are truthful." "Travel with your family at the dead of the night, and follow up behind them, and let none of you look back, and proceed as commanded." And We informed him of Our decree: the last remnant of these will be uprooted by early morning. And the people of the town came joyfully. He said, "These are my guests, so do not embarrass me." "And fear Allah, and do not disgrace me." They said, "Did we not forbid you from strangers?" He said, "These are my daughters, if you must." By your life, they were blundering in their drunkenness. So, the Blast struck them at sunrise. And We turned it upside down and rained down upon them stones of baked clay. Surely in that are lessons for those who read signs.

Comments: The writers of the Quran must have been very well trained in Jewish literature, yet they restate Genesis here in such a way as to promote their own objectives modifying the narrative.

Quran: The command of Allah has come, so do not rush it. Glory be to Him; exalted above what they associate. He sends down the angels with the Spirit by His command, upon whom He wills of His servants: "Give warning that there is no god but Me, and fear Me."

Comments: God or Allah or Yahweh would never say 'Give warning that there is no god but Me, and fear Me.' God does not want to be feared, He wants to be loved. He does need the love of His intelligent creatures, but rather the love of God is the path to happiness for His creatures.

Quran: Allah cites the example of a bonded slave, who has no power over anything; and someone to whom We have given plentiful provision, from which he gives secretly and openly. Are they equal in comparison? And Allah cites the example of two men: one of them dumb, unable to do anything, and is a burden on his master; whichever way he directs him, he achieves nothing good. Is he equal to him who commands justice, and is on a straight path?

Comments: What is this example where Allah cites a bonded slave? Seems like a fabrication by the authors of the Quran to make

Quran: Those who disbelieve and obstruct from Allah's path, We will add punishment to their punishment, on account of the mischief they used to make.

Comments: Again, who is 'We' and in this verse will add punishment to their punishment, it certainly cannot be God since that is against His nature.

Quran: Those who do not believe in Allah's revelations, Allah will not guide them, and for them is a painful punishment. It is those who do not believe in Allah's revelations who fabricate falsehood. These are the liars. Whoever renounces faith in Allah after having believed, except for someone who is compelled, while his heart rests securely in faith, but whoever willingly opens up his heart to disbelief, upon them falls wrath from Allah, and for them is a tremendous torment. That is because they have preferred the worldly life to the Hereafter, and because Allah does not guide the people who refuse.

Comments: 'Those who do not believe in Allah's revelations, Allah will not guide them, and for them is a painful punishment.' Such coercive, intimidating language. Perhaps, people don't believe that the so-called revelations to Muhammed were not from God and that is why they do not believe in his teachings.

Quran: He has forbidden you carrion, and blood, and the flesh of swine, and anything consecrated to other than Allah. But if anyone is compelled by necessity, without being deliberate or malicious, then Allah is Forgiving and Merciful.

Comments: God does not forbid any food. Prohibitions against certain type of food only come from men.

Quran: For those who are Jews, We have prohibited what We related to you before. We did not wrong them, but they used to wrong their own selves. And We conveyed to the Children of Israel in the Scripture: You will commit evil on earth twice, and you will rise to a great height. When the first of the two promises came true, We sent against you servants of Ours, possessing great might, and they ransacked your homes. It was a promise fulfilled. Then We gave you back your turn against them, and supplied you with wealth and children, and made you more numerous.

Comments: For people that do not know better and the history of the Jews, they may mistakenly believe these verses. But again, they are fabrications by the authors of the Quran to achieve some objective.

Quran: This Quran guides to what is most upright; and it gives good news to the believers who do good deeds, that they will have a great reward. And those who do not believe in the Hereafter, We have prepared for them a painful punishment.

Comments: These verses use a marketing strategy used often in the Quran to persuade readers and listeners to accept the Quran because it is good for them and not believing the Quran is bad for them. Sounds like snake oil selling techniques one hundred and fifty years ago.

Quran: When We decide to destroy a town, We command its affluent ones, they transgress in it, so the word becomes justified against it, and We destroy it completely. How many generations have We destroyed after Noah?

Comments: Again, who is the 'We' speaking in these verses. It cannot be God or angels for such stated actions are against their natures.

Quran: And do not kill the soul which Allah has made sacred, except in the course of justice. If someone is killed unjustly, We have given his next of kin certain authority. But he should not be excessive in killing, for he will be supported.

Comments: When is killing ever acceptable except for self-defense. What kind of so-called justice permits killing?

Quran: There is no city, but We will destroy before the Day of Resurrection, or punish it with a severe punishment. This is inscribed in the Book.

Comment: Destroying cities, punishing cities with a severe punishment - what book is this written in. And in destroying a city, one kills innocent children, this is not from God.

Quran: When We said to the angels, "Bow down before Adam," they bowed down, except for Satan. He said, "Shall I bow down before someone You created from mud?" He said, "Do You see this one whom

Quran: You have honored more than me? If You reprieve me until the Day of Resurrection, I will bring his descendants under my sway, except for a few."

Comments: These verses are repeated multiple times in the Quran and are from some mythological writings. They are fabricated.

Quran: We send down in the Quran healing and mercy for the believers, but it increases the wrongdoers only in loss.

Comments: Who is the 'We' who sent down in the Quran? God wants healing and mercy for all people, not just believers. God only want His children to love each other, help each other, and take care of each other.

Quran: Say, "If mankind and jinn came together to produce the like of this Quran, they could never produce the like of it, even if they backed up one another."

Comments: This is a very misleading verse. In fact, the Quran was written by men, not angels or God. Evidence of this is that the Quran contains contradictions, myths, and statements regarding to or referring to God that are contrary to His nature/

Quran: A Quran which We unfolded gradually, that you may recite to the people over time. And We revealed it in stages.

Comments: Who is the 'We' in these verses? It is certainly not God. And who is the 'you' in the statement 'that you may recite to the people over time.' The Quran does not come from God, but rather from men.

Quran: And to warn those who say, "Allah has begotten a son." They have no knowledge of this, nor did their forefathers. Grave is the word that comes out of their mouths. They say nothing but a lie.

Comments: These verses are an obvious criticism and condemnation of the Christian belief that Jesus was the Son of God. The Gospels cite miracles that Jesus performed, what miracles did Muhammed perform?

Quran: Whoever wills—let him believe. And whoever wills—let him disbelieve". We have prepared for the unjust a Fire, whose curtains will hem them in. And when they cry for relief, they will be relieved with water like molten brass, which scalds the faces. What a miserable drink, and what a terrible place.

Comments: These verses are coercing people into believing in the teachings of Islam as found in the Quran because if they don't, they will be damned to Hell. This is certainly not from God.

Quran: These will have the Gardens of Eden, beneath which rivers flow. Reclining on comfortable furnishings, they will be adorned with bracelets of gold, and will wear green garments of silk and brocade.

Comments: And continuing from the previous verses, those who believe are told that they will merit the Gardens of Eden (Heaven) where there will be comfortable furnishings and fancy clothes and jewelry. But are people who go to Heaven going to sit around all day and strut around in dazzling clothes and jewelry? The authors of the Quran are trying to entice people to believe in Islam based on earthly pleasures. This is not from God.

Quran: We said to the angels, "Bow down to Adam." So, they bowed down, except for Satan. He was of the jinn, and he defied the command of his Lord. Will you take him and his offspring as lords instead of Me when they are an enemy to you? Evil is the exchange for the wrongdoers.

Comments: Who is 'We' in these verses? It would appear to be God; however, Islam holds there is only one God. Again, this narrative is repeated multiple times in the Quran. And if the 'We' is not God then were does this information come from regarding a command to the angels to bow down to Adam? This narrative has no basis in truth and is a fabrication by the authors of the Quran.

Quran: A mention of the mercy of your Lord towards His servant Zechariah. When he called on his Lord, while in seclusion. He said, "My Lord, my bones have become feeble, and my hair is aflame with gray, and never, Lord, have I been disappointed in my prayer to you. "And I fear for my dependents after me, and my wife is barren. So, grant me, from Yourself, an heir. To inherit me, and inherit from the House of Jacob, and make him, my Lord, pleasing." "O Zechariah, We give you good news of a son, whose name is John, a name We have never given before." He said, "My Lord, how can I have a son, when my wife is barren, and I have become decrepit with old age?" He said, "It will be so, your Lord says, 'it is easy for me, and I created you before, when you were nothing.'" He said, "My Lord, give me a sign." He said, "Your sign is that you will not speak to the people for three nights straight." And he came out to his people, from the sanctuary, and signaled to them to praise morning and evening. "O John, hold on to the Scripture firmly," and We gave him wisdom in his youth. And tenderness from Us, and innocence. He was devout. And kind to his parents; and he was not a disobedient tyrant.

Comments: These verses are very similar to the Gospel of Luke, obviously indicating again that the authors of the Quran copied from Christian and Jewish literature. Since the narrative from the Gospel of Luke is probably fiction, it undermines the authenticity of the Quran as the Word of God.

Quran: And mention in the Scripture Mary when she withdrew from her people to an eastern location. She screened herself away from them, and We sent to her Our spirit, and He appeared to her as an immaculate human. She said, "I take refuge from you in the Most Merciful, should you be righteous." He said, "I am only the messenger of your Lord, to give you the gift of a pure son." She said, "How can I have a son, when no man has touched me, and I was never unchaste?" He said, "Thus said your Lord, 'It is easy for Me, and We will make him a sign for humanity, and a mercy from Us. It is a matter already decided.'" "So, she carried him, and secluded herself with him in a remote place. The labor-pains came upon her, by the trunk of a palm-tree. She said, "I wish I had died before this, and been completely forgotten." Whereupon he called her from beneath her: "Do not worry; your Lord has placed a stream beneath you. And shake the trunk of the palm-tree towards you, and it will drop ripe dates by you." "So, eat, and drink, and be consoled. And if you see any human, say, 'I have vowed a fast to the Most Gracious, so I will not speak to any human today.' "Then she came to her people, carrying him. They said, "O Mary, you have done something terrible. O sister of Aaron, your father was not an evil man, and your mother was not a whore." So, she pointed to him. They said, "How can we speak to an infant in the crib?" He said, "I am the servant of Allah. He has given me the Scripture and made me a prophet. And has made me blessed wherever I may be; and has enjoined on me prayer and charity, so long as I live. And kind to my mother, and He did not make me a disobedient rebel. So, Peace is upon me the day I was born, and the day I die, and the Day I get resurrected alive. "That is Jesus, son of Mary, the Word of truth about which they doubt. It is not for Allah to have a child; glory be to Him. To have anything done, He says to it, "Be," and it becomes.

Comments: These verses are a repeat of the announcement to Mary by the angel, Gabriel, that she would conceive a son through the Holy Ghost as expressed in the Gospel of Luke 1:26–38, though greatly exaggerated to fit the theme and objectives of the authors of the Quran.

Quran: It is not fitting for the Most Merciful to have a son.

Comments: Obviously a criticism of Christianity.

Quran: As for those who disbelieve and repel from Allah's path and from the Sacred Mosque, which We have designated for all mankind equally, whether residing therein or passing through and seek to commit sacrilege therein, We will make him taste of a painful punishment.

Comments: Again, who is the "We' in these verses. The statement 'We have designated for all mankind would imply that this is Allah or God speaking. Yet, Islam is totally opposed to the Christian belief in the Trinity of God. But the implication is that all mankind should be converted to Islam.

Quran: But those who disbelieve and reject Our revelations, these will have a humiliating punishment.

Comments: Who does 'Our' refer to? Is this supposedly God speaking? God would not impose a humiliating punishment on anyone who doubts or disbelieves that that the so-called revelations Muhmmed claimed to have come from God did come from God. There is reason to believe that these so-called revelations were fabricated by Muhammed and or the writers of the Quran.

Quran: Those who emigrate in Allah's cause, then get killed, or die, Allah will provide them with fine provisions.

Comments: This verse seems like an exhortation to follow Muhammed when he emigrated from Mecca to Medina in 622 to supposedly escape persecution. Once in Medina, Muhammad began to establish Islam as a political organization within the Arabian Peninsula. The question must be asked was Muhammed's move to Medina with a small group of followers based on religious motives or political ones?

Quran: Allah has never begotten a son, nor is there any god besides Him. Otherwise, each god would have taken away what it has created, and some of them would have gained supremacy over others.

Comments: Another criticism of the Christian belief that God exists as three persons in one being. Perhaps the authors of the Quran did not understand this Christian doctrine.

Quran: And tell the believing women to restrain their looks, and to guard their privates, and not display their beauty except what is apparent thereof, and to draw their coverings over their breasts, and not expose their beauty except to their husbands, their fathers, their husbands' fathers, their sons, their husbands' sons, their brothers, their brothers' sons, their sisters' sons, their women, what their right hands possess, their male attendants who have no sexual desires, or children who are not yet aware of the nakedness of women.

Comments: Obviously, these verses are the same commandments followed by Muslims even to today with enforcement by morality police. It also implies that Muslims had eunuchs based on the statement, male attendants who have no sexual desires. Does this mean that Islam allowed eunuchs, male slaves who were intentionally castrated? Slaves and forced castration are against the Natural Law of God.

Quran: Pray regularly, and give regular charity, and obey the Messenger, so that you may receive mercy.

Comments: One must obey the Messenger, Muhammed, in order to receive mercy. Who is supposedly saying this. Certainly, it is not God nor an angel who is saying this. It is probably Muhammed or the authors of the Quran who are saying this to coerce people into obeying Muhammed and the leaders of Islam.

Quran: The believers are those who believe in Allah and His Messenger, and when they are with him for a matter of common interest, they do not leave until they have asked him for permission. Those who ask your permission are those who believe in Allah and His Messenger.

Comments: Speaking to Muhammed is like speaking to Allah (God), an outrageous and arrogant claim.

Quran: Do not address the Messenger in the same manner you address one another. Allah knows those of you who slip away using flimsy excuses. So let those who oppose his orders beware, lest an ordeal strikes them, or a painful punishment befalls them.

Comments: Who is speaking here warning people to render obedience to Muhammed lest 'ordeal strikes them, or a painful punishment befalls them'? It is certainly not God. Rather it is probably the writers and editors of the Quran and possibly the leaders of Islam who were directing the writers and editors of the Quran.

Quran: Those who disbelieve say, "Why was the Quran not revealed to him at once?" Thus, in order to strengthen your heart thereby, and We revealed it in stages. Whatever argument they come to you with, We provide you with the truth, and a better exposition.

Comments: Misleading verses written to try to persuade the reader or listener of the Quran that it was intentionally revealed by God over a period of time, when it was fabricated by the authors over a long period of time.

Quran: You are receiving the Quran from an All-Wise, All-Knowing.

Comments: Here is an unsubstantiated claim that God wrote the Quran and who is making this statement? Another persuasive verse to mislead people into believing that God wrote the Quran and gave it to Muslims.

Quran: We gave Moses the Scripture after We had annihilated the previous generations; as an illumination for mankind, and guidance, and mercy, so that they may remember.

Comments: 'After We had annihilated the previous generations' is a fabricated statement written to mislead the reader or hearer into believing that God had annihilated people for some self-serving reason. God does not annihilate anyone; it is against His nature.

Quran: Those who disbelieved in Allah's signs and His encounter, these have despaired of My mercy. For them is a painful torment.

Comments: Another example of verses implying that disbelieving in the Quran merits Hell.

Quran: Muhammad is not the father of any of your men; but he is the Messenger of Allah, and the seal of the prophets.

Comments: Muhammed is the seal of the prophets? Does this imply that Muhammed completes the so-called revelations of all previous prophets?

Quran: O prophet! We have sent you as a witness, and a bearer of good news, and a warner. And a caller towards Allah by His leave, and an illuminating beacon. And give the believers the good news that for them is a great reward. And do not obey the blasphemers and the hypocrites and ignore their insults.

Comments: The question again must be asked, who is the 'We' speaking in these verses. Is it God? Whoever it is supposed to be, these verses are attempting to claim the role of Muhammed as the prophet and messenger of God. However, it is just a claim by the authors of the Quran and is based on the overall claim that the Quran was written by God or dictated by God. And such a claim is followed up by coercion that the reader or hearer must accept these claims or suffer eternally in Hell. This certainly does not come from God Who is Love and does not threaten.

Quran: O Prophet! We have permitted to you your wives to whom you have given their dowries, and those you already have, as granted to you by Allah, and the daughters of your paternal uncle, and the daughters of your paternal aunts, and the daughters of your maternal uncle, and the daughters of your maternal aunts who emigrated with you, and a believing woman who has offered herself to the Prophet, if the Prophet desires to marry her, exclusively for you, and not for the believers.

Comments: Are these verses implying that God granted special privileges to Muhammed concerning his wives and relatives? Polygyny is opposed to Natural Law since it denies the equality of the man and the woman because it implies superiority of the male over the female.

Quran: O you who believe! Do not enter the homes of the Prophet unless you are given permission to come for a meal; and do not wait for its preparation. And when you are invited, go in. And when you have eaten, disperse, without lingering for conversation. This irritates the Prophet, and he shies away from you, but Allah does not shy away from the truth. And when you ask his wives for something, ask them from behind a screen; that is purer for your hearts and their hearts. You must never offend the Messenger of Allah, nor must you ever marry his wives after him, for that would be an enormity with Allah.

Comments: These verses treat Muhammed like an arrogant king and actually belittle God for implying that offending Muhammed when he is acting childishly is supported by God.

Quran: If the hypocrites, and those with sickness in their hearts, and the rumormongers in the city, do not desist, We will incite you against them; then they will not be your neighbors there except for a short while. They are cursed; wherever they are found, they should be captured and killed outright. Such has been Allah's precedent with those who passed away before. You will find no change in Allah's system.

Comments: 'They should be captured and killed outright. Such has been Allah's precedent with those who passed away before. You will find no change in Allah's system.' God does not promote killing anyone especially those who are only hypocrites and rumormongers. These verses indicate a very poor understanding of the nature of God.

Quran: Allah has cursed the disbelievers and has prepared for them a Blaze. Dwelling therein forever, not finding a protector or a savior. The Day when their faces are flipped into the Fire, they will say, "If only we had obeyed Allah and obeyed the Messenger."

Comments: More coercive verses! God would not curse and condemn to Hell people who do not believe in the Quran and Islam.

Quran: As for those who strive against Our revelations, seeking to undermine them, for them is a punishment of a painful plague.

Comments: More coercive verses 'Our revelations' who is speaking here, certainly not God.

Quran: We have cited in this Quran for mankind every ideal, that they may take heed. An Arabic Quran, without any defect, so they may become righteous.

Comments: These verses imply that the Quran is for mankind and not just the Arabs at the time of Muhammed and the founding of Islam. And the statement 'an Arabic Quran without any defect' is very misleading. Any objective reader or hearer will see defects in the Quran, inconsistencies, repeated verses, statements contrary to the nature of God.

Quran: It is not for any human that Allah should speak to him, except by inspiration, or from behind a veil, or by sending a messenger to reveal by His permission whatever He wills.

Comments: God does not have physical characteristics and does not speak in the sense of these verses. God does inspire virtually everyone, and it is doubtful is God has ever sent a human messenger to people.

Quran: This Book of Ours speaks about you in truth. We have been transcribing what you have been doing."

Comments: These verses are very confusing and ambiguous. Who are we to understand 'Ours', 'you', 'We' in these verses. The lack of clarity in these verses represent a defect, perhaps intentional.

Quran: Recall when We dispatched towards you a number of jinn, to listen to the Quran. When they came in its presence, they said, "Pay attention!" Then, when it was concluded, they rushed to their people, warning them.

Comments: 'Recall when We dispatched towards you a number of jinn, to listen to the Quran.' This is very misleading since almost all readers and listeners will not be able to recall such an event since it did not happen.

Quran: Those who disbelieve and repel from the path of Allah, He nullifies their works. While those who believe, and work righteousness, and believe in what was sent down to Muhammad, and it is the truth from their Lord, He remits their sins, and relieves their concerns.

Comments: These verses imply that salvation is only through Muhammed, a very outrageous claim. And what about people who never are exposed to Islam and the Quran, will they all go to Hell?

Quran: When you encounter those who disbelieve, strike at their necks. Then, when you have routed them, bind them firmly. Then, either release them by grace, or by ransom, until war lays down its burdens. Had Allah willed, He could have defeated them Himself, but He thus tests some of you by means of others. As for those who are killed in the way of Allah, He will not let their deeds go to waste. He will guide them and will improve their state of mind. And will admit them into Paradise, which He has identified for them.

Comments: 'Killed in the way of Allah'. Allah (God) does not condone violence, fighting, killing, and war.

Quran: O you who believe! Obey Allah, and obey the Messenger, and do not let your deeds go to waste.

Comments: This verse is coercive and misleading. 'Obey the Messenger' implies that the Messenger represents God.

Quran: He who does not believe in Allah and His Messenger, We have prepared for the disbelievers a Blazing Fire.

Comments: This verse is coercive and misleading.

Quran: Those who disbelieved filled their hearts with rage, the rage of the days of ignorance. But Allah sent His serenity down upon His Messenger, and upon the believers, and imposed on them the words of righteousness, of which they were most worthy and deserving. Allah is aware of everything.

Comments: These verses imply that anyone who does not believe in the Quran and in Islam is ignorant and full of rage, while those who believe in the Quran and in Islam are serene, worthy, and righteous. Coercive!

Quran: Allah has fulfilled His Messenger's vision in truth: "You will enter the Sacred Mosque, Allah willing, in security, heads shaven, or hair cut short, not fearing. He knew what you did not know and has granted besides that an imminent victory."

Comments: 'Imminent victory'? Are these verses trying to connect Allah, Muhammed, and Islamic battles and wars? War is contrary to the nature of God.

Quran: It is He who sent His Messenger with the guidance and the religion of truth, to make it prevail over all religions.

Comments: Islam will prevail over all religions? This is a rather outrageous claim.

Quran: Muhammad is the Messenger of Allah. Those with him are stern against the disbelievers, yet compassionate amongst themselves. You see them kneeling, prostrating, seeking blessings from Allah and approval.

Comments: Again, these verses are coercive. And who is saying that Muhammed is the Messenger of Allah?

Quran: O you who believe! Do not place your opinions above that of Allah and His Messenger, and fear Allah. O you who believe! Do not raise your voices above the voice of the Prophet, and do not speak loudly to him, as you speak loudly to one another, lest your works be in vain without you realizing. Those who lower their voices before Allah's Messenger, those are they whose hearts Allah has tested for piety. They will have forgiveness and a great reward.

Comments: How can these verses be believed and upon whose authority? Who is speaking these verses?

Quran: I did not create the jinn and the humans except to worship Me.

Comments: Apparently, this is supposedly God speaking. However, God is not self-serving nor selfish. God is Love that continuously pours himself out to others. The verse is not from God, but rather from the authors of the Quran.

Quran: We made the Quran easy to remember. Is there anyone who would remember? We made the Quran easy to understand. Is there anyone who would understand? We made the Quran easy to memorize. Is there anyone who would memorize?

Comments: Again, who is the 'We' speaking here? The Quran has over 77,000 words and over 6,000 verses. That does not appear to be easy to memorize. As for easy to understand, it is not. The almost continuous change from first-person plural to first-person singular to third person makes it extremely difficult if not impossible to tell who is speaking. These verses appear to be a marketing technique to persuade people to try to memorize the Quran and to read the entire text.

Quran: In the name of Allah, the Gracious, the Merciful, the Compassionate. Has taught the Quran.

Comments: This is rather outrageous claim that Allah (God) taught the Quran. And the so-called basis for this statement is the claim by Muhammed or is this merely the claim of the writers and editors of the Quran?

Quran: What is the matter with you that you do not believe in Allah, when the Messenger calls you to believe in your Lord, and He has received a pledge from you, if you are believers? It is He who sends down upon His servant clear revelations, to bring you out of darkness into the light.

Comments: These verses again claim that Muhammed speaks on God's behalf without any proof or evidence.

Quran: We sent Noah and Abraham and established in their line Prophethood and the Scripture. Some of them are guided, but many of them are sinners. Then We sent in their wake Our messengers, and followed up with Jesus, son of Mary, and We gave him the Gospel, and instilled in the hearts of those who followed him compassion and mercy. But as for the monasticism which they invented, We did not ordain it for them, only to seek Allah's approval. But they did not observe it with its due observance. So, We gave those of them who believed their reward, but many of them are sinful.

Comments: These verses are trying to link Judaism, Christianity, and Islam through each of prophets or messengers from God in order to show some kind of continuity and equality. The criticism regarding Christian monasticism is rather strange given that there were Christian monasteries in the Arabian Peninsula at the time of Muhammed and some aspects of Islam seem to be copied from Monasticism especially the practice of praying five times a day.

Quran: Those who oppose Allah, and His Messenger will be subdued, as those before them were subdued. We have revealed clear messages. The unbelievers will have a demeaning punishment.

Comments: These verses are equating opposition to Muhammed as opposition to God. This claim is rather outrageous. And to state that those who oppose Muhammed must be subdued and will receive a demeaning punishment is also outrageous. How can any person within the religious organizations of Islam, Judaism, or Christianity equate themselves with God.

Quran: O you who believe! When you converse privately with the Messenger, offer something in charity before your conversation. That is better for you, and purer.

Comments: Do these verses imply that a person should give money to Muhammed before talking to him? And does this money influence Muhmmed in what he says or does to this person?

Quran: O prophet! If believing women come to you, pledging allegiance to you, on condition that they will not associate anything with Allah, nor steal, nor commit adultery, nor kill their children, nor commit perjury as to parenthood, nor disobey you in anything righteous, accept their allegiance and ask Allah's forgiveness for them.

Comments: Who is supposedly speaking to Mohammed? And the exhortation not to disobey Muhammed in anything righteous – who defines what is righteous – Muhammed? These verses are misleading. They are written to persuade or convince women to follow Muhammed because supposedly God wants them to do so. These verses are from men and not from God.

Quran: Allah loves those who fight in His cause, in ranks, as though they were a compact structure.

Comments: God does not love those who fight, and He has no cause that required fighting.

Quran: But as for those who disbelieve and denounce Our revelations, these are the inmates of the Fire, dwelling therein forever; and what a miserable fate!

Comments: What is the basis for a person believing so-called revelations – the claim of the person to whom the so-called revelations were made? And what is the evidence that these so-called revelations are from God and not just made-up by the so-called prophet?

Quran: O prophet! Strive hard against the disbelievers and the hypocrites and be stern with them. Their abode is Hell. What a miserable destination!

Comments: Who is supposedly telling the prophet (Muhammed) to 'Strive hard against the disbelievers and the hypocrites and be stern with them. Their abode is Hell. What a miserable destination'? It is neither God or an angel.

Quran: For those who reject their Lord, there is the torment of Hell. What an evil destination! When they are thrown into it, they will hear it roaring, as it seethes. It almost bursts with fury. Every time a batch is thrown into it, its keepers will ask them, "Has no warner come to you?" They will say, "Yes, a warner did come to us, but we disbelieved, and said, 'Allah did not send down anything; you are very much mistaken.'" And they will say, "Had we listened or reasoned, we would not have been among the inmates of the Blaze." So, they will acknowledge their sins. So, away with the inmates of the Blaze.

Comments: Rejecting the Lord is rejecting Love, it is not rejecting a man-made set of religious teachings that falsely claim that they came from God.

Quran: Say, "It was revealed to me that a band of jinn listened in, and said, 'We have heard a wondrous Quran. It guides to rectitude, so we have believed in it; and we will never associate anyone with our Lord.

Comments: What? What do the so-called jinn have to do with the Quran? The jinn are mythological creatures and what evidence is there for the existence of them? So, referring to the jinn actually undermines the veracity of the Quran. And who is 'me' that a band of jinn listed in.

ADDITIONAL COMMENTS ON THE QURAN

The above section contains only certain verses of the Quran with comments. A complete reading of the entire Quran will show to the reader that it, the Quran, seems to be a merged collection of verses from different authors. This will explain the replication of certain topics, often with almost the exact same words, and the apparent inconsistencies of similar topics.

The very frequent mixed use of points of view, first-person singular, first-person plural, second-person singular, second-person plural, and third person along with references to Allah and Muhammed, the Messenger, makes it difficult to understand who is speaking. This can all be explained by the probability that there were multiple authors and multiple editors of the Quran.

The frequent comparison of the Quran, Mohammed, and Islam to Noah, Abraham, Moses, and Judaism, and to Jesus, and Christianity is meant to support and promote the claims that the Quran represents direct revelations to Muhammed and that a person must abide by the teachings of Islam to merit Heaven and contrarywise that a person who does not abide by the teachings of Islam will merit Hell.

The writers of the Quran attempt to acknowledge the so-called revelations of Noah, Abraham, and Moses in order to somehow show or prove that the revelations to Muhammed are legitimate.

However, the narratives of Noah, Abraham and Moses are myths and there were no revelations from God to these mythical characters. So, these facts undermine the claim that God revealed teachings to Muhammed.

Similar to the Jewish Bible and the Christian Bible, the Quran is not the literal word of God. God did not write or dictate directly or indirectly these documents, they are works of men, but pious, devout, and mostly well-intentioned men. When reading or listening to Jewish literature, Christian literature, or Islamic literature, it is best to remember the Latin phrase caveat lector, let the reader beware. Read or listen in a critically thinking manner.

Similar to the Jewish Bible and the Christian Bible, the Quran contains both true verses and false verses. The true verses involve exhortations to virtuous actions and behaviors. The false verses represent attempts by the writers to promote specific beliefs and actions which are contrary to the Will of God because they go against the nature of God Who is all-loving because He is Love itself and because God considers all people, all people without regard to gender, age, race, nationality, educational level, economics status, health, head-covering, or social status as His children and because all people are God's children they are equal.

If the Quran is the word of God, then it should not contain any errors or inconsistencies with the nature of God, but it does.

There are very many verses in the Quran which can only be described as coercive, attempting to coerce the reader or listener to believe, submit and obey because the words are from Allah (God) and failure to believe, submit, and obey is punishable by eternal suffering in Hell.

Like Jews, Christians, Hindus, and Buddhists, all of whom have been misled and manipulated by their leaders and so-called religious guides, Muslims have been misled and manipulated by their leaders.

While Islam has produced holy and devout people since its founding, it has also produced prejudices, discrimination, hatred, murders, and wars. Even today the War by the Saud family, who claim to be highly religious Muslims, against Yemen, who are also Muslims, show that Islam promotes both peace and war.

HINDUISM

induism is a predominantly Indian religion that is found mostly but not entirely in India. It has extended outside of India by people emigrating to other countries such as England, Canada, and the United States. It is the world's third-largest religion, with approximately 1.3 billion followers. There are approximately 1.4 billion people in India with about 80 percent practicing Hindus.

Hinduism originated over 4000 years ago in the Indus Valley, an area spanning parts of modern Afghanistan, Pakistan, and northwest India. Hinduism has no one founder, rather it is a blend or a fusion of various beliefs that evolved over centuries from cultural practices, so-called sacred texts, teachings from various philosophies, local popular beliefs, rituals, and cosmological systems.

Hinduism prescribes duties incumbent on its followers such as honesty, refraining from injuring all living beings, patience, forbearance, self-restraint, virtue, and compassion. In practice, many of these prescriptions have not been followed. Instead, practices and rituals dominate Hinduism such as worship, fire rituals, prayers and incantations, chanting, meditation, sacrifice, ancestor homage, rites of passage, annual festivals, and pilgrimages.

Unlike other major religions, the Hindu religion does not claim any Prophets, it is not monotheistic, it does not believe in any one philosophy, but it does accept a set of sacred literatures. Because of these inconsistencies with the other major religions, Hinduism is sometimes considered more of a way of life than a religion

There are ten ethical rules, norms, or mandates in Hinduism, five political/social norms called Yamas, and five personal norms called Niyamas. These commandments are broad-based social and universal virtues in the form of moral restraints or social obligations according to Yoga philosophy.

The Vedic hymn (Rigveda 10.90) is one of many creation myths in the Vedas and describes how, at the beginning of time, the primordial person Purusha underwent a process of sacrifice that produced a four-part cosmos and its human counterpart, a four-part social order comprising Brahmans (priests), Kshatriyas (warriors and nobles), Vaishyas (commoners), and Shudras (servants). This is the basis for the infamous Hindu caste system. And it should be noted that the Hindu caste system is based on a myth, yet it has lasted for thousands of years and has led to almost countless social evils.

Rigveda (10.90)Ralph T.H. Griffith, The Hymns of the Rg Veda, 1896

"A thousand heads hath Purusha, a thousand eyes, and a thousand feet. On every side pervading earth, he fills a space ten fingers wide. This Purusha is all that has been and all that is to be. The Lord of immortality which waxes greater still by food. So mighty is his greatness; yea, greater than this is Purusha. All creatures are one-fourth of him, three-fourths eternal life in heaven. With three-fourths of Purusha went up: one-fourth of him again was here. Then he strode out to every side over what eats not and what eats. From him Viraj was born; again, Purusha from Viraj was born.

When gods prepared the sacrifice with Purusha as their offering, its oil was spring, the holy gift was autumn; summer was the wood. The balmed as victim on the grass Purusha born in earliest time. With him the dieties and all Sadhyas and Rishis sacrificed.

From that great general sacrifice the dripping fat was gathered up. He formed the creatures of the air, and animals both wild and tame.

From that great general sacrifice Ricas and Sama-hymns were born. Therefrom were spells and charms produced; the Yajus had its birth from it.

From it were horses born, and from it all cattle with two rows of teeth: From it were generated cattle, from it the goats and sheep were born. When they divided Purusha how many portions did they make? What do they call his mouth, his arms? What do they call his thighs and feet?

The Brahman was his mouth, of both his arms was the Rajanya made. His thighs became the Vaisya , from his feet the Sudra was produced. The Moon was gendered from his mind, and from his eye the Sun had birth; Indra and Agni from his mouth were born, and Vayu from his breath.

Forth from his navel came mid-air; the sky was fashioned from his head; Earth from his feet, and from his ear the regions. Thus formed the worlds.

Seven fencing-sticks had he, thrice seven layers of fuel were prepared, when the gods, offering sacrifice, bound, as their victim, Purusha.

Gods, sacrificing, sacrificed the victim: these were the earliest holy ordinances. The Mighty Ones attained the height of heaven, there where the Sadhyas, gods of old, are dwelling."

A person reading the above creation myth today would be amazed at the ridiculousness of this text. Yet, people for thousands of years believed this myth to be true and used it to promote the ridiculous idea of a segregation of society into classes or castes as though these castes were ordained by the gods and therefore legitimate. And the caste system is still prevalent in India today, based on this ridiculous creation myth.

Hindu so-called sacred literature is replete with other myths that unfortunately people accept as truths.

While Hinduism believes in Ahimsa or non-violence towards all living creatures, it really fails completely in this regard.

Disrespecting others (women, widows, the poor, the homeless, slaves) and exploiting others politically and economically is actually perpetrating violence against others. It is absolutely absurd that Hindus worship cows and avoid walking in grass for fear of stepping on an insect while at the same time having almost complete disregard for the poor, the homeless, and Dalits (Untouchables).

In addition, while Hinduism purports to be a religion focused on the practice of virtue, the prevalence of social evils within Indian society undermines this claim of Hinduism to be focused on virtue. The social evils include the caste system, poverty, the marriage of young girls without their choice and often to older men, the prevention of widows from remarrying and their isolation from society even for very young widows (these young and even very young widows would have to spend the rest of their lives in a widows' commune after their husbands died), widow sacrifice (Sati is the practice among some Hindu communities where a recently widowed woman either voluntarily or involuntarily commits suicide because of her husband's death), extreme male chauvinism, arranged marriages, female infanticide (preferring to have a male baby instead of a female baby led and lead the parents literally murdering their female baby), female abortions, the dowry system, the castigation of women divorcees, and the abuse (including rape, sadistic torture, and murder) of Muslims during the 1947 partition of India (it should be stated that Muslims were guilty of the same abuses)

Why have these social evils existed within a society which is imbued with Hindu philosophies, culture, religious practices, and religious rituals? Obviously, Hinduism has failed to prevent or eliminate these evils. Hinduism is an absolute failure in bringing about a just, peaceful, tolerant, kind, and loving society and nation. And in fact, as a practice, Hinduism has contributed to the social evils within Indian society.

The Caste System

For thousands of years, Indian society has been divided into five castes and while there have been some recent efforts to eliminate the caste system at least in India's larger cities, it still remains in rural areas. The Brahman are the priestly caste, the Kshatriya is the royal caste also considered to be the landowner, ruler, and warrior caste, the Vaisya is the worker or commoner caste, the Sudra is the slave caste representing the great bulk of the Indian population, and the Untouchable caste who are considered descendants of slaves or prisoners.

Even within the castes themselves there were and are numerous subdivisions, including 3,000 major castes and over 25,000 sub-castes, some with only a few hundred members and others with several million.

So strictly controlled has been the division of society into these castes, that inter-marriage between the castes was and is forbidden and if it occurred, the bride or groom would be shunned for life. In addition, caste decides a person's social circle and profession.

This concept of a caste system is surely not from God and is entirely against the Natural Law. Such a ridiculous concept can only come from men, arrogant men who want to control other people for their own selfish means.

The caste system also has and is well-suited for the ruling class because the Caste System actually supports the exploitation of people for economic means. This is one of the underlying reasons why there has been and is such a great economic disparity in India and great levels of poverty. Various estimates are that between 40 and 55 percent of Indians live in poverty. Unfortunately, the government of India and the ruling class of India (those individuals who own 75 percent of the wealth of India and represent only 1 percent of the population) have been working not so much to reduce or eliminate poverty, but rather to manage the statistics both from Indian agencies and global agencies. Of course, that also happens in many other countries where the government and the ruling class (which controls the government, all levels, and all branches) are more concerned with embarrassing statistics rather than the plight of the people.

The ruling class does not want to reduce or eliminate poverty because that would reduce their assets and their control of the country. And like the children's game 'the king of the hill' the ruling class is at the top of the hill and will resist any and all attempts by others to move to the top of the hill.

Throughout history Untouchables have been forbidden from entering Hindu temples and schools, and from touching members of other castes. They have had to drink from separate wells, sit on separate benches, use different cups and utensils from those used by members of other castes, sometimes served from coconut shells, or have water poured into their hands.

These are cases where Brahmans, Kshatriyas, Vaisyas, and Sudras would not even let the shadows of Untouchables fall on them and if that happened, they were required to take a special bath and perform a ritual to regain their purity because the shadow of an Untouchable fell on them. Untouchables have even been required to wear bells to alert upper class Hindus that they are coming so that the upper caste member could avoid them. And there were rules requiring Untouchables keep a certain distance away from members of the upper casts.

Untouchables in the country have been made to live apart from the upper castes. They had to use their own roads and could not live in areas downwind from where the upper castes lived so that their wind would not defile the upper castes. In the cities they had to live in separate slums. In some places higher caste Kshatriyas would deflower Dalit brides on their wedding in front of the helpless groom.

How can this be reconciled with Ahimsa? It cannot!

Dowry System

The dowry system in India refers to the jewelry, goods, cash, and other property that the bride's family gives to the groom, and the parents and relatives of the groom. This transfer is actually a condition of the marriage and the groom's family actually demands the dowry. So strict was and is the dowry system in India that the marriage may not occur if the dowry is not given. For poorer families, the dowry system can put great financial burden on the bride's family.

The dowry system coupled with the practice of arranged marriages undermines the natural idea that marriage is based on love and compatibility.

While the dowry system has been made illegal since 1961, it existed for thousands of years in India and Hinduism did nothing to try to eliminate the practice. In addition, the dowry system does still exist, and the 1961 legislation allows loopholes in that the penalty for giving or taking dowry does not apply if the transfer does not involve a demand for the property or a condition of the marriage. Because of these loopholes, the laws against the dowry system in India have been ineffective.

According to India's National Crime Records Bureau, more than 7,600 women were killed or moved to suicide in 2015 as a result of dowry harassment by their husbands or families of the husband. In addition, many of the approximately 8000 women murdered a year as the result of what is called 'bride burning' were killed for refusal to pay the groom or his family a dowry.

While the numbers are small within the context of the Indian Hindu population of 1.1 billion people, it shows that abuses of the dowry system have been ignored by the Hindu leaders and teachers: priests (Brahmins), gurus, and swamis. In addition, the number of cases of harassment that do not result in murder or suicide are likely in the hundreds of thousands and include physical, emotional, and sexual assault.

A Canadian documentary film called 'Runaway Grooms' released in 2005 explores the phenomenon of Indo-Canadian men who return to India seeking women to marry only for the bride's dowry who abandon the woman after having received her dowry.

Poverty

Poverty is an extreme evil that has affected India for literally thousands of years, and it still exists today impacting hundreds of millions of people. One of the underlying causes of this poverty is Hinduism, specifically its doctrine of the caste system. The caste system has been extremely favorable to the two upper casts the Brahmans and the Kshatriyas, and the benefits to these two classes have been at the expense of the lower castes the Vaisyas, the Sudras, and the Untouchables.

The question must be asked whether the doctrine of the Caste System found in Hindu so-called Sacred texts was developed out of a sense of religion or at the direction of the Ruling Class in India when the Sacred texts were written. In other words, was the original doctrine of the Caste System in Hindu Sacred texts fabricated by individuals who were employed by, directed by, and funded by the Ruling Class in India in order to fool, or trick, or deceive people into accepting such a ridiculous system that is absolutely contrary to Natural Law, the law of

Nature which imbues every conscious, intelligent individual and forms the natural basis for right and wrong.

So, was and is the Caste System a 'rigged system', rigged by and maintained by the Ruling Elite of India 1600 years ago to control the masses of people? And have the masses of Indians for the past 1600 years been duped into accepting such an absurd system? And has the likely fabricated religious basis for the Caste System been designed to not only control and exploit the vast majority of Indians for the benefit of the Ruling Class, but was it also intentionally designed to dissuade and discourage the masses from rebelling from such an unjust system?

Besides the Caste System, Hindu mythology, the doctrine of samsara, and the doctrine of karma have probably been designed and fabricated in order to allow the control of the Indian masses by the Indian Ruling Elite.

Lakshmi is one of the principal goddesses in Hinduism. She is the mythological goddess of wealth, fortune, power, beauty, fertility, and prosperity. The question must be asked, why did the writers of the myth involving Lakshmi, create or fabricate the idea of Lakshmi? What were their objectives in creating this goddess? Was it for people who naively accepted this myth to pursue wealth, fortune, power, beauty, fertility, and prosperity – and notice the emphasis on wealth, fortune, power, and prosperity, as though happiness can come from such selfish things.

Hinduism actually disparages poor people and blames the poor themselves and claims that bad karma is the cause of the person's poverty. In addition, the upper castes should not pity the poor and help the poor because it is their own fault that they are poor. This attitude is similar to the attitude of the wealthy in the Western world.

Poverty and the lack of adequate food to maintain health, the lack of healthcare, no or inadequate housing, the lack of education, no or poor means of transportation, and other social issues impacting an extremely high percentage of India's population, while at the same time having a very small percentage of the population with extreme wealth is due in great part to Hinduism itself. Was Hinduism fabricated to support the wealthy class's exploitation and control of the majority of the people?

Sati

It is very difficult to reconcile the Hindu practice of sati, the burning to death (either voluntarily or by use of force or coercion) of a widow on her husband's funeral pyre, with any other notion of a wife's love and devotion for her husband in any other religion or culture. While, the practice is illegal in current-day India, it still occurs and is regarded by some Hindus as the highest sign of wife's devotion.

While Sati is considered by some Hindus as the highest wife's sign of devotion to her husband, there is no corresponding practice for a husband to show his devotion to his wife. Obviously, these Hindus do not accept the saying 'what is good for the goose, is good for the gander'.

There are other forms of sati as well such as drowning. In addition, historically and currently there are many cases of suicide on the part of the wife after her husband's death, because the husband's wealth goes to his family and not his wife.

Child Marriage

While child marriage has existed for thousands of years and still exists in other cultures influenced by other religions, it is most prevalent within India influenced by Hinduism. It also happens that the marriage of children, usually girls, occurs between young girls and older men. These marriages are based on arrangements which usually involve financial incentives to the family of the girl.

Any marriage of a child (any individual below the age of 12 is in fact a child) is in fact 'child abuse' and against the Natural Law. Any person younger than 18 years old is not able to make a rational decision that involves a lifelong commitment to another person and this young person only goes along with this arrangement because of parental pressure or parental respect.

The 2006 movie, Water, by Deepa Mehta depicts an 8-year-old girl who marries a much older man (he appears to be at least fifty or sixty years old) and becomes a widow after her husband dies soon after their marriage. The movie, however, focuses on an equally ridiculous practice of 'widow shunning' prevalent in Indian society both historically and currently and supported by Hinduism. The very young widow is committed by her father to a widow's commune where she and the other widows are to live there not only segregated by society but also shunned by society for the rest of their lives. And what is their crime -being widows. Absolutely absurd!

And there is not a corresponding practice for widowers. How can Hinduism purport to be a religion or practice or way of life that leads to Nirvana (the same as Heaven in other religions) when it promotes and supports such ridiculous practices.

Arranged Marriage

Arranged marriage is a situation where the bride or the groom are selected by individuals other than the bride or grooms themselves, usually by family members such as the parents. In some cases, a professional matchmaker may be used to find a spouse for a young person where the individual reviews a catalog of potential matches provided by the matchmaker and then interviews the candidates he or she has selected.

Matchmakers are most often used by the man and his family rather than the women.

In some cases, the identification and selection of the proposed spouse takes place without any input or interaction by the to-be bride or the to-be groom and the bride and groom never meet in person before the actual wedding.

It is often difficult to determine whether the arranged marriage is based on force, coercion, or just obedience to the parents. The motivation for arranged marriages typically involve benefits to the parents or family members and not the good of the bride and groom.

Often there are negative consequences for the woman if she refuses to go through with the arranged marriage. She is often considered to have dishonored her entire family. In some cases, killing the woman is a way for the family to enforce the institution of arranged marriages, and such so-called honor killings are often done publicly and involve multiple family members. Again, it should be noted that this practice is usually one-sided and only involves the woman who refuses the arranged marriage and not the man.

Arranged marriages are based on duty and not on love and the long-term relationship between the husband and wife continues to be based on duty and not love during their lifetimes. And their relationship typically involves superiority and dominance by the husband over the wife.

Widows

The prevention of widows from remarrying and their isolation from society even for very young widows (these young and even very young widows would have to spend the rest of their lives in a widows' commune or on the streets after their husbands died), as noted above is a despicable practice. The non-existence of a corresponding practice for widowers point to another social evil involved with Hinduism, that is, the rather extreme male chauvinism of Hinduism. While not defending Hinduism, institutional and doctrinal male chauvinism also exists in Pauline Christianity, Judaism, and Islam.

Indian widows are shunned by society, considered 'unclean', and required to shave their heads and wear white clothing and not wear jewelry. By Hindu tradition, they cannot remarry. They are among poorest of the poor because are forced to beg for their income.

And what is their crime? How is it a crime if a women's husband dies? Typically, their sole means of support were their husbands, and with the deaths of their husbands and the property of the husband going to his family and not his wife, the widow has no means of support.

But how absurd is it for the husband's family and society in general to shun and ostracize a widow. How extremely sad it is for a woman but especially a young to be rejected by society for the death of her husband.

And why doesn't this apply to widowers? Is it because Hinduism was created by men and is imbued with male chauvinism?

Extreme Male Chauvinism and Toxic Masculinity

Dowries, almost always favorable to the man and his family, the cultural norm promoted by the Hindu religion that the new bride must move in with her in-laws and serve them, the desire to have male babies leading to female infanticide, the shunning of and discrimination of women divorcees and not male divorcees, domestic abuse by husbands against their wives, rape committed virtually always by men, and even murder where the perpetrator is male are some of the main indications of toxic masculinity in India.

The are many other expressions of violence against women due to Indian cultural values and beliefs were because of these beliefs women agree that their husband beating them is justified.

Any and every religion that supports and allows the dominance of a man over a woman runs contrary to the Natural Law and the Will of God who considers all humans equal and wants all humans to love and support each other.

It appears that Hinduism supports the domination of the rich over the poor, and the domination of a man over a woman because it was written by rich men or by men who were supported, directed, and sponsored by rich men.

Female Infanticide

The Indian practice of female infanticide and of sex-selective abortion is based on the preference to have a male baby instead of a female baby has led and continues to lead parents to literally murdering their female baby or fetus. It is based on the Hindu belief that males are superior to females which is also the basis for male chauvinism and the dowry system.

1947 partition of India

The Partition of India in 1947 divided India into two independent countries: India and Pakistan. It is estimated to have displaced between 10 and 20 million people along religious lines, and that between 200,000 to 1 million people died during the migration. There was widespread violence that occurred during the with partition with death estimates between 200,00 and 2 million people. The partition created hostility, contempt, and suspicion between India and Pakistan that continues to this day. In addition, there were abuses committed by both Hindus and Muslims during the partition that included rape, sadistic torture, and tortures leading to murder. The killings are sometimes considered to be 'ethnic cleansing' on the parts of the Hindus and Muslims.

Mahatma Gandhi opposed the partition of India and considered that it violated his vision of unity among Indians of all religions.

There are numerous eyewitness accounts of the maiming and mutilation of victims. The catalogue of horrors includes the disemboweling of pregnant women, the slamming of babies' heads against brick walls, the cutting off of the victim's limbs and genitalia, and the displaying of heads and corpses. While previous communal riots had been deadly, the scale and level of brutality during the Partition massacres were unprecedented.

BUDDHISM

Buddhism is one of the world's largest religions, originating about 2,500 years ago in India. It has over 500 million followers making it the fourth largest religion in the world.

Buddhism is the dominant religion in Bhutan, Myanmar, Cambodia, Mainland China, Hong Kong, Japan, Tibet, Laos, Macau, Mongolia, Singapore, Sri Lanka, Taiwan, Thailand, Kalmykia and Vietnam and there are large populations of Buddhist in North Korea, Nepal, India, and South Korea.

Buddhism originated out of Hinduism, and they both share doctrines on karma, dharma, moksha, and reincarnation. However, Buddhism rejects the priest, rituals, and the caste system. It is questioned whether Buddhism is a reformed type of Hinduism.

Buddhism teaches that human life involves suffering, which needs to be addressed and confronted through meditation, physical labor, and good behavior. Doing these things during life will lead to nirvana.

Nirvana is the ultimate goal of Buddhism and Buddhists. It is the same as Moksha for Hindus, it is similar to Heaven for Christians, and Jannah

(Paradise) for Muslims. Judaism does not have any clear teaching on life after death and it consists of in. According to Buddhism, Nirvana is a transcendent state devoid of all suffering, desire, and sense of self, where the individual is released from karma and the cycle of death and rebirth.

Buddhism is an Indian religion or philosophical tradition based on teachings attributed to the Buddha. The founder of Buddhism, Siddhartha Gautama Buddha supposedly lived over 2500 years ago. His legend tells his birth in Lumbini, Nepal, in about 567 BCE. He was supposedly the son of a king and was raised in an ostentatiously rich and luxurious environment with no lack for anything. He did not work. He was allegedly married, had one son, and was a Hindu.

The Legend of the Buddha

According to the legend of the Buddha, the prince was on a carriage ride outside his palaces when he encountered first a sick person, then an old man, and lastly then a dead person.

Comments: The statement 'the prince was on a carriage ride outside his palaces' implies that his father and he, himself, were extremely rich. And was his carriage pulled by horses or by slaves? And what was the source of his and his father's wealth? Did Siddhartha and his father own slaves? And how was it that the prince from his carriage was able to view and discern that a person was sick? Was the person lying on the road? And was the corpse lying on the road? And why didn't the prince offer any help to the sick person or render assistance to the dead person? If Prince Siddhartha saw a sick person, an old person, and a dead person on his carriage ride, these individuals must have been subjects within his father's kingdom, and if so, he had a responsibility to help them, but apparently, he did not. And what were these people doing outside on the road? It is very strange that a sick person and a dead person would be on the road with no one to care for them. So, was Siddhartha a good and kind person?

Continuing with the legend, the encounters with the sick person, the old person, and the corpse had a profound impression on him. Supposedly, the prince came to the realization that he too could become sick, and old, and some day die in spite of his wealth.

Comments: Who captured or wrote down this incident and these views by Siddhartha since the Buddha did not write anything and the writings about the Buddha did not start until 250 years after his death. While some of the teachings of Siddhartha Gautama could have been passed from generation to generation amongst his followers from the time of his death to those individuals who began to write about Buddhism, it is most likely that the creators of Buddhism where the authors who took the legend of the Buddha and some of these supposed teachings and expanded this information into Buddhism as a religion and philosophical set of doctrines. And lastly from the story, the Buddha was more concerned with his mortality than the good of the sick person, the old person, and the dead person.

After and because of his realizations regarding life based on his encounters with a sick person, an old person, and a dead person, as the story is written, the prince gave up his life as a prince and he began to seek out spiritual teachers and he became an ascetic engaging in extreme and prolonged fasts. After six years of this ascetical lifestyle, he had not found peace but only frustration and he probably renounced asceticism.

According to the legend, he then began to preach, going from village to village, attracting disciples along the way. During this time, he established orders of nuns and monks. He continued with this for the rest of his life.

Comments: Great story but is any of it true. What happened to his wife and son? Did he abandon them? And, if he did abandon his wife and son what does that tell us about his character, his teachings, and his philosophy? And did he renounce all of his wealth? And if Prince Siddhartha Gautama gave up all of his wealth, how did he support himself during the six years when he was practicing extreme asceticism and during his ministry? And while the legend states that the Buddha engaged in extreme and prolonged fasts, he is usually depicted in paintings and statues as a fat man.

It is most likely that the legend of the Buddha's life is not factually accurate and was fabricated by his biographers and the real creators of Buddhism who live 250 to 300 years after the death of the Buddha,

While Buddhism's doctrines are supposedly based on what it calls the Middle Way, which is a lifestyle that avoids the extremes of asceticism and hedonism, devout Buddhists tend towards ascetism and become Buddhist monks and sisters.

While Buddhism supposedly teaches peace and non-violence, practicing Buddhists have joined the war efforts of their respective countries.

Buddhism does not condemn the acquisition of wealth and encourages hard work to gain wealth. Is this a justification for wealthy and extremely wealth Buddhists to acquire wealth at the expense of others. Every economy is limited in the total amount of wealth. The more wealth that one person owns or controls, the less there is for others. Everyone cannot be a millionaire. Currently, there are at least 10 Buddhist billionaires in the world.

Buddhism is the predominant religion in Bhutan, Myanmar, Cambodia, Mainland China, Hong Kong, Japan, Tibet, Laos, Macau, Mongolia, Singapore, Sri Lanka, Taiwan, Thailand, Kalmykia and Vietnam and there are large populations of Buddhist in North Korea, Nepal, India, and South Korea.

What influence has Buddhism had both historically and currently on the societies, politics, and economics of these countries especially in those countries where Buddhism is the predominant religion?

While Buddhism condemns all violence, throughout history Buddhists have justified violence for various reasons. Buddhism has a history of violence going back to its beginning.

There have been many instances throughout its history involving acts of violence and aggression by Buddhists for political and social reasons as well as self-inflicted violence by monks for religious purposes. Buddhism must be judged, not based on its teachings, but on how it is and has been practiced by its members and its effect on society, politics, and economics within the countries where Buddhism is the dominant religion

Buddhists have sometimes marched out to war and Buddhist monks have also been involved in violence. And it is rather interesting that the martial art called Kung Fu originated from Buddhism and was promoted by Buddhist monks. While Kung Fu involves learning, discipline, focus, and practice which is also found in Buddhism, it is a martial art whose purpose is self-defense and military engagements, both of which seem to be contrary to the non-violence teachings of Buddhism.

Buddhist Warfare

While the monks who invented Kung Fu used their martial skills primarily for self-defense (it is rather strange that the monks created Kung Fu for self-defense unless they lived in very dangerous times), they were engaged in warfare, one example being in the sixteenth century when they fought against Japanese pirates at the request of the government.

But, if the government asked for help from the Buddhist monks, it must have been due to the monks' reputation for fighting. If this is true, it seems to be inconsistent with the supposed non-violent teachings of Buddhism. Or was and is the supposed non-violent perception of Buddhism just that, a perception that masks the real practice of Buddhism?

Warrior Monks and Militant Monks

Sōhei (monk soldiers or warrior monks) were Buddhist monks in Japan who held considerable power within the imperial government. These warrior monks protected land and fought rival Buddhist schools and were a significant factor in the spread of Buddhism in Japan. These historical examples seem to show inconsistencies between the teachings of Buddhism and the practice of Buddhism.

While Buddhism has been marketed as a non-violent, personal, gentle, sensitive, generous, warm, and kind religion, these violent, militaristic, and aligned to land-owner monks imply that actual Buddhism may be far different than what people think about Buddhism. And a better picture of Buddhism may be found in the social, political, and economic history of Buddhism rather than in the teachings of Buddhism.

During the Second Sino-Japanese War and World War II, Zen Buddhist organizations in Japan carried out funding drives to buy war material and even weapons. Many monks and other religious figures participated in the promotion of Japanese nationalism and warmongering. Instead of influencing the Japanese leadership with the non-violent teachings of Buddhism, the Japanese leadership influenced Buddhist practicing believers of Buddhism.

In recent times, Buddhist monks have promoted and participated in wars, particularly wars against religious minority groups in predominantly Buddhist nations. These monks see Buddhism as part of their national identity and consider any non-Buddhists in the population to be a threat to the nation.

This is certainly inconsistent with the teaching of the Buddha.

It certainly appears that Buddhism from a practical point of view is an absolute failure. Despite having existed for 2500 years, it has failed to improve the social, political, and economic lives of its members while at the same time safeguarding the ruling elites and their power bases in the countries in which Buddhism is the predominant religion.

Could it be that Buddhism is just like the other major religions in that it maintains the status quo, that is, the dominance of the ruling elite over the majority of people as Karl Marx stated, 'religion is the opium of the people (or masses)'. As opium takes away pain and makes the user with calm and peaceful and almost oblivious to what is happening around him or her, so religion seems to neutralize a person's desire to fight back against the unjust domination and control in the sphere of politics and economics of the ruling elite over the working class.

CONCLUSION

This work was not intended to offend the members of the Pauline Christian Churches, Judaism, Islam, Hinduism, and Buddhism. Rather it was intended to show the members of these major organized religions that they have been misled by their leaders for centuries. Instead of teaching people how to live good lives by doing and promoting good, avoiding evil, treating others in words and actions as you would have them treat you in words and actions which is also expressed in the Christianity of Jesus as 'love your neighbor as yourself', and respecting the absolute dignity and equality of each and every human being; the leaders of these religious organizations have promoted absolute allegiance to their religious organization, animosity to the other religious organizations, and financial support and obedience to the clerics of their organization. The leaders of various religious organizations are more focused in their own organizations rather than the good of their members and the good of all people.

Unfortunately, virtually all political leaders since the foundations of the various major religious organization have acted as though they are fervent believers and members of the dominant religion within the country or region over which they rule, and that is because it is politically expedient to do so. And this is still true today. In reality, the ruling elite are not really concerned with the beliefs, principles, and practices of the religion that they hypocritically and outwardly profess to believe in. And the ruling elite and the leaders of the major religious organizations are aligned in their goal of manipulating and controlling their respective members.

And where has this left society over the last two to four thousand years? The world today has been plagued by almost constant wars and the exploitation of the majority by the elite minority in every country who dominate virtually their country politically and economically, for their good and not the good of the majority of the people.

And what have the major religious organizations done to correct or offset this gross injustice and great moral evil? Absolutely nothing!

While Pauline Christianity, Judaism, Islam, Hinduism, and Buddhism have been successful in leading a few individuals to a virtuous and good life, they have all failed miserably with respect to the majority of their members and virtually all societies. Are the various societies of the world better today than they were before the major religious organizations were established? Absolutely not!

These major religious organizations have actually been successful in enabling the ruling elites over the last two to four thousand years to manipulate and control the masses of society.

And during the pain and suffering that the masses of society have experienced and are experiencing due to the actions of the ruling elites, the leaders of these religious organizations have told and continue to tell their members not to seek justice, goodness, and happiness in this life but wait for the next life.

Did God or Allah or Yahweh or Buddha really intend this life to be a life of happiness for the ruling elite and a life of misery at the hands of the ruling elite for the majority of people? Absolutely not!

The suffering and misery of this life by so many people is due entirely to the injustices that exist with the political and economic leadership of society and the moral corruption of the leaders of the religious organizations.

The phrase 'evil exists because good people do nothing' is false. Evil exits because there are too few good people to counter the evil. Evil is countered or offset by goodness. The prevalence and extent of evil in the world indicates the lack of good people to counter that evil. Good people need to remove the evil in evil people, not destroy evil people. And why are there so few good people in the world despite the existence of Pauline Christianity, Judaism, Islam, Hinduism, Buddhism, and their supposed influence over the majority of people?

Because Pauline Christianity, Judaism, Islam, Hinduism, Buddhism are absolute failures. They have not succeeded in bringing about a more just and a more loving world, but rather they have worked with the ruling elites throughout history and today in maintaining their unjust dominance of the majorities of virtually every nation.

God does not want prayers or rituals or fasts. God only wants people, all people to get along and treat each other as brothers and sisters, respect all people, and help all people.

www.ingramcontent.com/pod-product-compliance
Lightning Source LLC
Chambersburg PA
CBHW051130120626
46547CB00012B/742